The Animal
Rights Debate

POINT/COUNTERPOINT

Philosophers Debate Contemporary Issues
Series Editors: James P. Sterba and Rosemarie Tong

This new series provides a philosophical angle to debates currently raging in academic and larger circles. Each book is a short volume (around 200 pages) in which two or more prominent philosophers debate different sides of an issue. For more information contact Professor Sterba, Department of Philosophy, University of Notre Dame, Notre Dame, IN 46566, or Professor Tong, Department of Philosophy, Davidson College, Davidson, NC 28036.

Sexual Harassment: A Debate
    by Linda LeMoncheck and Mane Hajdin
The Death Penalty: For and Against
    by Louis P. Pojman and Jeffrey Reiman
Disability, Difference, Discrimination: Perspectives on Justice in Bioethics and Public Policy
    by Anita Silvers, David Wasserman, and Mary B. Mahowald
Physician-Assisted Suicide: Pro and Con
    by Margaret P. Battin, David Mayo, and Susan M. Wolf
Praying for a Cure: When Medical and Religious Practices Conflict
    by Margaret P. Battin, Peggy DesAutels, and Larry May
The Abortion Controversy: A Debate
    by N. Ann Davis and Janet Smith
Sexual Orientation and Human Rights
    by Laurence M. Thomas and Michael E. Levin
The Animal Rights Debate
    by Carl Cohen and Tom Regan

The Animal Rights Debate

CARL COHEN AND TOM REGAN

ROWMAN & LITTLEFIELD PUBLISHERS, INC.
Lanham • Boulder • New York • Oxford

ROWMAN & LITTLEFIELD PUBLISHERS, INC.

Published in the United States of America
by Rowman & Littlefield Publishers, Inc.
4720 Boston Way, Lanham, Maryland 20706
www.rowmanlittlefield.com

12 Hid's Copse Road
Cumnor Hill, Oxford OX2 9JJ, England

Copyright © 2001 by Rowman & Littlefield Publishers, Inc.

Distributed by NATIONAL BOOK NETWORK

British Library Cataloguing in Publication Information Available

Library of Congress Cataloging-in-Publication Data

Cohen, Carl, 1931–
    The animal rights debate / Carl Cohen and Tom Regan.
        p. cm. — (Point/counterpoint)
    Includes bibliographical references and index.
    ISBN 0-8476-9662-6 — ISBN 0-8476-9663-4 (pbk. : alk. paper)
        1. Animal rights. I. Regan, Tom. II. Title. III. Series.

HV4711 .C63 2001
179'.3—dc21   00-069044

Printed in the United States of America

♾ ™The paper used in this publication meets the minimum requirements of American National Standard for Information Sciences—Permanence of Paper for Printed Library Materials, ANSI/NISO Z39.48-1992.

Contents

Preface

The continuing debate over the moral status of animals is often characterized by more heat than light. Those who use animals, on farms and in laboratories, are thought callous and immoral by many who contend that animals have rights and that killing them in our interests cruelly infringes upon those rights. Those who defend the use of animals in science and agriculture often regard their critics as extremists who sometimes substitute terrorist acts for rational discourse. A great gulf separates the partisans of the two sides, and so deep has this gulf become that even the hope for genuine understanding of each side by the other is commonly lost.

We seek to rejuvenate that hope. We aim to create, with reasoned argument, an environment of mutual respect, in which the controversy over the moral status of animals may be pursued rationally and in good spirit. We, the two authors of this book, believe that the animal rights debate can be conducted—*must* be conducted—with reasoned discourse.

Do animals have rights? We stand at opposite poles in answering this question. As joint authors of this volume, we have sought to make our respective cases in turn, against animal rights and for them, in a manner that is appropriate in view of the importance of the issues that divide us. Our disagreements are profound, but we fully agree in this: that important moral questions like those explored in these pages can be resolved only if the inquiry is both patient and fair. We agree that *ad hominem* attacks are no substitute for reasoned argument; great care must be taken, we believe, to understand those with whom we differ most strongly. We agree that it is possible, and even obligatory, to show respect for persons whose values conflict with our own. When the moral conflict is very sharp, as in the issues here discussed, we think the need for thoughtfulness and goodwill is especially great.

Each of us is confident that rational deliberation—informed, balanced, and penetrating—supports his conclusion with overwhelming weight. Who is right we leave for readers to decide. We are content to have the two sides of the animal rights debate put openly and clearly before the public.

On issues of community concern, wise policy is most likely to result when the best arguments on all sides have been forcefully expressed and thoughtfully heard. Where disagreement is intense, as here, this is particularly true. "The beliefs we have most warrant for," writes John Stuart Mill in *On Liberty*, "have no safeguard to rest on, but a standing invitation to the whole world to prove them unfounded." We share that conviction.

Mutually we have devised a format that we think will support reasoned discourse. We write separately. The arguments on both sides, we believe, can be put clearly and forcefully in comparatively short compass, and with a minimum of jargon. In Part I (by C. C.) the case is made against animal rights; in Part II (by T. R.) the case is made in their defense. Each of us has the opportunity then to respond to the other—C. C. in Part III, T. R. in Part IV.

How we argue is in some ways as different as what we argue. And this, we agree, is unavoidable. Throughout we have each conceded to the other the unrestricted liberty to frame issues in the manner that he chooses. We are mindful of the fact that how the issues are approached is itself among the topics open to possible criticism.

Despite our many differences, we are of one mind in affirming the profound practical importance of the debate over animal rights. Our disagreements are theoretical, certainly, but they are much more than that. Decisions about the moral permissibility of how humans treat other animals must have great impact on our conduct in daily life. What we conclude about animal rights will have consequences for the food we eat and the clothes we wear, and it will have direct bearing on the kinds of science we think morally justifiable. Every one of us (we both believe) ought to deliberate thoughtfully in coming to judgment. Our shared hope is that this volume will make a genuine contribution to this process.

Carl Cohen
Tom Regan

Part I

IN DEFENSE OF THE USE OF ANIMALS
Carl Cohen

1

The Moral Problem of Animal Use

We humans use animals. We eat them, play with them, and wear their skins. Most important, we use them as the subjects of experiments in advancing medical science. Animals of many species—rabbits, dogs, pigs, monkeys, but in overwhelming proportion mice and rats above all—have long been used in scientific research. Such research has led to discoveries that have saved millions of human lives and have contributed to the safety and well-being of hundreds of millions of other lives, animal and human. In experiments aimed at the *discovery* of new drugs or other therapies to promote human health, animal subjects are essential. They are also indispensable in *testing* the safety of drugs and other products to be used by humans. Anesthetized, the animals serving in this way are seldom caused pain. Some do experience distress, however, and many are killed.

Animals are not stones. They live and they may suffer. Every honest person will agree that treating animals in some ways is inhumane and unjustified. But the good that has been done by medical investigations that could not have been undertaken without animal subjects is so very great as to be beyond calculation; this, also, every honest person must acknowledge. Using animals is an inescapable cost of most successful medical research. Bearing that in mind, we ask, Is this use of animals in medicine morally right?

Other uses of animals are common, obviously. Animals give companionship, provide transportation, serve as food and clothing, and so on; and within each kind of use there is an enormous variety of specific uses. For each specific use, as for each kind of use, it may always be asked, *Should* that be done? Is it right? The answer in medical science is very clear. Investigators there *cannot* do without animal subjects. All over the world medical centers and individual scientists, pharmaceutical companies and great research institutes, rely heavily—and must rely—on the use of animal subjects in testing candidate drugs for safety, searching for new cures, widening and deepening biological knowledge. This arena gives us the most powerful lens with which to examine the moral issues of animal use. The rightness or wrongness of using animals in medical science is the central focus of this book.

Critics contend that medical experiments unjustly infringe on the rights of animals. I ask, Do animals have rights? This philosophical question lies at the heart of the debate. We cannot evade it because, as we shall see, if animals do have rights, the use of them in medical experiments may have to be forgone. I emphasize: It is not the wearing of furs that is our chief concern here, or hunting for sport, or even the eating of meat. It is the use of animals in medical research, above all other uses, that compels us to think carefully about the moral status of animals.

Whether animals do have rights may be a provocative question, but is it of practical importance? Is it more than an exercise in theoretical dispute? The animal rights debate, some might say, is a set of quarrels so academic, so "philosophical," that it does not really concern most ordinary folks. After all, great industries and tens of thousands of jobs depend on animal use. Hundreds of millions of humans rely on animals as their food. Most humans in the world consume dairy products and fish and meat every day or every week; we wear leather shoes and wool clothing; we visit zoos and love our pets, and so on and on. Why take this "animal rights debate" seriously? Human reliance on animals is so pervasive, so deep and complete, that there would seem to be little point in asking whether animals have rights.

We have, in fact, very good reason to ask and answer that question. The morality of animal use is indeed a *philosophical* issue, but by no means is it arcane. Any position adopted regarding the alleged rights of animals will have a direct bearing on community policy and on the life of each of us.

The practical force of philosophical questions about animal rights is this: If what we (individually or as a society) are doing with animals is not morally justifiable, we ought to stop doing it, and we ought to seek to keep others from doing it. If animals really do have rights, those rights deserve protection, as do the rights of vulnerable humans. Laws may be adopted that forbid conduct that is now nearly universal; regulations may forbid acts and practices to which we have long been accustomed. Such laws and regulations may prove exceedingly inconvenient and very costly. But neither convenience nor cost can excuse us from fulfilling our obligations. I repeat for emphasis: If animals really do have moral rights, we humans have the moral duty to respect those rights. The controversy over the use of animals with which this book deals is therefore intensely practical. Whatever the moral status we conclude animals deserve, that conclusion will surely affect the range of things we are permitted to do with them—and will therefore play a significant role in guiding our personal lives.

I hold that most uses of animals in medical science, including some that result in the deaths of many animals, are fully justifiable. This position is very widely shared by ordinary folks. Defending this conclusion, formulating and explaining it, is a badly needed step in responding to emotional attacks on what animal rights advocates like to refer to as "vivisection." Those attacks by the defenders of "animal rights" are deeply and dangerously mistaken. Exposing and explaining their mistakes is an enterprise at once important and humane.

Animals do not have rights. This is not to say that we may do whatever we please to animals or that everything commonly done by humans to animals is justifiable. Not at all. It is morally right to use animals in medical research, but from this it does not follow that *any* use of them is right. Of course not. We humans have a universal obligation to act *humanely*, and this means that we must refrain from treating animals in ways that cause them unnecessary distress. Animals, to repeat what was said at the outset, are not lumps of clay, and they ought not to be dealt with as though they feel no pain.

In medical science the use of animals as experimental subjects will be shown to be morally right. Indeed, physician-investigators often have a *duty* to use animals in place of humans. Most of us don't seriously doubt this, yet the condemnation of animal research is now a widely popular cause. How is this to be explained?

Experiments using animals are sometimes condemned out of ignorance. Many who know little of the methods of biological research do not fully understand the central role that animals play in medicine; many who care deeply about animals do not understand why animal subjects are essential and not replaceable. For most of those who are troubled by experiments using animals, reservations will dissipate when the consequences of forbidding those experiments are fully understood.

But not all critics of animal use are ignorant. Some understand the role that animals have played in the history of medicine and may also be aware of research in progress that depends on animal use. These critics object to animal experimentation in spite of that knowledge, however, for reasons that (in their view) override all medical consequences. These critics of animal use condemn the practice on moral principle. They hold deep convictions about what is not ethically justifiable behavior; they believe that killing animals for human purposes, even killing rodents, is never justifiable in a sound moral system. Their moral fervor is found by many to be persuasive. Their arguments give rise to the animal rights debate. Their mistakes are the chief concern of this book.

Animal *welfare* is not at issue here. Basic care for animals is today a moral concern almost universally shared. Sentient animals must be treated with careful regard for the fact that they can feel pain; decent people will always exhibit that concern and will rightly insist that the animals we use be fed and housed properly, handled considerately. Regulations ensuring such humane treatment are not in dispute; they are entirely justified and (in this country) universally in force. Principles of good animal husbandry rule, as they ought to rule, among the scientists who rely on animals in their investigations. Every medical center, every pharmaceutical company, every research institute using animals has (and under American law must have) its own Institutional Animal Care and Use Committee whose legal duty is to ensure that the animals in that facility are cared for properly and that experiments using those animals are conducted humanely. Frequent inspections by federal agencies, as well as by professional peers, enforce and reinforce high standards for animal care and use. Reasonable persons do not dispute the wisdom of this protective machinery. This book is not about animal welfare.

Advocates for animals, however, often demand regulations that would do very much more than enforce humane and thoughtful care. These critics object to any use of animals *categorically*. They aim to bring to an end all uses of animals, most certainly including all experiments in which animals are subjects. They seek, in their own words, "not larger cages, but empty cages." Such persons describe themselves, with respect to animal experimentation, as *abolitionists*. The growing popularity of this abolitionist position, and the danger of it, oblige us to reexamine here the arguments for and against the use of animals in medical science. I will argue that the abolitionist view is gravely mistaken, indefensible; it would (if enforced) seriously damage human well-being.

Two branches of the abolitionist family must be distinguished. Both adopt as a central aim the cessation of all animal use, but the underlying moral arguments of the two branches are very different. The phrase "animal rights advocates" has been loosely but inaccurately applied to both, resulting in widespread misunderstanding. The appeal to *animal rights* is indeed the heart of one main branch of the abolitionist family, but by those in the other branch no such appeal is made. Allow me to explain.

The current crusade for animals was opened by an Australian professor of philosophy, Peter Singer, who was deeply troubled by the widespread maltreatment of animals, especially animals raised for slaughter. His 1975 treatise, *Animal Liberation*,[1] ignited widespread agitation over other animal uses as well. Experiments using animals, Singer believes, we are morally obliged to stop, as we are obliged to stop all production of animals for food, because of the horrendous cruelties inflicted on helpless and innocent creatures. The benefits we obtain from the use of animals, he contends, are rightly weighed, but they cannot justify the inhumanity our use of them imposes. The animal liberation movement made (and makes) no claims about the rights of animals. Singer is explicitly a *utilitarian* in philosophical method; *consequences* are what count for him. The movement taking its name from his book is built on the conviction that, all things considered, animal experimentation does more harm than it does good. The suffering inflicted on animals by medical experiments using them is so great, say the liberationists, that it outweighs any good consequences those experiments may produce.

This conclusion is certainly not correct, as I will show in some detail later. Here I note simply that this animal *liberation* movement is not correctly described as defending animal *rights*. The animal rights movement (strictly so-called) is the second branch of the abolitionist family, and it has a moral foundation that is very different, not utilitarian at all. All uses of animals—including medical and scientific uses—are to be condemned (on this second view) because they are *wrong*. To see that they are wrong, we have only to understand the true moral status of animals and then to apply universal moral principles to the human conduct in question. The evil of animal experimentation, for philosophers in this camp, lies not in the alleged outweighing of good consequences by bad ones. Rather, the use of animals is (for them) *intrinsically* immoral; it is conduct that violates, always and inevitably, the *rights* those animals possess. On this account, it does not matter how the advantages and disadvantages of animal experimentation balance out; using animals in science is morally wrong because it violates the rights of conscious beings that we have a compelling moral duty to respect. This branch of the abolitionist family, careful in formulating its claims, does indeed defend the existence and centrality of "animal rights." I will use the phrase "animal rights advocates" in the strict sense, to identify this second branch of the abolitionist family. *Animal liberation,* on the one hand, and the defense of *animal rights* on the other hand, need to be distinguished, as their thoughtful advocates very carefully do.

Both branches of the abolitionist family are zealous in their condemnation of animal use in science. Members of both are often highly principled vegetarians as well, committed to a thoroughly "vegan" way of life: wearing no leather shoes or belts, surviving on a diet free of all meat, milk, eggs, or other animal products, and so on. Shared objectives and enthusiasms cause the two groups of abolitionists, although sharply at odds in their ethical foundations, to be commonly lumped together and referred to collectively by journalists and others as "the animal rights movement." The amalgamation is understandable; whether relying ultimately on consequences or on rights, they do agree that *all* uses of animals for the sake of human ends ought to be halted.

But because underlying moral arguments of the two camps are profoundly different, the responses to the arguments of each are also necessarily different, and must be presented separately in what follows. Chapters 4 through 6 address the claims of the *animal rights* advocates that animals have rights as humans have rights and that experimentation on animals is morally wrong because it violates those rights. Chapters 7 through 9 address the claims of the *animal liberation* movement that (although animals may have no rights in the strict sense) the evils of experimentation on them outweighs all the goods that it may do.

The two camps are often very unhappy with one another. Members of each are distressed by the efforts of the other to advance worthy ends with what are thought to be bad arguments. For the liberationists, whose calculations are of pleasures and pains, moral claims regarding abstract animal rights are derided as fuzzy and untenable. The "rights" alleged are taken by liberationists to be matters of bitter contention, never firmly established. To stake the lives of animals on a foundation so fundamentally insecure, say the liberationists, is to invite disaster. But for the advocates of animal rights in the strict sense, the utilitarian arguments of the "liberation" camp are not only insecure but dangerous. In some cases, at least, the calculation of good and bad consequences of animal use is virtually certain to yield a result not favorable to the animals. But in such cases the liberationist defense of animals must collapse, resting as it does on the calculation of the worth of outcomes. This is an unacceptable result from the standpoint of those who defend animal *rights*. Animal experimentation, they say, along with the eating of animals and every other disrespectful use of animals, is to be condemned not conditionally but absolutely, not because it does more harm than good but because it is intrinsically and absolutely *wrong*.

The critical fears of both sides are well warranted. Abolitionist arguments based on the calculation of goods and evils are indeed mistaken, as I will show in reckoning the full consequences of animal uses. An unadulterated utilitarian analysis will indeed support the use of animals in science. And abolitionist arguments based on the alleged rights of animals do indeed have a foundation that is murky and untenable. Animals, whose welfare we protect, cannot have rights, as I will explain; rights arise in the sphere of human morality and apply to moral agents that are uniquely human.

The most distinguished representative of the animal liberation movement is Peter Singer, now a member of the philosophy faculty at Princeton University. Tom Regan, a professor of philosophy at North Carolina State University, is the most distinguished representative of the animal rights movement. Regan disdains the consequentialist defense of animals; he rejects utilitarianism utterly. He is a good and an honest man, the deepest and most thoughtful representative of the principled position that animals have rights that must be respected and that any human practices that infringe upon these rights are damnable. Regan's book in defense of animals, *The Case for Animal Rights*,[2] is far and away the leading treatise on which the ethical position of the animal rights movement is built. Two other accounts of animal rights will be examined briefly here,[3] but the main pillar of the animal rights movement is the work of Tom Regan, and it is therefore his work to which the most careful attention must be given.

A personal word is in order. Tom Regan and I are friends. We like and respect one another. We both love animals; we both know a good deal about animals; we both derive great satisfaction from the companionship of our dogs. We are both professors of philosophy whose studies have long been in moral philosophy. Each of us is thoroughly convinced that the other is deeply mistaken about the moral status of animals. One of us surely is mistaken, obviously, since our conclusions contradict one another.

The objectives of the animal rights movement are sweeping. Regan has formulated them succinctly, and it is well to set them forth here, in his own words. Readers need to know all that is at stake in this intellectual dispute. Regan writes:

> The animal rights movement . . . as I conceive it, is committed to a number of goals, including:
> - the total abolition of the uses of animals in science;
> - the total dissolution of commercial animal agriculture;
> - the total elimination of commercial and sport hunting and trapping. . . .
> You don't change unjust institutions by tidying them up.[4]

The sentiments that motivate these convictions are honorable, but the arguments that underlie them will be seen upon close examination to be without merit. The abolitionist argument based on animal rights (I will show) confuses and misuses the concept of right, mistakenly applying it in a sphere in which it has no proper application.

But the utilitarian arguments of Regan's liberationist cousins are equally frail, weaker (I will argue) than even Regan thinks them to be. All things considered, we will come confidently to the conclusion that the use of animal subjects in medical research is not only practically necessary but is *morally justifiable* from every point of view.

First in this reexamination will come a review of the factual setting of the controversy, then an exploration of some philosophical fundamentals. Following that we turn to the reasoning in this turbulent arena: Claims and counterclaims must be set forth and evaluated; developments in the world of medical science must be borne in mind. The case for the use of animals, to be presented at length in the chapters that follow, deserves a patient hearing.

Notes

1. Peter Singer, *Animal Liberation* (New York: Avon, 1975).

2. Tom Regan, *The Case for Animal Rights* (Berkeley: University of California Press, 1983).

3. Aside from Tom Regan's work, the most valiant efforts to defend the rights of animals appear in Bernard Rollin, *Animal Rights and Human Morality* (New York: Prometheus, 1992), and in Steve Sapontzis, *Morals, Reason, and Animals* (Philadelphia: Temple University Press, 1987). Neither of these defenses (discussed in chap. 6) has had more than a fraction of the influence of Regan's treatise.

4. Regan, *Case,* 13.

2

The Factual Setting of Animal Experimentation

In the summer of 1948, I was a counselor in a children's camp in western North Carolina; one of our young campers was stricken by polio, an event that befell summer camps around the country that year. The fear in the faces of parents who rushed to the camp to take their children from that dangerous place, reaching with their arms across the quarantine chains, is vivid in my recollection. They trembled; my parents trembled; all parents trembled every polio season, which was every summer, never knowing whether their children would prove to be among the random victims of that crippling and often fatal disease.

The epidemic did not soon relent. During the summer of 1952, more than fifty-eight thousand American youngsters contracted polio. Thousands of these children died; thousands more were sentenced to a lifetime in the cruel machine that we called "the iron lung."

A vaccine for polio had been under development for some time, but years would pass before its safety and reliability were established and it could become widely effective. By the late fifties, however, childhood vaccination for polio had become routine; by the close of that decade, the number of reported polio cases in the United States had been reduced to twelve—*one dozen*. Polio was totally eradicated from the Western Hemisphere not long after that, and as I write the disease is nearing eradication in other parts of the world as well.

The astounding success of that first polio vaccine was announced at the medical center of the University of Michigan, only blocks from where I live in Ann Arbor. Its impact has been global. How many have been spared misery and death by this one great step in medical science we can hardly guess.

11

But about this wonderful vaccine and its successors we do know one thing for certain: *It could not have been achieved without the use of laboratory animals.*

To prepare the culture from which the polio vaccine was made, animal tissue was indispensable. And with that new vaccine greatest caution was obligatory. Many candidate vaccines had earlier been tried and had failed. From those earlier vaccines some healthy children had actually contracted polio. That could not be allowed to happen again. To test the new vaccine before its administration to humans, animal subjects were absolutely essential.

This true story, close to us in time and place, is widely known. But there are a thousand stories like it of which we are mostly unaware: scientific victories over tuberculosis and typhus, the discovery of insulin rescuing diabetics from misery and death, the discovery of antibiotics and the development of anesthetics—uncountable advances that have proved to be of incalculable importance to human beings. All this and much more could not have been done without the use of animals in the key experiments. The absolutely critical role of animals in these investigations cannot be emphasized too strongly. It is not simply that animals were convenient in such work or that they speeded the results—although if only that were the case, the justification of their use would be strong enough, heaven knows. But it is not like that. Experiments using animals are not merely helpful; they were and remain a necessary condition for most critical advances in protecting human health.

New vaccines are always dangerous. Testing them (and testing many new drugs as well) unavoidably risks the well-being, sometimes even the lives, of the first experimental subjects. When a new vaccine or new pharmaceutical compound has been devised and is at last to be tried, whose lives shall we put at risk? Not the lives of my children, certainly. The lives of yours, perhaps? You are offended by the thought—rightly. Shall we then use the children of unsophisticated people in underdeveloped societies? Heaven forbid. What, then, are our alternatives? There are only two: We will use animals (by which I mean nonhuman animals, of course) in such biomedical experiments, or we will not do those experiments at all.

The philosophical dispute about animal use therefore concerns each of us directly, insofar as we ourselves use, or expect to have available for use, vaccines and drugs that are effective and safe. Respecting every vaccine and almost every new drug, we will use animals in the research process, or we will not develop and we will not have that vaccine or that drug for our use.

Much talk in recent years suggests that animals in biomedical experiments should be replaced. Let us use "tissue samples" instead of whole animals, it is said; let us use "computer simulations" of the disease or the experimental organism. In a very few restricted settings, such replacements are possible and appropriate. But in most medical investigations the replacement of live animals with tissue samples or computer simulation is simply out of the question. The reason is simple: Investigators must learn the impact of a new compound or a new vaccine on the living organism as a whole; side effects that may be dangerous can be investigated only in the living organism and its complicated network of constituent organs, as they actually function. Computers cannot give that information. The results of experiments using tissue samples, however favorable, will not be enough to warrant the use of a new drug in humans until we have done our very best to learn its full organic impact. We can learn that only by studying the outcome of its use on live animals who are not human.

The first use of a new compound on a living organism is inescapably experimental. The subject of that experiment will be a human or another animal. The use of humans in such experiments we will not permit, understandably. If, therefore, the use of nonhuman animals is also not permitted, there will be no such experiments.

The large-scale replacement of animals by tissue samples or computers or anything else is, to be blunt, a misleading fantasy. In this continuing discussion of the morality of animal use, all such wishful conjectures should be put aside. Where alternatives to the use of animals can yield the needed data, it is right to use them, and it is right to seek such alternatives, as we do. But romantic dreams cannot guide actual research and may prove dangerous if relied on. Professor Tom Regan (who condemns all animal experimentation as immoral) was asked publicly in Washington, D.C., what he would have medical investigators do if the use of animals were indeed forbidden. How should they proceed? His answer was that they must find alternatives somehow, somewhere. They must, Regan said, "set their imaginations on fire."[1] That is an embarrassing response, not very helpful advice from a philosopher to laboratory scientists. To those who labor for new treatments of stubborn diseases, and for those who suffer grave illness and who pray for relief and can only hope for the successful outcomes of investigations in which experimental animals are the key, "set your imaginations on fire" is close to insult. We use animals because in most medical contexts no known alternatives to animal use are available. It is virtually certain that no such alternatives will exist for a very long time at least, since none are even on the horizon. In fact, it is probable that there never will be feasible alternatives to the uses of animals in much of medicine.

The killer disease for which a vaccine is now most desperately needed is malaria, which infects about *three hundred million new victims each year,* of whom *more than two million die* every year, most of them children in Africa and Asia. Drugs to combat malaria have become less and less effective as new strains of the parasite, resistant to those drugs, arise and spread. In the United States also malaria is spreading, the number of cases in recent years up well more than 200 percent—attributable to people who return from visits in their home countries, where they find that they are not immune. Many vaccines have been tried—not recently on children, thank God—but have failed. The parasite that causes malaria, carried by the anopheles mosquito, is so resilient that scientists have long been unable to generate in any living organism the antibodies needed to ward off the disease.

Recently, however, some striking progress has been made in this battle. After decades of effort a vaccine has been developed and tested at the Naval Medical Research Institute in Bethesda, Maryland; it does inoculate with safety and complete success against malaria—*in mice.*[2] For humans we do not yet have a vaccine proven safe. But before very long we probably will have one, and we will get it, if we do, only because we were able to experiment on mice, many mice, who will have been deliberately killed by investigators to learn what must be learned for the development of that new vaccine. In developing a malaria vaccine, we will use mice (as we do in the study of cancer, and diabetes, and hundreds of other human diseases) *because there is no other way.*

Many wince at the thought of using animals in biomedical research because they think immediately of dogs and cats, whom they love. In this view we are misled. The controversy should be understood to be one that mainly concerns the use of rodents, and among rodents chiefly mice and rats. Dogs, pigs, and other mammals (almost always anesthetized) are also used when they are the most suitable models for the disease under investigation. But only in a small minority of studies is that the case. The number of dogs and cats killed each year as experimental subjects is less than one-fiftieth of the number of dogs and cats killed *in animal shelters by humane societies for convenience,* because we have no place for them. About ten million dogs and cats are put to death in the United States each year for no good reason save that nobody wants them. Bearing in mind this wholesale killing of strays and former pets in animal shelters, how ought we respond to academic philosophers like Tom Regan who strenuously protest the carefully limited use of mice by medical science? Of all the animals used in biomedicine, dogs and cats make up less than 1 percent and primates less than three-tenths of 1 percent. Pigs, rabbits, and chickens are used more—but they amount to an extremely tiny fraction of 1 percent of all those billions of pigs, rabbits, and chickens killed for use as human food.

The U.S. Department of Agriculture recently estimated the number of animals used in medical and pharmaceutical research to be about 1.6 million, of which the vast majority, approximately 90 percent, were rats, mice, and other rodents. These animals would not have come to exist had they not been bred specifically for biomedical use.

Meanwhile, in the world of everyday life outside science, the extermination of rats and other vermin that infest our cities is a perennial objective, difficult to achieve but important for the sake of human health. The rats that multiply in our central cities are dirty and dangerous animals, carriers of disease, and specially threatening to the poor. In Chicago, where until recently rats outnumbered people by more than two to one, an aggressive campaign to clean the lakefront of rats has had substantial success. Of the rat population of about six million in 1979, more than five million had been eliminated by 1997.

In Boston, a massive rat control enterprise, largely successful, has recently been made necessary by the Central Artery Tunnel project, called by locals "the big dig."[3] A *huge* population of rodents, whose ancestors have been burrowing and breeding in the vicinity of the old Boston harbor for centuries, might have been dislodged by the construction of the new tunnel/highway and forced into the central city. These sewer rats (*Rattus norvegicus*) are not the cute little pets to be found in preschool classrooms; they are large (over a foot long), ferocious, often filthy creatures laden with disease, rats that eat virtually anything—including human babies when given the opportunity. The feces and urine of wild mice (*Peromyscus maniculatus,* not these rats) have very recently transmitted the deadly hantavirus, resulting in many human deaths in the United States. Rats like those of concern in Boston transmitted bubonic plague, the "black death," in ages past.[4] Should those Boston rats have been protected, possibly chased into the alleys and basements of the crowded city center? Or should they have been poisoned, as they were? In my judgment, it would have been morally wrong to risk the invasion of the human habitations of Boston's poor by these rodents; it was right to kill them as humanely and as efficiently as possible. Readers are likely to judge similarly about any rats, possibly disease-laden, discovered in their own basements.

What, then, will be our considered view of the protection we owe to rats on moral grounds? This is not merely an abstract puzzle. Deciding what conduct is moral is, as Kant insisted, a very *practical* matter. What shall be our practice, our actions, in dealing with rodents? Do we seriously think it to be wrong to kill disease-carrying rats for the sake of human health? Wrong to use rats as the subjects of experiments designed to develop new drugs for cancer, new vaccines for malaria and other human afflictions?

Whether we are morally justified in using animals as we do in science must be decided in the light of what we know about safeguarding the healthy and curing the sick. The arguments in the continuing philosophical controversy that is the substance of this book should be evaluated in the light of the facts, often very unpleasant facts, of human and animal disease.

Notes

1. At a conference in which we both participated, on the moral status of animals, at Georgetown University in Washington, D.C., on 25 June 1995.

2. See Stephen L. Hoffman and others, "Protection against Malaria by Vaccination with Sporozite Surface Protein 2 Plus CS Protein," Science 252 (3 May 1991): 715–18.

3. See B. A. Colvin et al., "Planning Rodent Control for Boston's Central Artery/Tunnel Project," Proceedings, Fourteenth Vertebrate Pest Conference, University of California, Davis, 1990; and, more recently, F. Fothergill et al., "Control of Norway Rats in Sewer and Utility Systems," Eighteenth Vertebrate Pest Conference, University of California, Davis, 1998.

4. They do plenty of damage still. In New York City, where live millions of rats, eating virtually anything, hundreds of persons are bitten by rats each year. In spite of the fact that the rat control budget in the city rises steadily and is now about $13 million per year, professional exterminators in New York report that the rat problem there is worse than it has ever been. See "Rats Love New York" in the *New York Times,* 12 July 2000. If rats have rights, the vicious rats of New York and Boston, and of every other city, have them, too.

3

Rights and Interests

The central attack on animal experimentation comes from those who contend that animals have rights. Whether animals do have rights is a question of very great importance, because if they do, as these critics claim, those rights must be respected—and they must be respected (as we noted earlier) even if doing so imposes great costs or burdens on human beings. Rights count; they are dispositive; they cannot be ignored. The meaning of *right* is therefore absolutely critical in this debate; it deserves the most careful reflection at the outset.

A *right* is a valid claim, or potential claim, that may be made by a moral agent, under principles that govern both the claimant and the target of the claim.[1] Every genuine right has some *possessor* and must have some *target* and some *content*.

You, the reader, possess many rights, of course. The *content* of your rights may vary greatly: You may have a right to the repayment of a loan or deposit, a right to nondiscrimination by an employer on account of race, a right to noninterference by the state in some protected activity like political speech, and so on. The *target* against whom some rights claim of yours may be registered may also vary greatly. It can be a single person (say, your landlord), or a group (say, some profit-making corporation), or a community (say, the city in which you live). You may, conceivably, have a right against all humankind. To comprehend any genuine right fully, therefore, we must know *who* holds the right, *to what* it is a right, and *against whom* it is held.

Rights are very different from *interests,* and this distinction is of profound importance in moral reasoning. It may be much in my interest for you to employ me—and yet I may have a right to neither. I may have a very strong interest in the passage of some legislation or in having a particular

17

decision reached by a judge or jury—and yet have no right to those outcomes. I may have an interest in admission to some school or participation in some deliberative body, but have no rights to either. Some of my interests are of the very greatest importance to me, and some of your rights may be of little concern to you. But your rights, being valid claims, must be respected, while my interests, even when important, do not always command respect. Rights cannot be justly disregarded; interests may deserve to be disregarded in some contexts, and very often they will go unsatisfied.

If you have a right that conflicts with my interest, there can be no serious doubt how that conflict is to be resolved. Interests are for the most part transient and subjective. Rights are objective and commonly endure; they are legitimate demands made within a moral system. *Rights trump interests.* This is a point of the most fundamental importance. The animal rights movement takes rights very seriously, and so should we all.

Some illustrations of this common conflict may prove useful. You have a right to the return of the money you lent me, today if this be the date of repayment to which I had earlier committed myself. We both understand this. I may have a continuing urgent need for the money owed to you, and it may be very much in my interest to hold on to it. You may have little current need for it at all. But my convenience and your affluence are not to the point. You now have a *right* to the money you lent. Laws in a civil society are framed, and a system for their enforcement devised, partly to ensure that certain moral rights will receive the respect to which they are entitled. A body politic having legitimate authority may on occasion create rights by statute. But the true merit of any community's system of justice depends on the relation between the laws and the moral rights that ought to underlie them.

Many rights cannot be written into law. If I give you an earnest promise—say, to maintain complete confidentiality on some sensitive matter—you have a moral right to my keeping that promise even though there may be no court in which your claim could be enforced. It may be very much in my interest to break the promise I gave you, but my interests and the silence of the law do not override the obligation created by that promise freely given—a promise whose binding force we both well understood.

Those holding power in the state also often have important interests for the sake of which they might gladly override your rights—your right to travel freely, perhaps, or your right to publish sharp criticism. Their interests need not be nefarious; your rights may interfere with their genuinely benevolent intentions. But the protection of fundamental rights is one central function of a good constitution and is one reason, perhaps the chief reason, that we prize respect for our Constitution so highly. In a decent society (which we like to think ours is) the interests of the powerful are not allowed to trample rights, even the rights of the humble. Rights always trump interests.

Nazi doctors under Hitler, partly to support what they thought to be great national interests, were determined to learn all that they could about hypothermia, human freezing. Too many German soldiers were freezing to death on the eastern front; grave military needs impelled their inquiry. To advance these interests, they conducted scientific studies; they soaked Jews in cold water and put them in refrigerators, the better to learn how hypothermia develops and can be treated. Such experiments are outrageous, horrible, utterly repugnant on moral grounds. The scientific results obtained from these investigations will not even be referred to by many who think such uses of human beings to be unconscionable. Those Nazi doctors did in fact learn a good deal about hypothermia—but we have no difficulty in seeing that all scientists, no matter the importance of the interests they pursue, are forbidden to advance medicine in that way. The Jews who were the innocent victims of those atrocious experiments had rights, rights demanding respect. Those rights were cruelly violated, ignored; medical investigators who use humans with a callous disregard for their rights deserve to be the object of our moral loathing.

In that same spirit, all decent human beings condemn torture. Even criminals ought not be treated as though they were mere things. Felons convicted of the most heinous crimes, we will agree, ought not have their bodily organs forcibly harvested for transplanting. Every human being, we think, is the bearer of some rights, natural human rights. Some philosophers have contended that such natural rights are really no more than fictions, that what are commonly called rights are nothing but advantages to be gained or lost by one group relative to some other group.[2] But even those whose writings may deprecate rights will act with mighty determination in defense of their own rights when push comes to shove.

In all morality the key concept is that of *right*. In the life of the community what is most precious to its members are its rights. We have a weighty interest in protecting our rights, of course—but we certainly do not have a right to have all our interests satisfied. An interest, even if it is weighty, does not for that reason become a right. Rights have a commanding place in moral relations that interests cannot usurp. Rights, but not interests, are valid moral claims that other moral agents have the obligation to recognize and to respect.

Notes

1. This account of right expresses what most philosophers agree is essential to it. Some may argue with the formulation, but Professor Tom Regan, who fairly represents the animal rights movement, is not likely to quarrel with it; his account of rights is very similar. He writes, "To have a right is to be in a position to claim, or to have

claimed on one's behalf, that something is due or owed, and the claim that is made is a claim made against somebody, to do or forbear what is claimed as due" (*Case*, 271). Regan's views will be sharply criticized in what follows, but in holding that a right is at bottom a valid moral claim, there is no conflict between us.

2. Jeremy Bentham, the great utilitarian philosopher, in *Introduction to the Principles of Morals and Legislation* (London: Wickering, 1823) wrote, "Natural rights? Natural and imprescriptable rights? Nonsense. Nonsense upon stilts."

4

If Animals Had Rights

All that has been thus far said about rights applies to human beings. We humans certainly do have rights, and few matters are of greater importance to us than the protection of our rights. The words of the Declaration of Independence are more than rhetoric: "To secure these rights governments are instituted among men. . ." But the rights secured by governments are not created by governments; they are ours by nature, because we are human beings. The centrality of rights is understood everywhere; rights belong to all humans because they are humans; that is the point of the Universal Declaration of Human Rights, adopted unanimously by the General Assembly of the United Nations. Practice is not always consistent with profession, of course, but nearly all the nations of the planet profess the recognition of life, liberty, the security of person, and freedom of thought, conscience, and religion as universal human rights. Tom Regan and his followers in the animal rights movement accept that universality, too, and that far they are on solid ground.

But are those rights, all of the greatest consequence for humans, possessed by the lower animals as well? Do rats have rights? Here we reach the heart of the debate with which this book is concerned. Regan and company believe that animals are the bearers of rights, just as surely as those Jews the Nazis used in their hypothermia experiments were the bearers of rights. Not all the same rights, of course, but rights in the same sense. Animal rights advocates need not suppose (and generally, when they are sensible, they do not suppose) that animals have all the rights that humans do; that wouldn't even make sense, of course. That rats have the right to freedom of religion they do not urge. But they do earnestly believe that animals have some very important rights and that those rights that they do have, they have in the very same sense that the Jews

21

in Germany had theirs. And the rights of animals (they say), like the rights of Jews, *demand* respect. Some animal rights advocates therefore look on contemporary uses of animals by American medical researchers exactly as we look on the uses of Jews in the 1940s by Nazi medical researchers.

In pressing this analogy between the Jews in Hitler's Germany and the rats in the modern American laboratory, they are entirely consistent. Their point is this: Animals may not have all the rights that humans do, but if they have any rights at all, they certainly have the right not to be killed to advance someone else's convenience. If animals have any rights at all, they have the right to be respected as beings with rights, the right not to be used like inanimate tools to advance human interests. And this is true, they contend, no matter how important we think those human interests to be.

This animal rights position must be taken seriously because rights must be taken seriously. If animals have any rights at all, we do have the duty to respect those rights. Seeking to evade the force of this argument some will rejoin, "Well, they [the animals] may have rights, but we humans have rights, too, and our rights override theirs." This, unfortunately, cannot suffice to justify our killing the rats. No doubt we humans do have rights, and if animals have rights also, it may be true in some cases that our rights conflict with theirs and in such cases may be held to override theirs. But most of our uses of animals, and certainly our uses of animals in medical experiments, although they serve good purposes, are not essential to protect our rights. We want very much to devise a vaccine that will protect humans against malaria, and AIDS, and so on, and we do have a very weighty interest in learning how to achieve these objectives, as the Nazis had a serious interest in learning how to deal with hypothermia. But we don't have a *right* to learn, at any cost, what may be useful to us, any more than the Nazis had such a right. When animals (or humans) attack us, we have the right to defend ourselves and may in such cases be justified in killing, to preserve our lives. But the animals we kill in medical research are not killed in self-defense; to claim so would be flatly dishonest. The helpless and innocent mice that die in our efforts to understand and defeat cancer never did attack us.

In short, animal rights advocates make a very strong hypothetical point: *If* animals have any rights at all, they certainly must have the right not to be killed to advance the interests of others.

Therefore (in this animal rights view), what we did to animals in developing the polio vaccine and what we are doing to animals as we now try to learn how to immunize against malaria or AIDS or any other disease is as profoundly wrong, as plainly *unjust,* as what was done by Nazis to those Jews not so very long ago. This is not for them hyperbole. Animal rights advocates need not hold (and generally do not hold) that contemporary medical scientists are as vicious as the Nazis were. They simply believe that in the same way that what the Nazis did was morally unacceptable, what is being done to animals now is morally unacceptable. If it is wrong, there is no excuse for it. It will be no answer to explain how useful the results of doing it may prove to be. Rights trump interests.

The vast majority of animals used in biomedical investigations (as earlier noted) are rodents, guinea pigs and ferrets, but mainly mice and rats. The rat may be appropriately taken, and is generally taken by the animal rights advocate, as the best exemplar of animals whose moral status is in dispute. If rats have rights, then dogs and rabbits surely do, and so on. This use of the rodent as exemplar is very helpful; it enables us to grasp the sweep of the animal rights movement. The thrust of their attack on medical experimentation using animals is expressed dramatically in the work of the most celebrated advocate of animal rights. Tom Regan has no doubt that rats have rights and believes that because they do, they *may not* be used in biomedical investigations. Regan does not hide or cheat. He sees the consequences of his view and accepts them forthrightly. He writes:

> The harms others might face as a result of the dissolution of [some] practice or institution is no defense of allowing it to continue. . . . No one has a right to be protected against being harmed if the protection in question involves violating the rights of others. . . . [N]o one has a right to be protected by the continuation of an unjust practice, one that violates the rights of others. . . . Justice *must* be done, though the heavens fall.[1]

That last line echoes Immanuel Kant, who in turn had borrowed it from a venerable tradition: *Fiat justitia, et pereat mundus* (Let justice be done though the world perish). That is Regan's view: Doing justice entails protecting the rights of rats to life; he is not daunted by the consequences. Believing that rats have rights as humans do, that they are bearers of rights in the same fully moral sense, he concludes consistently (but not for the sake of consistency alone) that killing rats in medical research is "morally intolerable." Regan writes. "On the rights view[2] we cannot justify harming a single rat merely by aggregating 'the many human and humane benefits' that flow from doing it. . . . Not even a single rat is to be treated as if that animal's value were reducible to his *possible utility* relative to the interests of others."[3]

If Regan were correct in this, we are forbidden by morality from doing the experiments that alone might yield the vaccines, drugs, and other compounds and therapies that humans desperately need. Can this extraordinary conclusion possibly be true? It *is* true, say Regan and his followers; we *are* so forbidden. But (we answer) the result of your principles is that very many humans will suffer terribly; many humans will die who might otherwise live happy lives if (as on your view) the rights of rats trump human interests. Perhaps that is so (they rejoin), but if there are some things we will not be able to learn because animals have rights, well, as Regan puts it bluntly, "so be it."

These are the conclusions to which one is certainly driven if it be true that animals have rights. No compromise is possible here. If animals have rights, they have the right to be respected. If they have the right to be respected, they have the right not to be killed to advance our interests. The premise that animals possess rights may be utterly false, as indeed it is, but Regan reasons correctly once that premise is granted: If rats have the moral standing that gives them rights, we humans can have no right, ever, to kill them for our benefit—not in the laboratory or in our basements or in the back alleys of Chicago or Boston. A rat that attacks a human may be killed in self-defense. Medical investigations in which rats are routinely killed cannot be honestly described as self-defense. Scientific experiments relying on the use of rats, or mice, or any other animal subjects—and this will include most medical studies and nearly all the most important studies of certain kinds—must therefore come to an end, not gradually or eventually but immediately. Recall that the replacement of animal subjects by computers or by anything else (except human subjects) is, as a practical matter, out of the question. All biomedical investigations using animal subjects, and of course all uses of animals as food or clothing too, are morally forbidden and must *stop*.

Readers who reflect on the scientific impact of this conclusion are likely to think it bizarre. We might suppose that those who insist on such an outcome are out of their minds. But the fact that the consequences of the view are outrageous cuts no mustard for the zealots of the animal rights movement. They are not consequentialists. The consequences of animal use may be very good for us, they will allow, but it is wrong; acts that are morally wrong cannot be made right by listing the many good things they serve to bring about. The interests of humans—the universal human desire to be freed of disease and relieved of pain—are understood well enough by the animal rights movement. But from the perspective of its consistent members, of whom Tom Regan is the paramount example, these human interests cannot outweigh the rights of *a single rat*. The issue for them is one of simple justice, and the use of animals in medical experiments, in their view, is simply not just.

Talk about the rights of animals appears to many to be harmless. It's just a way to encourage the greater protection of innocent animals, many think. To say that animals have rights, they suppose, is no more than a formal recognition of the fact that there are some things we ought not do to animals. Not so. The supposition of animal rights entails very much more than that. The animal rights movement, as we have seen, explicitly aims for the *total abolition* of the use of animals in science and the *total dissolution* of commercial animal agriculture. These objectives are the logical consequences of believing that animals have rights. Seeing this clearly will give most of us good reason to think carefully before giving assent to claims about animals that appear superficially to be innocuous.

The inescapable consequences of imputing rights to animals are so very bad, so damaging to medical science, that we owe it to ourselves to weigh very skeptically what are put forward as arguments in support of that claim. Do you, the reader, believe that you and all other humans have the strongest moral obligation never to eat meat of any kind, never to use animal products of any kind? Do you believe that the scientific work done in eradicating polio and smallpox, along with the work of all other medical investigators past and present who rely on animal subjects, is morally wrong? Probably you do not. If you do not, you must reject the premise from which these fanatical convictions flow.

Do you approve of the scientific experiments using animals that have in fact resulted in the protection of millions of human beings, probably including yourself and your children, from diphtheria, hepatitis, measles, rabies, rubella, and tetanus? Do you believe that the scientific studies now in progress to combat AIDS, lyme disease, Alzheimer's disease, heart disease, diabetes, and cancer—almost all of those studies relying essentially on the use of animals—are morally justifiable? Probably you do. I surely do, with all my heart. If you would join me in support of the research that vulnerable humans desperately need, you will join me also in concluding that the central claim of the animal rights movement—that rats and rabbits and chickens possess rights in the same sense that humans do—is a profound and gigantic mistake.

Notes

1. Regan, *Case*, 346–47; emphases in the original.
2. Professor Regan regularly refers to his defense of animal rights as "the rights view." But of course many philosophers who take rights every bit as seriously as he does do not believe as he does that rights are possessed by animals; the position he refers to as "the rights view" is more correctly called "the Regan rights view."
3. Regan, *Case*, 384; emphases in the original.

5

Why Animals Do Not Have Rights

The consequences of holding that animals have rights are intolerable, as we have just seen, yet there is widespread reluctance to assert forthrightly that animals do not possess rights, for two reasons. One is the fear that we will be thought callous if animal rights are denied. Most of us care a great deal about animals, and we want not to undermine that reputation.

But the major reason we hesitate to deny that animals have rights lies in a widespread confusion about the relation between our obligations to animals and the claim that animals possess rights. Humans do have many obligations to animals, as I have earlier insisted and as all decent persons will agree. Does it follow from this that animals must have rights? Many assume that it does and therefore suppose that if animal rights were to be denied, the obligations owed to animals would need to be denied as well. This is a common and unfortunate mistake. Denying the reality of animal rights does not entail the denial of our obligations to animals. Most certainly it does not, as I will explain.

Reflect for a moment on the obligations we humans owe to others. Some of these obligations may be traced to the fact that we are the targets of their rights. My obligation to repay the money I borrowed from you is the obverse of the right that you have to my payment of the debt. So, plainly, *some* of my obligations do arise from the rights of others against me. But that is by no means true of all obligations. A correct understanding of the true relation between rights and obligations is absolutely essential for sound moral judgments.

The common readiness to assent to the proposition that animals have rights is mainly a result of the hasty supposition that if we have obligations to them (which we surely do), they must have rights against us. But this is not so. Recognizing (correctly) that we are not morally free to do anything we please to

animals, it is supposed (incorrectly) that they must therefore have "rights"—
and once that supposition is granted, all the problems discussed in the previous chapter unavoidably confront and confound us.

The premise that underlies such reasoning is the supposition of the *sym-
metrical reciprocity* of obligations and rights. It is a false premise, and its falsity
is easy to discern. Between rights and obligations the relations are not sym-
metrical. Rights do entail obligations on the targets of those rights, of course,
as earlier noted. If you have a right to the return of money you lent me, I have
the obligation to return that money, and so on. But we may not correctly infer,
from the fact that all rights impose obligations on their targets, that all obligations owed arise because one is the target of the rights of another.

A logical confusion underlies the mistake. From the true proposition that
all dogs are mammals we certainly may not infer that all mammals are dogs.
Universal affirmative propositions of the form "All dogs are mammals" or
"All rights entail obligations" cannot be *converted simply* and retain their
truth. *Some* mammals are dogs, yes, and *some* obligations do arise from rights.
But it is a confusion of mind to conclude, from the fact that all dogs are mammals, that all mammals are dogs. It is no less a confusion of mind to conclude
that, because all rights entail obligations, all obligations are entailed by
rights.

Very many of the moral obligations borne by each of us are owed to other
persons or other beings who have no *rights* against us; reflection on everyday
experience confirms this quickly. Our obligations arise from a great variety of
circumstances and relations, of which being the target of another's right is but
one. Illustrations of this rich and important variety are everywhere to be
found; here are some:

1. Obligations arise from *commitments* freely made by a moral agent. As a
   college professor, I promise my students explicitly that I will comment
   at length on the papers they submit, and from this express commitment
   obligations flow, of course. But my students understand that they have
   not the right to demand that I provide such comment.
2. Obligations arise from *the possession of authority*. Civil servants are
   obliged to be courteous to members of the public; presiding officers at
   a public forum ought to call on representatives of different points of view
   in alternation; arbitrators have the obligation to listen patiently to the
   arguments of parties disputing before them—but such obligations are
   not grounded in rights.
3. Obligations arise as a consequence of *special relations:* Hosts have an
   obligation to be cordial to their guests, but guests may not demand cor-
   diality as a right.
4. *Faithful service* may engender obligations: Shepherds have obligations

to their dogs, and cowboys to their horses, none of which flow from the *rights* of those dogs or those horses.

5. My son, eight years old as I write this, may someday wish to study veterinary medicine as my father did. I will then have the obligation to help him as I can, and with pride I shall—but he has not the authority to demand such help as a matter of right. *Family connections* may give rise to obligations without concomitant rights.

6. My dog has no right to daily exercise and veterinary care, but I do have the obligation to provide these things for him. *Duties of care* freely taken on may bind one even though those to whom the care is given have not got a right to demand it. Recognizing that a beloved pet is suffering great pain, we may be obliged to put it out of its misery, but the tormented animal has no claim of right that that be done.

7. An act of *spontaneous kindness* done may leave us with the obligation to acknowledge and perhaps return that gift, but the benefactor to whom we are thus obliged has no claim of *right* against us.

And so on and on. The circumstances giving rise to obligations are so many and so varied that they cannot all be catalogued. It is nevertheless certain, and plainly seen when we consider the matter with care, that it is *not only* from the rights of others that our obligations arise.

How, then, are rights and obligations related? When looked at from the viewpoint of one who holds a right and addresses the target of that right, they appear correlative. But they are plainly not correlative when looked at from the viewpoint of one who recognizes an obligation self-imposed, an obligation that does not stem from the rights of another. Your right to the money I owe you creates my obligation to pay it, of course. But many of my obligations to the needy, to my neighbors, to sentient creatures of every sort, have no foundation in their rights. The premise that rights and obligations are *reciprocals*, that *every* obligation flows from another's right, is utterly false. It is inconsistent with our intuitive understanding of the difference between what we believe we *ought* to do and what others can justly *demand* that we do.

This lack of symmetry is of enormous importance. It helps to explain how it can be true that, although animals do not have rights, it does not follow from this fact that one is free to treat them with callous disregard. It is silly to think of rats as the holders of moral rights, but it is by no means silly to recognize that rats can feel pain and that we have an obligation to refrain from torturing them because they are beings having that capacity. The obligation to act humanely *we owe to them* even though the concept of a right cannot possibly apply to them. We are obliged to apply to animals the moral principles that govern *us* regarding the gratuitous imposition of pain and suffering. We are the moral agents in this arena, not the rats. Act toward lesser creatures, as the saying goes, "not merely according to their deserts, but according to your dignities." We are restrained by moral principles in this way, but being so restrained does not suggest or suppose that the animals to whom we owe humane regard are the possessors of rights.

Animals cannot be the bearers of rights because the concept of right is *essentially human;* it is rooted in the human moral world and has force and applicability only within that world. Humans must deal with rats—all too frequently in some parts of the world—and must refrain from cruelty in dealing with them. But a rat can no more be said to have rights than a table can be said to have ambition or a rock to exhibit remorse. To say of a pig or a rabbit that it has rights is to confuse categories, to apply to its world a moral category that can have content only in the human moral world.

Try this thought experiment: Imagine, on the Serengeti Plain in East Africa, a lioness hunting to feed her cubs. A baby zebra, momentarily left unattended by its mother, becomes her prey; the lioness snatches it, rips open its throat, tears out chunks of its flesh and departs. The mother zebra is driven nearly out of her wits when at first she cannot locate her baby; finding its carcass at last she will not leave its remains for days. The scene may cause you to shudder, but it is perfectly ordinary and common in the world of nature. If that baby zebra had any rights at all, it certainly had the right to live; of all rights, that one is surely the most fundamental and the one presupposed by all others. So, if in that incident of natural predation, the prey has rights and the predator infringes those rights, we humans ought to intervene in defense of the zebra's rights, if doing so were within our power. But we do not intervene in such matters even when it is in our power; we do not dream of doing so. On the other hand, if we saw (or even suspected) that the lioness was about to attack an unprotected human baby playing at the edge of the forest, we would respond with alacrity, protecting the baby in every way possible.

Now I ask: What accounts for the moral difference between those cases? Not convenience, merely; protecting the baby may be dangerous, while intervening to save the baby zebra may be easy and safe. Humans are often in a position to intervene to avoid predatory killing, yet we deliberately refrain. Our responses to threatened humans differ fundamentally from our responses to threatened zebras. But why? No doubt we have greater empathy for the endangered human. But we also recognize, consciously or subconsciously, that profound differences exist between the moral status of the baby zebra and the moral status of the baby human. The human baby, we might say if later asked, has a right not to be eaten alive, and it has that right because it is a *human* being.

Do you believe the baby zebra has the *right* not to be slaughtered? Or that the lioness has the *right* to kill that baby zebra to feed her cubs? Perhaps you are inclined to say, when confronted by such natural rapacity (duplicated in various forms millions of times each day on planet earth) that *neither* is right or wrong, that neither zebra nor lioness has a right against the other. Then I am on your side. Rights are pivotal in the moral realm and must be taken seriously, yes; but zebras and lions and rats do not live in a moral realm—their lives are totally *amoral*. There *is* no morality for them; animals do no moral wrong, ever. In their world there are no wrongs and there are no rights.

One contemporary philosopher who has thought a good deal about animals puts this point in terms of the ability to formulate principles. Referring to animals as "moral patients" (i.e., beings *upon* whom moral agents like ourselves may act), he writes:

> A moral patient [an animal] lacks the ability to formulate, let alone bring to bear, principles in deliberating about which one among a number of possible acts it would be right or proper to perform. Moral patients, in a word, cannot do what is right, nor can they do what is wrong. . . . [E]ven when a moral patient causes significant harm to another, the moral patient has not done what is wrong. Only moral agents can do what is wrong.

Just so. The concepts of wrong, and of right, are totally foreign to animals, not conceivably within their ken or applicable to them, as the author of that passage clearly sees. His name is Tom Regan.[1]

Here is yet another thought experiment that illuminates our intuitive judgments about the moral status of animals: Imagine that, as you were driving to work the other day, a squirrel suddenly reversed its course and ran in front of your car. It being impossible for you to avoid hitting it, you clenched your teeth as you heard the telltale thump from beneath the automobile. Pained by the thought that the squirrel had been needlessly killed by your car, you silently express to yourself the hope that, if indeed it was killed, it was caused no great suffering; and you drive on. But now suppose that it was not a squirrel but a human toddler who ran into the path of your car and whom you hit through absolutely no fault of your own. Swerving in panic, we will suppose, you avoid a killing blow, but you cannot avoid hitting the child and it becomes plain that she has been badly injured by the impact. Anguish, fear, *horror* overwhelm you. Most assuredly you do not drive on but stop in wretched torment, to do what can be done for the injured child. You rush it to medical care; you contact her parents at the earliest possible moment, imploring their understanding. Nothing you could possibly have done would have avoided the terrible accident, you explain—and yet you express tearfully your profound regret. At the first opportunity you arrange to visit the recuperating child; you bring her a present, wish her well; her injury and her recovery will be forever on your mind. And so on.

What accounts for the enormous difference between the response you make to the death of a squirrel and to the injury of a human child, you being the cause of both, and in both cases entirely innocent of fault? Does that difference not spring from your intuitive grasp of the difference in the moral status of the two, your recognition that the one has rights, which you would not for all the world have deliberately infringed upon, while the other, although sentient and perhaps endearing, has no rights on which you could possibly infringe?

The obligation of scientists to act humanely no one will contest. But medical investigators, using animals in research to advance human well-being, can never violate the rights of experimental animals because, to be blunt, they have no rights. Rights do not apply to them.

Humans, on the other hand, certainly do have rights. And at this point we are likely to ask how this difference is to be accounted for. Rabbits are mammals and we are mammals, both inhabiting a natural world. The reality of the moral rights that we possess and that they do not possess we do not deny, and the importance of this great difference between us and them we do not doubt. But we are unsure of the ground of these rights of ours, their warrant, their source. Where do our rights come from? We are animals, too; we are a natural species, too, a product of evolution as all animals are. How, then, can we be so very different from the zebras and the rats? Why are we not crudely primitive creatures as they are, creatures for whom the concept of moral right is a fiction?

Philosophers and theologians have long struggled, and struggle still, to explain the foundations of natural human rights. In this book, dealing chiefly with the claim that animals have rights, it is not to be expected that a definitive account of the human moral condition will be given. I do not propose to offer here the resolution of the deepest questions confronting human beings. But the sharp divide between the moral status of animals and that of humans we can say something more about.

It will be helpful to reflect, if only briefly, on the *kinds* of explanations of human rights that have been given by the greatest of moral philosophers. What has been generally held to account for the fact that humans, unlike animals, do have rights?

Divine gift. Many have thought that the moral understanding of right and duty, by humans, is a *divine gift*, a grasp of the eternal law for which we have been peculiarly equipped by God. So thought St. Thomas of Aquinas, who argued tightly in defense of that view in the thirteenth century: All things, said he,

> are ruled and measured by the eternal law. . . . Now among all others, the rational creature is subject to divine providence in the most excellent way, in so far as it partakes of a share of providence. . . . Wherefore it has a share of the eternal reason, whereby it has a natural inclination to its proper act and end: and this par-

ticipation of the eternal law in the rational creature is called the natural law. Hence the Psalmist after saying . . . "Many say, Who showeth us good things?" in answer to which question he says: "The light of Thy countenance, O Lord, is signed upon us";[2] thus implying that the light of natural reason, whereby we discern what is good and what is evil, which is the function of the natural law, is nothing else than an imprint on us of the divine light.[3]

The power to grasp the binding power of moral law, and therefore the capacity to understand human rights and to respect them, is on this account divinely endowed. No one has put this view more cogently than St. Thomas. The account he gave was not new in his day, nor has it lost its authority for many today.

Long before St. Thomas marshaled such arguments, other fathers of the Church, perhaps St. Augustine most profoundly, had pointed out that if God has made us in his own image as we are taught, and therefore with a will that is truly free and "knowing good and evil,"[4] we, unlike all other creatures, must choose between good and evil, between right and wrong.[5]

Human moral community. Philosophers have very commonly distrusted such theological reasoning. Many accounts of the moral dimension of human experience have been offered that do not rely on inspired texts or supernatural gifts. Of the most influential philosophers, many have held that human morality is grounded not in the divine but in the human moral community. "I am morally realized," wrote the great English idealist, F. H. Bradley, "not until my personal self has utterly ceased to be my exclusive self, is no more a will which is outside others' wills, but finds in the world of others nothing but self." What Bradley called "the organic moral community" is, he thought, the only context in which there can be right. "Realize yourself as the self-conscious member of an infinite whole, by realizing that whole in yourself."[6]

Before him the great German idealist, Georg W. F. Hegel, accounted for human rights as a consequence of the self-conscious participation of human beings in "an objective ethical order."[7] And there have been many other such accounts of rights, accounts that center on human interrelations, on a moral fabric within which human beings must always act, but within which animals never act and never can *possibly* act.

Direct intuitive recognition. Such reasoning is exceedingly abstract, and many find it for that reason unsatisfying. A better account of rights, an account more concrete and more true to their own experience, some think to be that given by ethical intuitionists and realists who rely upon the immediate moral experience of ordinary people. Human moral conduct must be governed, said the leading intuitionist H. A. Prichard, by the underivative, intuitive cognition of the rightness of an action."[8] Would you know how we can be sure that humans have rights? Ask yourself how you know that you have rights. You have no doubt about it. There are some fundamental truths, on this view, for which no argument need be given. In that same spirit Sir David Ross explained our grasp of human right as our recognition of moral "suitability"—"fitness, in a certain specific and unanalysable way, to a certain situation."[9] And that was the view of my teacher and good friend of happy memory, Professor C. D. Broad. Rights surely are possessed by humans, he thought; by humans but never by animals the knowledge of right is immediately and certainly possessed.

Natural evolutionary development. For those who seek a more naturalistic account of ethical concepts, there are, among others, the writings of Marx and his followers who explicitly repudiated all moral views claiming to have their foundation in some supernatural sphere. "The animal," Marx wrote, "is one with its life activity. It does not distinguish the activity from itself. It is its activity. But man makes his life activity itself an object of his will and consciousness. . . . His own life is an object for him. . . . Conscious life activity distinguishes man from the life activity of the animals." Hence, humans can concern themselves with human*kind*, and humans alone can understand their species; humans, unlike animals, make judgments that can be "universal and consequently free."[10] Moral judgments are typically universal in this sense. That is why, Lenin later wrote, "There is no such thing as morality taken outside of human society."[11] Every conception of moral right, on this view, is a reflection of the concrete conditions of life, but always the conditions of *human* life.

A more sophisticated ethical naturalism was presented by the American pragmatists, John Dewey and George Herbert Mead, who shared the view that morality arises only in human community but who emphasized the development of self within that community. We humans create our selves, selves that develop and become moral, Mead wrote, only through "the consciousness of other moral selves."[12]

Which among all these families of moral positions is most nearly true? Readers will decide for themselves. Differing ethical systems have been very briefly recapitulated here only to underscore the fact that, however much great thinkers have disagreed about fundamental principles, *the essentially human (or divine) locus of the concept of right* has never been doubted. Of the finest moral philosophers from antiquity to the present not one would deny—as the animal rights movement does seek now to deny—that there is a most profound difference between the moral stature of humans and that of animals, and that rights pertain only to the former.

The extraordinary departure of the animal rights movement from near universal moral convictions may be exhibited in the following way. Protecting animals is viewed by many in that movement as a noble struggle against a brutal holocaust. A fiery leader in defense of the moral equality of all animal species is Ingrid Newkirk, long the codirector of the largest animal protection organization, People for the Ethical Treatment of Animals (PETA). In her view, it is cruelly wrong to give special consideration to the human species. Research using animal subjects, no matter its aim or beneficial outcomes, she calls "fascism" and "supremacism." Her belief, and that of her followers, is that there is no fundamental moral difference between animals and humans. "There is no rational basis [says she] for saying that a human being has special rights." But in this she is profoundly mistaken; there *is* a rational basis for this distinction, a distinction of the deepest importance. The failure to grasp and respect that distinction leads some zealots to interfere with medical research using animals in every way they find feasible.

The moral issue is epitomized by Newkirk's notorious and often-quoted remark: "A rat is a pig is a dog is a boy. They're all mammals." To be fair, she probably did not mean in saying this that rats and pigs and human boys are of equal importance in our lives; we care more about little boys, mother rats care more about little rats, of course. But she and PETA certainly do mean and contend unreservedly that humans do not possess rights in any way that rats and pigs cannot possess them equally. In *that* sense she really does believe that "a rat *is* a pig *is* a dog *is* a boy." This conviction—well meaning but deeply mistaken—pervades the animal rights movement. It is both dangerous and absurd.

The depth of the mistake will be appreciated more fully when we reflect on what it is that differentiates acts by humans from the acts of rats or rabbits. Returning as moral thinkers commonly do to the work of Immanuel Kant, we may say with him that critical reason reveals at the core of *human* action a uniquely moral will; we recognize the unique capacity of humans to formulate moral *principles* for the direction of our conduct. Human beings can grasp the maxim of the principles we devise, and by applying those principles to ourselves as well as to others, we exhibit the autonomy of the human will. Humans, but never rodents, confront choices that are purely moral. Humans, but certainly not pigs or chickens, lay down rules, moral imperatives, by which all moral agents are thought to be rightly governed, ourselves along with all others. Human beings are *self*-legislative, morally *auto*nomous.

To be a moral agent is to be able to grasp the generality of moral restrictions on our will. Humans understand that some acts may be in our interest and yet must not be willed because they are simply wrong. This capacity for moral judgment does not arise in the animal world; rats can neither exercise nor respond to moral claims. My dog knows that there are certain things he must not do, but he knows this only as the outcome of his learning about his interests, the pains he may suffer if he does what had been taught forbidden. He does not know, he cannot know (as Regan agrees[13]) that any conduct is *wrong*. The proposition "It would be highly advantageous to act in such-and-such a way, but I may not do so because it would be morally wrong" is one that no dog or rabbit, however sweet and endearing, however loyal or loving or intelligent, can ever entertain, or intend, or begin to grasp. *Right is not in their world*. But right and wrong are the very stuff of human moral life, the ever-present awareness of human beings who *can* do wrong and who by seeking (often but not always) to avoid wrong conduct prove themselves members of a moral community in which rights may be exercised and must be respected.

Every day humans confront actual or potential conflicts between what is in their own interest and what is just. We restrain ourselves (or at least we can do so) on purely moral grounds. In such a community the concept of a right makes very good sense, of course. Some riches that do not belong to us would please us, no doubt, but we *may* not take them; we refrain from stealing not only because we fear punishment if caught. Suppose we knew that the detection of our wrongdoing were impossible and punishment out of the question. Even so, to deprive others of what is theirs by right is conduct forbidden *by our own moral rules*. We return lost property belonging to others even when keeping it might be much to our advantage; we do so because that return is the act that our moral principles call for. Only in a community of that kind, a community constituted by beings capable of self-restricting moral judgments, can the concept of a *right* be intelligibly invoked.

Humans have such moral capacities. They are in this sense self-legislative, members of moral communities governed by moral rules; humans possess rights and recognize the rights of others. Animals do not have such capacities. They cannot exhibit moral autonomy in this sense, cannot possibly be members of a truly moral community. They may be the objects of our moral concern, of course, but they cannot possibly possess rights. Medical investigators who conduct research on animal subjects, therefore, do not violate the rights of those animals because, to be plain, they have none to violate.

One *caveat* of the utmost importance I repeat though it was earlier emphasized: It does not follow from the fact that animals have no rights that we are free to do anything we please to them. Most assuredly not. We do have obligations to animals, weighty obligations—but those obligations do not, because they cannot, arise out of animal rights.

An objection is sometimes raised to this view that deserves response and deserves also to be permanently put aside.

It cannot be [the critic says] that having rights requires the ability to make moral claims, to grasp and apply moral laws, because, if that were true, many human beings—the brain-damaged, the comatose, infants and the senile—who plainly lack those capacities must be without rights. But that is absurd. This proves [the critic concludes] that rights do not depend on the presence of moral capacities.[14]

Objections of this kind are common but miss the point badly. They arise from a misunderstanding of what it means to say that humans live in a moral world. Human children, like elderly adults, have rights *because they are human*. Morality is an essential feature of human life; all humans are moral creatures, infants and the senile included. Rights are not doled out to this individual person or that one by somehow establishing the presence in them of some special capacity. This mistaken vision would result in the selective award of rights to some individuals but not others, and the cancellation of rights when capacities fail. On the contrary, rights are *universally* human, arise in the human realm, apply to humans generally. This criticism (suggesting the loss of rights by the senile or the comatose, etc.) mistakenly treats the essentially moral feature of humanity as though it were a screen for sorting humans, which it most certainly is not. The capacity for moral judgment that distinguishes humans from animals is not a test to be administered to human beings one by one. Persons who, because of some disability, are unable to perform the full moral functions natural to human beings are not for that reason ejected from the human community. The critical distinction is one of kind. Humans are of such a kind that rights pertain to them *as humans;* humans live lives that will be, or have been, or remain *essentially* moral. It is silly to suppose that human rights might fluctuate with an individual's health or dissipate with an individual's decline. The rights involved are human rights. On the other hand, animals are of such a kind that rights never pertain to them; what humans retain when disabled, rats never had.

The contrast between these two very different moral conditions is highlighted in the world of medical experimentation itself. In addition to the animals used there, many humans are experimental subjects as well. But humans are capable of moral choice; therefore, humans must *choose* to allow themselves to be the instruments of scientific research, and where they have moral authority their choices must be respected. Humans do have moral authority over their own bodies, and thus we insist that humans may be the subject of experiments only with their informed and freely given consent. Investigators who withhold information from potential subjects or who deceive potential subjects, thereby making it impossible for them to give genuinely voluntary consent to what is done, will be condemned and punished, rightly. But this consent that we think absolutely essential in the case of human subjects is *impossible* for animals to give. The reason is not merely that we cannot communicate with them or explain to them or inquire of them, but that the kind of moral choice involved in giving consent is totally out of the question for a dog or a rat.

An objection of a different kind is raised by some advocates of animal rights. It goes like this:

> Animals have internal lives far more rich and complicated than most people realize; many animals are, as Tom Regan points out, "psychologically complex" beings. Therefore [this critic argues] the effort to distinguish the world of humans from the world of animals by pointing to some special capacity of humans cannot succeed. Although in lesser degree than humans, animals do have the capacities we commonly associate with humanity. Humans are rational, but animals can reason too; animals communicate with one another, not with languages like ours of course, but very effectively nonetheless. Animals, like humans, care passionately for their young; animals, like humans, exhibit desires and preferences. And so on and on. So there is no genuine moral distinction to be drawn.[15]

This objection has much popular appeal, but it misses the central point. *Cognitive* abilities, the ability to communicate or to reason, are not at issue. My dog certainly reasons, if rather weakly, and he communicates rather well. Nor is it *affective* capacities that are at issue; many animals plainly exhibit fear, love and anger, care for one another and their offspring, and so on. Nor is it the exhibition of *preference,* or memory, or aversion that marks the critical divide; no one doubts that a squirrel may recall where it buried a nut or that a dog would rather go on the walk than remain in the car. Remarkable behaviors are often exhibited by animals, as we all know. Conditioning, fear, instinct, and intelligence all contribute to individual success and species survival.

Nor is the capacity to suffer sufficient to justify the claim that animals have rights. They surely can suffer—that is obvious; they can feel pain. And because they are sentient in that way, they are properly a concern of morally sensitive humans; they are, we may say, morally "considerable." Of course. And that is why the moral principles that govern us oblige us to act thoughtfully, humanely, in our use of them.

But with all the varied capacities of animals granted, it remains absolutely impossible for them to act *morally,* to be members of a moral community. Emphasizing similarities between human families and those of monkeys, or between human communities and those of wolves, and the like, cannot ground the moral equality of species; it serves only to obscure what is truly critical. A being subject to genuinely moral judgment must be capable of grasping the *maxim* of an act and capable, too, of grasping the *generality* of an ethical premise in a moral argument. Similarities between animal conduct and human conduct cannot refute, cannot even address, the profound moral differences between humans and rodents.

Because humans do have rights, and these rights can be violated by other humans, we all understand that humans can and sometimes do commit *crimes.* Whether a crime has been committed, however, depends utterly on the actor's moral state of mind. If I take your coat from the closet honestly believing that it was mine, I do not steal it. A genuine crime is an act in which the guilty deed, the *actus reus,* is accompanied by a guilty state of mind, a *mens rea.* Humans can commit crimes not merely because we realize that we may be punished for acting thus-and-so but because we recognize that there are duties that govern us; to speak of such recognition in the world of cows and horses is literally nonsensical. In primitive times cows and horses were sometimes brought to the bar of human justice and punished there. We chuckle now as we look back on that practice, realizing that to accuse a cow of a crime marks the accuser as inane, confused about the applicability of moral concepts. Animals never can be criminals, obviously—not because they are always law-abiding but because "law-abiding" has no sense in this context; moral appraisals do not intelligibly apply to them. And that is why it is not true, and never can be true, that animals have moral rights.

The fundamental mistake is one in which a concept (in this case, moral right) that makes very good sense in one context is applied to another context in which it makes no sense at all. It may be helpful to reflect on other spheres, very distant from morality, in which mistakes of the same general kind have been commonly made at great cost.

The world of metaphysical thinking is riddled with mistakes of that kind. In his *Critique of Pure Reason,* Immanuel Kant explains at length the metaphysical blunders into which we are led when we apply concepts fundamentally important in one sphere to another sphere in which those concepts can have no grip. In our human experience, for example, the concepts of time and space, the relations of cause and effect, of subject and attribute, and others, are inescapable, fundamental. But these are concepts arising only within the world of our human experience; when we forget that we may be misled into asking: "Was the world caused, or is it uncaused?" "Did the world have a beginning in time, or did it not?" Kant explains—in one of the most brilliant long passages in all philosophical literature—why it *makes no sense* to ask such questions.[16] "Causation" is a concept that applies to phenomena we humans encounter; it is a category of our experience and cannot apply to the world as a whole. "Time" is the sequential condition of our experience, the way we experience things, not a container within which the world could have begun. In his discussion of the *paralogisms* of pure reason, and after that his analyses of the *antinomies* of pure reason, Kant patiently exhibits the many confusions arising from the misapplication of the categories of experience. Whatever our judgment of his conclusions about the limits of reason, his larger lesson in these passages is powerful and deep. The misapplication of concepts leads to fundamental mistakes, to nonsense.

So it is also when we mistakenly transfer the concept of a right from the human moral world in which it applies to the world of animals in which it has no possible applicability. To say that rats have rights is to apply to the world of rats a concept that makes very good sense when applied to humans, but makes no sense at all when applied to rats. That is why rats, like the other animals used in biomedical research, cannot have rights. Ascribing rights to animals is a mistake.

Notes

1. Regan, *Case,* 152–53.
2. The reference by St. Thomas is to Psalm 4, line 6.
3. St. Thomas Aquinas, *Summa Theologica,* First Part of the Second Part, Question 91, Second Article.
4. *Genesis,* chap. 3, verse 22.
5. St. Augustine, *Confessions,* book 7, 397 A.D.
6. Francis Herbert Bradley, "Why Should I Be Moral?" from *Ethical Studies* (Oxford: Clarendon, 1927).
7. Georg Wilhelm Friedrich Hegel, *Philosophy of Right* (1821).
8. H. A. Prichard, "Does Moral Philosophy Rest on a Mistake?" in *Moral Obligation* (Oxford: Oxford University Press, 1949).
9. Sir David Ross, *The Foundations of Ethics* (Oxford: Clarendon, 1939), chap. 3.
10. Karl Marx, *Economic and Philosophical Manuscripts* (1844).
11. V. I. Lenin, "The Tasks of the Youth Leagues" (1920), reprinted in *The Strategy and Tactics of World Communism,* Supplement I (Washington, D.C.: U.S. Government Printing Office, 1948).
12. George Herbert Mead, "The Genesis of the Self and Social Control," in *Selected Writings,* ed. A. J. Reck (Indianapolis: Bobbs-Merrill, 1964).
13. See n. 1.
14. Tom Regan makes this objection explicitly in "The Moral Basis of Vegetarianism" in *All That Dwell Therein: Animal Rights and Environmental Ethics* (Berkeley: University of California Press, 1982).
15. Objections of this kind are registered by Dale Jamieson, "Killing Persons and Other Beings" in *Ethics and Animals,* ed. H. B. Miller and W. H. Williams (Clifton, N.J.: Humana, 1983), and by C. Hoff, "Immoral and Moral Uses of Animals," in *The New England Journal of Medicine* 302 (1980): 115–18.
16. The analysis of these mistakes is given in what Kant calls the "Transcendental Dialectic," which is the Second Division of the Second Part (Transcendental Logic) of the Transcendental Doctrine of Elements. The position Kant is defending is deep and difficult—but the general point he makes in the Transcendental Dialectic is readily accessible. Confusions and errors resulting from the misapplication of concepts in thinking about our *selves* he treats in a chapter called "The Paralogisms of Pure Reason"; confusions and errors resulting from the misapplication of concepts in thinking about *the world as a whole* he treats in a chapter called "The Antinomy of Pure Reason"; confusions and errors resulting from the misapplication of concepts in thinking about *God* he treats in a chapter called "The Ideal of Pure Reason." In all three spheres the categories (of which causation is only one example) that make sense only when applied to phenomena in our direct experience cannot be rationally employed. His analyses are penetrating and telling; the metaphysical blunders he exposes result in every case from the attempt to use categories having applicability only in one sphere in a very different sphere where they can have no applicability whatever.

6

Why Animals Are Mistakenly Believed to Have Rights

Since animals *cannot* be the holders of rights, as we have seen, those who claim that animals do have rights must be mistaken. Tom Regan and others continue to assert that they have proved their case. Something is plainly amiss in the reasoning of those who think themselves to have given a proof of what cannot be. Where do their errors lie, and why do those errors remain widely seductive?

Their underlying mistake may be generally characterized as that of confusing the moral condition of animals with that of humans, then applying concepts and principles to animals that can correctly apply only to humans. Some variant of this mistake lies buried, sometimes well hidden, in the writings of all the leading advocates of animal rights.

The one book most often cited in defense of animal rights is *The Case for Animal Rights* by Tom Regan.[1] In it Regan contends that all animals used in medical research—rats and rabbits along with dogs and sheep—*possess rights in the same sense that human beings possess rights*. To his readers who may doubt that this is so he gives this blunt reassurance: "The best arguments are on my side." In fact this is very far from true, and it is important to see how and why the arguments he presents don't make the case for animal rights at all. Before addressing the particulars of Regan's arguments, however, it will be helpful to see how other philosophers, equally well meaning and equally unsuccessful in defending animal rights, also go astray. Sometimes they go wildly astray.

Two examples will suffice. The first is the defense of animal rights given by Bernard Rollin, a sensitive veterinarian whose great love of animals leads him to urge respect for the rights of spiders and worms.[2] The second is the defense of animal rights given by Steve Sapontzis, an academic philosopher who concludes

41

that in some cases we are obliged to defend animals against their natural preda-
tors and who also believes that insects as well as mammals may have a moral
right to our protection.[3] These claims are advanced seriously. How does it happen that thoughtful people are carried by their sympathies to such extremes?
This is a matter worth exploring.

Rollin begins with a premise that is not very controversial: that every living
animal has *interests,* that it needs things that matter to it. Animal expressions
of pain and pleasure, he contends, clearly indicate that this is so. His argument then advances as follows: The interests of every animal must flow from
the "*telos*" of the animal, its intrinsic nature. The spider is the animal Rollin
chooses as example. Every spider has interests "which are conditions without
which the creature, first of all, cannot live, or second of all, cannot live its life
as a spider, cannot fulfill its *telos.*"[4] But, he contends, every living thing that
has interests in this sense also necessarily "has some sort of conscious awareness,"[5] and we therefore cannot reasonably deny, Rollin concludes, that creatures that have nervous systems and withdraw from noxious stimuli must be
supposed to "enjoy a mental life."[6] These criteria (for the possession of a mental life), he asserts, "take us down, as we saw earlier, to insects, worms, and
perhaps planaria as animals with interests."[7] The reader may be relieved to
learn that Rollin does think it possible that bacteria, viruses, and plants are not
likely to warrant our moral concern.

Where does the argument go from there? Recall that Rollin's aim is to
defend the claim that animals have rights; the title of his book is *Animal
Rights and Human Morality.* So a leap must be made from animal *interests* to
animal *rights,* and that leap he makes without any recognition that a critical
step has been taken. Rollin writes, "[W]e have established that animals have
a very basic right, namely, *the right to be dealt with or considered as moral objects
by any person who has moral principles, regardless of what those moral principles
may be!*"[8]

He has established no such thing. But even if he had done so, the claim
would be innocuous if all that were meant by the principle is that we humans
ought to *consider* the pains of animals in so far as they are sentient. But for
him the principle means very much more than that. It becomes in his hands
a bludgeon, transforming a concern for animal pain into the flat assertion that
all animals with interests must have *rights,* and that among these rights there
are some that are "absolute, invariable, and inalienable."[9]

This beachhead once claimed, the rights alleged soon begin to swallow all
that is in their path. Since "being alive is the basis for being a moral object,
and [since] all other interests and needs are predicated upon life, then the
most basic, morally relevant aspect of a creature is its life."[10] The conclusion
so desperately wanted seems now within Rollin's grasp: "We may correlatively
suggest that any animal, therefore, has a *right to life.*"[11] Voilà!

From this point the attack on medical research using animals, and indeed on most uses of animals by humans, goes forward with gusto. We may be justified in killing a rat about to bite our child, he allows, just as we may be justified in killing human terrorists who are threatening the lives of hostages. But without reasons of that kind, grounded in self-defense, the rights of animals to live must be respected just as the rights of humans to live must be respected. Rollin concludes that the argument of the vegetarian who refrains from eating meat as a moral principle is powerful and (he suggests) perhaps irrefutable: "[H]umans can live and live well without taking animal life; therefore the taking of animal life for food is unnecessary and correlatively unjustifiable, and our mere gustatory predilection for meat does not serve as sufficient grounds for violating the basic right to life."[12]

The moral equivalence between animals and humans is "established," on the ground that both plainly have interests. From this Rollin concludes that "moral reasoning involved in making [the decision to kill an animal] utilizes exactly the same weighing of principles and consequences that our moral deliberation about human rights does."[13] Therefore, "it is wrong to poison the rabbits eating one's garden lettuce when one can trap them without harm and deposit them elsewhere (conceivably, in someone else's garden!)"[14] Rollin reports with pride the forbearance of one of his colleagues who "will kill insects, but only when they pose a danger to the ecosystem. As a result she has killed only six grasshoppers during one growing season that was literally infested with them."[15]

Because grasshoppers, rabbits, and humans are (in his view) all animals with rights, Rollin finds himself unable to deny that, at least in some contexts, these various species are morally equivalent. That is a foolish claim, of course, and even Rollin cannot stomach his own conclusions regarding their moral equality: "I find myself unable," he confesses at one point, "to directly respond to the argument about animals having no concept of death. If, indeed, most animals do not understand the concept of death, that would seem *prima facie* to be a morally relevant difference between humans and animals regarding their right to life."[16] Yes, it surely would. And so would many other essential features of human moral life to which Rollin does not attend, features totally beyond the capacity of rats and spiders.

But the rights of animals are so precious to the zealot that intellectual problems like these will not be allowed to put them at risk. The *telos* of wasps, Rollin tells us, requires respect for their right to live. He reports with approval the conduct of people who "will chase a stinging insect, such as a bee or a wasp, out of the house rather than kill it. In this case the person clearly sees the animal's right to life as trumping their own danger of being stung."[17]

Rollin's passage from plausible beginnings to absurd conclusions teaches an important lesson. Animals do have interests, of course—but from that everyday observation one cannot extract the conclusion that the possession of *rights* by animals has been established. Once the leap is made from the (correct) recognition that humans may have obligations to animals to the (incorrect) supposition that animals have *rights,* the consequences that may then be spun out will boggle the mind.

In the world of medical research, Rollin tells us, his reasoning has immediate application. His *"rights principle,"* he reminds us, is "pivotal to our ethic and asserts that in the context of research, *all research should be conducted in such a way as to maximize the animal's potential for living its life according to its nature or* telos, *and certain fundamental rights should be preserved regardless of consideration of cost."*[18] This means that "we must attend to the animal's rights following from its nature."[19] These rights include the right to be free from pain; moreover, since the animal's *"telos"* requires that it *live,* Rollin's "rights principle" effectively puts an *end* to virtually all research using rats, mice, and any other animals that may have to be killed in the effort to advance human medicine.

Will this outcome have damaging consequences for medical science? Never fear, he answers. We must "force ourselves to look more carefully at the logic of the medical research we fund."[20] Then follows a chain of questions in which Rollin, too clever to assert flatly what he knows to be very dubious, uses deliberately loaded questions to strongly suggest what is false, while expressly committing himself to nothing. The entire enterprise of medical research, he insinuates, is distorted, misdirected by scientific myth. He asks:

> How much of it [i.e., medical research] is simply legitimized by the myth [of its scientific merit] with little theoretical coherence or defensibility? . . . Could the money be better spent in other ways? Are we supporting research that can really lead to curing disease, or are we simply perpetuating an industry that has assumed a life of its own?[21]

The current medical emphasis on illness as "biological fact" is a mistake, says he. It is based on a "reductionist" model of biology that may "work" in keeping us alive, but if so it works on "undesirable terms. . . . Does the cancer victim whose life is prolonged 1.2 years . . . enjoy a higher state of well-being than the person whose cancer took him swiftly?"[22] For the members of a group called the Incurably Ill for Animal Research—persons whose diseases have no known remedy and whose only hope for cure, or even survival, lies in medical investigations using animal subjects—Rollin's question may be offensive. No doubt he does not mean to offend, but those whose lives are genuinely at risk may justifiably think him light-headed when he disparages animal research in medicine on the grounds that it deals with illness as though it were a biological fact. It *is* a biological fact.

The loss to medicine if animal research were stymied, Rollin suggests, would be more than made up for by the alternative views of health such a loss will encourage. "The movement toward holism in medicine is a good public protest against excessive mechanism. . . . [Other factors such as] love, touch, and companionship"[23] play an important role in health. Needing *evidence* that animal research is misdirected, he provides what he takes to be compelling: "Recent studies, for example, indicate that having a pet may be a major factor in preventing recurrence of heart attacks."[24] That is probably true. Finding ways to eliminate the plaque that—as a biological fact—blocks blood vessels, discoveries achieved mainly through research using rats, may prove even more helpful than having a pet.

Rollin is careful to say that he does not seek the abolition of medical research; no one would seek that, of course. He does *not* say that he does not seek the abolition of medical research using animals. His argument, if taken literally, would have exactly that result. This outcome would not greatly trouble him. Here is his summary view of medical research:

[T]he cheap and plentiful supply of overly simplistic "animal models" for the study of illness, which has been a major factor in medical research, may also be a source of the blinders that the medical community wears, and that stops it from seeing the more holistic and subtle factors involved in health and illness. Worse, the overemphasis upon animal research may well be a major source of a stunted and dwarfed concept of illness and health, which results in profound suffering for those who live in its shadow.[25]

Readers of this book or their loved ones who become seriously ill are not likely to seek help from the likes of Bernard Rollin, who disdains most current efforts to identify the causes and cures of disease. Most diseases are biological facts. We will turn—and he, too, when in critical need will turn—to those knowledgeable physicians and medical researchers who, having learned much of what they know about human disease through investigations using animal subjects, offer antibiotics and other pharmaceutical compounds that really do cure and that really do give release from human misery and pain. (Much more about the actual scientific results of research using animals will be reported in chapter 9.)

Bernard Rollin is a very decent man; he is sensitive; he exhibits an affection for animals that many of us share. But his defense of the rights of animals is an intellectual catastrophe. His moral position, which entails not only that rats and rabbits have the right to live but that spiders and worms do also, and that no animal with interests may be killed without a justification as strong as that we would need to kill a human, is—to mince no words—preposterous.

The argument he gives in defense of that position is utterly fallacious. From the reasonable conviction that we ought to seek to cause animals no pain, Rollin takes a series of giant leaps, to the unreasonable claim that all animals with interests have rights, and then to the claim that all animals have a right to life and therefore that all animals deserve the moral respect that the right to life entails.

The critical failing of this argument, like that of most arguments for animal rights, is the well-meaning but mistaken passage from the moral *consider-ability* of animals (that few would deny) to the claim that they have *rights*. If animals feel pain (and certainly mammals do, though we cannot be sure about insects and worms), we humans surely ought cause no pain to them that can-not be justified. Nor ought we kill them without reason. The truth of this rests not on any claim of right, but because we, as moral human beings, have the duty not to be cruel. The jump to animal rights is a blunder, and on that blun-der is built a towering pile of mistaken conclusions.

Do animals have interests? Of course they do. Every living creature, even the most lowly, strives to realize itself, to continue in life, to reproduce, to be what it can be. And is there value in those lives all animals lead? Yes, there is. Each animal is unique and therefore cannot be perfectly replaced by any other thing. Animals, all animals, are quite wonderful, and it is not surprising that people who work with animals, or who care much for them, feel that wonder when contemplating their lives. But we must see that this regard for animal life does not yield, cannot possibly yield, a foundation for the reality of ani-mal *rights*. The fact that animals have *interests* has absolutely nothing to do with rights of any kind. Animal interests may indeed be of concern to us in view of our moral principles, but they warrant no moral claims by worms and spiders; they do not convert the worm or the spider (who surely do have inter-ests!) into moral agents. The absurd conclusions into which Bernard Rollin topples should clearly warn us: *the fact that animals have interests does not in any way support the claim that animals have rights.* Animals *cannot* have rights; *rights are essentially human, and only humans can possess them.*

A point of view similar to Rollin's, backed by a similar reliance on the fact that animals have "interests" but also grounded in the capacity of animals to have "feelings," leads Steve Sapontzis, viewing himself as flag bearer for his own version of "animal liberation," to claims about animal rights that are as extreme as those of Rollin, and perhaps even more distant from good sense. Here is his credo:

> Animal liberation[26] seeks to eliminate being human as a necessary condition for having moral rights and to substitute sentience, having interests of one's own, or feelings of well being as not only the necessary condition but also, as long as the individual is innocent of crime, a sufficient condition of having moral rights. . . . [This would be] a fundamental and pervasive change in our moral attitudes toward animals and in our daily dealings with them, for it would require that they no longer be treated basically as means for satisfying human interests. That would put an end to the routine sacrifice of their interests in favor of ours.[27]

Sapontzis's revolutionary goal is put forthrightly: "all beings with interests of their own [are to have] the sort of moral respect for and protections of their interests currently enjoyed only by humans." The advancement of this objective, he declares, justifies the use of "the rhetoric of 'liberation' and 'rights.' "[28] The outcome of such respect for animals he does not doubt: "[A]nimals ought (morally) to share in the right to life."[29] We may not kill animals, we may not eat animals, and we may not use them in the service of humans without their consent.

But where do these universally protective animal rights come from? How does he defend the notion that animals are entitled to moral respect equally with humans? At first it appears that for Sapontzis, as for Rollin, the moral foundation is to be the *interests* that animals exhibit. "*All and only beings with interests can have moral rights,*" he declares.[30] And when does an animal have an interest? If it feels pain, or feels fit, or has feelings of fulfillment or of frustration, or

> the many other feelings that contribute to or detract from the enjoyment of or satisfaction with life. Now, the "animal" in "animal liberation" and "animal rights" refers to all and only those beings that meet the interest requirement. The phrase "sentient being" or "sentient animal" is sometimes employed to make this reference.[31]

There is no denying, he allows, that "animals are incapable of entering fully into the [moral] community that humans can enjoy with each other."[32] Nevertheless, there is nothing that "justifies our denying moral rights to animals and continuing to consume them."[33] He cannot bear the thought of eating meat.

Sapontzis's arguments sometimes rely on what he calls the "moral rights of the powerless against the powerful."[34] Animals do have such rights, he is confident, but of course they do not have (because they *can*not have) "correlative duties of the powerless to the powerful. . . . Therefore, since animals are vastly weaker than we [humans] are, *fairness requires that animals have moral rights against us.*"[35]

Armed with this vision of animal life he uncovers moral rights in creatures of very different kinds. Too often overlooked in the animal world, according to Sapontzis, are insects that have interests, and therefore rights. All those *insects*

> that can meet the interest requirement must, if animal liberationists are to be consistent, be included in the concerns of this movement. . . . There may be good reason, if we take an unbiased look at the evidence, to believe that at least some insects have feelings of well-being. . . . [And] if some insects have feelings of well-being, then a morality that attempts to respect all sentient beings will be more complicated [than the moral status quo].[36]

Readers will be again relieved to learn that plants may, at least for the present, be eaten. "To date," Sapontzis reassures us, "there has been no serious evidence to show that plants have feelings of well-being."[37] Should such evidence come to light we will find ourselves in a terrible pickle, no doubt. With meat precluded, the immorality of eating vegetables might leave us very hungry. But, as Sapontzis observes, morality is always more complicated when we enlarge the body of rights-holders who are due respect. "To one degree or another, we probably all share a yearning for a simpler life, but [the fact] that practicing a revolutionary morality would be more complicated than resting content with the status quo does not indicate that that revolutionary morality is ridiculous."[38] That is correct. The ridiculousness of this view does not stem from its complexity.

In the course of his argument Sapontzis changes his emphasis. He begins, like Rollin, by calling attention to the fact that animals have interests. But it turns out that it is really *sentience,* the capacity to feel, that is the moral foundation of his claim that animals have rights. Late in his book this passage appears:

> Since sentient beings are the source of values in the world, each sentient individual is valuable in itself, whether or not it is the object of evaluations by other valuers. Furthermore, each sentient individual enjoying life is also valuable in itself, whether or not it reflects on its condition, since . . . feelings of well-being are a form of evaluative self-consciousness.[39]

Sapontzis cannot be certain which animals (insects? bacteria? shellfish?) do have interests; mammals surely do; for animals in other categories the possession of interests is "an open question."[40] In any case, he is determined to protect all those animals that do have interests or experience feelings. He would even prefer to replace the expression "animal rights" with the expression "sentient rights" and the expression "animal liberation" with "interest liberation." But this replacement would not be politic. "Although employing [these new terms] might allow us to communicate more precisely at a philosophical conference, they would hardly do as slogans for a movement that is at least as much a popular one as a professional philosophical movement."[41]

Predatory slaughter is a serious problem for all who claim that animals have rights. Natural life in the wild—in the jungles or the oceans—is saturated by predation; the killing of animals by other animals is ubiquitous and unrelenting. Sapontzis grapples with this problem almost tearfully. The animals that are eaten by other animals are plainly sentient: the baby zebra ripped open by the lioness feels the pain, the millions upon millions of little fish eaten by bigger fish flee murderous jaws if they are able. And so it follows, Sapontzis believes, that the killing of one animal by another, although not *always* wrong, is *often* wrong and to be avoided. What is going on throughout nature, we must conclude from his argument, is a moral holocaust that it is our obligation to ameliorate so far as is within our power. One chapter in his book is entitled "Saving the Rabbit from the Fox."[42] Sapontzis is not completely mad; he observes that, as a strategic matter, since attempts to fulfill our obligation to prevent predation are likely to prove unsuccessful, animal rights activists would do better, "for the foreseeable future," to direct their efforts elsewhere.[43]

Among those other targets, medical research is perhaps the most suitable for animal rights activists, Sapontzis thinks, because "research with animals ought (morally) to be governed by the same ethical concerns and principles as research with human subjects." Now the principles that govern research with humans have been well worked out: humans must give their informed consent, freely and autonomously. But aren't the animals used in research individuals, too? They are; and on his account "individuals ought (morally) to be free to direct their lives according to their own values."[44]

It is therefore time, in his judgment, to recognize the moral autonomy of the laboratory rat. Humans participate in medical research only as volunteers, after giving their informed and uncoerced consent. For the mice and rats in medical laboratories Sapontzis demands the same respect. Can animals give informed consent? Of course they can, says he, from *their* point of view, which he takes himself to understand. But animals (he reports) commonly withhold consent because "what they fear and seek to escape is all that participating in the research holds for them, namely, frustration, distress, and death."[45] If the experiment is directly beneficial to the animals involved, therapeutic, or entirely innocuous, their consent may not be essential—but otherwise the use of them is simply not permissible. Animal subjects, after all, are entitled to

> the same sort of moral protection for their interests that we humans currently enjoy for ours. In the area of research, the principle that experiments can be performed only on those who freely and with understanding consent to participate in them . . . expresses at least an important part of the animal rights attack on the morality of animal research.[46]

Respect for what underlies the consent principle, the recognition of the rights of individuals, Sapontzis points out with satisfaction, "would put an end to virtually all animal research."[47]

This defense of animal rights, like that of Rollin, relies on strained inferences from reasonable beginnings to conclusions that may be generously described as mistaken. Consider the underlying argument. Are animals sentient? Of course they are. Some animals, crustaceans (barnacles, lobsters, etc.) or insects, may not feel pain; we cannot be sure. But the rodents and other mammals commonly used in medical research certainly are sentient; no one seriously doubts that. This explains the universal practice of anesthetizing animal subjects where that is scientifically feasible. Humans have a moral obligation not to cause unjustified pain; that far all agree.

But what may one reasonably *infer* from animal interests, from the fact of animal sentience? Advocates of animal rights like Sapontzis rely heavily on conclusions drawn from "sentience" or the presence of "interests" that have no warrant. May we conclude, because animals can experience pain, that they are moral individuals having the same *rights* as humans? Not at all. Because animals seem to exhibit feelings of well-being may we suppose that they have the right to live and not ever be killed? We may not. Animals—ticks and clams and mosquitoes, as well as rats and chickens—surely do have interests. Must we therefore respect them as moral "individuals" and protect their "right" to live their lives "according to their own values"? Seek their consent before using them in medical research? The argumentative leap is astonishing. Not one of these conclusions follows from the fact that animals are sentient or have interests. Claim after claim is put forward with the same underlying confusion operative throughout: Animals feel; therefore, animals are morally no different from humans in deserving moral respect; and animals have lives to live; therefore, they are the equal of humans in the enjoyment of rights.

The great majority of those who think of themselves as defenders of animal rights are very much like Rollin, or Sapontzis, in this: they fasten on some feature of animal life that is shared with humans—the possession of interests or the capacity to feel. This shared feature is then taken, explicitly or implicitly, to justify the moral equation of animals and humans. From that equation the absolute protection of the animals must follow. Humans do undeniably possess rights; so, on all these accounts, rats and rabbits must possess them, too.

Of these two advocates here presented as illustrative, it is difficult to decide which is the more wrong-headed: Sapontzis, whose concern for animal sentience results in the obligation to do what we can to save little fishes from big ones and rabbits from foxes, or Rollin, whose sensitivity to animal interests suggests that we must avoid the reckless killing of grasshoppers, wasps, and worms. They are driven to results like these by the force of their own arguments once having made the passage from interests to moral entitlements. They reap the consequences of insisting that animals have *rights*.

But in truth animals cannot be the bearers of rights. Ascribing rights to them, equating their moral position with that of humans, leads quickly to absurdity, as a careful reading of what these zealots write makes very clear. Their conclusions may seem outrageous; they understand that. But those conclusions must be embraced, as they explain at length, because they follow from the possession of rights. The most thoughtful defenders of animal rights convict themselves.

Of all the defenses of animal rights the most influential has been given by Tom Regan, my friend and colleague; to his arguments in *The Case for Ani-*

mal Rights I now turn. Regan's book is long and tortuous and in places obscure. The report of his views here must be compressed, of course, but I promise to be fair and to hold Regan responsible for nothing that he does not clearly say. Regan *must* have gotten off the track; we can be certain of that if we agree that rats do not have the *right* not to be killed by us. Examining his argument closely, let us find and identify the faulty switch.

Much of *The Case for Animal Rights* is devoted to a general treatment of ethical theory, to discussions of animal consciousness and animal awareness, and to detailed critiques of the views of others whom Regan thinks in error. That we humans do have some obligations to animals is a premise—a true premise—from which he begins. Regan seeks to show, patiently and laboriously, that to justify these existing obligations to animals it must be the case that animals have rights, because (he claims) there can be no other satisfactory explanation of them.

Some persons contend that our obligations to animals are simply a by-product of our duties to other humans. Regan calls these "indirect duty views" because the duty (in such views) is owed not directly to the animal but to another human by way of animals. This account of obligations to animals he holds inadequate. Nor can our obligations to animals be accounted for by "direct duty views," which hold that duties are owed directly to the animals concerned. Direct duty views (Regan thinks) fall into two families: those depending on the obligation to be kind or not to be cruel, and those depending on some kind of utilitarian calculation. But these views also—and especially utilitarian calculations—will ultimately fail to protect animals, he fears. No account of our obligations to animals can be sufficient, Regan is convinced, unless it is grounded on respect for their *rights*.

Counterargument of this sort makes up well more than half of Regan's lengthy treatise. With great patience and voluminous detail, Regan responds or seeks to respond to a variety of philosophers who would explain our moral relations with the animal world in ways other than his. But a critique of the arguments of his opponents cannot by itself establish his affirmative conclusion, the conclusion that animals do have rights, unless Regan had proved both that his listing of all the alternative conflicting views was exhaustive, which he does not even attempt to do, and had proved also that every such possible view is untenable, which he surely does not do.

So the counterarguments, the intellectual sparring and jousting that make up most of *The Case for Animal Rights,* are largely smoke. If there is a case *for* animal rights, Regan must surely be expected to put it squarely before us, to provide an affirmative defense of animal rights. This is a very long time coming. There is not even a single *mention* of animal rights (save in the Preface) in the first two-thirds of his big book, nor is there any argument, in those hundreds of pages, that even begins to show that animals actually do have rights. About rights in general, as they apply to the *human* condition, Regan does have a great deal to say. Justice and equality among humans are discussed at length in his seventh chapter.[48] But where is that central "case" for the rights of *animals*?

"The Rights View" is the title of the eighth chapter of Regan's book. (It should be called "The Regan Rights View," of course.) Its opening sections provide additional discussions of allegedly mistaken philosophers, the details of his quarrels with them, and yet another attack on utilitarianism, for which Regan has no sympathy whatever. But no reference to animals appears until we get to its fifth section. Here, in three paragraphs on two pages, the critical affirmative argument is at last put forward.[49] From this point on, the rights of animals are treated as though established beyond doubt. All the ramifications of animal rights—the absolute condemnation of the use of animals in science and in medical research, the universal moral obligation to be a scrupulous vegetarian, and so on—are supposed thereafter to be inescapable. How, one asks, is this remarkable proof accomplished so very crisply?

Regan's case is built entirely on one principle, a principle that allegedly carries over almost everything earlier claimed about humans and their rights to mice and rats and almost all other animals. What principle is that? It is the principle, put in italics but given no name, by which "moral agents" (humans) and "moral patients" (animals) are held unconditionally equal. Regan writes (the italics are his): "*The validity of the claim to respectful treatment, and thus the case for the recognition of the rights to such treatment, cannot be any stronger or weaker in the case of moral patients than it is in the case of moral agents.*"[50]

If this assertion were true, Regan would be home free, of course. What it says, in erudite and appropriately "philosophical" language, is that humans and animals are in fundamental respects equals, that they have rights equally, and that the rights they have are equally entitled to moral respect. But why in the world should anyone think this principle to be true? Why should one think the moral patient, the animal, is in precisely the same moral situation as the moral agent, the human?

In addition to the profound differences discussed at length in my preceding chapter ("Why Animals Do Not Have Rights"), very weighty reasons are given *by Regan himself* to believe "moral patients" and "moral agents" not equal. Earlier in his book, where Regan first presents his view of "moral patients," he allows that some of them are, although capable of experiencing pleasure and pain, lacking in other capacities.[51] But, he says there, he is chiefly concerned for those moral patients, those animals, which are like humans in having "inherent value." This is the key to Regan's argument for animal rights: *the possession of inherent value.* This concept and its uses are absolutely critical to the success of his defense of animal rights.

The argument fails completely. It fails because, as close scrutiny reveals, "inherent value" is an expression used by Regan with two very different senses—and in one of these senses it may be reasonable to conclude that those who have inherent value have rights, while in the other sense of the term that inference is wholly unwarranted. The argument gives the appearance of plausibility because the key phrase, "inherent value," does have some intelligibility in both the human and the animal context—although its meaning in those two contexts differs greatly. By shifting from one meaning of "inherent value" to another meaning of the same phrase, by equivocating, Regan appears to accomplish, in two pages, what his case for animal rights depends utterly upon.

The equivocation works like this: The concept of "inherent value" first enters Regan's account in the seventh chapter of his book, at the point at which his principal object is to fault and defeat utilitarian moral arguments.[52] Utilitarians, with lesser or greater sophistication, depend ultimately on some calculation of the pleasures and pains that moral agents experience. But, Regan argues there, the real value of human beings must rest not in their experiences but in them*selves*. It is not the pleasures or pains that go "into the cup" of humanity that give value, but the "cups" themselves; all humans are in a deep sense equal in value because of what they are: moral agents having *inherent value*. That is what underlies the principle of human equality. We are, all of us, equal in being *persons* who have this inherent value. This is a very plausible approach to the moral condition of human beings. Regan calls it the "postulate of inherent value"; all humans, "the lonely, forsaken, unwanted, and unloved are no more or less inherently valuable than those who enjoy a more hospitable relationship with others."[53] And all moral agents (he contends) are "equal in inherent value."[54]

This view of humanity is essentially that of Immanuel Kant; it has been adopted by many philosophers since Kant, of course, and is very widely defended still. Most of us, with Kant (and Regan), are likely to affirm that humans, by virtue of their moral autonomy, are indeed beyond all price, that they have a dignity that flows from their inherent moral worth, and that in the moral world humans occupy a unique position as agents having the capacity to act rightly or wrongly, and to pass moral judgment on the acts of others. This is *inherent value* in sense 1.[55]

The expression "inherent value" has another sense, however, a very different sense that is also quite intelligible and also commonly invoked. In this second sense my dog has inherent value too, and so does every wild animal, every lion and zebra, every fish and helpless stranded whale—because each living creature we know to be unique, in itself not replaceable by another creature or by any rocks or clay. The recognition of inherent value in this second sense helps to explain our repugnance for the hunting of animals for mere amusement, and for the wanton slaughter of elephants and sea turtles, tigers and eagles, and all endangered species, including even kinds of fish or lizards we ourselves have never seen. Animals, like humans, are not just inert matter; they *live*. As unique living creatures, they, like the magnificent trees whose needless cutting pains us so and the coral reefs and tracts of wilderness we hope to preserve for our children, have value in themselves, *inherent value*. This is inherent value in sense 2. That all animals possess inherent value in this second sense is an important truth, one also likely to meet with agreement by most thoughtful persons.

But used in this second sense the phrase "inherent value" means something entirely different from what is meant by those who use it in the first, Kantian sense earlier described. Inherent value in sense 1, characterizing humans and warranting the claim of rights by humans, is very much more than inherent value in sense 2, which (possessed by every living creature) warrants no such claim. The uniqueness of animals, their intrinsic worthiness of consideration as individual living things, is properly noted, but it does not ground the possession of rights, has nothing whatever to do with the moral condition in which rights arise. Tom Regan's argument reaches its critical objective with almost magical speed because, having argued (sensibly) that beings with inherent value (in sense 1) have rights that must be respected, he quietly glides to the assertion (putting it in italics lest the reader be inclined to express some doubt) that rats and rabbits also have rights, since they, too, have inherent value (in sense 2). Rats and rabbits do have inherent value, but their inherent value cannot yield rights.

The argument for animal rights that is grounded on their "inherent value" is utterly fallacious, an egregious example of the fallacy of equivocation—that informal fallacy in which two or more meanings of the same word or phrase are confused in the several propositions of an argument.[56] For example: were we to conclude from the fact that a hospital patient, old and sick, who is *incompetent* because physically unable to care for herself is therefore *incompetent* to consent (or refuse consent) to some invasive treatment proposed for her, we would be reasoning very badly indeed. "Incompetence" may refer to either physical or mental incapacity (or both), and we are plainly not entitled to infer that one who is incompetent in one sense of that term is incompetent in the other. The fallacy that underlies such equivocal arguments is often inadvertent; in some instances it is a deliberately deceptive maneuver. But whether it be deliberate or accidental, an argument that employs when convenient (as Regan's does) alternative meanings of a key term is dreadfully unsound. Recognizing that there has been an unmarked shift from one meaning of "inherent value" to another, we see immediately that the argument built on that shift is worthless. The "case" for animal rights evaporates.

Why is this slippage—from the Kantian sense of inherent value as possessed by humans, to the generic sense of inherent value as possessed by all living creatures—not seen at once? There are several reasons. Partly the equivocation slips through because everyone knows that the phrase "inherent value" is often used loosely, and so Regan's readers are not prone to quibble about its introduction or use. Furthermore, the two uses of the phrase he relies on are (as we have seen) both intelligible, and both commonly encountered, so neither by itself signals danger. Moreover the fallacy is partly obscured because inherent value in sense 2, the wide generic sense, is indeed shared by humans who also possess inherent value in sense 1, the Kantian sense. Also helping to conceal the error is the fact that the phrase "inherent value" is woven into Regan's account of what he calls, elsewhere in the book, the "subject-of-a-life criterion,"[57] a phrase of his own devising for which he can stipulate any meaning he pleases, of course, and which also facilitates while it obscures the shift between the sphere of genuine moral agency and the sphere of animal experience.

But perhaps the main reason this equivocation between the two uses of the phrase "inherent value" goes widely undetected by many readers of Regan's book (and possibly by its author, too) is this: Regan's assertion that animals have rights, when at long last it comes to the surface near the end of his book, is never defended forthrightly. It enters only *indirectly*, as the outcome of the application of the italicized claim of his, earlier quoted, that "moral patients" are entitled to the *same respect* as "moral agents"—a claim that does not appear in the book until long after the important moral *differences* between moral patients and moral agents have been recognized. But it is only with the application of this later claim of equality that the equivocation becomes operative—although there is a great mass of distracting philosophical argument presented between that earlier discussion of the moral differences between patients and agents, and the later emphatic assertion that the case for the rights of patients (animals) "*cannot be any stronger or weaker*" than the case for the rights of agents (humans). The reasons for the falsehood of this central claim are thus conveniently buried.

This central equivocation in Regan's argument, an equivocation fatal to his "case" for animal rights, I invite readers to trace out for themselves in *The Case for Animal Rights*. To those who have not the patience for this laborious task I give this assurance: there is no argument or set of arguments in *The Case for Animal Rights* that successfully makes the case for animal rights. Indeed, there could not be, for the same reason that no book, however long and convoluted, could make a tenable case for the emotions of oak trees, or the criminality of snakes.

Animals do not have rights, cannot possibly have them. Right does not apply in their world. Animals do have interests, obviously; they live and it is in their interest to continue to live and prosper. Animals are sentient, of course; they feel pain and we have many obligations to them, including the obligation to cause them no unjustified pain. I honor Tom Regan's appreciation of the uniqueness and the sensitivities of animals. I honor also his seriousness of purpose and his always civil and always rational spirit. But he, like Rollin and Sapontzis, is profoundly mistaken in ascribing rights to animals.

Finally, I would observe that, had these badly mistaken views about the rights of animals long been accepted, most of the successful medical therapies recently devised—antibiotics, vaccines, prosthetic devices, and other compounds and instruments on which we now all rely for saving and improving human lives and for the protection of our children—could not have been developed. Were Regan's views now to become general or to guide public policy (an outcome that is unlikely but possible), the consequences for medical science and for human well-being in the years ahead would be nothing less than catastrophic.

Advances in medicine absolutely require experiments, some of which are dangerous. Dangerous experiments absolutely require living organisms as subjects. Those living organisms, we all agree, certainly may not be human beings. Therefore, most advances in medicine will continue to rely on the use of nonhuman animals, or they will stop. When Bernard Rollin responds by telling us that medical research is mistakenly directed anyway and that when we cease to treat illness as a biological fact, we won't lose very much, he is rightly laughed out of court. Tom Regan is more realistic and less obtuse. Great scientific losses may result if animals may not be used; Regan sees this plainly. Nevertheless, he answers, there are some things we may not learn if learning them involves disrespect for the lives of rodents. His answer, when pushed to the point, is a verbal shrug: if, because we protect the rights of animals as we must, we cannot learn what we would like to learn, "so be it."

Tom Regan is free to shrug. If the cessation of most medical research is an unfortunate by-product of his moral convictions, he can ignore the point, or minimize it. We must not join him in that. Before we accept as unavoidable (as he does) the dreadful antiscientific result his convictions entail, we should demand from him a case in defense of the rights of mice and rats that is utterly compelling. In fact, the case he puts forward for the rights of animals is entirely unpersuasive. Arguments seeking to establish the rights of animals— as exemplified by those of Regan, Rollin, and Sapontzis, and others whose love of animals overwhelms their good sense—prove on careful examination to be without merit.

Notes

1. Regan, *Case.*
2. Rollin, *Animal Rights.*

3. Sapontzis, *Morals*. Others, whose work will not be addressed here, have sought to defend the rights of animals with arguments essentially like those of Regan, Rollin, and Sapontzis and in some cases with arguments like those of Peter Singer, to be discussed in the following chapter. Among these others are Stephen R. L. Clark, *Animals and Their Moral Standing* (London: Routledge, 1997), and Richard D. Ryder, *Victims of Science: The Use of Animals in Research* (London: Davis-Poynter, 1975). But all that needs to be said about the arguments for animal rights may be said with reference to the work of the three philosophers here taken as exemplars.

4. Rollin, *Animal Rights*, 75.

5. Rollin, *Animal Rights*, 77.

6. Rollin, *Animal Rights*, 77.

7. Rollin, *Animal Rights*, 78. This will not come as good news to public health agencies charged with pest control or to campers on vacation and other mosquito killers. If they could grasp it, however, it would be glad tidings to the hundreds of billions of fire ants and termites infesting the American South, swarming in the streets of New Orleans, causing injury and damage beyond calculation as they fulfill their *telos*.

8. Rollin, *Animal Rights*, 83; emphasis in the original.

9. Rollin, *Animal Rights*, 83.

10. Rollin, *Animal Rights*, 84.

11. Rollin, *Animal Rights*, 84.

12. Rollin, *Animal Rights*, 85.

13. Rollin, *Animal Rights*, 87.

14. Rollin, *Animal Rights*, 87. The parenthetical insertion is in the original!

15. Rollin, *Animal Rights*, 87.

16. Rollin, *Animal Rights*, 86.

17. Rollin, *Animal Rights*, 88.

18. Rollin, *Animal Rights*, 196; emphasis in the original.

19. Rollin, *Animal Rights*, 196.

20. Rollin, *Animal Rights*, 199.

21. Rollin, *Animal Rights*, 199.

22. Rollin, *Animal Rights*, 203.

23. Rollin, *Animal Rights*, 203.

24. Rollin, *Animal Rights*, 203.

25. Rollin, *Animal Rights*, 204.

26. This use of the term "animal liberation" is very different from that of Peter Singer, as explained in chapter 1. Saponzis admits that he adopts that term in part because of its rhetorical ring.

27. Saponzis, *Morals*, 87.

28. Sapontzis, *Morals*, 87.

29. Sapontzis, *Morals*, 196.

30. Sapontzis, *Morals*, 74; emphasis added.

31. Sapontzis, *Morals*, 74.

32. Sapontzis, *Morals*, 157.

33. Sapontzis, *Morals*, 157.

34. Sapontzis, *Morals*, 144.

35. Sapontzis, *Morals*, 144; emphasis added.

36. Sapontzis, *Morals,* 74–75.
37. Sapontzis, *Morals,* 74.
38. Sapontzis, *Morals,* 75.
39. Sapontzis, *Morals,* 258–59.
40. Sapontzis, *Morals,* 74. How far down the phylogenetic order the possession of rights extends is a question often asked of the advocates of animal rights. Tom Regan, when asked this question, commonly responds by confessing honest uncertainty, then adds, "But wherever you draw the line, draw it with a pencil." Consistent defenders of animal rights, including the rights of animals to life, may be obliged to protect creatures—say, mollusks—whose moral standing is very questionable.
41. Sapontzis, *Morals,* 74.
42. Sapontzis, *Morals,* 229–48.
43. Sapontzis, *Morals,* 247.
44. Sapontzis, *Morals,* 214.
45. Sapontzis, *Morals,* 215. How a creature may fear and seek to escape from something of which it has (as Rollin points out) and can have no concept whatever, like death, is not explained.
46. Sapontzis, *Morals,* 209–10.
47. Sapontzis, *Morals,* 215.
48. Regan, *Case,* 232–65.
49. Regan, *Case,* section 8.5, "The Rights of Moral Patients," 279–80.
50. Regan, *Case,* 279.
51. Regan, *Case,* section 5.2, "Moral Agents and Moral Patients," 151–56.
52. Regan, *Case,* sections 7.2–7.6, 235–50.
53. Regan, *Case,* section 7.2, 237.
54. Regan, *Case,* section 7.3, "All Animals Are Equal," 239–41.
55. Walter Lippmann, distinguished journalist and moral philosopher, formulated this view eloquently in 1927:

> There you are, sir, and there is your neighbor. You are better born than he, you are richer, you are stronger, you are handsomer, nay you are better, wiser, kinder, and more likeable; you have given more to your fellow men and taken less than he. By any and every test of intelligence, of virtue, of usefulness, you are demonstrably a better man than he, and yet—absurd as it sounds—these differences do not matter, for the last part of him is untouchable and incomparable . . . a spiritual reality behind and independent of the visible character and behavior of a man. (*Men of Destiny,* 49–50)

56. For an analysis of this fallacy, see Irving M. Copi and Carl Cohen, *Introduction to Logic,* 10th ed. (Upper Saddle River, NJ: Prentice Hall, 1998), 191–93.
57. Regan, *Case,* section 7.5, "Inherent Value and the Subject-of-a-Life Criterion," 243–48.

7

The Moral Inequality of Species:

Why "Speciesism" Is Right

Animal Liberation, a 1975 treatise by an Australian philosopher, Peter Singer, is the most famous of all attacks on the human use of animals.[1] Singer and his followers—the animal liberation movement—do not claim that animals have rights; they focus on animal suffering and endeavor to avoid all talk of rights. This is the second of the two large groups that strongly oppose the use of animals in biomedical research. The moral foundations of the two parties—animal *rights* advocates, and animal *liberation* advocates—are indeed very different, but the two are often confused in the popular mind because they share many convictions, including the conviction that the consumption of animal products as food is morally wrong, and the conviction that the *use* of animals to develop new drugs or to test new compounds for safety—virtually all uses of animals by humans, if not every single use—is morally unacceptable. The animal rights debate is our chief concern in this book, but Singer's arguments, the arguments of the animal liberation movement of which he is the theoretical leader, cannot be ignored here.

For liberationists the central truth in this controversy is the fact that animals are *sentient,* that they feel pain. No one seriously disputes this, of course. Liberationists then advance to a good principle: we ought to refrain from imposing pain on sentient creatures so far as we reasonably can. But by combining this principle with premises far more dubious, they develop arguments against animal research that are very bad. The objectives of medical investigators may be worthy, they allow, but just as those objectives would not justify imposing agonies on humans, they cannot justify imposing agonies on the lower animals. Liberationists conclude that the biomedical uses of animals, except in very rare cases in which experiments promise huge benefits, must be brought to a complete stop. Singer writes, "[A]n experiment [using animal subjects] cannot be justifiable unless the experiment is so important that the use of a retarded human being would also be justifiable."[2] This position effectively forecloses all animal research.

Liberationists avoid reference to "rights" because their arguments are explicitly *utilitarian*.[3] Objections to the eating of animals, and above all to the use of animals in science, are grounded on their calculation of the worth of the *outcomes* of such uses, measured in pains and pleasures. They frequently quote the great utilitarian philosopher of the eighteenth century, Jeremy Bentham. Comparing horses and dogs with other sentient creatures, Bentham remarks, in a spirit shared by contemporary liberationists: "The question is not, Can they *reason?* nor, Can they *talk?* but, *Can they suffer?*"[4]

Animals certainly can suffer, and surely they ought not to be made to suffer needlessly. That far the liberationists speak for us all. But the conclusion that biomedical research using animals is morally wrong, most certainly cannot be derived from that premise alone. Other premises, tacit or explicit—premises that are utterly false—are imported to reach that result. Two great errors pervade the liberationist critique of animal use, each of which by itself is damning; together they are devastating. I address the first of these errors in this chapter, the second in the next.

First and most fundamentally liberationists assume, mistakenly, that in calculating the balance of pains and pleasures to which alternative policies lead we must consider all sentient creatures as *equals*, attending to the pains and pleasures of all with equal concern. The pains of a rat and the pains of a human, on this view, although they may differ, do not differ in any way that counts morally. Justice demands equal treatment for all sentient creatures. Let us be fully fair to Singer, a sophisticated and learned man who does not make absurd claims—although some of his conclusions will be judged far-fetched by most of us. The equality he defends does *not* entail that all interests of humans and other animals are to be given equal weight, no matter what those interests may be. That would be a silly claim, and Singer is very careful to point out that he does not make it.[5] What he does say, very expressly, is that *when the interests of humans and animals are of similar kind, there is no reason to favor the human over the animal.* Singer writes, "The animal liberation movement . . . *is* saying that where animals and humans have similar interests—we might take the interest in avoiding physical pain as an example, for it is an interest that humans clearly share with other animals—those interests are to be counted equally, with no automatic discount just because one of the beings is not human."[6]

But if that is true, liberationists argue, then giving greater consideration to the pains of humans than to the pains of the lower animals is simply not just. Our assumption that the suffering of members of our species is somehow more important than the suffering of members of any other species is morally arrogant, and that arrogance has resulted in the most dreadful conduct.

Consider the larger picture, from their perspective: Preference for the interests of one group over the interests of another, they point out, has led throughout human history to insensitive cruelty and to rapacious exploitation. We see this clearly when the groups in question are the human races or the two sexes. The interests of white humans deserve no more regard than the interests of humans who are black or brown; males deserve no preference over females. But preference by race or by sex has marked all of human history; it was and it is morally wrong. At long last we are coming to see that all such group preference is intolerable.

The preference given to the interests of humans over the interests of nonhuman animals is (they say) no more than yet another form of group favoritism. In this case it is a murderous favoritism, resulting in indiscriminate animal slaughter. When (as in our relations with animals) the favored group is not a race but a *species*, our own species, and the pleasures of this species are held to be more worthy, and the pains of this species are held to be more dreadful, than the pleasures and the pains of other species, such unjust preference may be labeled *speciesism*.

On the liberationist view, no species deserves preference over any other. All policies or acts supposing a moral inequality among the species are flatly wrong. *All species are equal,* they contend, and the interests of all in avoiding pain are therefore rightly given equal attention, equal concern. The principle expressing this equality was given its classical statement by Peter Singer in *Animal Liberation:*

> The racist violates the principle of equality by giving greater weight to the interests of members of his own race when there is a clash between their interests and the interests of those of another race. The sexist violates the principle of equality by favoring the interests of his own sex. Similarly the speciesist allows the interests of his own species to override the greater interests of members of other species. The pattern is identical in each case.[7]

This argument is worse than bad. It *assumes* the equality of species, which is the very point at issue, and therefore can prove nothing, of course. But it serves (as it is meant to serve) as a rhetorically effective accusation because the label with which Singer brands his opponents carries very nasty overtones. This is deliberate.[8] The word *speciesism* was *chosen* to convey the thought that its practitioners exhibit moral insensitivity no less crude, no less brutal and perhaps more brutal, than that of racists or sexists. Reprobate defenders of white supremacy and male supremacy we all know to be morally wicked; for reasons of precisely the same kind, this name insinuates, defenders of the supremacy of humans over rats are wicked, too. That the term *speciesism* was devised to link it with racism is a fact emphasized by one of Singer's colleagues, Richard Ryder, who writes, "I use the word 'speciesism' to describe the widespread discrimination that is practiced by man against the other species, and to draw a parallel with racism. Speciesism and racism are both forms of prejudice . . . and both forms of prejudice show a selfish disregard for the interests of others, and for their sufferings."⁹

But the cases are *very* far from parallel; the analogical argument is insidious. Racism is evil because humans really are equal, and the assumption that some races are superior to others is false and groundless. Giving advantages to some humans over others on the basis of skin color is outrageous. Being more respectful of one race than another is unconscionable. The consequences of such racism have been and remain utterly without justification. Racism is pernicious precisely because there is no morally relevant distinction among human ethnic groups; there is even serious doubt whether racial categories as applied to human beings have any worth or validity whatever. Claims of differences among human races bearing in any way on moral status are *lies,* and liars about race have perpetrated almost unimaginable horrors. The same may be said, perhaps in lesser degree, of the historical oppression of women by men, neither sex being entitled by right to greater respect or concern than the other. There is no serious dispute about all this.

But among the species of animate life—between humans and rats, between dogs and sea urchins—the morally relevant differences are enormous, and almost universally appreciated. Sea urchins have no brains whatever, while dogs have very powerful brains. Humans engage in moral reflection, while rats are somewhat foreign to that enterprise. Humans are morally autonomous; the lower animals are not. Humans (as noted earlier) are members of moral communities, recognizing just claims even when those claims work against their own interests. Human beings have rights by nature, and those rights do give humans a moral status very different from that of sea urchins, rats, or dogs.

"Speciesism" may be taken as one way of expressing the recognition of these differences—and in this sense speciesism, in spite of the overtones of the word, is a correct moral perspective, and by no means an error or corruption. We incorporate the different moral standing of different species into our overall moral views; we think it reasonable to put earthworms on fishhooks but not cats; we think it reasonable to eat the flesh of cows but not the flesh of humans. The realization of the sharply different moral standing of different species we internalize; that realization is not some shameful insensitivity but is rather an essential feature of any moral system that is plausible and rational. In the conduct of our day-to-day lives, we are constantly making decisions and acting on these moral differences among species. When we think clearly and judge fairly, we are all speciesists, of course.

If a neighbor of ours were to insist on exhibiting the same moral concern for rats as for human beings, we would be likely to think him unbalanced. A neighbor who would have us treat dogs as we treat worms we would find abhorrent; we would have her arrested. The liberationist denial of fundamental differences among species is a terrible mistake; it is a gruesome moral confusion that encourages insensitivity, interferes with reasoned conduct, and may lead to unwarranted cruelty. We *ought not* respect rats as we respect humans; we *ought not* treat dogs as we treat worms.

Although the analogy drawn between "speciesism" and "racism" is insidious, it does often succeed in winning converts. The emotional overtones injected by the insinuating words interfere with sound moral thinking. If we are to act justly, we *need* to recognize the morally relevant differences among species and to incorporate that recognition into our habits and patterns of conduct. Making balanced judgments about what we owe to others *requires* some grasp of the nature of the beings to whom those things are owed. Therefore, the moral view that urges us to refrain from attending to these moral differences is pernicious; if adopted, it must result in our failing to apprehend our true obligations—obligations to human beings that differ very greatly from the obligations we owe to rodents or to chickens.

If all species of animate life—or only vertebrate animal life?[10]—must be treated equally, and if therefore in evaluating a research program the pains of a rodent count equally with the pains of a human (as Singer explicitly contends), we are forced to conclude either (1) that what we may not do to humans we may not do to rats or (2) that what we may do to rats we may do to humans also. At least one of these two propositions must be defended by those who insist on the moral equality of species. Both are absurd, and the animal liberation movement affirms them both.

I certainly do not mean to suggest that the pain of animals is unworthy of consideration. Their pain *is* morally *considerable*, of course; animals are not machines. I note this again with emphasis. But in making a calculation of long-term utility, it is one thing to say that the pains of animals must be *weighed,* and another thing entirely to say that all animal and human pains must be weighed *equally.* Accepting the truth that lower animals are sentient surely does not oblige one to accept the liberationist conviction that animal experiences are morally equivalent to the experiences of humans.

Humans, I submit, owe to other humans a degree of moral regard that cannot be owed to animals. I love my dog very much, but it would be very wrong for me to protect my dog at the cost of the life of my neighbor's child or of any human child. Obligations are owed to humans that are not owed to dogs.

Some humans, moreover, commit themselves willingly to care for others, and in doing so they consciously take on weighty obligations to do what is necessary to cure and to prevent disease, often in animals as well as in humans.

Medicine is a calling—and a stern calling, too. The duties of physicians and veterinarians go beyond the duties of nonmedical folks; those duties often become central in their lives. Medical investigators are sometimes obliged, for the sake of their patients, to sacrifice animals in the conduct of their research. If they were to abandon the effective pursuit of their professional objectives because Peter Singer had convinced them that they may not do to animals what the needs of human beings require, they would fail, objectively, to do their duty. More than permissible, the use of animals is therefore sometimes morally obligatory. One of the very greatest of American philosophers, John Dewey, put this point vigorously long ago:

> When we speak of the moral right of competent persons to experiment upon animals in order to get the knowledge and the resources necessary to eliminate useless and harmful experimentation upon human beings and to take better care of their health, we understate the case. Such experimentation is more than a right; it is a duty. When men have devoted themselves to the promotion of human health and vigor, they are under an obligation, no less binding because tacit, to avail themselves of all the resources which will secure a more effective performance of their high office.[11]

Human subjects in experiments are of course knowingly involved; medical investigators are strictly obliged to enlist their participation only when those subjects have given their informed consent. To ensure that human subjects are treated fairly, every medical center in this country is now legally obliged to have what is called an Institutional Review Board (IRB) whose duty it is to review all experiments imposing any possible risks on human subjects, to ensure that the consent sought from subjects is freely given and fully informed. Occasions arise, not rarely, during the debate over the relative risks and benefits of some proposed research involving human subjects, when an IRB will deny approval to an investigation proposed on the ground that what that investigator seeks to learn may be learned as well, and far more safely, through the use of some animal subjects. Institutional Review Boards consist mainly (but not exclusively) of physicians; these reviewing doctors sometimes say, in effect, to the investigator whose project is before them, "Stop. You could devise an experiment with which your aims may be achieved putting only pigs or rabbits at risk, thereby avoiding the dangers to humans that your research will inevitably impose. Do that; try your new drug, or procedure, on some suitable animal species that can serve as a model replacing humans. If later you find that progress in your research absolutely requires further studies in which the subjects are human volunteers, we will be happy to reconsider your proposal."[12]

When medical investigations are proposed, even if to confirm very promising hypotheses, in which the safety of the experimental compound or device under evaluation has not yet been fully tested using animal subjects, is it not *right* to ask the principal investigators to do all that they can to eliminate risks to humans? Before you or your children take that drug, would you not want its safety and efficacy given preliminary review using some species of rodent? Of course you would. It is morally right to proceed in that way because our duties to human subjects are of a different moral order from our duties to the rodents we use. We would not cause the death of subject animals—even rats—carelessly or wantonly, of course. But it does not require great learning to see that it is far better that risks of injury or death be imposed on animals if they can helpfully replace human beings in research. Medical scientists are speciesists, a fact for which all of us may be thankful.

Opportunities to increase human safety in this way are often missed. There are spheres in which risks could be shifted from humans to animals, yet that opportunity is occasionally overlooked or foregone. Why? For three reasons mainly. First, using animals as subjects has become *more costly,* in time and in money, than using human subjects. Regulations governing the involvement of dogs are in some ways more restrictive and more burdensome than those governing the involvement of humans. Specially bred laboratory animals are expensive, while payments to human subjects for the inconvenience caused them are quite modest. Second, using animal subjects has become much more *inconvenient* (their care and use being closely regulated) than human subject involvement. Access to suitable human subjects is generally easy for investigators, whereas access to appropriate animal subjects is not. Finally, animal use can be *hazardous.* Researchers who do use animal subjects are not rarely the target of zealous protesters. It is understandable that medical investigators are sometimes reluctant to proceed with animal studies that may prove awkward to their families and at times even border on the dangerous. The upshot is that humans are not infrequently subjected to risks that animals could have borne, and should have borne, in their place.

The assumption of the moral equality of species is the first and most fundamental error of the animal liberation movement. It is an assumption that unites it in spirit with those who hold that animals have rights as humans do. "Animal liberationists," said a leader of that movement (in a notorious remark discussed also in chapter 5) "do not separate out the human animal. . . . A rat is a pig is a dog is a boy."[13] This is more than a battle cry. She meant what she said, and the animal liberation movement she represents embodies this conviction. That all the species are fundamentally equals in a moral sphere is a deeply mistaken belief. Taken seriously in the realm of medicine, this mistake would be gravely damaging. But in the laboratories of medical centers and pharmaceutical companies, it is not and cannot be taken seriously, of course; it is preposterous. Scientists who seek to learn how to cure and how to prevent illness could not do the work they must do if there were any truth in the fantasy that "a rat is a pig is a dog is a boy." Speciesism, which asserts straightforwardly that all species are *not* equals, is not a vice but a demand of morality.

Notes

1. *Animal Liberation.* Peter Singer was appointed professor of philosophy at Princeton University in 1999.

2. Singer, *Animal Liberation*, 78. Some think that Singer's view of retarded humans is callous, but that is probably unfair to him. Rather, he thinks of animals as having all the merits of retarded humans and therefore uses our judgments about retarded humans as a standard for the judgments we ought to make about rats. The laboratory rat, he points out, "is an intelligent, gentle animal . . . and there can be no doubt that the rats do suffer from the countless painful experiments performed on them."

3. Singer's forthright utilitarian moral principles are made plain in an essay he wrote in 1985, reaffirming his earlier convictions: "Ten Years of Animal Liberation," *New York Review of Books* 31:46–52.

4. Bentham, *Introduction to the Principles of Morals and Legislation* (London: Wickering, 1823).

5. Peter Singer, *In Defence of Animals* (New York: Blackwell, 1985), 5.

6. Singer, *In Defence of Animals*, 9. Singer also holds, however, that "the life of a newborn [human] is of less value than the life of a pig, a dog, or a chimpanzee," because, he writes in his book *Practical Ethics* (Cambridge: Cambridge University Press, 1979; 2d ed., 1993), "Human babies are not born self-aware, or capable of grasping that they exist over time. They are not persons." The greater value of adult pigs and dogs, in his view, is due to the fact that they are unlike human babies in being self-aware.

7. Singer, *Animal Liberation*, 9.

8. "[T]he attitude that we may call 'speciesism,' by analogy with racism, must also be condemned. . . . It should be obvious that the fundamental objections to racism and sexism . . . apply equally to speciesism. If possessing a higher degree of intelligence does not entitle one human to use another for his own ends, how can it entitle humans to exploit nonhumans for the same purpose?" Singer, *Animal Liberation*, 7.

9. Ryder, *Victims of Science*, 16.

10. Some liberationists are tempted to distinguish vertebrate from invertebrate animals, perhaps on the ground that their central nervous systems differ so greatly that the latter do not feel pain as the former do. Of course our knowledge of the experience of the lower animals is imperfect, but it seems plain that even insects and fish experience physical distress; the equality of species urged by the animal liberation movement is their own petard. In chapter 6 we saw that those who suppose that the possession of "interests" underlies animal rights reluctantly admit that they may be obliged to recognize the rights of wasps and spiders. Likewise, those who suppose that every species is the moral equal of every other are compelled to account for a realm of pains and pleasures that is incomprehensibly vast.

11. In "The Ethics of Animal Experimentation," *Atlantic Monthly* 138 (September 1926): 343–46.

12. Such responses by IRB members to protocols submitted for approval are not rare. I have served on the Institutional Review Board at the Medical Center of the University of Michigan, in Ann Arbor, for more than twenty years. The data from research with animals, often expected to precede research with human subjects, are very often a matter of scrupulous concern by an IRB. In some contexts, of course, preliminary research using animals is simply not feasible. But where it is feasible, as is commonly the case, and yet the report of such investigations does not appear in the submission, the IRB will be very reluctant to permit investigators to put humans needlessly at risk.

13. Ingrid Newkirk, chairperson of People for the Ethical Treatment of Animals, in an interview with a reporter from the periodical, *The Washingtonian*. The significance of the remark was explored earlier in connection with the claims of the animal rights movement.

8

Spurious Scientific Arguments against the Use of Animals

The animal liberation movement bases its condemnation of animal experimentation on moral arguments that are expressly and fundamentally *utilitarian*. Such reasoning, if cogent, must take into consideration *all* consequences of the acts and policies in question—the negative and the positive consequences of the use and of the nonuse of animals in laboratory research. Animal liberationists fail to do this; that failure is their second great error. Their weighing of the advantages and disadvantages of animal experimentation is woefully incomplete. Indeed, when the long-term utilities of animal experimentation are thoroughly laid out and weighed, the arguments relied on by Peter Singer and his followers backfire.

Rights are not the issue here. Opponents of animal experimentation who believe that such investigations unjustly violate the rights of animals may consistently argue that however great the benefits of such research it is wrong for reasons having nothing to do with its results. For such critics (e.g., Tom Regan) the possession of rights is dispositive, and therefore all interests, even weighty human interests, must give way if animals do have rights. That argument was discussed at length in chapter 5.

But liberationist critics, whose objections are grounded on the merits and demerits of consequences, may not consistently take that stance. Their view demands the weighing of all the advantages as well as the disadvantages of animal experimentation, for all parties, over the long term. Not only the pains of animals but all the known benefits of animal use as well must be taken into account. Everything that may reasonably affect our judgment of the overall value of alternative possible outcomes must be put on honest utilitarian scales, including all the achievements of research that very probably would not have been attained had animals not been used, and all the likely future achievements in medicine that are attainable (so far as we can now determine) only by way of experiments in which animals are used as subjects.

About the positive outcomes of animal use in medicine I shall have much to say in the next chapter. But the general conclusion of a fair and thorough weighing may be registered summarily here: The elimination of horrible disease, the increase of longevity, the avoidance of great pain, the saving of endangered lives, and the improvement of the quality of lives (for humans and for animals) achieved through research using animals are so incalculably great that the argument of utilitarian critics, consistently and honestly pursued, establishes the very opposite of the conclusion they urge. *To refrain from using animals in biomedical research is, on utilitarian grounds, morally wrong.*

Some negatives result from the use of animals in research. Animal lives are inevitably lost, and that loss is regrettable and ought to be minimized. It would be dishonest to deny that. But it would be equally dishonest to deny the extraordinary benefits that have been achieved through the use of animals in science. Even if every animal pain were the moral equivalent of a human pain, the fair balancing of all pleasures and all pains must not fail to take into consideration the great human suffering that would have resulted, and would be experienced now and for the foreseeable future, had animals not been used to advance medicine. Almost every new drug discovered, almost every disease eliminated, almost every vaccine developed, almost every method of pain relief devised, almost every surgical procedure invented, almost every prosthetic device implanted—indeed, almost every modern medical therapy is due, in part or in whole, to experimentation using animal subjects.

The history of scientific medicine renders these truths undeniable—but the historical record is very inconvenient from the viewpoint of those who would abolish all animal experiments. To ward off the impact of this historical record, liberationists contend that there are "scientific" reasons to believe that animals are not as important in medical science as they seem to be. If that were true, or if the uses of animals could be shown to be scientifically counterproductive, the apparent benefits flowing from their past use might not outweigh the disadvantages of their continued use. But those claims, commonly made by animal liberationists, are most assuredly not true. The arguments against animal use presented by liberationists as "scientific" are the very reverse of that. Three such fallacious arguments are frequently heard; in this chapter I deal with each of these three in turn.

First Fallacious Argument

Most common is the claim that although animals may indeed have been used by medical science in the past, they *need no longer* be used, because recent technological developments make it possible to replace them; the critical experiments in which animal subjects previously were used may now go forward, it is said, without using live animals. If animals can be replaced in medical experimentation without harm to humans, the argument runs, they should be. They can be so replaced. Therefore, they should be replaced, forthwith.[1]

But, in fact, the critical premise of this argument is simply false. Animals can*not* be adequately replaced. Substituting nonanimal methods for testing in medical research (by using computer simulations, or by using experiments on pieces of tissue *in vitro*, or by using existing clinical data, etc.) is possible in a few limited contexts, but in most medical research it is wishful fantasy. Where sound experimental methods are possible that do not entail the expenditure of animal lives and that do yield results as reliable as those got through the use of animal subjects, we ought to employ those alternatives, of course. In those special circumstances such replacements are indeed already made. But in the vast majority of biomedical investigations, there are absolutely no satisfactory replacements for animal subjects, and there are none even on the horizon, *because the safety and efficacy of an experimental drug or procedure must be determined by assessing its impact on a whole, living organism*. No computer simulations, no manipulation of cells or tissue samples in test tubes, can give reliable evidence about the impact of the experimental therapy upon a living being. Therefore, the general replacement of animals in medical research is simply out of the question, now and for the foreseeable future.

This conclusion is forcefully re-confirmed by the recent discovery that humans, in spite of our immense complexity, have vastly fewer genes than had long been supposed. Our responses to most stimuli, therefore, cannot possibly be traced to any single gene. Investigators who need to learn how an organism will react will very likely be misled, therefore, if they examine only its pieces out of the full organic context. The noted zoologist Stephen Jay Gould writes: "The key to complexity is not more genes, but more combinations and interactions generated by fewer units of code–and many of these interactions (as emergent properties, to use the technical jargon) must be explained at the level of their appearance, *for they cannot be predicted from the separate underlying parts alone*. So organisms must be explained as organisms, and not as a summation."[2]

At issue is the balance of goods and evils. The claim that animals are generally replaceable is important to animal liberationists because, if that were true, the evils of animal use now and in the future (whatever the benefits of their past uses may have been) might outweigh its good consequences. But the realities of medical science demolish this argument. A new drug to combat cancer or to fight infection or to combat depression must have a great variety of impacts on the many integrated systems of the organism to which it is administered. Some of those impacts may be anticipated; others may be wholly unexpected. There is no possible way in which all the consequences of some new compound can be fully measured by computers no matter how powerful computers become; no tissue samples or organ samples can yield the outcomes needed when a new drug is to be tried. Whole organisms are not replaceable in medical research, which means that animals are not replaceable in medical research. Therefore, the claim that the negative consequences of using animals need no longer be borne is utterly false.

The liberationist counters: Perhaps it is impossible to *replace* animals in experimentation, but it is often possible to *reduce* the number of animals used, and that alone will save many animal lives.

This is true but not relevant. Where it is possible to conduct reliable experiments with a reduced number of animals, that should be done, of course, so long as the validity of the results is not impaired. In testing the toxicity of experimental compounds, or the efficacy of promising new drugs, the number of animals used should be no greater than the number required for scientific reliability. Determining that number is a technically complicated statistical problem with which medical investigators are perennially concerned. But the statistical demand cuts both ways: we certainly should use no *more* animals than are needed for safe and reliable results, *and* we certainly should use no *fewer* animals than are needed for safe and reliable results. Eliminating wastage in the uses of animals is morally right; this gives no support to the claim that animals can be generally replaced and certainly gives no support for the abolitionist position.

Second Fallacious Argument

A frontal attack is launched against the usefulness of animals in medicine. Their use, liberationists commonly contend, has no scientific reliability at all. It is "junk science." Animal experiments are worse than unnecessary because they mislead investigators and actually hinder scientific advance.

This criticism of animal use is widely repeated by persons who, ignorant of the ways in which biomedical research is actually carried on, would like to think it true. It is utterly false. The role of animal experiments in medical research is not misleading but central; in many branches of medicine, it is the most rewarding and the most essential research tool. The ways in which animals are actually used merit a brief account here.

"He who knows anything knows this, that he need not search far for an instance of his ignorance."[3] Nsowhere is this truth more vexing than in the world of medicine. Much is known, but all that we know is bounded by wide fields of ignorance. On every front medical investigators chip away, laboriously, at the uncertainties that pervade human disease and disorder. Some major achievements receive wide acclaim: a new understanding of an old disease, a new vaccine, a new antibiotic, a new surgical technique. Most medical advance, however, does not come as thrilling breakthroughs but in tiny and gradual increments. Knowledge expands slowly as the product of laborious and patient inquiries into what is hoped will prove to be improvements in drugs or other therapies. For any single advance, the process is likely to require a great number of small steps and years of work.

Suppose indications are found that pharmaceutical compounds of a certain general kind have an effect that *may* prove helpful in alleviating a disorder for which no cure is presently known. That possible new drug, however promising, must be approached with great caution. Varieties within that family of compounds must be meticulously examined; all the dangers of that set of compounds must be explored with greatest care; in experimental trials all their effects in living organisms, beneficial and adverse, must be recorded in scrupulous detail.

Toxicity is the first great concern. On first investigation the dangers of a new compound cannot be fully known. We must learn through the actual administration of the compound, and long before seriously planning its use in human beings, that the new drug is not poisonous. This we learn in the only way possible: by administering the drug, in repeated and meticulously planned trials, to a pool of live experimental subjects. Who shall they be? Only by using animals, of course—most commonly mice or rats—can we do the preliminary testing that will determine whether the compound is toxic. Animal testing does not determine safety absolutely, of course; successful administration to mice does not guarantee harmlessness, but it certainly does avoid a very great deal of risk and injury to humans.

If repeated trials confirm the conclusion that the compound is not toxic, it remains to determine—again using animals—the *dose level* at which it may be safely administered. The first principle for all physicians, taught early to all medical students, is this: *Primum non nocere*—first, do no harm. So experimental doses very much larger than those envisaged for eventual human use are first administered to rodents much smaller than humans; testing of this kind is a critical step in preparing for the first trials of the drug with humans.

But long before human trials are begun, there must be years of work to determine the *efficacy* of the new compound. Does it do what was hypothesized? How does its effectiveness compare to that of other drugs already in use to achieve the same or a similar objective? Winnowing out what is not reliable, or not a significant improvement over what is already in hand, is an exceedingly burdensome task, expensive and time-consuming. Even when early results are very promising, the animal trials must be many times repeated to determine whether in fact the proposed improvement is genuine, its hoped-for consequences probable.

Preliminary trials of the new drug, randomized and statistically very sophisticated, move laboriously forward, through phase after phase: toxicity, dose level, effectiveness, each step undertaken first with one animal model, and then often with a second animal model to increase safety and confidence yet further and to determine efficacy yet more surely. Only after the investigators' hypotheses concerning the safety and efficacy of the drug are repeatedly confirmed *in animals* may the testing of that drug reach the point at which the approval of federal agencies may be requested for the commencement of the first phase of clinical trials on human beings. Very, *very* few of all the compounds investigated as candidates ever do reach the point at which testing in humans may begin—and if they do so, it is only because *years* of preliminary experimentation using animals have paved the way.

Is this use of mice and rats "junk science"? Of course it is not; it is the very best science we know. Critics make much of the fact that in spite of every precaution taken in this process, the judgment of the new compound is sometimes mistaken. That is true. It may turn out, after extended experimentation involving hundreds or thousands of preliminary tests, that a drug shown to be effective in treating some animal model proves ineffective in treating humans. It may even turn out—although it happens very rarely—that what had been shown nontoxic in animals proves toxic in humans. To avoid such errors investigators go to the most extraordinary lengths—but there can be no absolute certainty before the tests on humans begin.

What should we conclude from this? Do such occasional failures show that drug trials using animal subjects are *generally* misleading? Certainly not. The animals used to test for efficacy are chosen because (in view of their known anatomical similarities to humans, and in light of extensive previous experience with animals of that species) they are believed to be good *models* for the human organism. Of course, no model is perfect. But better by far to work with an imperfect model first than to use no model at all.

The closeness of the animal model to the human condition is a continuing scientific concern. That is why different species of animals are used for different kinds of investigations. For example: Recent research with mice has enabled scientists to create mice with fully functioning human immune systems, by replacing the bone marrow of the mice with human bone marrow.[4] The spongy red marrow in bones produces not only the red blood cells that carry oxygen, and the platelets that help blood to clot, but also the disease-fighting white blood cells, the main pillar of the body's immune system. At the Weizmann Institute of Science in Israel, investigators destroyed the bone marrow cells of mice using radiation, thus erasing the ability of the mice to combat the introduction of foreign marrow, and at the same time creating the needed cavity for the growth of new marrow. Human bone marrow cells were then dripped into the veins of those mice, cells that quickly moved into the bones of the mice and took up residence there. The new marrow—*human marrow thriving now in mice*—functions perfectly, producing the full array of circulating human immune cells, white blood cells and antibodies that protect the mice, and new red blood cells as well. The method is simple and easy to replicate. An immunologist at the University of California at Los Angeles observed that with such mice we can "test AIDS drugs, test vaccines, test anything immunological that we now do in humans." These mice, he says, are in effect "humans with fur."[5]

But even with excellent animal models like these, no serious investigator will claim that results in preliminary experiments using animals can *prove* a drug effective in human use or that such experiments can prove with certainty that it is entirely safe for human use. Differences between animals and humans remain; these differences are well understood and make it essential, *after* all the animal data have been collected and refined, to conduct new trials, very cautiously, in which the compound (for whose safety and efficacy there is now substantial evidence) will be administered to volunteer humans subjects in closely supervised "phase 1" clinical trials. Again the process is painstaking; again toxicity and dose level must be investigated to determine safety before all else. *Primum non nocere.*

If things go well in the first stages of these clinical trials, a second and then a third phase will be undertaken in which efficacy will be the central concern. In the end it may turn out that the new compound does offer some substantial benefit or perhaps only a modest but still a genuine improvement over the existing standard treatment for the condition in question. If things go badly in the early clinical stages, the candidate compound will be put aside; investigators may return to their search for a drug in that promising family of compounds, or will perhaps abandon that family and search for a compound of a wholly new kind, or may seek an entirely different approach to the target disease.

This laborious process goes on endlessly. In any major center for medical or pharmaceutical research, during any given year, thousands upon thousands of new drugs, new ideas, new procedures are to be found at some stage of this arduous passage from conception through trials to possible realization. The very backbone of this process, the heart of it, is research using animals.

Animal studies thus make two absolutely critical contributions to the advance of medical science, the first *eliminative,* the second *suggestive.*

First, animal trials *eliminate* a wide range of drugs or other therapies whose risks and attendant miseries never need to be tried on humans. We cannot learn with certainty, from animal studies alone, that promising drugs are indeed useful. But we can learn, with a very high degree of probability, that toxic compounds are indeed toxic, and that what may have been thought promising is likely to be a biological dead end.

Before administering any new drug to any human being, we must have substantial evidence that the experimental compound is not poisonous, and the only way we can gather good evidence for that belief is through the results of prolonged trials using live animals. Toxicological studies using animals, most commonly rodents, are the first and toughest hurdles any new drug must overcome. Long before investigators can even begin to measure the effectiveness of a new drug in humans, they must have good reason to believe that it is safe. To this end animal subjects *must* be used.

It happens on rare occasion that a new compound makes it through to the stage of clinical testing on humans but is found later to be dangerous; the outcome can be tragic. But were it not for animal tests, the number of dangerous compounds *not* weeded out would be vastly greater. There are hundreds, thousands of drug *candidates* that animal experiments eliminate from consideration long before humans become involved, compounds that never will be tested in human patients because they were first tested in mice. Many mice are killed in this process, and that is no good thing; yet great human suffering is avoided by such animal screening, and that *is* a good thing, good almost beyond quantification.

Second, animal trials *suggest* new compounds and other therapies whose efficacy in treating rats or monkeys may be well enough confirmed to justify the cautious exploration of those or related compounds in treating humans—first experimentally, of course, with fully informed human volunteers.

Liberationist critics are scornful because, when all the animal testing is done, experiments using human subjects are still essential. Indeed, they are essential—but that is no justifiable cause for scorn. Without animal trials a very great deal that we have learned in modern medical research would have gone *un*discovered. And the cost of what would have been learned, had animals not been used, would have been mercilessly high. The number of unidentified human subjects *protected* from needless injury by preliminary animal screening is exceedingly great.

Responds the critic:

> You miss my point. It isn't merely that some animal experiments mislead by encouraging the trial of drugs that will not work for humans but that they mislead dangerously, by encouraging the trial of drugs that, although safe enough for rats, are deadly for humans. Thalidomide is a good example. Devised to reduce nausea during early pregnancy, it passed muster in animal tests—and wrought havoc among humans by causing the birth of many horribly deformed babies. This happened because investigators were misled by experiments using animal models that did not yield reliable predictions about the adverse effects of thalidomide in humans. The animals used in medical research are not human beings and therefore cannot serve as rational guides to the impact of drugs upon humans. Experimentation using animal subjects [the argument concludes] is therefore worse than useless—it is dangerous.

A very few dangers are not screened out by animal trials, as we have seen. But anecdotes prove nothing, and used in this way an anecdote can be seriously misleading. Misfire on rare occasions certainly does not justify the conclusion that animal trials increase danger. It is wrong-headed to refrain from using animals to protect humans from *any* of the dangers entailed in the development of new drugs because we cannot with certainty protect them against *all* such dangers. The horrors of teratogenic compounds such as thalidomide do drive home a lesson, but not the lesson the liberationist intends. The real lesson is this: New drugs can be dangerous; no research tool at our disposal must be rejected that can help determine the likelihood of disastrous consequences *before* administering new drugs to humans. The elimination of animal testing would not reduce the incidence of such disasters. It would, on the contrary, *increase* their number because, without background animal data, human trials would begin (if ever they did begin) in a condition of far greater ignorance.

The critic rejoins again:

Some dangers may perhaps be avoided through the use of animals. But there is one scientific failing of animal tests to which that answer will not suffice. Because animals represent the human organism imperfectly, they mislead in another way: The animal subjects may exhibit no response to drugs that would in fact be highly efficacious if used by humans. *False negatives* are as misleading as *false positives—* and we cannot know how multitudinous are the cases in which good drugs have been bypassed or discarded because of misleading negative results in animals.

This complaint is based on the false assumption that animals are generally not good models of human disease. In fact, they are often excellent models, and commonly they are the only models we have. The physiological differences between humans and animals are obviously great, for which reason inferences drawn from results in the one context to probable results in the other must be treated always as tentative. But decades of experience, and thousands upon thousands of trials in which are studied the effects of compounds upon parallel conditions in animals and humans, establish beyond serious doubt that we can use animal results in devising therapies for humans and that the contributions made by preliminary animal studies are usually very reliable and often seminal.

Animals of different species are used in investigations of different human disorders, of course, the disease in question and the models used carefully matched. For research into the toxicity of new drugs, for the preliminary testing of chemical compounds designed to combat cancer, and for many genetic disorders, mice and rats have repeatedly proved to be excellent models.[6] For the testing of new treatments for heart disease and vascular diseases, the great similarity of the cardiac systems of the human and the pig render swine excellent models. To determine the efficacy of newly developed vaccines, the species selected must be one known to be subject to the disease for which the proposed vaccine has been devised. And so on and on. No animal is a perfect model of the human. Animal results are indicative but not dispositive, and the results of animal trials must be used with great circumspection. All this is clear. But the great body of research in medical centers around the world now makes it also clear that there is no guide to the development of new treatments for human sickness that is more suggestive or more reliable than the testing of the treatments of parallel conditions in animals.

Hypotheses for the treatment of diseases or disorders having no current treatment must often be far-reaching; new approaches must be speculative, even revolutionary. To confirm or disconfirm such speculations, the use of humans is likely to be out of the question. One scientific approach—sometimes a failure but sometimes also brilliantly successful—has been to breed special animals, to develop new animal strains (usually of mice) whose special characteristics make possible research that would be otherwise impossible. The logical patterns employed in this approach to discovery illuminate the necessity and the unique value of animal subjects.

1. The classic and most common pattern is that of developing an animal that contracts a disease very similar to the human counterpart disease for which no cure is yet known. Those humanlike animals are then inbred, and their genetic strains become rich platforms for research on that disease. For example, research on diabetes has long relied critically on what is known as the *nonobese diabetic mouse.* Diabetologists call it "a wonderful friend of mankind."

2. A second pattern is the creation of animal models by developing what is called the *nude mouse*—an animal specially inbred so as to be completely without an immune system. Because these mice have no immune defenses, human (and other animal) tissues and tumors may be grafted on to them and can then be studied in the living bodies of those mice after grafting, without the threat of immune rejection—and without danger to humans.

3. A third pattern is the use of *transgenic mice,* in which there has been a germ-cell transfer into the mice, the *addition* of some human gene that is known to produce a protein that is suspected of involvement in some puzzling disease. These mice are then inbred, and a model is created in which the added human gene is *expressed* so that the role of that suspect protein in the living body of the mouse may be carefully studied.

4. A fourth pattern is the use of *knockout mice,* in which a specific gene, whose protein product is thought to be involved in some puzzling dis-

ease process, is *deleted* from the genome of the mouse. Animals so treated are then inbred. Studies are then conducted in those living organisms on processes relevant to the disease in question in the *absence* of that suspected protein.

This fourth pattern is an exceedingly powerful research technique. With the completion of the Human Genome Project now at hand and the genome of the mouse also decoded, knockout mice become central in many medical investigations.[7] The genomes of the two species (human and mice) are about the same size, and most human genes have counterparts in the mouse genome, recognizable because of the similarity of their DNA sequences. But the actual roles of most human genes (of which there are tens of thousands) are not yet known. Understanding the genes of mice has thus become an essential tool in interpreting the genes of humans. Researchers, dealing with some human gene whose function is a mystery, locate the counterpart mouse gene on the mouse genome; they then create a strain of mice that *lacks* that gene—mice in which it has been "knocked out"—and observe what such mice can no longer do. The impact of the deletion of a gene on the organic functions in the mouse, experimentally shown, gives very fruitful leads to the role of the analogous human gene in question.

This technique is real, not hypothetical. A vivid illustration of the contribution made by knockout mice is exhibited by very recent investigations into the still mysterious causes of lupus—a potentially fatal immune disorder. The human body's waste disposal system is disrupted in lupus; hypothesizing that this in turn is caused by the deficiency of a certain enzyme called DNaseI, Swedish researchers turned off the gene that encodes DNaseI in specially bred mice and found that 73 percent of the mice without the DNaseI gene were indeed showing clear symptoms of lupus. This technique has given clear evidence that a known genetic mutation blocking the ability of the organism to mop up dying cells contributes directly to the cause of lupus, a result that could be obtained only in this way. [8] Advances in the science of human genetics rely ever more extensively on the uses of knockout mice.

The third and fourth of these patterns are powerful illustrations of what logicians call the "method of agreement" and "the method of difference," among the most fundamental analytical tools for the confirmation of scientific hypotheses. Using the method of agreement, causal relationships suspected but not established are explored by creating assorted sets of circumstances having one potentially critical factor *in common;* using the method of difference, causal relationships suspected are explored by creating assorted sets of circumstances alike in all relevant respects *except* one: the absence (or the anomalous presence) of what is suspected to be the cause, or a critical part of the cause, of the phenomenon under investigation. When that phenomenon is a disease, the method of agreement could not be used on *human* subjects, for it would involve introducing some factor suspected of causing disease. And when the phenomenon is some critical organic function that we seek to control by eliminating (an hypothesized) necessary condition, using the method of difference, research of that kind on humans, involving deliberate damage to the organism, would be outrageous. Medical progress requires live organisms in which suspected causal factors may be safely manipulated—introduced or removed—to confirm (or disconfirm) new hypotheses. Only animal subjects can serve in this way.[9]

In sum: The claim that animal experimentation is "bad science" is wildly false. Old anecdotes are repeated endlessly to excite fears that are born of ignorance. The belief that animal experimentation is misleading or unnecessary arises from the failure to appreciate the great caution with which medical investigations go forward, and the failure to understand the key theoretical role of animal models in the confirmation or disconfirmation of medical hypotheses. In the investigations of medical scientists—laborious, prolonged, meticulous, and often intellectually adventurous—experiments using animal subjects are absolutely essential.

Third Fallacious Argument

Some abolitionists contend that even if animal research does yield results helpful in treating human disease, it ought to be abandoned because the advances it produces encourage the large-scale misdirection of medical resources. The liberationist argument goes like this:

> The widespread dependence of medical science on research with animals is a consequence of a conception of medical care that is wasteful and largely useless. The entire medical establishment must be redesigned, restructured. The vast majority of human diseases and disorders result from the failure to *prevent* disease, and that should be our overriding goal. Our proper targets are not cures or palliatives but *bad diets* resulting from poverty, *destructive environments* caused by ill-considered industrialization, and *injurious habits* encouraged by profit-driven corporations. The medical research industry thrives on animal research, but its achievements are minimal and transitory. If the enormous resources now devoted to medical research and the care of the acutely ill were directed instead to prevention and to the creation of a genuinely humane environment, many of the "cures" we now seek would be unneeded because the illnesses would not have arisen. Humankind would then be vastly better off, and the killing of innocent animals in the name of science could be stopped. Animal experimentation [this argument concludes] is but one unseeing arm of a huge system needing wholesale redirection, a system that thrives on sickness yet does little to eliminate it.

When this great system has been fully reconstructed, research with animals will be seen to have been a misguided and foolish expenditure of money, effort, and animal lives.

This argument deserves little respect. It is the desperate resort of animal liberationists who see no way to deny that animals do in fact greatly serve the interests of the human sick. These are ideological enthusiasms, and political complaints, but not serious scientific criticisms of medical practice. It is probably true that, in the large, too little energy and money is expended in the effort to prevent disease, as compared with the energies and funds expended to cure it. Were bad diets improved, environmental deterioration reversed, unhealthy habits corrected, and so on, humans in general would no doubt enjoy far better health than they now do. But from this we may not rationally conclude that efforts to cure those who are sick, whatever the cause of their present sickness, are misguided.

If cigarette smoking, for example, could be eliminated, the boon to global human well-being would be enormous. Much heart disease and very many cancers (and other ailments) now sure to develop would in that case never arise. But it certainly does not follow that we ought to diminish the intensity of research efforts aimed at curing or mitigating existing conditions caused in part by smoking. If nutrition could be universally improved, overpopulation and poverty overcome, humankind would be hugely benefited, no doubt—but this truth cannot justify the cessation of our efforts, including efforts using animals as models, to find ways to alleviate the miseries of those who now suffer from diseases that might, in that envisioned world, be much reduced.

The number of persons who suffer from diseases and disorders for which cures are not yet known is very great. It will remain very great even if the vision that underlies this abolitionist criticism of the present medical system were one day to be realized. If good nutrition and good habits eventually eliminate many of the diseases from which humans now suffer, mortality will not be overcome, disease will not disappear. Disorders and afflictions now having lesser impact would come to have a greater role in human decline, and these conditions in turn would become our chief medical concerns.

As an argument against the use of animals in medical research, the wholesale condemnation of contemporary medical science as misdirected is preposterous. A vision of the world in which preventive medicine has largely replaced curative medicine is commendable but totally unrealistic. Our world is very far from that condition, obviously, and the suffering condition of most humans makes it very unlikely indeed that the search for cures will soon cease to be pressing. On planet Earth for many generations to come, hundreds of millions, even billions, of human beings will suffer gravely from diseases for which research with animals offers the principal hope. Even in a world in which medicine has been revolutionized on some utopian model, needs will still remain—there will *always* remain needs—for medical treatments whose design or improvement will depend on scientific research using animals.

Notes

1. One version of this argument runs as follows: "Since animals are innocent, and since it cannot be right to harm the innocent unless one has conscientiously explored the alternatives to doing so, it is wrong to use animals for scientific purposes if (a) this harms the animals and if (b) a conscientious effort has not been made to explore the alternatives." But, the authors of this complaint continue, "a conscientious effort to avoid using animals has not been made"; therefore, "we must conclude that, as things stand, at least most and possibly all use made of animals for scientific purposes harmful to them is morally wrong." See D. Jamieson and T. Regan, "The Case for Alternatives to Laboratory Animal Experimentation," *Lab Animal* 11, no. 1 (January–February 1982): 21–22. The false premise in this variant is the claim that conscientious efforts to replace animals have not been made. In fact, entire scientific institutes are devoted to precisely this enterprise, such as the Johns Hopkins Center for Alternatives to Animal Testing, the University of California Center for Animal Alternatives, and the European Research Group for Alternatives in Toxicity Testing—all seeking, in the words of their Interagency Coordinating Committee, to "encourage the refinement and reduction of animal use in testing, and the replacement of animals with nonanimal methods and/or phylogenetically lower species, when scientifically feasible" (*Newsletter of the Center for Alternative to Animal Testing* 13, no. 1 [Fall 1995]: 5). There has been no failure to seek alternatives to the use of animals in science; there has been a failure, by no means deliberate, to find them. Replacements for animals are nearly impossible to devise except in very special contexts.

2. "Humbled by the Genome's Mysteries," *The New York Times*, 19 February 2001 (emphasis added).

3. John Locke, *An Essay Concerning Human Understanding* (1690).

4. See Yair Reisner and others, "Engraftment and Development of Human T and B Cells in Mice after Bone Marrow Transplantation," *Science* 252 (19 April 1991): 427–31.

5. Dr. Andrew Saxon, quoted in the *New York Times*, 19 April 1991. Even *fish* can serve as useful models in the exploration of some human diseases. Investigators at the University of Texas and at Southwestern Texas State University have collected and are breeding pure strains of certain species of fish (swordtails and platies) that produce melanoma cells strikingly similar to those produced by the human body. Melanoma is a particularly deadly kind of cancer, and the powerful weapons needed to attack it are difficult to develop if only humans can be the experimental subjects. Happily, that may no longer be true. But are fish among the species whose pains must be weighed as morally equivalent to the pains of humans? About that members of the animal liberation movement are ambivalent.

6. Geneticists now report that the gene pool in mice is essentially the same as that

in humans, although arranged differently. A molecular geneticist at Princeton University, Dr. Lee Silver, puts it this way: "Every gene in humans seems to have a homologue in mice. It doesn't always do the same thing, but if you look at the size of the mouse genome [you find that] it's the same size as the human genome," and with the rearranged pieces of mouse genome, "you can make the human genome." Quoted in the *New York Times,* 26 December 1995.

7. The Human Genome Project is being completed as this book is published; the full decoding of the mouse genome is being completed simultaneously.

8. These lupus studies, also conducted by researchers in German laboratories in Essen and Bochum, were reported in *Nature Genetics* (June 2000).

9. Additional illustrations of these research techniques will be found in the following chapter.

9

What Good Does Animal Experimentation Do?

No one takes pleasure in the sacrifice of animal lives. Experiments using animals do cause the death of many rodents and some other animals as well. Most of these animal subjects suffer no pain or distress, but a few do, and these are consequences that need to be justified. Do the results of animal studies provide that justification? Yes, they are justified a thousandfold. Remarkable advances in medical science, achievements precious to human beings beyond calculation, but possible only through the use of animals in laboratory research, far outweigh the loss of animal lives entailed.

This point was made earlier in general form: very few of the great advances in modern medicine, I noted, could have been achieved without animal experiments. But readers will want to know specifically what animal research is good for *now*, what is being accomplished at the present time, and what we, in our lifetimes, may reasonably expect to be accomplished through research using animals.

Experiments using animals to advance human well-being are so many and so complex that a full account is impossible to present; it would require a medical library to report. Almost all drugs, all vaccines, and all medical treatments that are now in wide use or now under development would not be available to us, or to our children, had there been no animal experiments to establish their safety and efficacy.

My task here is to give this claim concreteness. In the ten sections that follow I give illustrations, current and genuine, of the progress being made, and being made possible, through animal research. Tens of thousands of drugs and treatments are in the research pipeline as I write; only a fraction of these will be realized in fact. But of those that are realized, virtually none could enter human service without a foundation of animal research upon which they are built. Almost all of the avenues of medical research opening now would *close* if experiments with animals were to be forbidden. This is so because we certainly may not do with humans what we may do with animals; without animals most of these inquiries simply could not be undertaken.

The examples selected bear on health concerns that are widely understood. Recounting the role of the animal research involved in these studies requires brief background explanations of a technical sort, for which the reader's patience is required. Citations for the scientific studies referred to will be provided in endnotes for readers who may wish to review one or more of these inquiries in more detail. These citations will be mainly the reports of research in scientific journals, but where those reports are likely to be indigestible by a general readership, more accessible accounts of the research in question may be provided in their stead. Much of the best work in progress cannot be reported here because its explanation would require far too much complex biological detail. The reports that follow, however, are not mere dreams—these are the exciting medical and biological investigations that are under way *now*, in the effort to cope with human disease.

Heart Failure

The leading cause of death in the developed world is heart disease.[1] Poor diet, smoking, lack of exercise, genetic predisposition—there are many culprits, but their common product is *atherosclerosis*, the clogging and stiffening of arteries that brings on circulatory stoppage and death. To overcome this clogging, more than half a million operations are done each year in the United States, some to bypass closed arteries, others to clear out obstructed arteries with what is called *angioplasty*, in which the obstructing material on the artery walls is pressed or scraped away using inserted catheters.[2]

By removing the obstructions, angioplasty improves blood flow, but it also unavoidably injures the walls of those arteries. As the body repairs these minor injuries, new cells proliferate at the site, and this gathering of cells on artery walls often causes new blockages, *restenosis*. So what was designed to open clogged arteries frequently results, shortly thereafter, in their more complete clogging.

To advance the healing of wounds the body produces a substance called *platelet-derived growth factor*, or PDGF. Because platelets clog the arteries it was hypothesized that PDGF plays a significant role in promoting restenosis. Two questions then arise: (1) How does one determine with confidence that PDGF is a major cause of blockage after angioplasty? (2) If it is, how shall we use that knowledge to combat excessive growth on the artery wall after angioplasty?

To answer the first question, it was necessary to introduce an antibody that would neutralize the action of the growth factor and then test to see whether that neutralization had the hypothesized effect. Neutralizing agents could first be developed only using nonhuman animals. Human PDFG was injected into goats; the goats' immune system produced the needed antibody. To test the effects of this antibody—not on humans, of course—angioplasty was performed on rats, using catheters exactly like those used in human angioplasty, though far smaller. Damage was caused by the catheters to the inner wall of the neck arteries of the rats, just as it is caused by catheters in human arteries. Half the experimental rats received doses of the PDGF antibody to reduce cell multiplication; the other half, used as controls, were injected with an antibody also produced in goats but one that does not neutralize PDGF. The arteries of the control rats thickened and narrowed as human arteries commonly do after angioplasty, but of those rats in which the PDGF antibody had been injected, 41 percent developed *no blockage* at the angioplasty site.[3]

The thickening of artery walls remains a serious threat to human patients after bypass surgery or angioplasty. We now know, thanks to Dr. Russell Ross, and to the antibodies he produced in goats and injected into rats, that it is PDGF that promotes excessive growth on the artery wall, whose effects must be counteracted.

The goat antibody used in this study cannot be used in humans because it would be recognized as foreign and destroyed by the human immune system before it could work. In rats, however, the theory could be tested because long experience with laboratory rodents has made it possible to breed mutant strains with abnormal immune systems[4] in which the antibody is tolerated.

Knowing that it is the action of PDGF that must be blocked, researchers sought some way in which that knowledge, gained in work with rats, might be applied to the arteries of humans. One very clever system has been devised to *slow* the injurious cell growth at the site of the wounds on the arterial wall caused by angioplasty. This is a system using not an antibody but a gene—the *retinoblastoma* gene, known (from earlier animal studies) to slow the growth of cancers. But how to get this critical gene to the precise place where it is needed?

Investigators at the University of Chicago hypothesized that the needed gene might be introduced by embedding it in a virus, one made safe by being modified so that it could not spread. Human subjects could not possibly be used in the first experiments, of course. Angioplasty was performed on rats and on pigs using catheters whose balloons had been coated with the gene-laden virus. Rats were used because a great deal is already known about restenosis in rats on whom angioplasty has been performed; pigs were used because their coronary arteries are so very similar to those of humans. The results were startling: *new blockage was reduced by 50 to 60 percent* with no adverse side effects.[5] Samples of the arteries of the experimental animals, sacrificed for detailed examination, showed that the retinoblastoma gene had taken hold within one day after its introduction on the catheter, that it had lived for about two weeks until the virus carrying it died, and that this interlude had been long enough to interrupt the cell growth that eventually causes restenosis. These results have been replicated at the University of Michigan, and the laboratory investigation of this technique continues. Trials on humans may not be begun before there is very solid, very well-confirmed results in animals.

It is reasonable to hope, as Dr. Claude Lenfant, past director of the National Heart, Lung and Blood Institute of the National Institutes of Health, has said, that restenosis—a very serious threat to human patients after bypass surgery or angioplasty—will before long become preventable. When that happens, it will be because the essential techniques for suppressing excessive tissue growth in arteries were developed using rats and pigs. The lives of hundreds of thousands of people, perhaps millions of people, will eventually be saved. The cost in animal lives—not animal pain, since the animals used are completely anesthetized—will have been very modest. Is that a price we should be unwilling to pay?

Ideally, of course, the cleaning out of arteries would be unnecessary if only we could learn how to avoid blocking them in the first place. That will require a better understanding of the way in which the high-density lipoproteins (HDL) bearing cholesterol carry away fatty substances, while the low-density lipoproteins bearing cholesterol are taken up by and accumulate on the walls of blood vessels. One critical question, long unanswered, is how does HDL do its good work?

The answer is now known, thanks to recent research with mice and rats at the Southwestern Medical Center in Dallas and at MIT.[6] The molecule that serves as the cell-surface receptor has been identified at long last; it is a protein known as SR-B1; it binds with the HDL cholesterol and influences the transfer of cholesterol from the blood to specific tissues that need HDL-bound cholesterol to make steroid hormones.

In mice it was found (by using marked antibodies) that SR-B1 was concentrated in the liver and adrenal glands and in the ovaries of female mice—the places where HDL-bound cholesterol primarily is used to make hormones. From this it could be deduced that SR-B1 was indeed that long-sought HDL receptor. These animal experiments provide no cure for atherosclerosis, of course, but they make it possible to study, to understand, and eventually to cope with cholesterol and its role in arterial health. Progress is possible now in the understanding of vascular disease that would not have been possible without that work with mice. Millions of people die each year from heart failure due to blocked arteries. What is the balance of goods and evils in this case?

Vaccines

One of the most wonderful achievements of modern medical science has been the development of vaccines that protect healthy human children (and also adults and animals) against serious illnesses. The number of lives that have been saved and the amount of suffering that has been avoided by vaccines are beyond calculation. Not long ago, large families were thought necessary partly because parents had to presume that some among their children would fall early victims to some dreaded disease. But now nearly all children (including the children of those who oppose the use of animals in research!) are vaccinated as a matter of course against a host of diseases that, years ago, might decimate local populations.

Sadly, in parts of the world childhood vaccination is very far from routine, and the killer diseases afflicting children are among those for which no vaccine is yet available. There populations are decimated still.

The development of safe immunization—vaccines that work in preventing deadly diseases and that cannot themselves cause those diseases—is a dangerous enterprise; it cannot go forward without the use of experimental animals. Zealots who now demand the cessation of research using animals are also in effect demanding the cessation of virtually all serious efforts to devise new vaccines or to improve old ones. *Medical research in the field of immunology depends absolutely on the use of animals.*

First a backward look: Influenza caused an estimated *twenty million deaths* during the international pandemic of 1918; it was finally brought under control during World War II by vaccines developed using laboratory animals. One of the researchers deserving credit for that achievement was Dr. Jonas Salk. Paralytic polio, afflicting hundreds of thousands of Americans almost randomly during the 1940s and '50s, became Salk's target after World War II. The eventual victory over polio—it was eradicated completely in the United States some years ago, and global eradication is now approaching—was recounted briefly in the opening chapter of this book. That victory would have been impossible without using animals.

Earlier efforts to immunize against polio had failed very badly; some experimental immunizations had caused paralysis in humans rather than preventing it. Human trials of any vaccine for polio were considered by many investigators too risky to undertake. Salk and his research team began by making a thorough survey of the many polio viruses, establishing unequivocally that an effective vaccine would have to cope with three distinct types of polio virus—then called the Brunhilde, Lansing, and Leon strains—but not more than those three. These viruses would have to be grown in the laboratory and then killed for use.

Viruses can be cultured; that had been demonstrated by John Enders at Harvard, in research winning a Nobel Prize. But the technique requires cell tissue taken from animals and can be very tricky. Salk, often in conflict with his more senior colleagues, had to find a way to apply that technique to the culture of polio viruses so that they could be used to produce the vaccine he sought. The task may be compared to Thomas Edison's famous quest for the particular filament that would make possible a successful incandescent electric light. After a great number of tries, Salk at last found the host tissue on which the polio viruses could be successfully cultured: kidney cells taken from monkeys.[7]

Field trial of the monkey-cell product on humans—which could begin only after the safety of the new vaccine had been well confirmed in tests on animals—was the climax of the work of the National Foundation for Infantile Paralysis. Some 440,000 American children received the Salk vaccine; an approximately equal number not vaccinated served as controls. On 12 April 1955, at a news conference at the University of Michigan in Ann Arbor, Dr. Thomas Francis, one of Salk's colleagues who had supervised the field research, announced the wonderfully successful result: a safe and effective vaccine for polio had been found. "This," said the chairman of the board of directors of the American Medical Association, "is one of the greatest events in the history of medicine." It was made possible only by the extensive use of laboratory animals.

Now a forward look: Any proposed vaccine for AIDS will be dangerous just as polio vaccines were dangerous, until animal trials give solid grounds to believe it safe. AIDS is the acronym for *acquired immunodeficiency syndrome,* a collapse of the immune system that results in deterioration and death from a variety of infections that the body, infected by the human immunodeficiency virus (HIV), has become incapable of warding off. Transmitted through blood products and sexual relations, AIDS is lethal; there is no cure, and no one has yet been known to recover from it.

HIV has infected some thirty million people worldwide at the time of this writing. Of these, most reside in thirty-four sub-Saharan countries in Africa, where approximately *one quarter of the population* will soon die from AIDS. In Zimbabwe, one out of every five adults is infected. In Botswana, life expectancy, which was sixty-one years in 1993, has dropped below forty-seven and will soon fall to forty-one years.[8] In Asia, according to the World Health Organization, the number of those afflicted is now approaching twelve million; on that continent alone some *ten million people* will die of AIDS in the next fifteen years. Each day there are about seven thousand new infections. AIDS is pandemic. A vaccine against HIV is a very high priority for medical science.

Any live organism on which an experimental HIV vaccine is to be tested will be put in very serious danger. Besides humans, the only animals in which some form of HIV causes disease are primates. But the early HIV vaccine candidates that did protect adult monkeys (against SIV, the simian form of HIV) actually caused the disease, killing the baby monkeys it was designed to protect.[9] So risky to the experimental subjects were those early tests that the prospect for any vaccine effective in human beings was thought dim. With such risks, how could even the most promising candidate ever be evaluated?

But there is reason for a little optimism that this difficulty may be overcome.

Some recent experiments appear to show that monkeys can be vaccinated safely. The technical hurdle was to develop a vaccine that would protect both against cells infected with the virus *and* against particles of the virus that are free of cells. That has now been done. The new vaccine, tested successfully on macaques, produced remarkable results, reported by the investigators thus:

> Eight cynomolgous macaques inoculated with attenuated simian immunode-ficiency virus (SIV) were challenged (four each) with cell-free and cell-associated SIV. All were protected; whereas eight controls were all infected [and died of AIDS] after challenge. These findings show that live-attenuated vaccine can confer protection against SIV in macaques.[10]

The extrapolation of these results to humans is not yet possible. The British researchers write, "The use of live-attenuated HIV as an AIDS vaccine in man is fraught with problems of safety. [This approach] could not be used in man without extensive safety investigations. Nevertheless, our results show that an effective AIDS vaccine is feasible and can prevent infection with [both] cell-associated and cell-free virus."[11]

A vaccine that will successfully protect against the human immunode-ficiency virus, HIV, remains a goal medical researchers are struggling to achieve. The vaccine used successfully on monkeys for SIV gives a little promise. When that promise is one day realized, a safe and effective HIV vaccine devised, humankind will be saved incalculable misery and pain. That goal cannot possibly be achieved without the use of animals as experimental subjects, some of whom will die in the process. To avoid those animal deaths, shall we stop this research?

Many diseases remain for which no vaccine yet exists. If we are to expand the range of diseases from which humans can be protected, we must use animal tests. In research with mice, new vaccines, using the techniques of genetic engineering, are now being devised. These have great advantages: having been administered to more than two billion people around the world, they have been proved remarkably free of adverse side effects; they are cheap to produce, and the new design permits fifty-year protection from many different diseases to be packed into one vaccine. Best of all, vaccines of this new kind can be administered to newborns—this is of great importance because for children in developing nations, contact with any kind of health care system is often limited to the day of their birth. Such vaccines may eventually prove to be one of the great contributions of animal research.

Against measles, whooping cough, polio, and other viral ailments for which standard vaccines (also developed using animals) already exist, the new vaccines will offer better protection than is now available. But even more promising is the likelihood that vaccines of the new kind can stimulate the body's immune system to prevent diseases that have thus far proved invulnerable to vaccines of the traditional sort. The key to the new approach is the use of recombinant DNA technology: investigators insert into bacteria the genes that manufacture critical bits of proteins taken from a variety of micro-organisms that cause disease. These bacteria are then cultured in fermentation tanks to produce the needed protein fragments that induce immunity but cannot cause disease. These protein fragments are purified and made into vaccines. With high-tech vaccines of this kind, the immune systems of human children may soon be stimulated into the development of defenses against leprosy, Lyme disease, malaria, and even possibly AIDS and other diseases that have thus far evaded all treatment.

Will this system really work? It is being perfected. The serviceability of the bacterium serving as vehicle has already been established. The insertion of genes into that bacterium for wide protection against disease was first tested on mice—not on humans, of course—and in those mice the new technology certainly does work. The immunities developed in experimental animals were described by one leading investigator as nothing short of "miraculous."[12]

Two groups of mice were challenged with injections of infective organisms that resulted in serious disease for the control group. The group that had been earlier given recombinant DNA vaccines, however, exhibited immune systems that responded magnificently: in those mice antibody proteins were produced to neutralize the antigens, white blood cells were marshaled to destroy them, and special signaling compounds were produced that quickly sent the responding immune system into high gear. This vigorous response was, moreover, permanently etched into the memory of the animals' immune system, ready to be called on if at any future time their bodies were to be confronted with that antigen in microbes carrying genuine disease. None of the work resulting in the development of this new kind of vaccine—or indeed new vaccines of any kind[13]—is feasible without experiments on animal subjects.

Alzheimer's, Parkinson's, ALS, and Other Neurodegenerative Diseases

Terrible disorders resulting from the degeneration of cells in the nervous system are widespread. Senility is now known to be most often due to Alzheimer's disease, whose cause is a degeneration of the cells of the brain involved in learning and memory. Alzheimer's patients gradually lose their memory, then their ability to reason, and then even the ability to think clearly; complete incapacitation comes all too soon. This terrible disease—the fourth leading cause of death (after heart disease, cancer, and stroke) in the developed world—afflicts about *four million* Americans each year.

The mechanical cause of Alzheimer's is the accumulation of plaques of *beta-amyloid* (a fragment of a normal protein) in the critical regions of the brain and the loss of nerve cells there. But research on this disease is unavoidably dangerous because it must involve intervention in brain function. If effective treatment for Alzheimer's is ever to be found (none is known at present), first some *safe* method of testing the new drugs must be devised to combat it. Safety demands a good model for the disease, a living animal in which that same deterioration of the brain takes place. Such a model has recently been created, using mice, into whose DNA the critical gene has been inserted.

Animals that reliably exhibit true Alzheimer's disease may serve as very useful models of the human sufferers of that condition. These mice, just like humans who develop Alzheimer's, appear to be fine when young, but their brains, just like the brains of afflicted humans, become riddled in middle age with those tell-tale balls of beta-amyloid plaques. The mice suffer, just as humans do, the loss of brain cells that characterizes Alzheimer's patients.[14]

Progress in treating this dreadful disease is at last possible thanks to animal research. Successful treatment can be developed only if there are animals on which the compounds that may alleviate brain degeneration can be tested. Such animals we do now have—those very special mice carefully bred by the hundreds. Humans otherwise destined for the most humiliating deterioration of old age—millions of humans—may one day benefit from their use. The research will require that many mice be killed (without pain) in order that their brain cells be microscopically and chemically examined. Is the sacrifice of those animal lives justifiable?

Amyotrophic lateral sclerosis (ALS, also known as Lou Gehrig's disease) is a degenerative disorder from which about thirty thousand Americans suffer; it has no known cure. In ALS the motor neurons of the brain and spinal cord degenerate, leading to progressive weakness, then paralysis, and eventually a horrible death. The sufferer may remain fully conscious and yet be trapped in a body that (in the later stages of ALS) is completely immobile, unable to move as much as a finger or an eyebrow.

Nerve cells do not regenerate as cells in most of the human body do. But to rescue those who suffer from ALS and other brain disorders, human nerve cell regeneration must somehow be stimulated. Is that possible? Perhaps. This regeneration has been achieved in experimental animals, using a substance called *glial-cell-derived neurotrophic factor,* or GDNF, which works specifically on the dopamine-producing nerve cells. Experiments involving neurotrophic factors are dangerous; one such experimental substance earlier caused ALS patients great pain and suffering. But researchers using GDNF with mice have shown that the dopamine-producing cells, which help to regulate movement throughout the central nervous system and whose degeneration is involved in both Parkinson's disease and ALS, can be rescued.

At the Karolinska Institute in Stockholm, mice were first treated with a toxin that kills dopamine-producing cells. A week later GDNF was injected, with a positive response. A large number of those critical cells regained health and grew new connections in the animals' nervous system. When GDNF was injected *before* the toxin was administered, the result was yet better: full protection for the dopamine-producing cells.[15] In a second experiment dopamine-producing cells in mice were severed; half the mice whose cells were cut were treated with GDNF and half were left untreated. In those untreated, 50 percent of the neurons survived; in those treated, 85 percent of the neurons survived.[16] In a third experiment the motor neurons (critical in ALS) of newborn rats were severed. In rats left untreated, only 6 percent of those neurons survived; in rats treated with GDNF, 100 percent of the neurons survived.[17]

Neurotrophic factors are substances produced in tissues throughout the body; transported to the spinal cord and the brain they play a critical role, especially during infancy, in making the connections between the brain and the outer nerve circuits that control the body throughout life. The protective and healing powers of these remarkable substances, produced in humans as they are produced in rats, are the targets of experimentation now in progress around the world.[18] It is too early to say that treatment with glial-cell-derived neurotrophic factor will succeed in combating human nerve degeneration; various types of neurons may require different combinations of neurotrophic factors. But in this sphere of medical research, where progress is very difficult, recently confirmed results with GDNF are wonderfully promising. None of this work, *none of it,* could have been done without using live animals in research.

Neurodegenerative diseases have been particularly difficult to study because humans who suffer from the target disease may not be experimented on, and there have generally been no available animal subjects who exhibit the same nerve degeneration. In the research just recounted, for example, the effectiveness of a treatment for cell regeneration could only be tested after the nerve cells of mice had been deliberately damaged. But in the case of ALS, researchers at Northwestern University have done better, creating, through genetic engineering, mice that naturally develop an inherited form of that disease.[19]

It works like this: There are certain toxic chemicals, oxygen-free radicals, that are implicated in neurodegenerative disorders. The enzyme that rids the body of these toxic chemicals is produced by the instruction of a gene; that gene is known. When mutations of that gene *cancel* the functions of the critical enzyme, the gene itself becomes malevolent, promoting degeneration. What is needed are animal models in which this calamitous process takes place naturally. These animals now exist, mice that have been bred to express the genetic mutations that have precisely this damaging effect. Using these mice, researchers can study the process of degeneration and explore new ways to combat it. A leader of the research group achieving this result, Dr. Mark Gurney, points out that this development is "a key step" in finding a cure for the disease. "Now we can rapidly test therapies with greater safety and also less expensively."[20]

When the spinal cord is damaged, as in an automobile accident or an athletic injury, the regeneration of nerve tissue presents a special challenge to medical researchers because wounds to the spinal cord have long been thought irreversible and uncontrollable. This pessimism has been mitigated by recent research with chickens.

Nerve fibers, axons, are normally covered with a protective substance called *myelin,* one of whose functions is to stabilize the nerve pattern laid down during the early development of the organism.

When the spinal cord is injured, as in an automobile accident, a biological chain reaction begins in which myelin (which has a useful function in the very early development of an organism) begins to form in the wounded region, permanently blocking needed nerve regeneration. How can the formation of myelin in those regions be temporarily suppressed, so as to allow the injured nerve fibers to regenerate?

Investigators at the University of British Columbia have done this. Protein compounds have been devised that contain an antibody that targets myelin; these are attached to enzymes that then disrupt the formation of the myelin coating immediately after injury. When a "protein cocktail" of this kind was injected into chickens whose spinal cord had been cut, spinal nerve fibers that previously could not regenerate *did* regenerate.[21]

Hundreds of thousands of Americans suffer partial or total paralysis resulting from spinal cord injuries; more than ten thousand such injuries are reported each year in the United States, of which most are in the vulnerable lower back. The victims of catastrophic automobile or sporting accidents are sentenced to a lifetime of immobility and pain. Research with chickens may lead to a substantial reduction in this human toll. Objection to this research by the advocates of animal liberation must attach a very great value to the lives of chickens.[22]

Obesity

Obesity is a serious medical condition—a substantial risk factor for a great many human diseases, dangerous in itself, and a source of physical and mental distress for very many people. Most commonly it is the consequence of gluttony in weak-willed humans, but sometimes it is the product of a metabolic disorder. Recent research with obese mice has at last opened the way to the possible treatment of some forms of this disorder, treatment at once life saving and life improving, that may reduce weight quickly and sharply.[23]

The key to the problem appears to be the absence or insufficiency of a key hormone, recently discovered in mice, called *leptin*. Injecting it into mice deficient in leptin causes the animals to lose excess fat quickly and thoroughly.

Thirty years ago it was found that if the circulatory systems of genetically obese mice were hooked together with those of normal mice, the obese mice quickly regained normal weight. Something carried by the blood of the normal mouse, missing in the blood of the obese mouse, was plainly causing that rapid loss of fat. But what and why? The mystery substance was not detectable at that time because, as animal research has very recently shown, the weight control factor is present in the blood of mice in almost unbelievably tiny quantities, just *billionths of a gram* per milliliter of blood.

Identifying that weight control factor required recently developed techniques for the manipulation of mouse DNA. The first step was to find the specific gene in the makeup of the normal mouse that, when *in*activated, results in the *gain* of weight. This was done at the Rockefeller University in New York in 1994 by Dr. Jeffrey Friedman and others; eliminating the critical gene, they proved that they could cause mice to grow very fat.

The next step was to identify the weight control gene in humans, almost perfectly identical to the weight control gene in mice. Leptin, the hormone this gene produces, was thought likely to play a key role in the weight control system of the body of both organisms.

This hypothesis had then to be tested—on mice first, of course. Would injections of additional amounts of leptin force the mouse body to shed its fat? The results of these experiments have been stupendous. In mice that produce no leptin of their own and are therefore genetically obese, injections of leptin caused the mice to lose 30 percent of their body weight in two weeks. They ate less; they burned calories at a faster rate; they began to move around their cages like normal mice—and the diabetes that accompanied their obesity simply disappeared as they lost weight. But it is not only on those genetically peculiar mice that leptin works its wonders. Lean mice given additional leptin also lose weight, and the more leptin they receive, the more weight they lose. If the level of leptin naturally found in the blood was doubled, the mice lost virtually all of their body fat (reducing it from 12.2 percent of body weight to 0.67 percent of body weight) in four days. The critical gene has been patented by Rockefeller University, and a major pharmaceutical company, Amgen, paid them a very large sum for a license to use the gene to develop a treatment for human obesity. By 1998, the success of synthetic leptin produced by Amgen had been established.[24] Leptin does not work for everyone, since obesity has many causes, nor does it have as dramatic an impact on humans as on mice. But weight loss increases as dosage with the new drug increases, which proves the effectiveness of the treatment and the importance of the discovery.

Another firm (Hoffman–La Roche, whose researchers had simultaneously reported similar results in mice given leptin) is seeking a method to embed leptin in pills for simpler administration. How many millions of human beings are likely to find such pills worth the life of some experimental mice?

Exactly how leptin works is not yet known. It is produced throughout the body by fat cells and released into the bloodstream in the most minuscule quantities. The level of leptin in the blood appears to be monitored by the hypothalamus, a region of the brain in which the body's metabolic rate is set and the appetite controlled. The experiments with which leptin was identified were done only on mice, but human fat cells produce a hormone so closely similar that human leptin, injected into mice, works perfectly in eliminating their excess fat.[25]

Leptin—whose receptor in the brain was identified using laboratory rodents some six months after the research just described was conducted—is only part of a very complicated story. Another protein, called *glucagon-like factor-1* (GLP-1), has also been found in rats to play a key role in signaling the body when to eat or to stop eating. Leptin keeps body weight at an even level over the long term; GLP-1 acts quickly to affect the perceived need for food. GLP-1 is active in the stomach and the intestines where, after a meal, it is released into the bloodstream, prompting the release of insulin, which helps metabolize sugar. Researchers in Hammersmith Hospital in London hypothesized that the injection of GLP-1 would reduce the desire to eat—and that it does, rapidly. Rats receiving injections of the protein as they nibble food pellets *immediately* appear satiated and lethargic, as if they had just finished a large meal.[26]

GLP-1 is to be found in the human gut and brain; indeed, it has been found in identical form in every vertebrate species examined, from fish to mammals. If, using laboratory animals, a way could be found to mimic its effects or to slow the breakdown of GLP-1, the amount of food eaten by overweight humans would be reduced without injury or distress.

Obesity may be countered by causing a loss of appetite; being fat is often the result of simply eating too much. So, naturally, the pathway in the brain that is responsible for appetite, and for the production of fat, is a natural target for researchers. And indeed it turns out that an experimental drug, called C75, has a dramatic effect on this pathway. At Johns Hopkins University scientists have shown that that chemical, without any apparent damage to the health of the experimental mice, causes an almost immediate drop in appetite, while metabolism does not slow, and fat continues to be burned. The mice simply stopped eating until the effects of the drug wore off. Said the leader of the research team, Dr. Frank Kuhajda, "The mice drop their weight like a stone, losing 25 percent of their body mass in a couple of days." These animal results, he concluded, "give us some hope" that we may find a new way to fight obesity.[27]

The use of "knockout mice" (in which some genetic elements have been deleted) has uncovered what may prove to be valuable information about the genetic roots of appetite. Researchers at the University of Dentistry and Medicine of New Jersey have bred mice in which the gene known as Hgmic has been stripped away. That gene, it now appears, must play a central role in helping mice store fat. Mice that do not have the gene, this research team discovered, could eat and eat with impunity—and not get fat![28]

Research with chickens, as well as with mice, gives strong indications that the presence of some viruses also affect obesity. At the University of Wisconsin researchers found that the bodies of animals inoculated with adenovirus-36, a human virus associated with colds and diarrhea, contained twice as much fat (after the passage of several months) as control animals without the virus. And that adenovirus, they discovered, is much more prevalent among those humans who are overweight.[29] With results of this sort, medical science chips away at the disorders and diseases that afflict human beings.

The body systems of humans and rats, it turns out, are in many respects very similar; from experiments on rodents, a great deal can be learned about human weight control. More than *half* of all Americans are overweight; half of these—about 25 percent of our population—are medically obese. How many rats may we justifiably kill to find a way to remedy human obesity?

Sleep

The daily cycles of human wakefulness and sleep are controlled by many small clumps of specialized cells in the forebrain and in the brain stem, but the interconnections of these cells, and the master switch that controls them, have not been fully understood. In all mammals, the circuits that control sleeping and waking are known to be closely similar. When the front part of the hypothalamus of rats is cut, it has been shown that the rats cannot sleep, while when the back part of the hypothalamus is cut they become comatose. But, within the hypothalamus, the location and chemical nature of the unit that turns off and turns on all the brain cells involved in sleep and awareness remained a mystery. No longer. Dissecting the brains of rats, investigators at Beth Israel Hospital in Boston have found that master switch.[30] For the treatment of human insomnia and other sleep disorders, this discovery opens a new and promising domain.

Experimenting on rats in various stages of sleep and wakefulness, and tracing a protein called *fos* that is found in cells only when they are active, the master control system for sleep in mammals was found in a region of the hypothalamus called the *ventrolateral preoptic neurons.* Here, it was learned, the hypothalamus produces a neurotransmitter that inhibits the firing of other brain cells and also stimulates the connections that send arousal signals to every part of the cerebral cortex, thus keeping us awake.

This advance in the understanding of sleep and wakefulness in the human organism was possible only through brain research that could not possibly have been done on humans. Building on this knowledge, physicians at Concordia University in Quebec[31] and at Harvard University in Cambridge[32] have learned how to reset the internal clock in humans who suffer sleep disorders. The exploration of the sleep control mechanisms of the human brain continues at many medical centers, and many rats are killed in the process. Is the knowledge gained not worth the lives of those rats?

Organ Transplants

Can animals be used to supply new organs—hearts and livers and kidneys—for humans who will die without them? Not yet, but the prospects are good. *Xenotransplantation,* the human use of animal organs, is a very active field of medical research; its potential is enormous.

Transplanting organs from human cadavers is now common and very successful, but the supply of organs from that source falls very far short of the need; while the waiting lists for new organs lengthen, the number of people who die while waiting for an organ increases. Here are the figures for human-to-human organ transplants (in the United States only) for 1994:[33]

Kidneys: 11,390 kidney transplants were performed; 27,498 patients remained on the waiting list; 1,376 people died while waiting for a new kidney.

Hearts: 2,340 heart transplants were performed; 2,933 patients remained on the waiting list; 723 people died while waiting for a new heart.

Livers: 3,653 liver transplants were performed; 4,059 patients remained on the waiting list; 646 people died while waiting for a new liver.

Lungs: 737 lung transplants were performed; 1,625 patients remained on the waiting list; 281 people died while waiting for new lungs.

If organs from animals could be safely transplanted into humans, very many human lives could be saved.

Xenotransplantation cannot yet be done successfully for the same reason that transplants from human donors commonly failed when first tried: the immune system of the recipient identifies the new organ as a foreign body and rejects it. There are two ways of dealing with this threat. One is by suppressing the recipient's immune system. This works but has serious drawbacks: a weakened immune system opens the way to diseases of other kinds, and the essential regime of immunosuppressive therapy is burdensome, expensive, and perpetual. The drugs that are successful in suppressing the immune system of organ recipients—cyclosporine is the one now most widely used—eventually have dangerous side effects on other organs of the recipient's body.

But there is another strategy to counter the rejection of a donated organ. If the new organ can somehow be altered so as to cause the recipient's body to find it tolerable, the threat of rejection may be overcome. That is why the "matching" of donors and recipients is important in transplant medicine. But donor organs naturally matching the recipient's system are very hard to come by, and when the donor is not a human the match-problem is magnified. That difficulty, plus the threat of cross-species infection when the donor animal is a baboon or a monkey, had led many to conclude that xenotransplants would not prove feasible. But three recent developments have dramatically transformed the prospect for the near future.

First, xenotransplant efforts have been redirected from primates, whose use creates a genuine risk of interspecies infection, to pigs, which (although their organs are similar) are so different from humans that the risk of cross-species infection is virtually eliminated.[34]

Second, genetics has made it possible to breed pigs that can more safely serve as the donors of hearts, or lungs, or livers, or kidneys, because human DNA, inserted into fertilized pig eggs, results in pigs that produce human counterpart proteins instead of the pig proteins that excite rejection and whose organs therefore do not provoke the acute rejection that befalls ordinary pig organs. Pig organs are similar in size to human organs and therefore pigs may serve as a nearly unlimited source of transplantable organs—if ways can be found to avoid the rejection of the organs by the immune system of the human host. To achieve this objective, the porcine donors need to be genetically engineered to make their immune systems more closely match the immune systems of humans. This explains the race to clone pigs. Creating genetically identical animals is not the main objective; the cloning is a mechanism that permits efficient genetic manipulation and thus holds enormous promise for humans. The cloning of pigs became a reality in the year 2000.[35] Hopes for the successful transplantation of pig organs into humans, without immune system rejection, are now very high.

Effecting the specific changes that will be needed in donor animals is also an enterprise being rapidly advanced. The company that is famous for having cloned the sheep Dolly recently announced that it had produced two healthy lambs from genetically modified cells—cells in which new DNA and the eggs of sheep had been fused. These lambs prove that a transgene, a gene from another species, can be introduced at a preselected site in the genome of animals other than mice. With this technique unwanted genes may be eliminated, or genetic modifications may be introduced that have therapeutic or nutritional applications.[36] And, of course, this will permit researchers to knock out those genes in pigs or other animal cells that cause the rejection, by humans, of transplanted organs.[37]

Third, animal research has led to the enhancing technology of *pre*treatment, in which the body of the recipient is given a very small amount of the donor animal's bone marrow well before the transplant. The recipient's immune system is in this way gradually prepared for an organ from an identified animal and thus made far more tolerant of the organ to be transplanted. It is no longer, as one researcher puts it, "like you're waiting for someone to fall off his motorcycle."[38]

This combination of the new type of donor animal, the genetic alteration of the donor animal, and pretreatment of the recipient holds great promise. Monkeys receiving pig organs have been proved able to survive for years, even without suppression of their immune systems after the first thirty days. Human patients who desperately need new organs, and for whom human organs are not and will not be available, may yet have a chance to live.

Using the *parts* of animals in surgery on humans is a well-established practice; the intestines of sheep are used routinely as surgical sutures; and insulin taken from pigs has been saving the lives of human diabetics for many years. Not so widely known is the fact that pigs have long been bred to provide heart valves for humans, many of whom now survive only because of a pig valve grafted into their vascular systems. Grafts of this kind are being rapidly improved; a normal pig heart valve is stripped of all the cells that could cause rejection or transmit disease, and the collagen structure that remains is then implanted into the human heart—and the patient's own cells then grow in and on the collagen structure and build new collagen. It becomes the patient's own heart valve, able to withstand the wear and tear of constant use. The routine use of pig valves for humans needing new heart valves is soaring.

On another experimental front, the transplantation of brain tissue from pig embryos into human brains, to replace the dopamine-producing cells whose loss has resulted in advanced Parkinson's disease, has already been experimentally undertaken, with encouraging results.[39] Research aiming at the similar use of hearts and livers is going forward briskly; the temporary uses of pig organs to keep patients alive while a suitable human organ donor is sought is now clearly envisaged; genetically altered pig organs will be experimentally grafted into humans very soon; competing biotechnology companies are racing toward what they confidently believe will be a new realm of human therapy.

In addition, promising new research[40] has shown that cells of one kind can be transformed into cells of another kind. Cells from the bone marrow of rats (like those of humans) that would normally grow into bone or muscle or fat have been redirected, converted into nerve cells. But of course the tinkering that is possible with live rats cannot be done on humans. Yet this research has what some scientists think to be revolutionary implications, including even the possibility of correcting the most intractable health problems with new cell replacements. There remains a very long way to go in this undertaking, of course, but so extraordinary is the potential of this animal research that one leading neuroscientist expressed his response very simply, saying, "It's really beautiful."[41]

Other experiments with mice have exhibited (in a different way) a plasticity in the cells of the mammalian body that is both amazing and cause for great hope that damaged or defective human tissues may one day be repaired or regenerated.

From what are called *stem cells* other differentiated cells are produced; it had long been thought that each organ of the body had its own brand of stem cells from which that organ's specialized cells develop. But experiments in 1999 with mice, by Dr. Angelo L. Vescovi and others at the National Neurological Institute in Milan, prove that stem cells from one portion of the body can metamorphose into stem cells of another portion.[42] Using radiation to destroy the blood-making cells of the bone marrow of the mice, researchers injected stem cells (with an identifying genetic tag) from the nervous system of other mice, which found their way to the defective bone marrow and began to produce new blood cells bearing the identification of the donor mice. The long-held theory that the cells of blood and brain are permanently committed to the realm from which they come has thus been disconfirmed.

This is a dramatic result, for the following reason: Stem cells taken from human embryos had been isolated in 1998; this gave hope that faulty tissue might eventually be produced from such cells. But because their use requires the destruction of an embryo, the barriers to such work seemed very high. If, as the most recent work suggests however, ordinary stem cells from the skin or the blood can be acquired from a given patient and used for the production of needed tissue elsewhere in the body of that patient, we may enter a new era of medical advance. This work in mice may make it possible, with perfected technique, to harvest skin stem cells from a patient and insert them into the bone marrow of that same patient for the making of blood or into the brain of that patient for the making of cells lost in Parkinson's disease. No problem of rejection by the immune system will arise, since the cells introduced would be the patient's own.

Animal research may one day make possible the repair of human disorders previously thought entirely impossible to treat by regenerating organ tissue within the human body. "The resource to heal a sick body," says the very hopeful Dr. Vescovi, "lies in the body itself."

In sum: New organs, new tissues, replacements for the defective or damaged parts of human beings are in very great demand. The search for them grows more and more pressing; for those in mortal danger, it is a desperate search.

This need cannot be met by donations from human cadavers. It will not be met until ways are found to grow or make replacements, or until, using animals in different ways, we find new sources for organs that are safe and durable. Thousands of human lives are at stake. It is morally wrong to refrain from this research, whose rewards may prove so very great, to save the lives of pigs.

Diabetes

A terrible disease that often results in dreadful complications (blindness, circulatory failure resulting in amputations, etc.) and in early death, diabetes is a disorder in which the victim needs what his defective pancreas does not supply: the release of insulin in appropriate quantities at appropriate times, to enable the body to utilize essential sugars in food. The principal tool of medical researchers now working with diabetes is the carefully bred diabetic mouse, whose use has made possible some dramatic improvements in treatment.

The discovery of insulin resulted from experiments with dogs. In 1923 Dr. Frederick Banting received the Nobel Prize for that discovery—although it was not until the 1950s that Rachmiel Levine, again working with dogs, revealed how insulin works: not within the cell but on the outside of it, unlocking the cell membrane and thus permitting the transport of glucose and other sugars. These early animal studies have been the foundation for subsequent decades of research on diabetes. Animal studies have always been central in diabetes research. New ideas, new modes of treatment for diabetics—of whom there are many *millions* in the United States alone—depend utterly on research with animals, now mainly mice.

It is very common today for diabetics to receive daily injections of insulin, much of which comes from pigs.[43] It would of course be far better if the patient could produce his own insulin, which suggests that the transplantation of a pancreas from a human cadaver might prove effective as treatment. But such transplants, which have indeed often succeeded, involve not only major surgery but also the permanent suppression of the patient's immune system to ward off the rejection of the foreign organ. This suppression is burdensome and also dangerous. Three paths are now being pursued—all involving the use of animals—to overcome this obstruction.

First, some researchers seek to provide the subject with the needed insulin by inserting an artificial pancreas—a plastic device about the size of a miniature hockey puck within which are stored insulin-producing islets obtained from pigs. The heart of this device is a coil containing the insulin-producing cells and a selectively permeable membrane through which the patient's blood circulates. The islet cells are nourished, and the insulin penetrates the membrane to join the circulating blood. It works in dogs. The promise of such a device lies in the fact that it is not rejected by the host because the cells of the immune system, the lymphocytes that attack foreign tissue, are too large to pass through the membrane lining the coil. So the patient can retain the device in the lower abdomen indefinitely, without the need for immunosuppression.

But this system remains flawed because of a decline, over time, in the amount of insulin produced within the coil. Of course, its improvement will require extended use of both the pigs from which the insulin-producing islets are taken and the dogs on which the device must be extensively tested. But hope remains that such a system may yield effective long-term treatment for human diabetics.[44]

Second, more promising than any mechanical device is the transplantation of the islet cells themselves, in such a way that they take up residence in the patient and are not rejected as foreign. Investigations leading to this outcome require the sacrifice of many mice. Very recently there has been heartening progress on this front. Dr. James Shapiro and a team of researchers from the University of Alberta in Edmonton announced in May 2000 that they had been able to achieve long-term insulin independence in a small group of severely diabetic patients who received pancreatic islet cell transplants. All of the subjects—seven out of seven—remained free of the need for insulin injections for at least one year. The immunosuppressive regime required was simple and relatively very safe. This advance was possible only after a very long period of transplant research with mice and primates. So important was this development that the *New England Journal of Medicine* announced the finding six weeks in advance of the publication of the results of the full study.[45]

Third, very shortly before this book goes to press, yet another development has thrilled diabetics and diabetes researchers around the world. No suppression of the immune system will be required if, by genetic manipulation, we can devise a way to cause cells in the body of the patient to become insulin producing, while also being appropriately responsive to sugar levels, so that insulin is released in the right quantities at the right times. In December 2000, a team of researchers—also at Edmonton, and with the cooperation of researchers at the University of Tennessee and Boston Medical Center—reported that they had succeeded in causing cells in the gut of experimental mice to produce human insulin—insulin that was released in the right quantities at the right times, protecting those mice from diabetes even after their native insulin-producing cells had been destroyed![46] No such development would have been remotely possible without the use of mice. But now, with those remarkable animal studies completed and others under way, we may reasonably hope, as Dr. Shapiro put the matter, that a *cure* for insulin-dependent diabetes may be achieved before long.

Meanwhile, another quite different approach to diabetes is under way, in this case seeking to reduce the damage already done to the sufferer's tissues by high glucose levels—damage done in exactly the same way to the tissues of diabetic mice. The wounds that diabetes produces, if they heal, heal very slowly. Research with diabetic mice at the University of Michigan has revealed a way to speed the healing of those lesions. A substance called *fibronectin* is the key to the wound-healing process; by isolating, modifying, and injecting a tiny drop of a peptide (called *PHSRN*) that has been found to stimulate wound-healing cells in fibronectin, the healing of wounds in diabetic mice has been speeded up enormously. This is certainly no cure for diabetes, but to the very many humans afflicted with the complications of diabetes, it offers great hope for relief.[47]

Consider now, from the perspective of the millions upon millions of diabetics, the question raised by the book in hand: Do the established benefits and the probable gains of these investigations using pigs and dogs and mice outweigh their costs in animals' lives? Perhaps that question is best answered by the children (and adults) who suffer from this common and debilitating disease—and by their parents.

Genetic Diseases

Thousands of genetic disorders afflict humans; many of them do their damage to the fetus before birth, resulting in blindness, mental retardation, disfiguring skull malformations, and other skeletal anomalies. The cause of some of these is known: the absence of a particular gene or the presence of an imperfect gene. If those missing or defective genes could be replaced much human misery would be avoided. But the needed gene, even if it is identified and isolated, must somehow be implanted in the organism. Might it be possible to introduce genetic replacements of this kind into the embryo before birth, thus eliminating the genetic disease before it takes hold?

The needed genetic therapy must first be perfected in animals, and on that front substantial progress has been made.[48] By connecting a readily identified gene to microscopic bubbles of fat, and then injecting those fat bubbles into the tail veins of pregnant mice, selected genes can be implanted in mouse embryos in utero. Because of the way in which the mother's placenta handles those fatty bubbles, the genes remain active in the mice when newborn.

There is always the danger, in genetic therapy, that the inheritance of future generations may be affected by what has been done. But this research has shown that such threats can be avoided because, using this technique, the inserted genes remain separate from the animal's gene pool and therefore cannot be passed on to the offspring of the newborn mice. The implanted genes did their good work during pregnancy, but fourteen months after the mice were born, the genes were no longer detectable. Yet they had been operative long enough to overcome the developmental deficiencies of defective genes for which they were replacements.

Many genetic disorders in humans (e.g., malformations of the skull and other skeletal problems) may become preventable in the womb using this technique. The number of mice involved is small, the number of humans great. "We'd be talking," says Dr. Richard Leavitt of the March of Dimes Birth Defects Foundation, "about a very substantial number of individuals." Who finds this use of mice to present a moral problem?

Sickle-cell anemia is a genetic disorder in which red blood cells containing an abnormal form of hemoglobin cause those cells to stiffen and contort into jagged shapes when deprived of oxygen. These sickle-shaped cells then block and damage blood vessels and injure their linings. This is a serious disorder that in the United States afflicts mostly African Americans and people of Hispanic descent. For many years, scientists have been seeking some animal model that would make it possible to screen new compounds as potential treatments.

Finally, the first true model of sickle-cell anemia, a genetically altered mouse laboriously created by cooperating research teams from the University of Alabama in Birmingham and the University of California at Berkeley, has been created.[49] Using genetic engineering, these researchers added human genes for sickle hemoglobin to some animals, producing transgenic mice that secrete the abnormal human protein. They also developed a strain of knock-out mice in which genes for normal hemoglobin production had been deleted. Cross-breeding these two strains, they obtained offspring all of whose hemoglobin genes had been replaced by the mutant human sickle genes, mice that exhibit the tissue damage and cell death and other symptoms seen in the human disease: severe anemia, blocked blood vessels, injured and enlarged hearts and kidneys, and vascular congestion in the lungs. Now at last treatments for sickle-cell disease can be screened and tested for safety and efficacy. Experiments with mice are much easier than experiments with humans, of course; but more important, as one of the California researchers observed, "You can try things [in mice] that are impossible to do in humans. These models should really open up sickle cell research."

Loss of hair, known to have genetic causes, can be a devastating condition, especially for women. One disorder of this kind, *alopecia areata,* leads to the loss of clumps of hair and eventually to complete baldness. Studying victims of this condition, investigators narrowed the search for the responsible gene to a region on human chromosome 8. But the region is large; finding the villainous gene seemed nearly impossible.

Then, partly by accident, they obtained pictures of mice that have a mutant gene that leaves them hairless. Like the humans who suffer from alopecia areata, these mice are born with hair but soon lose it. The structure of the responsible gene in the mouse was already known; very many genes in mice are known to have nearly identical counterparts in people. The search began for a version of the hairless mouse gene in human DNA; it was located and then mapped to the same stretch of chromosome 8 that research had earlier identified. The cause of that genetic disorder had been found.

The gene in question carries the code for a type of protein molecule known as a transcription factor, which "turns on" the other genes—in this case, turns on the genes that make hair. In defective or mutant form, as in mice and humans suffering abrupt hair loss, the transcription factor is missing. Much remains to be done to provide healthy replacement genes for those who suffer from alopecia areata, but the understanding of its genetic foundation, and a good deal more concerning factors that control the growth of hair, was achieved directly through the study of mutant mice.[50]

Cancer

The most dreaded cancers—including the solid malignant tumors of the lung, breast, pancreas, brain, larynx, and malignant melanomas—have one feature in common: they *grow*, and their growth depends absolutely on the support of new blood vessels formed in the body to sustain them. *Tumor angiogenesis* is the name for this process. If some way could be found to inhibit that new vessel growth, a powerful anticancer weapon would be in hand.

Research with human cancers implanted in chickens and mice, at the Scripps Research Institute, has confirmed the effectiveness of a new and powerful technique to achieve this result, forcing the regression of already established tumors. By blocking the formation of new vessels, protein compounds newly developed in experiments with animals choke off the tumors' blood supply.[51]

Fragments of a wide variety of human tumors were grafted first into chicken embryos; new blood vessels quickly began to form in the tumor fragments. Some of the experimental animals were injected with a substance (a genetically engineered monoclonal antibody) that blocks only the material that binds the cells lining the blood vessels. In embryos so treated there was a dramatic reduction in the number of vessels that fed the tumors; the cancers regressed, and all the embryos developed normally. In those embryos left untreated as controls, blood vessels supporting the tumors continued to form copiously, and the tumors grew and spread throughout the animal. The same experiment was then tried in mice, with the same encouraging results.

Many drugs work well against cancers at first—but the tumor cells mutate, develop resistance. But the capillary-making cells are normal and therefore do not develop resistance to repeated doses of these compounds, called *angiostatin* and *endostatin*. A very encouraging result of this technique when used in mice is the fact that although tumors at first grew back when the drugs were withheld, they did not recur after two or more repetitions.[52] Further confirmation of the efficiency of theses "statins" using rabbits and other animals is now being sought. Clinical trials of this technique on humans cannot begin until extensive toxicological tests have been completed in animals, of course, to determine what adverse effects, if any, these compounds may have.

This approach to cancer is very promising. First reports of a breakthrough are often too optimistic, but in this case subsequent reports have been heartening.[53] When angiogenesis has been blocked there is an indubitable shrinkage of tumors; some primary tumors are actually eliminated. Beyond that, this technique is likely to prevent the metastatic spread of tumor cells by eliminating their access to a blood supply.

Additionally, it has been recently shown that in mice, when the radiation of tumors is enhanced by the concurrent use of angiostatin, the combination can be exceedingly effective.[54] This has changed much thinking about the way radiation works. Radiation therapists had formerly focused on trying to kill as many tumor cells as possible; now it appears that "a significant part of the benefit from radiation comes from killing the blood vessels that supply a tumor's growth."[55] This much at least is certain: whatever human gains eventually come by cutting off the blood supply of cancers will come only after those techniques have been tested repeatedly on animals first.

Cancer becomes deadly when it whirls out of control. Not only does it grow, but it spreads throughout the body. This spreading from the primary site, called *metastasis,* causes 90 percent of all cancer deaths. But what causes a potentially deadly tumor to metastasize?

Combining information gathered from the Human Genome Project and extensive experimental investigations in mice, scientists at the Center for Cancer Research at MIT asked this question about one of the most feared forms of cancer, malignant melanoma. They have been able to identify thirty-two genes that are active in malignant cells but not in nonmalignant cells. The cancer had first to be introduced into the mice; then extensive tests on those afflicted mice revealed that one gene, RhoC, makes melanoma cells *fifty times more invasive* than those in which that gene is absent. Two other genes, they found, play important supporting roles: one of these enables the traveling cancer cells to put down new roots, and the other helps establish a blood supply for the new colony of the tumor.[56] The cure for malignant melanoma we do not have, but we do have, as a result of these studies in mice, clearly established targets for future treatments.

Prostate cancer afflicts a substantial percentage of the male population aged sixty and above. Human prostate cancer tumors can be grafted onto mice, and by carefully controlling the diet of those mice with a degree of accuracy not possible in humans, the effect of reducing fat intake has been carefully measured. At the Sloan-Kettering Cancer Center in New York, researchers demonstrated that prostate cancers grew *twice as fast* when the diet was 40 percent fat (the approximate normal fat content of the average American male adult's diet) as they did when the diet was 21 percent fat.[57]

Diet has thus been proved to have a marked effect on cancer. Mice were specially bred to permit the establishment, in them, of human prostate tumors. Four experimental groups were then created, each receiving a different level of dietary fat, from a high of 40.5 percent to a low of 2.3 percent. After eleven weeks, the mice were killed and the tumor growth measured. "What we found," said one of the investigators, Dr. William R. Fair, "was astonishing to us. Tumors didn't disappear, but the decrease in growth rate was really impressive." Because human prostate cancer generally appears in older men, the rate of growth is particularly important in selecting which cancers to treat aggressively. "If we are able to tell a 60-year old," Dr. Fair points out, "that he could do something to slow the growth of his cancer for 30 years, that's the same as a cure for most men. . . . It is possible that many men wouldn't need anything more than dietary manipulation."[58]

Prostate cancer can be lethal and can cause excruciating pain. Devising effective ways to treat it may prove a boon for *millions* of human males. Is it wrong to kill mice in the effort to achieve this end?

Leukemia is a deadly cancer. One of its forms, chronic myelogenous leukemia, is known to be caused by a genetic abnormality in the blood-producing cells of the bone marrow. Bone marrow transplant for such patients is often unavailable or unsuccessful. But a very successful treatment, a form of gene therapy for this condition, has been developed in mice. Two genetic traits are added to the bone marrow cells of the afflicted animal, after which they behave like normal cells. Remaining unaltered malignant cells are then killed, and the treated cells introduced gradually provide healthy replacements for the leukemic stem cells that are so fatally defective.[59]

Will this treatment work on humans? We do not yet know. We do know that when malignant cells from people with leukemia were injected into mice, nearly all the animals died within a hundred days. But if the cells injected were first given the new genes and then injected, three quarters of the animals were still alive and healthy a hundred days later. There is always difficulty, in such gene therapies, in effecting the uptake of the new genes by the afflicted patient. So no cure is in hand, but experiments with mice have given new hope to persons suffering from chronic myelogenous leukemia, who can expect, without treatment, to live no more than three or four years.

Treatment of a cancer is much advanced by knowing its cause. The cause of the second most common blood cancer in this country,[60] multiple myeloma, appears to be a virus—Kaposi's sarcoma herpes virus—discovered among individuals who had AIDS and the cancer called Kaposi's, which affects the skin and the internal organs. That virus was found, in a study at the

Veteran's Affairs Medical Center in Los Angeles, in all myeloma patients tested—but not in patients with other cancers or in healthy volunteers.[61] If this causal connection is ultimately established, the consequences are great: new therapies aimed at that virus might be devised, and it may even be possible to develop a vaccine to prevent myeloma.

But the causal connection is still only hypothetical. It must be tested. How is that to be done? We want to know whether that virus is the cause of that cancer in humans, but to inject humans with the virus to prove that it does cause cancer would be outrageous. How, then, is this very promising hypothesis to be confirmed? The answer is plain: repeated studies in which mice and rats are injected with the suspected virus will have to be conducted. On this front, as on so many fronts in the war on cancer, experiments with animals are the key to advancing knowledge.

What is the *cause* of these assorted malignant growths, these various cancers that are so deadly and so hard to fight? The standard view of cancer has long been that, at some points, for reasons unknown, the normal growth of the body's cells goes out of control, whereupon new growth simply runs amok. A different view of cancer, well supported by recent work with mice, suggests that cancerous growth is a consequence of the breakdown of the normal system causing cell death, *apoptosis*. The problem (on this account) is not so much excessive cell *vitality* as deficient cell *mortality*.

All normal cells die and are replaced with some frequency; the cells of mice are very much like those of humans in this respect. Research with mice has demonstrated that a gene that produces a protein called *p53* controls the proliferation of cells and is thus central to the life cycle of all cells. It does this by binding to a pivotal spot on the DNA of the cell and thereby blocking any further cell division. Recent mouse studies at Stanford University have revealed another function performed by the healthy gene p53: when it encounters an aberrant cell, it activates a self-destruct mechanism that causes the deviating cell to disintegrate. P53 is therefore known as a tumor-suppressor gene. When p53 is not healthy, we suffer the absence of what triggers normal cell death and thus uncontrolled cell growth—cancer.[62]

Experiments on rodents reveal two facts about this critical gene that suggest new weapons against cancer. First, the production of normal p53 protein is stimulated by the lack of oxygen; the center of solid tumors are regions where oxygen levels are very low, and in mice those tumor centers have been found to be full of dead or dying cells whose self-destruction was triggered by their p53 gene. The second significant discovery is that in some cancerous cells the p53 gene has been mutated—and this mutation in a low-oxygen environment, resulting in what may be thought of as a "brake failure," gives enormous competitive advantage to the mutated cells. Indeed, in human cancers, it turns out that p53 is one of the most commonly mutated genes. Malignant cells not dying as they normally would soon come to dominate the central regions of solid tumors. This helps to explain why radiation and chemotherapy are so frequently unavailing: they work by damaging the DNA of the cancer cells, so as to promote p53 production and cell death—but in cells where p53 has mutated, this approach cannot succeed. When the p53 gene mutates cell death slows; the tumor that may have been growing very slowly at first then gradually spins out of control. One key to the problem of cancer, now eagerly sought, is some technique for controlling genetic mutations of the kind revealed by this research with mice.

One gene critical in the development of breast cancer, BRCA1, has been certainly identified. It generates a protein secreted from breast tissue that mixes with the fluid between breast cells. When this gene is healthy, its protein interacts with surrounding cells to keep all in balance. But BRCA1 too often goes awry, mutates; a defective BRCA1 gene is now believed to be the chief culprit in tumors that account for about 90 percent of all breast cancers. Research with mice, at Vanderbilt University in Nashville, has proved the therapeutic impact of transferring healthy BRCA1 genes onto existing tumors.[63]

Human breast tumors were first cultivated in the abdominal cavities of ten mice. Half of these mice then received injections of viruses containing healthy copies of the BRCA1 gene; the other half received nonfunctional versions of the same gene. The viruses—*viral vectors,* they are called—deliver their cargo by penetrating the cells of the cancer-ridden mice. All the mice treated with nonfunctional BRCA1 died in a week, killed by huge malignant tumors. The mice given working copies of BRCA1 survived, and of these some mice *had no detectable tumors left,* dying eventually of pneumonia.

In humans the delivery of healthy copies of BRCA1 will not be so simple. But knowing the critical gene, and knowing the effects of the protein it produces, there is reasonable hope that chemically based drugs can be devised (tested extensively on animals first, of course) that will give therapeutic benefits similar to the production of the protein encoded by the BRCA1 gene. The next step is to find the mechanism by which the secreted protein is taken up; that will require much more work with rodents. Once that receptor is identified, drugs that can mimic the product of BRCA1 may be designed and cancerous growths obstructed. There is a very long way to go. But *tens of thousands* of women who suffer from breast cancer may ultimately owe their lives to research done with a few mice.

Emphysema

A distressing chronic disease that afflicts millions of Americans to varying degrees, ultimately leaving them unable to breathe, emphysema is one of those pulmonary disorders, caused mainly by cigarette smoking, which are together one of the leading causes of death in the United States. Tissue damage to the lungs, caused by the loss of elasticity in the many little sacs (called *alveoli*) in which oxygen and carbon dioxide move between the lungs and the bloodstream, makes breathing ever more difficult. Normally new air sacs are not created in the lungs after childhood. But might there be some way to stimulate the regeneration of the alveoli?

Studies using rats give emphysema sufferers a glimmer of hope. Some time ago it had been shown that treating normal newborn rats with retinoic acid increases the size of their alveoli. Very recently investigators at the Georgetown University School of Medicine used the enzyme elastase to cause lung damage in adult rats similar to that seen in some forms of emphysema. These rats were then given injections of retinoic acid (a derivative of vitamin A and beta carotene) for twelve days, after which they were killed and their lungs examined. Treated rats were found to have grown new air sacs, in structures very like those of normal rat lungs.[64]

No cure for emphysema in humans is at hand, of course. But a very promising avenue for the treatment of this dreadful disorder has been opened, a discovery confirmed by experiments that entailed the killing of rats.

Elsewhere, seeking to understand how emphysema is caused, scientists at Washington University in St. Louis have proved, using mice, that it is the body's own chemicals, mustered to defend against irritants, that bring on the inflammation and the cell destruction that is so gravely injurious. Two groups of mice were exposed to cigarette smoke twice a day, six days a week. (The mice came to enjoy their smoke treatments, "running" into the chambers where the treatment was applied.) Half of the animals tested were ordinary mice and soon contracted emphysema.

But the other half were knockout mice in which the gene used to produce that body chemical called *elastase* (which can destroy the elastin that keeps the alveoli resilient) had been deleted, knocked out. These mice did not suffer the lung damage that the smoke had caused in the normal mice.[65]

These animal studies show that in the development of emphysema, the body responds to the constant irritant of smoking with an overreaction, creating large quantities of elastase. Under normal conditions, elastase helps to break down damaged tissues to clear the way for repair—but the constant presence of cigarette smoke makes the body produce far too much elastase, which then destroys the lung cells it is trying to rebuild.

A cure for emphysema we do not have, but its mechanics we do now know, thanks to those smoking mice. That knowledge is essential for the eventual development of some effective treatment.

The absolutely critical role of animals in current medical research is entirely beyond doubt. An account of all the diseases presently being attacked through animal studies, the research avenues being opened using laboratory animals, the knowledge being accumulated in the interest of human well-being through the many uses of animals, could not be contained in one book. The investigations briefly summarized in the ten sections here, bearing on vascular diseases, vaccines, neurodegenerative diseases, obesity, sleep, organ transplantation, diabetes, genetic disorders, cancer, and emphysema, are only a very few of those thousands in progress as this is written. These illustrations can give no more than a glimpse of the ways in which laboratory animals contribute to human health and well-being.

Some of the paths followed in these investigations or suggested by them will probably stymie researchers and perhaps be abandoned. Advances in medicine are never steady, never sure. Investigations approaching targets from different directions with different hypotheses will be essential for progress over the long term. By the time this brief account is being read, new and even more promising results using animals may well have been produced for human benefit. But the reader should recognize the serious consequences of the conflicting philosophical positions presented in this book. If the advocates of animal rights and the defenders of animal liberation were ever to have their way, the overwhelming majority all of this heartening progress in biomedical research would be brought to an immediate halt.

Notes

1. In the less developed world, the leading causes of death are infectious diseases, tuberculosis and malaria, for the treatment of which animal research has long been central.

2. On the very day on which this is being written, 18 March 1999, Dr. Russell Ross, perhaps the greatest of modern researchers into human artery disease, died in Seattle, Washington. Dr. Ross was the first to theorize that the chief causes of blockage in arteries lay not in the contents of the blood but in the walls of the arteries themselves. His theory, which came to be known as the "response-to-injury" hypothesis, led to a virtual revolution in the treatment of artery disease, a revolution made possible only by experimentation with animals because, to test his hypothesis, living arteries had to be deliberately damaged—a step that could hardly be taken with human subjects.

3. Russell Ross and others, "Inhibition of Neointimal Smooth Muscle Accumulation After Angioplasty by an Antibody to PDGF," *Science* 253 (6 September 1991): 1129–32.

4. See the account, in chapter 8, of investigative strategies using mice whose immune systems have been disarmed.

5. Jeffrey M. Leiden and others, "Cytostatic Gene Therapy for Vascular Proliferative Disorders with a Constitutively Active Form of the Retinoblastoma Gene Product," *Science* 267 (27 January 1995): 518–22.

6. Susan Acton and others, "Identification of Scavenger Receptor SR-B1 as a High Density Lipoprotein Receptor," *Science* 271 (26 January 1996): 518–20.

7. Salk used a vaccine in which the virus had been killed. Great controversy soon arose concerning the relative merits of a killed vaccine like his and an attenuated live vaccine, of the sort later developed by Dr. Albert Sabin. In the latter, which has proved more satisfactory and has now supplanted the killed vaccine, the live virus is modified in the laboratory so that it can cause no damage although it still does effectively stimulate the needed immunity.

8. Figures are from a report of 28 October 1998, issued by the Population Division of the United Nations.

9. Research results reported in the *New York Times* on 3 July 1998 are similarly disappointing. Dr. Ruth Ruprecht, at the Dana Farber Cancer Institute in Boston, began a series of trials in 1993, injecting nine newborn monkeys with the weakened SIV vaccine developed by Dr. Ronald Desrosiers at the New England Primate Center in Southboro, Massachusetts. But by 1998, five of these monkeys had died, and the remainder were very sick. Tests of the vaccine on adult monkeys then resulted in death and sickness nearly as dismal. Testing new vaccines is very dangerous.

10. A. Almond and others (at Britain's National Institute for Biological Standards and Controls), "Protection by Attenuated Simian Immunodeficiency Virus (SIV) in Macaques against Challenge with Virus-infected Cells," *Lancet* 345 (27 May 1995): 1342–44.

11. Almond et al., "Protection." But see the disappointing 1998 report in note 9.

12. Dr. Barry R. Bloom, of the Howard Hughes Medical Institute at the Albert Einstein College of Medicine, in New York City, quoted in the *New York Times*, 6 June 1991.

13. A very promising chemical vaccine, to immunize against addiction to cocaine, has recently been tested successfully on rats at the Scripps Research Institute in La Jolla, California. This vaccine stimulates the immune system to produce antibodies that bind to cocaine and block its psychoactive effects while not interfering with normal brain chemistry. In rodents it has been proved, at the National Institute on Drug Abuse, to reduce the amount of cocaine reaching the brain by more than 70 percent. The vaccine is not yet usable on humans, but it opens new avenues in dealing with drug addiction. See M. Rocio, A. Carrera, and others, "Suppression of Psychoactive Effects of Cocaine by Active Immunization," *Nature* 378 (14 December 1995): 727–30.

14. Dora Games and others, "Alzheimer-type Neuropathology on Transgenic Mice Overexpressing V717F Beta-Amyloid Precursor Protein," *Nature* 373 (9 February 1995): 523–27.

15. A. Tomac and others, "Protection and Repair of the Nigrostriatal Dopaminergic System by GDNF *in vivo*," *Nature* 373 (26 January 1995): 335–39.

16. T. Alexi and others, " Mesencephalic Dopaminergic Neurons Protected by GDNF from Axotomy-induced Degeneration in the Adult Brain," *Nature* 373 (26 January 1995): 339–41.

17. Q. Yan and others, "In vivo Neurotrophic Effects of GDNF on Neonatal and Adult Facial Motor Neurons," *Nature* 373 (26 January 1995): 341–44.

18. Among the centers at which such research is in progress are these: the National Institute of Neurological Diseases and Stroke of the NIH, the Albert Einstein College of Medicine in New York City, the Johns Hopkins School of Medicine in Baltimore, and the Karolinska Institute in Stockholm.

19. Mark E. Gurney, and others, "Motor Neuron Degeneration in Mice That Express a Human CuZn Superoxide Dismutase Mutation," *Science* 264 (17 June 1994): 1772–74.

20. Quoted in the *New York Times,* 21 June 1994.

21. This trauma research on chickens, conducted by Professor John D. Steeves of the Department of Neurobiology, in Vancouver, was reported at the Third International Neurotrauma Symposium, Toronto, July 1995.

22. A professor of neurosurgery at Case Western Reserve University, Dr. Robert J. White, adds strong support for animal research:

I have treated and operated on hundreds of spinal-cord-injured patients and for years undertook research supported by the National Institutes of Health on the damaged spinal cord of the subhuman primate. Our limited understanding of neural tissue injury has been almost exclusively derived from animal studies. . . . The linkage between animal research and clinical investigation has resulted in a drug that can improve neurological functioning in these patients.

From a letter to the *New York Times,* 19 August 1995.

23. Three scientific papers, published together in *Science* 269 (28 July 1995), report the details of the obesity research here briefly described. See Jeffrey M. Friedman and others, "Weight-Reducing Effects of the Plasma Protein Encoded by the *obese* Gene," 543–46; Mary Ann Pelleymounter and others, "Effects of the *obese* Gene Product on Body Weight Regulation in *ob/ob* Mice," 540–43; and L. Arthur Campfield and others, "Recombinant Mouse OB Protein: Evidence for a Peripheral Signal Linking Adiposity and Central Neural Networks," 546–49. All the experiments critical in these landmark studies required the use of experimental mice.

24. Reported by Dr. Andrew S. Greenberg, director of obesity research of the New England Medical Center in Boston, at the June 1998 meetings of the American Diabetes Association.

25. That a defective leptin-producing gene does account for some cases of obesity has been proved in studies at Cambridge University, reported in the *New York Times,* 24 June 1997. While the genetic cause of obesity is not common, the 1994 identification of leptin as critical in weight control, discovered through research with mice, is now beyond doubt.

26. Stephen Bloom, reported in *Nature,* 4 January 1996.

27. Reported in *Science,* 30 June 2000.

28. Reported in *Nature Genetics,* April 2000.

29. Reported in the *International Journal of Obesity,* August 2000.

30. C. B. Saper and others, "Activation of Ventrolateral Preoptic Neurons During Sleep," *Science* 271 (12 January 1996): 216–19.

31. Shimon Amir and Jane Stuart, "Resetting of the Circadian Clock by Conditioned Stimulus," *Nature* 379 (8 February 1996): 542–45.

32. Charles A. Czeisler and others, "Dose-Response Relationships for Resetting of Human Circadian Clock by Light," *Nature* 379 (8 February 1996): 540–42. Dr. Czeisler concludes, "Our results . . . support the conclusions that [humans] are not qualitatively different from other mammals in their mechanism of circadian entrainment."

33. Figures come from the United Network for Organ Sharing (UNOS).

34. Other species, similarly presenting little risk of cross-species infection, have also become the source of organic materials precious for human use. Goats have been bred in whose milk is carried antithrombin iii, a human blood protein that prevents

clotting in people; sheep have been bred whose milk secretes a drug called alpha anti-trypsin, which is used to treat cystic fibrosis; cows have been bred whose milk contains lactoferrin, a human protein usable in treating infections in humans. For transplantable solid organs, pigs remain the most promising species.

35. A Rockefeller University team reported in *Science*, in August 2000, the successful cloning of a pig (named Xena!) by injecting the genetic material of a skin cell into an egg cell stripped of its genetic material.

36. Such as the elimination of the protein in cows' milk to which 10 percent of all infants are allergic.

37. Reported in *Nature*, 29 June 2000. The same company has also cloned pigs, using a technique of its own. Xenotransplantation using the organs of genetically engineered pigs is on the near horizon.

38. Dr. David White, the director of a biotechnology firm called Imutran, in Cambridge, England, as reported in the *New York Times*, 5 January 1996.

39. This effort to reverse the course of Parkinson's disease using pig tissue was carried out in the spring of 1995 at the Lahey Hitchcock Clinic, in Burlington, Massachusetts, under the direction of Dr. James M. Schumacher. Earlier efforts to treat Parkinson's using the dopamine-producing cells from human fetal tissue were reported, but because there are many objections to the use of human fetal tissue, rapid progress has not occurred on that front. Even if human tissue could be used, some sixty to eighty aborted fetuses must be examined to find enough of the dopamine-making cells in human remains to supply the transplant material for just one patient. Pig embryos are abundant, and it has been shown (by Dr. Ole Isacson, of McLean Hospital in Belmont, Mass.) that because immune system defenses are weak in the brain, the transfer of brain tissue from one species to another can be effected with relative ease and safety.

40. At the Robert Wood Johnson Medical School, in Piscataway, New Jersey, under the direction of Dr. Ira Black, as reported in the *Journal of Neuroscience Research*, August 2000.

41. Dr. William Greenough, of the Beckman Institute for Advanced Science and Technology of the University of Illinois, quoted in the *New York Times*, 15 August 2000.

42. Reported in *Science*, 22 January 1999.

43. An interesting example of animal use that is being in some degree replaced. Insulin used to be extracted from the pancreases of pigs and cows as a slaughterhouse byproduct. Now it is largely human insulin that is used—because, having isolated the insulin gene, we can insert it into bacteria that can be cultivated, rendering them capable of producing human insulin. Thus, we reduce that need to use animals to save human lives. But the techniques that make such replacement possible had themselves to be developed on animals, of course.

44. Susan J. Sullivan and others, "Biohybrid Artificial Pancreas: Long-Term Implantation Studies in Diabetic Pancreatectomized Dogs," *Science* 252 (3 May 1991): 718–22.

45. A. M. J. Shapiro, "Islet Transplantation in Seven Patients with Type 1 Diabetes Mellitus Using a Glucocorticoid-free Immunosuppressive Regime," *New England Journal of Medicine* 343 (2000): 230–38.

46. A. T. Cheung and others, "Glucose-Dependent Insulin Release from Genetically Engineered K Cells," *Science* 290 (8 December 2000): 1959–62.

47. Reported in the *University Record*, Ann Arbor, Michigan, 19 June 2000.

48. At the National Cancer Center Research Institute in Tokyo and at the Chiba University School of Medicine in Japan. See *Nature Genetics,* March 1995.

49. Reported by Drs. Timothy M. Townes and Thomas M. Ryan at the University of Alabama, and Drs. Chris Paszty and Edward M. Rubin at the University of California, in *Science,* 31 October 1997.

50. Reported by Dr. Angela Christiano, of Columbia-Presbyterian Medical Center in New York, in *Science,* 30 January 1998.

51. David A. Cheresh and others, "Integrin alpha *v*–beta*3* Antagonists Promote Tumor Regression by Inducing Apoptosis of Angiogenic Blood Vessels," *Cell* 79 (30 December 1994): 1157–64. Credit and acclaim for the first development of the angiogenesis inhibitors, angiostatin and endostatin, is universally given to Dr. Judah Folkman, of the Children's Hospital, in Boston.

52. Reported in *Nature,* 27 November 1997. Commenting on this result, Dr. Noel Bouck, of the Northwestern University Medical School, says, "For years we thought you could hold tumors in check with angiogenesis inhibitors, but to actually cure them is amazing." And Dr. Robert S. Kerbel, in a commentary in *Nature,* remarks that the ability of endostatin to make mouse tumors regress without developing resistance is "unprecedented and could herald a new era of cancer treatment." If that era comes, we will owe a great deal to those experiments with mice.

53. On the CBS TV news magazine *60 Minutes,* 4 April 1999, the first-phase trials of another angiogenesis inhibitor, SU5416, at the UCLA Medical Center, were shown to have splendid results in patients with very advanced and otherwise untreatable cancers. All such trials must be preceded, of course, by trials with animals, usually mice. The *60 Minutes* episode was entitled "Could It Be Possible?"

54. Reported in *Nature,* 16 July 1998.

55. Dr. Jay Harris, chief of radiation oncology at the Dana Farber Cancer Institute in Boston, quoted in the *New York Times,* 16 July 1998.

56. Reported in *Nature,* 3 August 2000.

57. Yu Wang and others, "Decreased Growth of Established Human Prostate LNCaP Tumors in Nude Mice Fed a Low-Fat Diet," *Journal of the National Cancer Institute* 87 (4 October 1995): 1456–62.

58. Quoted in the *New York Times,* 4 October 1995.

59. Reported by Dr. Catherine Verfaillie, of the University of Minnesota, in the journal *Blood,* 13 December 1997.

60. The most common blood cancer is non-Hodgkins lymphoma.

61. Reported by Dr. James R. Berenson and Dr. Matthew B. Rettig in *Science,* 20 June 1997.

62. Amato J. Giaccia and others, "Hypoxia-Mediated Selection of Cells with Diminished Apoptotic Potential in Solid Tumours," *Nature* 379 (4 January 1996): 88–91.

63. Roy A. Jensen reported these results in two widely acclaimed papers appearing in *Nature Genetics,* March 1996.

64. Reported by Dr. Gloria De Carlo Massaro and Dr. Donald Massaro in *Nature Medicine,* June 1997.

65. Reported by Dr. R. Dean Hautamaki, Dr. Steven D. Shapiro, and others, in what has been called a landmark paper in *Science,* 26 September 1997.

10

The Proven Accomplishments of Animal Research

I conclude with a brief backward look. Animal research is promising for the future precisely because we know how very great its accomplishments have been in the past, the recent past, and the long history of medicine. Here again it is impossible to report all contributions because they have been so many and so varied. Even a list would be too long.

So I propose, in what follows, to exhibit the historical impact of animal research by noting how central animal studies have been to those who were awarded the Nobel Prize for medicine during the century that has just ended. The overwhelming majority of these Nobel awards have been made to scientists whose research was done using animal subjects.

In 1901, the Nobel Prize was awarded (to Emil von Behring) for the development of the antiserum to diphtheria, dependent on experiments with guinea pigs. In 1996, the Nobel was awarded (to Peter Doherty and Rolf Zinkernagel) for explanations of the workings of the human immune system in combating viruses, dependent on experiments with mice. In the years between, chickens and frogs, rabbits and monkeys, horses and rats, pigs and dogs, fish and sheep, as well as other species have contributed to Nobel Prize–winning research. This research has ranged from the monumental discovery of insulin for the treatment of diabetes (Frederick Banting and John Macleod in 1923 using dogs, rabbits, and fish) to the development of the yellow fever vaccine (Max Theiler in 1951 using monkeys and mice). The antibiotic streptomycin was developed using guinea pigs, resulting in the Nobel Prize for 1952 to its discoverer, Selman Waksman. Organ transplantation, to which thousands of humans now owe their lives, would have been impossible without the experiments of Joseph Murray and E. Donall Thomas using dogs, for which they received the Nobel Prize in 1990. The understanding of cholesterol and the regulation of fatty acids in humans was made possible by studies with rats, resulting in the Nobel Prize to Konrad Bloch and Feodor Lynen in 1964. How cancers can be induced by tumors, and treated with hormones, resulted in the Nobel Prize being awarded to Charles Huggins and Francis Rous in 1966 for their experiments with rats, rabbits, and hens. The role of adrenal hormones in combating arthritis was uncovered in studies using cows, for which the Nobel Prize was awarded to Edward Kendall, Philip Hench, and Tadeus Reichstein in 1950. Surgical techniques that are now taken for granted, the grafting of blood vessels and techniques of suture, could not have been developed without animal subjects, in this case dogs, in studies that resulted in the Nobel Prize award to Alexis Carrel in 1912. The understanding of the genesis of typhus, a deadly disease for most of human history, came only with experiments on pigs, mice, and rats by Charles Nicolle, who received the Nobel Prize for that work in 1928. And the genesis of tuberculosis, long the leading killer of humans, came only with experiments on cows and sheep, resulting in the Nobel being awarded to Robert Koch in 1905.

Fundamental understanding of the workings of the human body has repeatedly advanced by way of investigations with animals: the understanding of the central nervous system (using horses and dogs); of immunity (using rabbits and guinea pigs); of the role of vitamins (using chickens); of the function of neurons (using dogs and cats); of the working of the inner ear (using guinea pigs); of the processes of vision (using chickens, rabbits and crabs); of the genetic code (using rats); of antibacterial drugs (using mice and rabbits); of the specific functions of nerve cells (using cats); of the chemical structure of antibodies (in guinea pigs and rabbits); of the processing of visual information by the brain (using cats and monkeys); of the functional organization of cells (using chickens and rats)—for every one of which the Nobel Prize in medicine has been awarded. Almost endlessly the central role that animals have played in the history of medicine can be recounted. This very quick review gives evidence enough that animal subjects have been absolutely indispensable in medical research.

Readers of this book, including those who criticize animal research, owe their personal safety and well-being, and the well-being of their children, to the animal research that some would have us shut down. Vaccines, antibiotics, prosthetic devices, therapeutic drugs of every description, the basic science that will make possible advances not yet dreamed of, as well as the safety of products we consume every day, are owed to animal research.

This momentous role that animals play in medical investigation is not widely enough understood. Unfamiliar with the reliance of research on animal subjects, unaware of the full range of its consequences and unprepared to cope with the technical complexities of human disease, too many give their support too readily to organizations quite mistakenly suggesting that animal investigations can be replaced by computers or by human clinical studies. That supposition is utterly false. A committee consisting of fourteen of the most distinguished living physicians, the Council on Scientific Affairs of the American Medical Association, concluded categorically in 1989, "Research that involves animals is essential to improving the health and well-being of the American people."[1]

Not only humans but animals as well have benefited enormously from animal studies. Every pet owner, as well as all those who work with horses, sheep, or cows or other species in animal husbandry, and also those concerned to protect and preserve animals in the wild, may be grateful for the research that has been done using animals to keep animals healthy and to extend their lives.

Some of the critical advances in veterinary medicine have been these: vaccination against distemper, rabies, parvovirus, infectious hepatitis, anthrax, tetanus, and feline leukemia; treatment for animal parasites; corrective surgery for hip dysplasia in dogs; orthopedic surgery and rehabilitation for horses; treatment for leukemia and other cancers in pet animals; detection and control of tuberculosis and brucellosis in cattle; control of heartworm infection in dogs; treatment of arthritis in dogs; protection and preservation of endangered species through vaccinations and improved fertilization. The dean of the Tufts University School of Medicine, Dr. Franklin M. Leow, summarizes the matter forcefully: "Most drugs, diagnostic tests, and surgical techniques used in veterinary medicine today have come either directly from animal research or from human medical or surgical practice that was originally based on animal research."[2] Not for the sake of humans only are animals used in research. If the well-being of animals themselves is to be our concern, research using animals must not be impeded.

Do all these reports of the treating and healing of human beings, and of animals, not give reason enough on any utilitarian calculus to use the mice, or the rabbits, or the chickens such research requires? How many lives must we save, how much agony must we avoid, how much profound human unhappiness must we overcome before all will come to agree that there is little, in science or in any other sphere, that is of more direct and powerful service to humankind, and to animals, than medical research using laboratory animals?

The hopeless effort to ascribe *rights* to animals has been largely abandoned. The claim that mice and chickens have rights as humans do was examined with care in the earlier chapters of this book and shown there to be completely untenable. No satisfactory case can be made for animal rights. Only in a sphere in which moral right and wrong are understood and respected, a human sphere, can agents have rights or do wrongs. "Animal rights" is a popular slogan for the ignorant, but speaking thoughtfully it makes no sense.

Recognizing this, the "animal liberation" movement has shifted emphasis from entitlements to pains, urging that we think not about rights but about *consequences.* Consider the merits and demerits of the alternatives, say they; calculate the balance of goods and evils resulting from animal use; ask whether the gains of research using animals outweigh the losses.

Let us do as they ask. Death is inflicted, and some pain, too, on the rats and other animals whose lives are used in medical research. But human death and human pain count at least as much, and probably a good deal more. The misery that humans suffer, and that animals suffer, too, from diseases and disorders now *curable* as the result of laboratory animal research is so great as to be beyond calculation. Add to these what will soon be possible as a result of animal studies now in progress. And put on the scales, in a fair weighing, those medical achievements not yet even well conceived but likely to be realized one day—if research is not crippled by ignorant zealotry. And on the scales put also, with unflinching honesty, all of the horror, and pain, and excruciating misery of human sickness that would certainly have been suffered, and from which we and our children would be suffering now, had animals not been used to bring us to our present circumstances.

Each reader of this book is urged to make this utilitarian calculation. Attend, in fairness, to every bad thing that research with animals entails: its occasional misfires, its risks, the inevitable death of many rodents and rabbits and other animals, and the distress unavoidably caused to some of these creatures. Attend, with equal fairness, to every good thing that research with animals has achieved, is now achieving, and is likely to achieve—every vaccine, every antibiotic, every prosthetic device, every surgical procedure, every successful drug, every advance in medical understanding that has been made possible only by using animals. Consider the saving of lives and the easing of pains that this research has produced. Consider the aims and probable achievements of current research relying on animal use. Consider all the facts, weigh all the arguments carefully, and decide.

Notes

1. "Animals in Research," *Journal of the American Medical Association* 261, no. 24 (1989 June 23/30): 3602–06. In this powerful statement, the Council on Scientific Affairs goes on to list, in some detail, many recent and current advances depending *essentially* on investigations with animals. Most of the work referred to in this listing goes far beyond the account I have presented in this and the preceding chapter. The medical topics under which the council provides this detailed list of animal dependent research include aging; acquired immunodeficiency syndrome (AIDS); anesthesia; autoimmune diseases; basic genetics; behavior; cancer; cardiovascular system; childhood diseases; cholera; convulsive disorders; diabetes; gangliosidosis; gastrointestinal tract surgery; hearing; hemophilia; hepatitis; infection; malaria; muscular dystrophy; nutrition; ophthalmology; organ transplantation; Parkinson's disease; pul-

monary disease; rabies; radiobiology; reproductive biology; skeletal system, fracture, and related studies; spinal cord injury; toxoplasmosis; trauma and shock; yellow fever; virology.

The council concludes:

Animals have proved to be invaluable in the pursuit of knowledge in the life sciences, and the knowledge gained often benefits both animals and humans. . . . Many of today's most vexing health problems will be solved by research on animals. Acquired immunodeficiency syndrome [AIDS], Alzheimer's disease, coronary heart disease, and cancer represent but a few of the nation's most troubling health problems. [With continued support for animal experimentation] new pieces of information directed toward the conquest of these and other diseases continue to emerge.

2. *ILAR News* (Fall 1988).

Part II

THE CASE FOR ANIMAL RIGHTS
Tom Regan

11

From Indifference to Advocacy

I am an advocate of animal rights, active in the animal rights movement. This movement, as I understand it, is abolitionist in its aspirations. It seeks not to reform how animals[1] are exploited, making what we do to them more humane, but to abolish their exploitation. To end it. Completely. More specifically, the movement's goals include

- the total abolition of commercial animal agriculture,
- the total abolition of the fur industry, and
- the total abolition of the use of animals in science.

I am fully aware that some people view these abolitionist ideas as radical, even extreme. Had it not been for certain events and the timely influence of various people in my past, the same would probably be true of me.

I was born and raised in a working-class neighborhood of Pittsburgh, Pennsylvania. Education was a luxury the older people living there could not afford. By the time my parents were fourteen, they had quit school and, like the rest of their brothers and sisters, were trying to help their families make ends meet by earning whatever money they could. Soon after they married, the nation plunged into the Depression, the worst economic time in our history. Work was scarce; wages were meager; scrimping and saving, they survived. This period of special hardship helped shape my parents' character. Fifty years after my father found steady work, my parents were still living as if the Depression was a fact of everyday life.

While shopping the bargains was their shared passion, food was one indulgence they allowed themselves. My father was proud to be our family's provider, and one tangible way he measured his success was by what he was able to put on our plates. For him—and the same was no less true of my mother—meat was more than something you ate; meat was a symbol of success. To be able to eat food that, during the Depression, poor people could not afford meant my parents were living the American dream. Meat became the centerpiece of much of what we ate: bacon or ham at breakfast on Sundays; salami, bologna, and other lunch meat sandwiches most days for lunch; pot roast, pork chops, chicken, sometimes even a leg of lamb for the evening meal; and a robust, big-breasted turkey to celebrate Thanksgiving. In my case, questions regarding the ethics of diet not only were not answered; they were not asked. I dined eagerly at the trough of tradition. When the need arose for me to earn money to help offset the costs of going to college, I was not the least bit morally uncomfortable working in a butcher shop. Back then, I did not find butchering bloody, only bloody hard.

Fashion—being stylish, in a high-brow sort of way—never was, is not now, and never will be on my screen. Not that I have been totally indifferent to my appearance. Over the years I have worn everything from pegged pants to bell-bottoms, Mr. B to button-down collars, penny loafers to low-cut tennis shoes, all in the name of being "in style." But *haute couture* was, is, and will remain oil to my water. Understandably, therefore, when the subject is fur, with few exceptions, it has had little purchase on my life.

What few exceptions there were saw me mainly as witness, not agent. Pittsburgh winters are cold. For some of the older women I knew, cold weather meant fur weather. Two of my aunts could hardly wait to don their fox stoles, and some of the women who attended my church were eager to make a fashion statement, flaunting their low-end furs for all the blue-collar parishioners to see, the unmistakable odor of mothballs lingering in their wake as they glided haughtily down the aisle. All this I observed, as if at a distance, like a spectator at a ball game. Much later in my life, when I wanted to show my wife, Nancy, how much I loved her, I bought her a smart-looking mink hat. She looked sensational, like Julie Christie in the Academy Award–winning movie *Dr. Zhivago*. My only regret was that I lacked the money to buy her a full-length mink coat. Beautiful women *deserve* fur. That's why mink exist. At least this is what I thought at the time.

While in high school, and also during my years in college, I found myself in biology classes where students were required to dissect animals. It never occurred to me to raise a moral objection; judging from their silence, it never occurred to any of the other students, either. I remember fumbling through two sessions; in one, I was given a worm; in the other, a frog. The product of my inept labors proved I had no talent with the tools of the trade. I think I received a C− for my clumsy depredations. I know I did not like the smell of the specimens we were given, or the sticky feel they left on my fingers. But I cared not a whit for the dead creatures whose bodies gave way to my crude invasions. During this time of my life, the worm and the frog might just as well have been globs of Silly Putty.

First Steps

In large measure, then, my beliefs about and attitudes toward animals were quite unremarkable throughout my youth. In fact, it was not until much later, after I had completed my graduate work in philosophy and joined the faculty at North Carolina State University, that I began to think about ethics and animals. The war in Vietnam was then being waged, and many people of my generation, not to mention many more of college age, actively opposed it. Nancy and I were no exceptions. Together with a handful of others, we organized North Carolinians against the War, a statewide grassroots group that sought to end U.S. involvement.

It occurred to me at the time that war in particular and the topic of violence in general might be areas worthy of philosophical investigation. The writings of the great Indian pacifist, Mahatma Gandhi, were among the first resources I explored. What a fateful choice! For Gandhi challenged me to make sense of how I could oppose unnecessary violence, such as the war in Vietnam, when *humans* were the victims and support this same kind of violence—unnecessary violence—when the victims were *animals*. After all, there was no denying that parts of dead animals were chilling away in the Regans' freezer or that, most days, their cooked remains could be found on my plate. Eating animals, eating meat, as I did, certainly supported their slaughter—a truly horrible, violent way to die, something I would later come to know firsthand when, despite having a strong aversion to doing so, I watched hogs, chickens, and cows meet their bloody ends.

Moreover, from what I had learned about nutrition, I knew that my good health did not require animal flesh in my diet. So the logic was fairly obvious: the violent slaughter of animals for food was unnecessary. Was my fork, like napalm, a weapon of violence? Should I become a vegetarian, for ethical reasons? This was not an idea I wanted to embrace. Change, especially when it means altering the habits of a lifetime, is never a welcome prospect. So I did what any rational human being would do: I tried to avoid coming to terms with the question that was really troubling me. Instead, I threw myself into asking bigger, impersonal questions—about the justice of capitalism, the future of civilization, the threat of nuclear annihilation. But even as I tried to find a comfortable place for my gnawing sense of moral inconsistency, bedded down in the dark recesses of my unconscious, Gandhi's ghost would not go away. We never resolve conflicts of conscience by pretending they do not exist.

As it happened, it was during this same time that Nancy and I had to deal with the death of a special friend. Early in our marriage, before our children were born, we shared our life with a wonderful dog. For thirteen years, Gleco was our beloved, our all but constant companion. Then, one day, he was dead. Gone forever. Such grief Nancy and I shared! So many tears! Emotionally, we were a mess, our sense of loss so great.

From my reading of Gandhi I had learned how some people in India regard *eating cow* as unspeakably repulsive. I realized I felt the same way about cats and dogs: I could never *eat them*. How, then, could I justify eating cows and pigs, chickens and turkeys? Are moral right and wrong simply what the traditions of one's culture say they are? I knew I did not think that. Are they simply what your emotions say they are? I knew I did not think that, either. Besides, why should I feel differently about cows and pigs than I did about cats and dogs? If my emotions were really in focus, would I not feel sympathy and compassion for these animals, too? The more I thought about it, the more convinced I became that something had to give: *either* I had to change my beliefs and feelings about how companion animals should be treated, *or* I had to change my beliefs and feelings about the treatment of farm animals. In time, unable to find a way around the dilemma—and, given the power of old habits and the gustatory temptations associated with lamb chops, fried chicken, and steak grilled on the barbee, I have to confess that I fairly desperately wanted to find one—I chose the latter alternative.

So it was a combination of the life and thought of Gandhi, on the one hand, and the life and the death of a four-legged canine friend, on the other—a classic combination of the head and the heart—that first led me to ask ethical questions about the food I ate. The answers I reached in the early 1970s resulted in my decision to become an ovolacto vegetarian, a position I defended in my earliest professional publication in the area of animal ethics. Somehow, back then, I was able to convince myself that while it was wrong to eat animals, it was all right to eat eggs and dairy products as part of my everyday diet.

A Larger Consistency

That first step toward including nonhuman animals in my moral universe was soon followed by others. You might say Leo Tolstoy predicted as much. In his classic essay "The First Step," Tolstoy writes that one way people can attempt to grow in the direction of a more peaceful, less violent way of life is to stop eating animals.[2] Tolstoy does not mean that giving up meat necessarily makes one a better person; he does not even mean that meat eaters necessarily are bad people. What he means is that the decision to become a vegetarian, when rooted in the quest for a less violent way of being in the world, is a first step some people can take.

Once having taken that first step, Tolstoy believes that those who start this journey (and Nancy was alongside or ahead of me throughout the years of change) are all but certain to attempt to move in the direction of a larger consistency. The more I studied the animal ingredients in popular brands of household cleaners and cosmetics, for example, and the more I learned about the painful tests manufacturers routinely perform on animals, the more committed I became to using cruelty-free products: detergents and cleaners, shampoos and deodorants, soaps and toothpastes, for example, that do not contain anything of animal origin and that have not been tested on animals. I also realized that fur was not compatible with the kind of life I wanted to live. A mink hat might be warm, it might be stylish, and some women might look stunningly beautiful wearing one. All this I knew. But that did not make the violent death of fur bearing animals any less unnecessary. Such is the human mind's capacity for self-deception, however, that even as purchasing fur had become unthinkable, I continued to find no inconsistency in wearing leather belts, gloves, and shoes or in buying wool pants, sweaters, and jackets. I was in my bell-bottom, penny-loafer phase.

As for the use of animals in science, that was the last question I approached, and my first thoughts stopped well short of the abolitionist ones I hold today. Even while I called for "a vast reduction in research involving animals,"[3] I left open the possibility that some of this research could be justified. What sort of research would this be? Where did I draw the line? Suffice it to say that during this period of my life, hard as it is to understand today, I defended major auto manufacturers, like General Motors, when they killed baboons in crash tests designed to make seat belts safer.

The preceding few pages should go some way toward suggesting just how far the "radical," "extreme" abolitionist views I hold today are from those I accepted while I was growing up; and how much they differ, too, from what I believed when I first began asking ethical questions about how we humans treat other animals. I was not born an animal rights abolitionist, but, along with Nancy, I have become one, not all at once, but gradually. Animal rights advocacy was the unanticipated destination toward which a line of reasoning and transforming experiences would lead us. A dog's death was one of those experiences; watching animals bleed to death at their slaughter was another; still others, in which we learned more about the terrible things human beings do to animal beings, were to follow.

How *do* we treat other animals? What actually happens to them on the farm, in the wild, and at the research lab? While it is not possible to give anything like complete answers to these questions, it is necessary to provide some of the relevant facts. When the topic is animal rights, we are not dealing with imaginary beings like Winnie the Pooh or E.T.; we are dealing with flesh-and-blood creatures who breathe the same air and who live and die on the same planet as we do. Granted, facts about their treatment do not prove that animals have rights. What these facts can suggest is the magnitude of the evil that is done to them, *if* they do. Chapter 12 makes good on the need to provide some of the relevant facts by highlighting aspects of how animals are treated in the food industry, the fur industry, and the research industry.

Beginning with chapter 13, the discussion takes a philosophical turn. In the not too distant past, the topic of animal rights was laughed out of the court of serious philosophical discussion. In the latter part of the eighteenth century, for example, the distinguished English philosopher Thomas Taylor published *A Vindication of the Rights of Brutes,* a comic proposal meant to satirize the idea that women could have rights. More than a hundred years later, Father Joseph Rickaby spoke for the dominant philosophical orthodoxy of the time when he characterized the moral standing of animals as being "of the order of sticks and stones."[4]

Times have changed. More has been written on the rights of animals in the past thirty years than had been written on this topic in the previous three thousand. Today, asking whether animals have rights is recognized as a serious, challenging philosophical question. This is the spirit in which this question is explored in these pages, a question that, most obviously, cannot be given the kind of systematic attention it deserves in the absence of at least a working knowledge of what moral philosophers mean when they speak of individual rights. In chapter 13 I attempt to provide the necessary clarification. As I hope to be able to explain, the logic of rights requires abolitionist responses whenever those who have them are routinely treated as means to others' ends, whether the bearers of rights are humans or other animals.

While there are exceptions to the rule, moral philosophers as a group aspire to offer general accounts of moral right and wrong; fundamentally, what they want to know is not whether this or that particular action, policy, or law is right or wrong but what makes any action, policy, or law right or wrong. Some influential ways to think about moral right and wrong at this level deny rights across the board: animals do not have rights, they say, but neither do humans. Other positions, while they deny rights to animals, affirm them in the case of humans. Representative examples of these moral outlooks are examined in chapters 14 and 15. Each of the views considered has something to recommend it. No moral philosophy—none with which I am familiar, in any event—fails to say something true, something important; so even while I explain where and why I think each of these views has various weaknesses, I also think each has strengths worth preserving.

Having explained some of the deficiencies of the moral outlooks discussed in these two chapters, I then, in chapter 16, explain how some of these weaknesses can be overcome if human rights are recognized. The conclusions reached in this chapter are essential to how I think about morality, not only because of the role they play in my cumulative argument for animal rights but also because of the importance human rights occupy in my life and thought. As the pages ahead attest—clearly, I hope—my commitment to human rights, including the rights of infants, children, people with disabilities, racial and ethnic minorities, and other vulnerable members of the extended human family, is as central to my moral outlook as is my commitment to animal rights.

After making my case for human rights, I turn to the topic of animal rights and explain how recognition of their rights emerges from, and is dependent on, the conclusions reached in the preceding three chapters, including in particular my argument for human rights. This final chapter also contains replies to a variety of objections voiced against the idea of animal rights and draws together themes and topics considered along the way, including the "radical," "extreme" nature of my abolitionist beliefs. Sometimes, I argue, radical, extreme ideas are where the moral truth lies, the abolitionist implications of animal rights being a case in point. Or so I believe, and thus will I argue. First, though, we turn to some facts about how animals are treated, not in exceptional circumstances but as a matter of everyday, ordinary practice.

Notes

1. Although I frequently follow prevailing usage and use the word *animal* to refer to animals other than the human, I note that we humans are animals.

2. Tolstoy wrote "The First Step" as the introduction to the Russian edition of Howard Williams's *The Ethics of Diet,* published in 1892. Excerpts from "The First Step" are included in Kerry S. Walters and Lisa Portness, eds., *Ethical Vegetarianism: From Pythagoras to Peter Singer* (Albany: State University of New York, 1999), 97–105.

3. My early essay on vegetarianism is "The Moral Basis of Vegetarianism," *Canadian Journal of Philosophy* 5, no. 2 (October 1975): 181–214, and reprinted in *All That Dwell Therein: Essays on Animal Rights and Environmental Ethics* (Berkeley: University of California Press, 1982), 1–39. "Animal Experimentation: First Thoughts," the essay in which I called for "a vast reduction in research involving animals," will also be found in *All That Dwell Therein,* 65–74. For a more thorough examination of all the issues examined, both in those essays and in these pages, see my *Case for Animal Rights* (Berkeley: University of California Press, 1983).

4. Father Rickaby's views are summarized in Tom Regan and Peter Singer, eds., *Animal Rights and Human Obligations* (Englewood Cliffs, NJ: Prentice Hall, 1976), 180–81.

12

Animal Exploitation

We humans kill billions of animals every year, just in the United States. Frequently what we do causes them intense physical pain; often they are made to live in deplorable conditions; in many, possibly the majority of cases, they go to their deaths without having had the opportunity to satisfy many of their most basic desires. Readers interested in gaining a more complete grasp of animal exploitation, both in the United States and globally, are encouraged to consult the works cited in the notes for this chapter. What follows is at most a thumbnail sketch of some of the ways human beings treat animal beings in three institutional contexts: agriculture, fashion, and science.

Animals as Food

Veal, especially so-called "pink" or "milk-fed" veal, is the centerpiece in what some people regard as the finest dishes, prepared by the finest chefs, and served in the finest restaurants, especially French and Italian restaurants. Famous for its tenderness, milk-fed veal can be cut with a fork. No gristle. No muscle. Just soft, unresisting meat that melts in your mouth. When it comes to good dining, many people find it hard to imagine how it can get any better than this.

The situation is different for the calves who end up being veal. Veal calves (or "special fed veal," as they are also known) are surplus calves born to dairy herds. Because it is not economically viable for farmers to permit the number of milk producers in their herds to grow indefinitely, only a certain number of the female calves can be kept for purposes of milk production. While most of

135

the surplus calves, both male and female, are raised and sold as beef, approximately eight hundred thousand annually enter and exit a U.S. market of their own.[1] That market is known as the special-fed or milk-fed veal industry.

Calves who enter this industry are taken from their mothers hours or days after they are born and then sold at auction or delivered to contract vealers. Throughout most of history, demand for pink veal outstripped supply. Calves were slaughtered when they were very young, before they consumed too much iron-rich foods, like their mother's milk or grass, which would turn their flesh from pink to red and reduce consumer demand.

Understandably, these young animals were not large, weighing in at only about ninety pounds. Because they were so small, the supply of their tender, pink flesh was limited and the price per pound high. Predictably, premium veal found its way onto the dinner plates only of the wealthy. In time things changed, first in Europe, in the 1950s, then in the United States, in the 1960s. A new production system was introduced that enabled veal calves to live four or five months, during which time they more than tripled their birth weight, without the calves' flesh losing its desired pale color and tenderness. With the advent of larger calves, the industry offered milk-fed veal to an expanded market by selling it at a more affordable price.

For the system to work, milk-fed veal calves are permanently confined in individual stalls. Recommended stall dimensions in the United States are twenty-four inches wide by sixty-five inches long. Because calves lick their surroundings, because metal box stalls contain iron, and because extra iron can help turn their flesh red, the stalls are made of wood. *The Stall Street Journal*, a now defunct veal industry newsletter cited by Peter Singer is his landmark book *Animal Liberation*, explains, "Color of veal is one of the primary factors involved in obtaining 'top dollar' returns from the fancy veal markets. . . . 'Light color' veal is a premium item much in demand at better clubs, hotels and restaurants. 'Light color' or pink veal is partly associated with the amount of iron in the muscle of calves."[2]

Of course, if iron is totally eliminated from their diet, the calves' life could be placed in jeopardy, as would the farmers' financial interests. So *some* iron is included in the total liquid diet—a combination of nonfat powdered milk, vitamins, minerals, sugar, antibiotics, and growth-enhancing drugs—that the calves are fed twice a day, throughout the duration of their short lives. This, not their mother's milk, is the dietary history of so-called "milk-fed" veal.

To withhold real milk and other plentiful sources of iron from veal calves makes perfectly good sense to veal producers. In the words of *The Stall Street Journal*, "the dual aims of veal production are firstly, to produce a calf of the greatest weight in the shortest possible time and, secondly, to keep its meat as light colored as possible to fulfill the consumers' requirement."[3] For calves, this means being raised in a chronically iron-deficient (i.e., a chronically anemic) condition.

When the calves are small and able to turn around in their stall, a metal or plastic tether prevents them from doing so. Later, when they are three or four hundred pounds and too large to turn around in their narrow enclosures, the tether may be removed. Whether tethered or not, the animals are all but immobilized. Calves are notorious for their friskiness. We all have seen these boisterous youngsters gamboling across spacious pastures, their tender muscles firming up to support their increasing weight. Not so the calves raised in veal crates. The conditions of their confinement ensure that their muscles will remain limp so their flesh retains the degree of tenderness that, in the words of the *Journal*, "fulfill[s] the customers' requirement."[4]

The stalls in which individual calves are confined have slatted floors made of either wood or metal covered with plastic. In theory, the openings between the slats prevent urine and excrement from collecting. The theory does not work well in practice. When the animals lie down, they lie in their own waste. When they stand, their footing is unsure on the slippery slats. Unable to turn around, the calves cannot clean themselves. Unable to move without the prospect of slipping, they learn to stand in one place for long periods of time, a passive adjustment to their surroundings that takes its toll on their anatomy, especially their knees, which often are discernibly swollen and painful.

Independent scientific observers have confirmed what people of plain common sense already know. Veal calves suffer, both physically and psychologically. Physically, they suffer because the majority of these animals endure the pain and discomfort of swollen joints, digestive disorders, and chronic diarrhea. Psychologically, they suffer because their life of solitary confinement is characterized by abject deprivation. Throughout their lives they are denied the opportunity to suckle and graze, denied the opportunity to stretch their legs, and denied the fresh air and sunlight they naturally enjoy.

In a word, calves raised in veal crates are denied virtually everything that answers to their nature. That they display behavioral patterns (e.g., repetitive movements and tongue rolling) associated with psychological maladjustment should surprise no one.[5] These animals are not well, not in body, not in mind. When the day arrives for them to go to their foreordained slaughter, not as the frolicsome creatures they might have been but as the stunted "fancy" meat machines their producers and consumers have made them, death arguably offers these forlorn animals a better bargain than the life they have known.

Compared with the other animals raised for human consumption, the total number of "milk-fed" veal calves who end up on America's dinner plates is small—approximately eight hundred thousand of the more than *nine billion* animals slaughtered annually. But while their number is small, the life of "milk-fed" veal calves is a microcosm of the larger reality of commercial animal agriculture as it is practiced today.

The myth of Old McDonald's Farm dies hard. Whatever the reasons, and in the face of years of media exposure to the contrary, many people persist in believing that farm animals live in bucolic conditions. The truth is another matter. The vast majority of animals who enter and exit through the doors of today's commercial animal industry live lives not very different from those of veal calves. Intensive rearing systems ("factory farms") are the rule, not the exception. Hogs, chickens, and other animals raised for human consumption, not just veal calves, have become so many biological machines. Readers who doubt this or who want more by way of confirmation are encouraged to read the relevant books referenced in the accompanying notes.[6]

The reasons behind the ascendancy of factory farming are not hard to find. The profit motive, aided by government subsidies and price supports, drives the industry. Animal agriculture is a business, after all, whose object is to maximize financial return while minimizing financial investment. The key to financial success is a variation on the main theme found in veal production.

Factory farming requires that animals be taken off the land and raised indoors. This is important. Indoor farming enables a comparatively few people to raise hundreds, sometimes (as is true in the case of laying hens and broiler chickens) hundreds of thousands of animals, something that would be impossible if the animals were free to roam.

Next, farmers must do whatever is necessary to bring the animals to market in the shortest possible time. Measures that might be taken include limiting the animals' mobility, manipulating their appetite so that they eat more than they would in natural conditions, and stimulating their weight gain by including growth-enhancing hormones in their feed. In the words of *The Stall Street Journal,* it is essential "to produce a calf [or a chicken, turkey, or hog, for example] of the greatest weight in the shortest possible time." Those farmers who fail the test, fail in the marketplace of commercial animal agriculture. And many do. Unable to compete with their large corporate neighbors, powerless against the economies of scale and massive government assistance enjoyed by the multinationals, Old McDonalds' Farms are an endangered species. As is true of farming in America in general, when it comes to raising animals for human consumption, agribusiness has replaced agriculture.

Animals as Clothes

The most common justification of meat eating is that it is "necessary." Every red-blooded American knows that we have to eat meat. Without three or more ample portions a day, we will not get enough protein. And without enough protein, we will end up either sick or dead. That is certainly what I was taught while I was growing up. And this is what I continued to believe well into young adulthood.

The "protein myth" ("You have to eat meat to get your protein") once enjoyed wide currency among the general public. Times have changed. Today, more and more people understand that all the protein humans need for optimal health can be obtained without eating meat (a vegetarian diet) and without eating meat or any other food derived from animals, including milk, cheese, and eggs (a vegan diet). Even the United States Department of Agriculture (USDA), no friend of vegetarianism in the past, today waves a dietary flag of truce. In its most recent assessment, the USDA acknowledges that vegetarianism and veganism offer positive, healthy dietary options.[7]

Still, one thing meat eating historically has had in its favor is its presumed necessity for achieving two very important human goods: health and survival. The same is not true in the case of another ongoing chapter in the history of human exploitation of nonhuman animals: wearing their fur. True, wearing fur might be necessary for health and survival if we are Inuits living in the far North. But in the case of people on the streets of New York? The shopping malls of Chicago or Atlanta? The ski lodges of Aspen? No, neither health nor survival explain wearing fur in these places. The reason is *fashion*. And, truth to tell, when it comes to making a fashion statement, in some circles nothing speaks louder or clearer than fur.

The number of animals utilized by the fur industry has varied over time. In 1994 (the most recent year statistics were available at the time of this writing), approximately 4.5 million animals were killed for fur, just in the United States. Mink is the most common source, accounting for roughly 80 percent of all retail fur sales.[8]

Where does fur originate? In the not too distant past, trappers were the primary source of fur pelts, but recent years have seen a major shift in methods of procurement. Today, the majority of animals destined for the fur trade (2.5 of the 4.5 million in 1994) are raised on fur "ranches," a word that conjures up *bucolic* images associated with Old McDonald's Farm, only this time for mink and other fur-bearing animals. As it happens, a fur ranch is as close to an actual ranch as a veal stall is to a pasture.

Fur ranches throughout the world share the same architecture. They consist of long rows of wire mesh cages raised several feet off the ground. The cages have a roof overhead, and the entire structure is surrounded by a fence. (The fence ensures that any animals who happen to fall through or free themselves from their cage will not escape.) A ranch might contain as few as one hundred or as many as one hundred thousand animals. Among the furbearers raised on ranches are mink, chinchilla, raccoon, lynx, and fox.

In the case of mink, breeder cages, which house mothers and their kits, can contain as many as eight animals. Except for the tracks they leave behind, mink in the wild are rarely seen. Nocturnal creatures, they spend most of their time in water, and their reputation for being excellent swimmers is well deserved. Confined in cages, ranched mink are like fish out of water. Much of the waking hours finds them pacing, back and forth, back and forth, the boundaries of their diminished life defined by the path they repeat, over and over again, in their wire-mesh world.

As was noted in the discussion of veal calves, repetitive behavior of this sort is a classic symptom of psychological maladjustment. Other forms of repetitive motions (e.g., jumping up the sides of cages and circling their heads) attest to the same thing. Unnaturally confined as they are, and denied an environment in which they can express their natural desires to roam or swim, ranched furbearers give all the appearances of being neurotic at best, psychotic at worst.

Whatever its severity, the mental state of ranched fur-bearing animals is of no direct economic concern to those who raise them. By contrast, the condition of an animals' coat is, and necessary steps are taken to preserve the coat's integrity. For example, under the stress of close confinement, fox in breeder cages will sometimes attack one another. Cannibalism among fox, unknown in the wild, is not unheard of on ranches. Ranchers respond to this problem by reducing cage density from eight to four or even two. In the worst cases, "problem" animals are destroyed.

The premium placed on not spoiling the coat carries over to the methods of killing. No throat slitting here, as is true in the case of the slaughter of veal calves. Noninvasive methods, none of which involves the use of anesthetics, are the rule. In the case of small furbearers, mink and chinchilla in particular, a common practice is to break the animal's neck; however, because this method is labor-intensive, even these small animals, as is true of most of the larger ones, frequently are asphyxiated through the use of carbon dioxide or carbon monoxide. In the case of fox, anal electrocution may be the method of choice. It works this way. First a metal clamp is fastened around the animals' muzzle. Next one end of an electrified metal rod is shoved up the fox's anus. Then a switch is turned on and the animal is electrocuted to death, from the inside out. When properly done, these methods yield unblemished pelts.

Whereas damaged pelts do not pose a serious problem for fur ranchers, they can be a nightmare for those who trap fur-bearing animals in the wild. The fur of these animals can be so bloody and gnarled that it is economically useless. Sometimes this "wastage" (as it is called) results because a trapped animal is attacked by a natural predator. At other times potential pelts are ruined because of the frenzied efforts of the trapped animals, as they attempt to free themselves. In other cases, trapped animals chew through their trapped leg ("wring off," in the language of trappers) before crawling away, leaving no pelt at all. Friends of Animals (FOA), an organization that has for many years aggressively campaigned against fur, estimates that a quarter of those animals trapped for their fur are lost to wring-off. FOA's literature would give us to believe that trapped animals certainly would have enough time to chew themselves apart. Whatever the species, FOA estimates that these animals can spend up to a week (fifteen hours is given as the average) before they die or are killed by a trapper tending the lines.[9]

In the United States, the steel-jawed and Conibear are the most widely used traps. The Conibear entraps animals by their head, neck, or upper body; the steel-jawed, by a leg. The design of the latter is simplicity itself. The steel jaws of the trap are held apart by a spring. A pressure-sensitive weight pan is baited. When the animal reaches for the bait, the spring is released and the trap slams shut.

The physical trauma a trapped animal experiences has been likened to slamming a car door on a finger. According to the animal behaviorist Desmond Morris, the shock experienced by trapped animals "is difficult for us to conceive, because it is a shock of total lack of understanding of what has happened to them. They are held, they cannot escape, their response very often is to bite at the metal with their teeth, break their teeth in the process and sometimes even chew through the leg that is being held in the trap."[10]

Various attempts have been made to design a more "humane" trap. In place of steel jaws, for example, traps with padded jaws have been tried. None of these humane alternatives has caught on in the United States, and the steel-jaw leghod trap continues to be used (how often is unclear) by America's estimated 120,000 to 150,000 trappers. In the fifteen nations that comprise the European Union, by contrast, use of the steel-jaw leghod trap became illegal in 1995.

Whatever the type of trap used, the device itself obviously cannot distinguish between fur-bearing and so-called "nontarget" animals, including ducks, birds of prey, companion animals, even humans. Because trappers are not required to collect and report such data, hard numbers are hard to come by. FOA estimates the total number of nontarget animals that die in traps at between four and six million annually. Even if this figure is high, the number cannot be inconsiderable.

Semiaquatic animals, including mink and beaver, also are trapped in the wild. In their case, underwater traps are common. Mink can struggle to free themselves for up to four minutes; beaver, over twenty. Eventually, the trapped animals drown. Comparatively speaking, there is very little wring-off or wastage in the case of animals trapped underwater.

Whether made from ranched or trapped furbearers, fur coats require a lot of dead animals—the smaller the animals, the more required. FOA estimates that a forty-inch fur coat, depending on the type, requires sixteen coyote, eighteen lynx, sixty mink, forty-five opossum, twenty otter, forty-two red fox, forty raccoon, fifty sable, eight seal, fifty muskrat, or fifteen beaver. Of course, the suffering and death of *trapped* animals used to make fur coats is only part of the story. The number of *nontarget* animals needs to be added, and the time trapped land animals suffer before dying (fifteen hours, as we have seen, is FOA's estimate) also should be factored in. When the necessary computations are made, a forty-inch fur coat made from coyote, for example, equals sixteen dead coyotes, *plus* an unknown number of dead nontarget animals, *plus* more than two hundred hours of animal suffering. Similar calculations can be made for the remaining target animals. As is true of many things in life, when it comes to fur coats, there's more than meets the eye.

Animal as Models

While humans have been eating animal flesh and wearing the skins of animals for tens of thousands of years, the practice of using them for scientific purposes is by all accounts a comparatively recent development, inaugurated with deadly seriousness by Galen, in the second century B.C.E. Galen was much respected in the Rome of his day, and his four humors theory of human disease, based partly on his vivisection of nonhuman animals, continued to influence human medicine well into the seventeenth century. However, it is in the person of the nineteenth-century French physiologist Claude Bernard that the use of the "animal model" arguably finds its most ardent advocate. "I consider hospitals only the entrance to scientific medicine," Bernard writes, adding:

> They are the first field of observation which a physician enters; but the true sanctuary of medical science is a laboratory; only there will he seek explanations of life in normal and pathological states by means of experimental analysis. . . . In leaving the hospital, the physician . . . must go into his laboratory; and there, by experiments on animals, he will account for what he has observed in patients, whether about the action of drugs or about the origin of morbid lesions in organs and tissues. There, in a word, he will achieve true medical science.[11]

Whatever else we might think about Bernard's vision, there is no denying its simplicity. The *only* true way to learn the origin and proper treatment of human disease is to experiment on nonhuman animals. Today, it is doubtful whether any respectable scientists who use the animal model in their research would endorse Bernard's view. Still, it is fair to say that the majority of these scientists believe that the use of the animal model is *a* way, and no doubt many also believe that this is the *best* way, to advance knowledge about the origin, prevention, and treatment of human diseases.

Not everyone, even including highly trained scientists and physicians, agrees. For a variety of reasons, critics of animal model research think that extrapolating what is learned from nonhumans to humans is unreliable at best, misleading (and, sometimes, tragically so) at worst. I shall return to this topic in my reply to Professor Cohen. Here I am content to point out that some of the most trenchant criticism of this way of approaching human morbidity and mortality comes not from "outsiders" (people who have no advanced scientific or medical training) but from "insiders" within the research and medical communities.[12]

The utilization of animals in science usually is divided into three categories: research, testing, and education. At best there is a fine line separating the second from the first: when a toxicologist uses animals in an attempt to determine the possible harmful effects of drugs designed to lower blood pressure, for example, what is being done can be described equally accurately as "conducting research" or "conducting a test." Whichever description is preferred is less important than the recognition that using animals in research or testing differs from using them in education. In the latter case, their classic use is as a tool to impart what is already known; in the former cases, they are used as a tool to discover new knowledge. I shall confine my remarks to their use outside educational contexts.

In the United States, various federal and state laws apply to the use of animals in science. At the federal level, the Animal Welfare Act (AWA), enacted in 1966 and amended in 1970, 1976, 1985, and 1990, is the most comprehensive. The AWA addresses only the care and treatment of animals; it explicitly removes the federal government from playing any role in the "design, outlines, guidelines, or performance of actual research or experimentation by a research facility as determined by such a research facility." Moreover, the AWA defines "animal" to mean "any live or dead dog, cat, monkey (nonhuman primate), guinea pig, hamster, rabbit, or other such warm-blooded animal as the Secretary (of the Department of Agriculture) may determine is being used, or is intended for use, for research, testing, experimentation or exhibition purposes." Conspicuously absent from the list are rats and mice, as well as all birds and farm animals, which together account for approximately 90 percent of the animals used in a research context.

At the time of this writing, efforts are under way to have mice, rats, birds, and farm animals recognized for what they are: animals. Government officials to date have indicated their reluctance to do so, citing the increase in costs of new inspection as the main reason for retaining the status quo.

No one really knows how many animals are used for scientific purposes. U.S. government statistics for 1994 place the number at 1,618,194, but this total is not reliable, for at least three reasons.[13] First, without imputing treacherous motives to researchers, one can reasonably doubt that all those publicly funded research institutions that are legally required to report to the government do so accurately and fully. Second, thousands of private sector research institutions and other facilities use animals but are not required to report to the government. Finally, not all animals qualify as animals, given the perverse logic of current federal and state laws. Indeed, as already noted, the very animals who are used most frequently do not qualify and thus do not need to be included in a research facility's report to the government.

Still, everyone agrees the number of animals used is large. A 1986 Office of Technology Assessment review, conducted for the U.S. Congress, placed that number at between ten million and a hundred million. So the dispute is over how many million. Fifteen? Fifty? Somewhere in between? Somewhere in between, somewhere between twenty-five and fifty million, may not be an unreasonable estimate.

Enforcement of the Animal Welfare Act is entrusted to the United States Department of Agriculture, through its Animal and Plant Health Inspection Service (APHIS). Facilities that do not use any of the regulated species are exempt from the act, as are those facilities that do not receive federal funds and utilize animals they raise themselves. Despite these limitations, roughly eight thousand research facilities, animal dealers, animal shippers, and others are legally subject to inspection for compliance.[14] It has been estimated that APHIS inspectors, whose primary responsibility is to prevent interstate shipments of diseased plants and livestock, devote a maximum of 6 percent of their time to enforcing the AWA.

As a result of steadily increasing budget cuts, the first half of the 1990s witnessed more than a 20 percent decline in the number of APHIS inspections performed. Internal audits of APHIS, conducted in 1992 and 1995 by the Office of the Inspector General, found that "APHIS was still not able to make all the required inspection visits" to facilities *already* reported in violation of AWA. In response, APHIS officials noted that "some of the follow-up visits were not made due to staffing limitations and budgetary cutbacks." Past violators were thus able to continue to treat animals in ways that (in APHIS's own words) could "jeopardize the health and safety of their animals without APHIS intervention."

All considered, then, the legally mandated and enforced protection afforded animals in labs is modest at best. Certainly it would be naive in the extreme to assume that "all is well" behind the locked doors blocking the day-to-day activities in America's laboratories from public view. Even APHIS, which hardly qualifies as a radical animal rights group, would deny the credibility of such an assurance.

When the topic is the use of animals in science, most defenders allude to lifesaving cures and other improvements in human health whose discovery, it is claimed, would have been impossible without relying on animal models. Whether the claims made in behalf of utilizing animals for this purpose are accurate or exaggerated is something about which informed people of good will can disagree. Often forgotten in these partisan debates are other uses to which animals routinely are subjected. It will be useful, as a corrective to the tendency to marginalize these other practices, to consider a utilization of the animal model that is not restricted to attempts to advance medical knowledge.

Toxicity tests are one of the many ways animals are used in the name of science. These tests aim to establish a given substance's likely harmful effects on human beings by first administering the substance to nonhuman animals. What the test substance is varies, from potentially therapeutic drugs to pesticides, drain cleaners, industrial solvents, paints, or hair sprays. The methods used also vary. Sometimes animals are forced to ingest the substance, sometimes they are made to inhale it, and in other cases the substance is applied to the skin or the eye. Though the exact figure is not known, there is no doubt that millions of animals, mostly mice and rats, but sometimes dogs and monkeys, are used in toxicity tests. For example, current plans call for the chemical industry to conduct five types of animal-based toxicity tests on three thousand chemicals over the next six years; these tests alone, assuming they are carried out as they have been in the past, will require utilization of hundreds of thousands of animals; and this is only one among the many ongoing and planned animal-based toxicity studies the future holds. In the general area of toxicity assessment, the number of animals used is hardly inconsiderable.

Toxicity tests are carried out in the name of product safety, with a view to minimizing the known risks consumers run when they use items available in the market. Some government agencies (e.g., the Consumer Product Safety Commission) require that manufacturers conduct toxicity tests before their products can be legally merchandised. Requirements of this type are the exception, not the rule. In the great majority of cases, toxicity tests are not legally required. However, because product liability law is premised on the idea that manufacturers will do whatever is reasonably necessary to prevent consumers from running unreasonable risks, manufacturers who are not legally required to conduct toxicity tests may choose to conduct them anyway.

Throughout the past sixty years, one common toxicity test conducted on animals is the LD50. "LD" stands for "lethal dose," "50" for "50 percent." As the words suggest, the LD50 seeks to establish at what dosage the test substance will prove lethal (i.e., will kill) 50 percent of the test animals.

The LD50 works this way. The test substance is orally administered to the test animals, some of whom are given the substance in more, others in less, concentrated forms. In theory, anything and everything has a lethal dose. Even water has been shown to be lethal to 50 percent of test animals, if enough is consumed in a short enough period of time.[15] To control variables, and because the animals themselves will not "volunteer" to swallow such things as paint thinner or Christmas tree spray, a measured amount is passed through a tube and down the animals' throats. Variables are also controlled by withholding anesthetic. Anywhere from ten to sixty animals are used. Observation of their condition may last up to two weeks, during which time the requisite 50 percent normally die, after which the remaining animals are killed and their dissected bodies examined. Depending on the results, the test substance is labeled as more or less toxic if swallowed in full or diluted concentrations. Products are not kept out of the market even if they prove to be highly toxic for test animals; instead, tests like the LD50 are the invisible history behind the "Harmful or fatal if swallowed" labels on cans of such items as brake fluids, household lubricants, and industrial solvents.

That manufacturers have a responsibility to inform consumers about the safety of their products is an idea no sensible person would dispute. Whether reliance on the LD50 test discharges this responsibility to consumers, and whether using animals to discharge this responsibility is morally worth the cost to the animals, are matters sensible people would do well to pause to consider.

Scientific critics of the LD50, including many who are part of the regulatory toxicity industry, find the test to be badly flawed. Results have been shown to vary from one lab to the next, and even within the same lab from one day to the next. The sex, age, and diet of the test animals have been shown to skew the outcome, as has their species. Even if the results were regularly reproducible in the case of the test animals, their usefulness for humans is negligible at best. Doctors and other hospital personnel who work in emergency rooms, where the majority of accidental poisonings are dealt with, do not consult LD50 results before treating their patients. To suggest otherwise reflects profound ignorance of the practice of emergency medicine.

The consequences of utilizing animals in toxicity tests, when we consider the animals, are far from negligible. For them, life in a laboratory can be a living hell. In the case of LD50 tests, for example, animals frequently become quite ill before they die or are killed. Symptoms include diarrhea, convulsions, and bloody discharge from the mouth, eyes, and rectum. Richard Ryder, a former experimental psychologist who used animals in his research while at Cambridge and Columbia Universities, characterizes the plight of animals used in LD50 tests of cosmetics as follows:

> Because most cosmetic products are not especially poisonous, it necessarily follows that if a rat or a dog has to be killed this way, then very great quantities of cosmetic must be forced into their stomachs, blocking or breaking internal organs, or killing the animal by some other physical action, rather than by any specific chemical effect. Of course the procedure of force-feeding—even with healthy food—is itself a notoriously unpleasant procedure, as suffragettes and other prisoners on hunger-strike have testified. When the substance forced into the stomach is not food at all, but large quantities of face powder, make up or liquid hair dye, then no doubt the suffering is very much greater indeed. If, for the bureaucratic correctness of the test, quantities great enough to kill are involved, then clearly the process of dying itself must often be prolonged and agonizing.[16]

Lest we think that, in the majority of cases, the animals used are "only rats" or "only mice," it should be recalled that neither rats nor mice are classified as "animals" under the Animal Welfare Act and thus are not covered by extant federal legislation. We should also note that, unlike those animals who are covered, neither mice nor rats are able to vomit and so cannot find even the temporary relief this mechanism provides.

The use of "animal models" for scientific purposes involves much else besides their utilization in toxicity tests in general, their use in the LD50 test in particular. Nevertheless, the same questions can be asked about toxicity tests as can be asked of any test or research that uses the animal model. Questions arise about their *scientific validity:* Is it scientifically credible to believe that what is discovered by using a cat or a dog, a mouse or a rat can be extrapolated to human beings? Or might it be true that the use of the animal model is a bankrupt scientific methodology? These are the basic scientific questions.

The basic moral questions are two. First, if animal model tests or research is scientifically indefensible, then how, morally, can their continued use be justified? Second, even if this methodology is scientifically defensible—indeed, even if, by relying on it, important human interests in safety and health are advanced to a degree that would be otherwise unobtainable—does that make animal model tests or research right?

I consider the first question in my reply to Professor Cohen. As for the second, it cannot be answered in a philosophical vacuum. Whether use of the animal model is right or wrong depends on general considerations about moral right and wrong. This is hardly unique to the issue at hand. Consider moral controversies that have nothing to do with animals—abortion and physician-assisted suicide, for example. Different people have deeply felt opposing views about the morality of these practices, with both sides mounting passionate arguments in their defense. Which side is correct is hard to say. Nevertheless, separated though they are by the judgments they make, there is one point on which all can agree: it makes sense to ask *why* people believe what they do—to ask for, and to expect to be given, *reasons* that support the moral judgments they make. If in response we are told that *there are no reasons,* the person *just knows* where the truth lies, we are wise to walk away. Our positions about controversial moral issues, whatever these positions might be, are never self-evidently true; without exception, our answers to controversial moral questions require careful, informed, fair, and well considered rational support.

Which among the possible reasons given in support of our moral convictions really do the job—really do show that we are justified in believing what we do? When we rise to this level of inquiry, we are not asking whether an individual action or a particular practice is morally right or morally wrong. We want to know what makes *any* action or *any* practice morally right or morally wrong. This is what I meant earlier, when I said that the morality of using animals for scientific purposes cannot be assessed in a moral vacuum. To attempt to assess the morality of *this* practice necessitates asking and answering questions about the morality of *any* practice; it requires exploring the possible merits of competing moral philosophies. The next four chapters explore some of the most influential moral outlooks favored by philosophers over the centuries.

Notes

1. The estimate of eight hundred thousand milk-fed veal calves slaughtered is for 1995; see *Meat Facts* (Washington, D.C.: American Meat Institute, 1995). Other numerical estimates are those of the United States Department of Agriculture at www.usda.gov/nass/pubs/ histdata.htm.

2. Peter Singer, *Animal Liberation,* 2d ed. (New York: New York Review of Books, 1990), 133.

3. Singer, *Animal Liberation,* 130–31.

4. Singer, *Animal Liberation,* 131.

5. Repetitive motion and other behavioral signs of maladjustment of animals in intensive rearing systems were first documented in 1965 by an independent government-appointed committee, headed by zoologist Professor F. W. Rogers Brambell. See *Report of the Technical Committee to Enquire into the Welfare of Animals Kept under Intensive Livestock Husbandry Systems* (London: Her Majesty's Stationery Office, 1965). A second study, *Animal Welfare in Poultry, Pig and Veal Calf Production* (London: Her Majesty's Stationery Office, 1981), submitted by the House of Commons' Agriculture Committee, was highly critical of the intensive rearing methods that continue to dominate contemporary American animal agribusiness. A brief overview of scientific studies of animal welfare is Joy A. Mench, "Thirty Years after Brambell: Whither Animal Welfare Science," *Journal of Applied Animal Welfare Science* 1, no. 2 (1986): 91–102. A more detailed account covering the same period is Richard Ryder, *The Political Animal: The Conquest of Speciesism* (Jefferson, N.C.: McFarland, 1998); see, in particular, chapter 3, "The Science of Animal Welfare." Ryder was the first person to use the word *speciesism.*

6. General surveys of factory farming include Michael W. Fox, *Farm Animals: Husbandry, Behavior, and Veterinary Practice* (Baltimore, Md.: University Park Press, 1984), and Jim Mason and Peter Singer, *Animal Factories* (New York: Crown, 1980).

7. For the USDA's position on vegetarianism and veganism, see *Dietary Guidelines for Americans,* 4th ed. (Washington, D.C.: U.S. Government Printing Office, 1995), which is also available at www. nalusda.gov/fnic/dga/dga95/cover.html.

8. Most of the statistics concerning fur production come from the Fur Industry of America and can be confirmed at www.fur.org/furfarm.html. The estimate of the number of trappers I owe to Merritt Clifton, who bases this figure on two state-by-state censuses, one conducted by the Animal Welfare Institute, the other by the Humane Society of the United States.

9. Friends of Animals literature on fur can be obtained on request from Friends of Animals, 777 Post Road, Darien, Connecticut 06820, or www.friendsofanimals.org.

10. The quote from Desmond Morris appears in Mark Glover, "Eye of the Beholder," *Animals' Voice Magazine* 5, no. 4 (1992): 33. Morris also addresses trapping in *The Animal Contract: An Impassioned and Rational Guide to Sharing the Planet and Saving Our Common World* (New York: Warner, 1990), 116–18. My thanks to Laura Moretti for locating these sources.

11. Bernard, *Introduction to the Study of Experimental Medicine: Volume 1* (Paris, 1926), 35.

12. The Physicians Committee for Responsible Medicine, the Association of Veterinarians for Animal Rights, and the Medical Research Modernization Committee are among the groups of medically trained professionals who oppose using animals in research.

13. For information concerning the number of reportable animals used in research, see www.aphis.usda.gov/oa/pubs/awrpt97.html.

14. Data about the number of facilities subject to APHIS inspection, and the shortcomings of these inspections, are quoted from Office of the Inspector General's *Animal and Plant Inspection Service Enforcement of the Animal Welfare Act*, Audit Report No. 33600-1-Ch (Washington, D.C.: U.S. Government Printing Office, January 1995. An informed overview of APHIS practices will be found in Michael Budkie, "Are Laboratory Animals Protected in the U.S.?" *Animals' Voice Magazine* (Spring 1996): 6–9. Gary Francione offers a sustained critique of the Animal Welfare Act and APHIS's enforcement of its provisions in *Animals, Property, and the Law* (Philadelphia: Temple University Press, 1995).

15. For a classic discussion of the variability in LD50 results because of environmental and other factors, see R. Loosli, "Duplicate Testing and Reproducibility," in Regamay, Hennesen, Ikic, and Ungar, *International Symposium on Laboratory Medicine* (Basel: Karger, 1967).

16. Richard D. Ryder, *Victims of Science: the Use of Animals in Research* (London: Davis-Poyter, 1975), 36.

13

The Nature and Importance
of Rights

What makes right acts right? What makes wrong acts wrong? Some moral philosophers believe that the best answers to these questions require the recognition of moral rights. This is the position I favor, and it is also the one favored by Professor Cohen, at least in the case of human rights. It will therefore be useful to say something about the nature and importance of rights; to do so here will make it possible to highlight some areas where Professor Cohen and I agree and others where we do not.

The idea of the "rights of the individual" has had a profound and lasting influence, both in and beyond Western civilization. Among philosophers, however, this idea has been the subject of intense debate.[1] Some philosophers deny that we have any rights (moral rights, as they are commonly called) beyond those legal rights established by law; others affirm that, separate from and more basic than our legal rights, are our moral rights, including such rights as the rights to life, liberty, and bodily integrity. The framers of America's Declaration of Independence certainly believed this; they maintained that the sole reason for having a government in the first place is to protect citizens in the possession of their rights, rights that, because they are independent of, and more basic than, legal rights, have the status of moral rights.

People can agree that humans have moral rights and disagree over what rights are. They can even agree that humans have moral rights, agree about what rights are, and still disagree when it comes to saying what rights humans have. For example, some proponents of moral rights believe humans possess only *negative* moral rights (rights not to be harmed or interfered with), while others believe we also have *positive* moral rights (rights to be helped or assisted).

Most of these debates, as important as they are, lie outside the scope of our present interest. Professor Cohen and I agree that human beings have negative moral rights (about which I will have more to say momentarily). We also agree on how the idea of moral rights should be understood (about which I will have more to say in chapter 16). Where we disagree—at least this is our most obvious difference—is over the question of whether any nonhuman animals possess rights of the same kind: negative moral rights. I offer reasons for an affirmative answer in chapter 17. Here, in the present chapter, I will assume that humans have such rights, leaving open the question of whether other animals do as well. My purpose in this chapter is to explain why the idea that humans have negative moral rights and why the possibility that animals have them are the important ideas they are.

"No Trespassing"

Possession of moral rights (by which, again, unless otherwise indicated, I mean negative moral rights) confers a distinctive moral status on those who have them. To possess these rights is to have a kind of protective moral shield, something we might picture as an invisible "No Trespassing" sign.[2] If we assume that all humans have such rights, we can ask what this invisible sign prohibits. Two things, in general. First, others are not morally free to harm us; to say this is to say that, judged from the moral point of view, others are not free to take our life or injure our body as they please. Second, others are not free to interfere with our free choice; to say this is to say that others are not free to limit our choices as they please. In both cases, the "No Trespassing" sign is meant to protect those who have rights by morally limiting the freedom of others.

Does this mean that it is always wrong to take someone's life, injure them, or restrict their freedom? Not at all. When people exceed their rights by violating ours, Professor Cohen and I agree that we act within our rights if we respond in ways that can harm or limit the freedom of the violators. For example, suppose you are attacked by a thief; then Professor Cohen and I agree that you do nothing wrong in using physical force sufficient to defend yourself, even if this harms your assailant. Thankfully, in the world as we find it, such cases are the exception, not the rule. Most people most of the time act in ways that respect the rights of other human beings. But even if the world happened to be different in this respect, the central point would be the same: what we are free to do when someone violates our rights does not translate into the freedom to violate their rights without justifiable cause.

Professor Cohen and I also agree on a related point: to act in ways that are respectful of individual rights is to act in ways that are respectful of the individuals whose rights they are. It is because humans have rights to life, bodily integrity, and liberty that serial murderers commit grievous moral wrongs when they take the lives of their victims, child molesters act wrongly when they injure their victims, and kidnappers wrong their captives when they deprive them of their freedom. In each of these and all analogous cases, there is an essential moral sameness in the wrong that is done: when our individual rights are violated, individual human beings are treated with a lack of respect.

"Trump"

The moral limits possession of rights places on the freedom of others extends to society at large. Even if society in general, not a particular individual, would benefit if the rights of a comparatively small number of its members were violated, that would not make violating their rights morally acceptable to any serious defender of human rights, Professor Cohen and myself included. The well-known and justly condemned Tuskegee syphilis study provides a tragic example of this general point. Here, in brief, is one of the most shameful stories in the history of medical research in America.

The time: 1932. The place: Tuskegee Institute, among the nation's oldest, most respected African American institutions of higher learning. The participants: approximately four hundred African American men who had volunteered to receive what they were told was "special treatment" for their "bad blood," not knowing that in fact they suffered from syphilis and that the "medicine" they were given would have no therapeutic effect. Also unknown to them was the reason for the study: it was not to help them recover from their illness; it was not even to find a cure for syphilis; instead, the study was conducted to determine how long it would take the men to die if their condition went untreated. To learn this, the researchers thought, would be important for understanding syphilis, which might benefit those who suffered from this disease in the future. Remarkably, in a country founded on "the rights of man," this study was carried out on uninformed, trusting men from 1932 to 1972—for *forty* years—with funds from, and with the knowing support of, the United States government.

Did those who conducted this study show respect for the bodily integrity of the men they studied? No. Did they show respect for the lives of the victims who died? No. More generally, were the participants treated with the respect to which all humans are morally entitled, as a matter of moral right? No. When, in 1997, President Clinton, speaking for the nation, apologized to the few surviving human "guinea pigs" used in the Tuskegee study and to the descendants of those who had died, the apology came more than sixty years too late.

Proponents of human rights categorically deny the permissibility of treating human beings in the way these men were treated. When actions that would advance the collective good clash with the rights of the individual, then the individual's rights "trump" (to use an expression coined by the philosopher Ronald Dworkin[3]). Even if thousands, even if tens of thousands of future syphilis sufferers benefited from the Tuskegee study, that would not justify violating the rights of the men who participated. We are not to do evil that good may come, and one way of doing evil is to violate somebody's rights.

Animal Rights?

It is when viewed against this larger moral backdrop that the importance of the debate over animal rights comes into sharper focus. *If* animals have moral rights of the sort under review (such negative rights as the rights to bodily integrity and to life), then the way they are treated on farms and in biomedical research, for example, violates their rights, is wrong, and should be stopped, no matter how much humans have benefited from these practices in the past or how much we might benefit from having them continue in the future.

Professor Cohen agrees. "[I]f animals have any rights at all they have the right to be respected, the right not to be used as a tool to advance human interests . . . no matter how important those human interests are thought to be." In particular, if nonhuman animals have moral rights, biomedical research that uses them is wrong and should be stopped. Professor Cohen even goes so far as to liken the use of animals, in the development of the polio and other vaccines, to the use Nazi scientists made of Jewish children during the second World War. "[I]f those animals we used and continue to use have rights as human children do, what we did and are doing to them is as profoundly wrong as what the Nazis did to those Jews not long ago."[4] Clearly, what is true of the morality of relying on the animal model in scientific research would be no less true when evaluating the morality of commercial animal agriculture and the fur trade. These, too, would be "profoundly wrong", *if* animals have rights. On this point, without a doubt, Professor Cohen would agree.

But *do* animals have rights? Professor Cohen maintains that they do not; more, he maintains that they cannot. I shall postpone explaining where and why I believe his arguments go wrong for my Reply. Here I note that my argument for animal rights cannot be made in twenty-five words or less. Why animals have rights can be understood only after critically examining ways of thinking about morality that deny rights to animals and, sometimes, to humans, too. Once we understand the weaknesses of these positions, we can understand why human rights must be acknowledged; and once we adopt this latter position, then—but not before, in my judgment—we can understand why we must acknowledge animal rights as well.

In the nature of the case, therefore, as I indicated earlier, and as I will have occasion to say again, my argument for animal rights is cumulative in nature, arising, as it does, in response to weaknesses in other ways of thinking about morality. What these other ways are, where some of their weaknesses lie, are explored in the following pages.

Notes

1. Different philosophers understand rights differently. Professor Cohen and I understand rights as valid claims. What this means is explained in chapter 16. In my judgment, the most powerful defense of viewing rights in this way will be found in the work of Joel Feinberg, including his classic essay, "The Nature and Value of Rights," *Journal of Value Inquiry* 4 (Winter 1970): 243–57.

2. The idea that negative moral rights are like invisible "No Trespassing" signs I owe to Robert Nozick. See his *Anarchy, State, and Utopia* (New York: Basic Books, 1974).

3. Ronald Dworkin, *Taking Rights Seriously* (Cambridge, Mass.: Harvard University Press, 1977).

4. Carl Cohen, "Do Animals Have Rights?" *Ethics and Behavior* 7, no. 2 (1997): 92.

14

Indirect Duty Views

Most people like animals. Very few are indifferent to their suffering, and fewer still would intentionally mistreat a cat, dog, or any animal, for that matter. When children torment a puppy or kitten, most parents and other grown-ups are quick to reprimand them. We want our children to empathize with, not be the cause of, another's pain. For many children, one of life's earliest lessons in empathy concerns the suffering of animals.

But while almost all of us are of one mind when it comes to opposing the mistreatment of animals, most people evidently believe we do nothing wrong when we make them suffer or die in pursuit of various human interests. At least this is the verdict supported by the behavior and judgments of the majority of Americans. According to the latest available polls, somewhere in the neighborhood of 99 percent eat meat; a clear majority (70 percent) approves of using animals to test medical treatments; and the public is somewhat divided when it comes to wearing fur (50 percent against, 35 percent for, and 15 percent undecided).[1] How is it possible for people to oppose mistreating animals and, at the same time, to support practices they know cause animals pain and involve deliberately killing them?

Moral philosophers, as well as other people of conscience, are not short on possible answers. One influential explanation favored by some philosophers grants that we have duties *involving* animals but denies that we have any duties *to* them. It will be useful to give a name to moral outlooks of this type. For reasons that will become clearer as we proceed, I refer to them as *indirect duty views*. The present chapter examines two views of this type and explains why, in the end, despite the important contributions they make, indirect duty views are unsatisfactory.

157

An example should help clarify the basic logic of indirect duty views. Suppose you share your life with a dog, whom you love dearly. Your next door neighbor does not share your affection. He regards your dog as a nuisance and makes no effort to conceal his feelings. One day, without provocation, you see him deliberately break her leg. Proponents of indirect duty views will agree that your neighbor has done something wrong. But not to your dog. The wrong that has been done, they will say, is a wrong to you. After all, it is wrong to upset people and, by injuring your dog, your neighbor has upset you. So *you* are the one who is wronged, *not* your dog. Or again: By breaking your dog's leg, your neighbor damages your property. Since it is wrong to damage another person's property, your neighbor has done something wrong—to you, that is, not to your dog. Your neighbor no more wrongs your dog by breaking her leg than he would wrong your clock if he broke its hands.

While all indirect duty views deny that we have duties to animals, there is room for disagreement concerning why this is so. People who accept indirect duty views might deny direct duties to nonhuman animals because these animals are not created in the image of God, for example, or because animals, unlike us, are not able to use abstract principles when they make decisions. When we classify a position as an indirect duty view, therefore, we leave important moral questions open. What makes right acts right, what makes wrong acts wrong, remains to be explained, and the explanation given will depend on the particulars of the indirect duty view being reviewed. One basis common to a variety of indirect duty views involves the idea of interests. Because this idea plays a central role in all the moral outlooks discussed in the sequel, it will be useful to say something more about it here.

Two Kinds of Interests

The interests people have are of two kinds. *Preference interests* refer to what people are interested in, what they want to do or possess. Interests of this kind often differ greatly among different individuals. For example, some people would rather golf than play tennis; some prefer the opposite; and others, liking neither, would rather curl up with a book or spend their free time surfing the net. People also differ when it comes to the things they want. For example, some people are not satisfied unless they have closets full of clothes, while others think having the basics is enough. Not only do the preferences we have help define who we are; they also help describe how we differ.

Welfare interests are conceptually distinct from preference interests. Welfare interests refer to what is in our interests, those things and conditions that are necessary if we are to have a minimally satisfactory existence. Food, shelter, and health are welfare interests we all share, differ though we do when it comes to our preference interests. Logic suggests, and experience confirms, that the two sorts of interests can conflict, sometimes with tragic consequences. For example, people with serious drug problems can ruin their life by sacrificing their most important welfare interests to the preference interests that define their addiction.

Some advocates of indirect duty views deny that we have duties directly to animals because of how they understand human and animal interests. The interests animals have, if in fact they have any, it is claimed, are of no direct relevance to morality, whereas human interests, meaning both our preference interests and our welfare interests, are directly relevant. Because we cannot have direct duties to those whose interests are not directly relevant to morality, this way of viewing interests yields the conclusion that we do not have direct duties to animals. This in turn would explain why your neighbor did not violate a duty he owed to your dog. Because your dog's interest in avoiding pain, assuming she has this interest, is of no direct moral relevance, your neighbor's hurting her is not directly morally relevant, either. That being so, the idea of your neighbor's having a duty directly to your dog and, in general, the idea of any human being ever having a duty directly to a nonhuman animal emerge as morally empty.

Why would anyone think that animal interests have no direct relevance to morality? If your dog suffers because your neighbor has broken her leg, how could any rational person deny that her pain is directly morally relevant? Logic suggests, and this time history confirms, that one way to defend this position is to deny that nonhuman animals *feel* anything, pain included. That such a proposal goes against the grain of common sense is too obvious to require proof. Still, as is famously said, common sense tells us the world is flat. So perhaps we are just as mistaken about what animals experience as flat-Earthers are about the shape of our planet. Remarkably, some philosophers think we are.

Cartesianism: Then and Now

As was just noted, one way to support an indirect duty view is to deny that animals are aware of anything. It is important to grasp the full meaning of what is being proposed. We are not being asked to believe that nonhuman animals experience the same things we do only less intensely or that they experience different things than we do that we cannot begin to understand or even imagine. Instead, we are being asked to believe that animals do not experience anything, that their mental life is totally nonexistent. Given such a view, animals are as mindless as wristwatches, and questions about how they should be treated are on a par with asking about my duty to your Timex. From the moral point of view, we do not have duties *to* animals, just as we do not have duties *to* watches, only duties to humans that sometimes involve animals and watches.

Now, there was a time, owing to the influence of the seventeenth-century French philosopher René Descartes, when many scientists enthusiastically embraced the view that nonhuman animals are mindless, totally devoid of any conscious experience.[2] Nicholas Fontaine, a contemporary of Descartes, captures the reigning ideology of the times in these words:

> The [Cartesian] scientists administered beatings to dogs with perfect indifference and made fun of those who pitied the creatures as if they felt pain. They said the animals were clocks; that the cries they emitted when struck were only the noise of a little spring that had been touched, but that the whole body was without feeling. They nailed the poor animals up on boards by their four paws to vivisect them to see the circulation of the blood which was a subject of great controversy.[3]

Descartes offers several arguments to support his view that animals are not aware of anything, the most important of which deals with the ability to use language. We humans learn about one another's mental life because we are able to communicate. I describe what I see and hear and feel; you do the same in your case. Unlike us, animals are unable to do this. Because they lack the ability to use a language such as French or English, Descartes maintains that animals offer no compelling evidence that they are aware of anything. And because they fail to offer such evidence, Descartes concludes that animals lack any sort of mental life. Animals are (to use his words) "nature's machines," bodies without minds, biological wind-up toys as lacking in mental awareness as the Energizer Bunny.

Descartes's views are so patently at odds with common sense that they have attracted few adherents over the last three centuries. It may therefore come as a surprise to learn that the past several years have witnessed something of a renaissance of the Cartesian denial of animal awareness. The English philosopher Peter Carruthers is representative of the neo-Cartesians.[4] Following in Descartes's footsteps, Carruthers argues that because animals are unable to use language, they are unable to think; and because they are unable to think, they are not conscious of anything. Notwithstanding the fact that a coyote caught in a steel-jawed leghold trap behaves as if she suffers terribly, the animal has no interest in avoiding what she does not experience. On Carruther's view, animal pain is "unconscious."

Descartes's and Carruther's language argument for denying conscious experience to nonhuman animals will not stand up under logical scrutiny. For example, consider: Human children *must* be aware of things before they learn to use a language. If they were not—if they could neither see nor hear nor feel things, prior to learning to talk—they could never learn to talk. There would be no point—there *could* be no point—holding up the cat and, while pointing, saying "kitty," if preverbal children were unable to see the kitten or hear our voice. Human children *must* be preverbally (and thus *nonverbally*) aware of the world if they are to become linguistically proficient. This last point is crucial. Unless matters are prejudged arbitrarily, once we concede the *reality* of nonverbal awareness in humans, we must acknowledge the *possibility* of nonverbal awareness in animals. And once we acknowledge this latter possibility, we cannot deny mental awareness to animals merely because they are unable to use a language like French or English.

Of course, only a comparative handful of people out of the many billions who have lived have denied conscious awareness to nonhuman animals; only a very small minority have claimed that these animals, like wrist watches, have no interests. The Cartesian's ability to suspend belief to the contrary, the rest of us, with Professor Cohen included in our numbers, are people of common sense, people who both recognize our psychological kinship with other animals and who naturally sympathize with their pain and distress.

Science and Animal Minds

But it is not just common sense that declares that other animals are our psychological kin. Our best science supports the same conclusion. Darwin sees this clearly in the case of evolutionary theory.[5] *Naturam non facit saltum* (nature does not make jumps) is central to his understanding of how existing species of life, including the human, have come into being. Evolutionary theory teaches that what is more mentally complex evolves from what is less mentally complex, not that what is more mentally complex, the human mind in particular, springs full-blown from what lacks mind altogether. If that were true, nature would make some very big jumps indeed. Viewed in evolutionary terms, other-than-human minds populate the nonhuman world.

This clearly is Darwin's outlook. "There is," he writes, "no fundamental difference between man and the higher animals in their mental faculties." The difference in the mental life of human beings, other mammals, and birds, he goes on to observe, is "one of degree, not of kind." What Darwin means, I think, is that these animals are like us in having a rich, unified mental life. Darwin himself catalogues the mental attributes he finds in animals, basing his findings on his own and others' observations of their behavior. It is an impressive list, including—in addition to the capacity to experience pleasure and pain (sentiency)—such emotions as terror, suspicion, courage, rage, shame, jealousy, grief, love, and affection, and such higher-order cognitive abilities as curiosity, attention, memory, imagination, and reason.

For Darwin, there is nothing the least bit irrational or antiscientific in the belief that coyotes and veal calves remember events from the past, anticipate what will happen in the future, and are able to act deliberately, with the intention of satisfying their preferences in the future. It is only when we ask *how much* they remember or anticipate, or *how many things* they want to have and do, that differences emerge.

Our knowledge of the past, for example, extends beyond the limits of our own experience. The life of Plato. The fall of Rome. The Hundred Years War. The forced internment of Japanese Americans during World War II. No animal other than the human has such knowledge, just as no animal other than the human worries about the stock market, rejoices in a Steeler victory, or (to quote Darwin again) is able to "follow out a train of metaphysical reasoning, solve a mathematics problem, or reflect on God." Even so, there is sameness beneath the differences. In many important, though of course not in all, respects, the mental lives of humans and other animals are fundamentally similar.

The truth of Darwin's teachings finds further corroboration in comparative anatomy and physiology. Human anatomy and physiology are not in every way unique. On the contrary, as Darwin observes, "man bears in his bodily structure clear traces of descent from" other species of animals. These similarities of structure and function in the anatomy and physiology of humans and other animals are too obvious to be denied, their importance too great to be ignored. Thus may we ask, in the words of the seventeenth-century French philosopher Voltaire in his sarcastic rejection of Cartesianism, "Has nature arranged all the means of feeling in the animal, so that it may not feel? . . . Do not suppose this impertinent contradiction in nature."[6]

As the preceding discussion reflects, the grounds for attributing minds to animal beings are analogous to those we have for attributing minds to one another. Common sense supports it. How they behave supports it. Their physiology and anatomy support it. And their having a mind, their having a psychology, is supported by well-established scientific principles. Not one of these considerations by itself need be claimed as "proof" of animal minds; it is when they are taken together, as they are in Darwin's hands, that they provide compelling grounds for attributing a rich, unified mental life to other than human animals.

We may conclude, therefore, that our common sense belief in animal minds has good reasons on its side. Sheep and hogs, mink and beaver, mice and birds are not only in the world; they are aware of it, and aware, too, of what happens to them. They share with us a family of cognitive, attitudinal, emotional, and volitional capacities. On the cognitive side, they are able to form beliefs about the world (about what is happening now, what happened in the past, and what will happen in the future), while on the attitudinal side they are able to take an interest in things, wanting and desiring, as they do, different things, some more than others. In addition, mammals and birds (at least) respond emotionally to what transpires in their life and, given the freedom to do so, are able to use their cognitive capacities when making choices with a view to satisfying their interests. These animals are our psychological kin, and their minds are not unsophisticated by any means. Any plausible account of the moral status of animals must be consistent with the convictions of common sense, bolstered by the findings of an informed science.

Simple Contractarianism

For the most part (Carruthers being among the few exceptions), contemporary philosophers who hold indirect duty views grant that animals have various conscious experiences, including some that are painful, others pleasant. In other words, most indirect duty theorists are not Cartesians. How do these philosophers justify their position? Among this question's most influential replies are those favored by philosophers known as contractarians.

Here is the basic idea.[7] When two people negotiate a contract, both parties seek to advance or protect what is best for themselves. Contracts are entered into for the good of each person who signs, and no one should sign unless convinced that it is to that person's advantage to do so.

For contractarians, morality shares these essential features of contracting (hence the name: contractarianism). From a contractarian perspective, morality consists of a set of rules that all the contractors should follow because doing so is in each contractor's rational self-interest. For example, contractors might recognize that it is to their personal advantage to limit their freedom to increase their security. I agree not to steal your things if you agree not to steal mine; each of us voluntarily surrenders some of our freedom, but both of us reap the benefit of added security.

What makes right acts right? What makes wrong acts wrong? Contractarian answers generalize on the example of theft. Acts are right if they conform to a valid rule, wrong if they fail to conform to (if they break) a valid rule, the validity of the rules to be determined by the self-interest of the contractors. Valid rules are rules that advance the rational self-interest of the contractors if everyone who participates in framing the contract actually follows them.

It is important to recognize why, according to this form of contractarianism, referred to here as "simple contractarianism," the contractors enjoy a moral status that many humans lack. The interests of those who take part in framing the contract are directly morally relevant because their interests form the basis of the contract; this is why the framers are owed direct duties. By contrast, the interests of those who do not take part in framing the contract, because their interests do not form the basis of the contract, are not directly morally relevant; this is why no direct duties are owed in their case. This difference means a lot if you are a young child, for example. Because young children are unable to discern what is in their rational self-interest, they cannot participate in framing the contract; thus, *their* interests are not directly morally relevant; in their case, therefore, no direct duties are owed. Does this mean that contractors are morally free to treat children any way they please? Not necessarily. If the contractors have self-interested reasons in seeing that their own children are well treated (e.g., because they will want their children to look after them in old age), we can understand why rational, self-interested contractors would include rules that require that children should be well treated. There would thus be duties *involving* children but no duties *to* them. Our duties in their case would be indirect duties to the rational, self-interested persons who devise the contract.

As for animals, since they cannot understand contracts, they cannot participate. Accordingly, what interests they have are not directly relevant to morality. This much granted, the conclusion that they are not owed direct duties comes as no surprise. Still, like children, some animals are the objects of the sentimental interests of others. Those animals whom enough contractors care about (cats, dogs, whales, baby seals), though they will not be owed any direct duties, will have some indirect protection. For example, there might be a rule against eating cats and dogs because contractors find this practice upsetting, and another rule that protects baby seals because contractors find them adorable. In the case of other animals, where no or little sentimental interest is present—the millions of rodents used in laboratories and the billions of chickens slaughtered to be eaten, for example—what indirect duties there are grow weaker and weaker, perhaps to vanishing point. The pain and death these animals endure, though real, are not wrong if no one cares about them.

Evaluating Simple Contractarianism

Simple contractarianism has its attractions. Because it emphasizes a central role for reason in the determination of moral right and wrong, it distances itself both from views that reduce morality to our unreflective feelings and from outlooks that equate what is right and wrong with the reigning customs of the society into which we happen to be born. These are among simple contractarianism's strengths. As for its weaknesses, only two will be noted here. The first concerns how the position distorts the notion of justice; the second traces some of the morally unacceptable implications this distortion allows.

Concerning the matter of distortion: Morality, the simple contractarian tells us, consists of rules that rational, self-interested people agree to follow. Which people? Well, those who create the contract. This is all well and good for those who participate in framing the rules, but not so well and good for those who are excluded. And there is nothing in simple contractarianism that explains why it would be wrong to exclude some rationally competent human beings from participating in the formulation of the contract. Only a gross distortion of elementary justice would allow this.

To make this point clearer, consider what elementary justice requires. Elementary justice requires that we treat everyone fairly, not giving to some people more than they deserve, not withholding from others that to which they are entitled. In the case of welfare interests, for example, to use interests of this type for purposes of illustration, if my interests in having access to food and shelter are equal to your interests in having access to food and shelter, then, assuming that morality is based on interests and that other things are equal, it would be unfair to count my interests as being of greater importance than yours. Equal interests count equally. So says the voice of elementary justice, of fairness, when applied to interests.

Simple contractarianism is not bound by elementary justice. Because what is just and unjust, fair and unfair is *what the contractors decide,* there is no reason why the interests of some people might be ignored altogether, while the interests of others are given much greater weight or importance. For this reason alone, simple contractarianism cannot claim our rational assent.

But it is not for this reason alone that simple contractarianism should be rejected. The distortion of justice just noted (and here I turn to my second criticism) has morally unacceptable implications. This becomes clear when we ask which people might be denied the opportunity to participate in framing the moral contract. In the nature of the case, they would be people the contractors have self-interested reasons to exclude. An obvious candidate would be a racial minority whose members would best serve the contractors' interests if those in the minority were bought, sold, and forced to carry out slave labor. The same could be true of other people who belong to other vulnerable groups (e.g., those who are physically disadvantaged or mentally impaired), provided the contractors have self-interested reasons to exclude and exploit them.

As should be evident from these examples, simple contractarianism can have alarming implications, sanctifying the most blatant forms of social, economic, moral, and political injustice, ranging from a repressive caste system to systematic racial or ethnic discrimination. Let those who are not covered by the contract suffer as they will; it matters not so long as the contractors have decided that the suffering of "outsiders" does not matter morally. Such an outlook takes one's moral breath away, as if, for example, there would be nothing wrong with enslaving an African American minority if the moral contract was drawn up by a majority of bigoted whites.

A way of thinking about morality that has so little to recommend it when it comes to how other humans may be treated cannot have anything more to recommend it when it comes to the treatment of other animals. Simple contractarianism's implications for animal beings, we know, are both clear and unsurprising. Because they lack the requisite abilities, animals are not able to participate in framing the contract, and contractors have no direct duties to them. Indeed, the interests of animals are not in any way directly morally relevant and, if the contractors decide to do so, can be ignored completely. Elementary justice can therefore be transgressed just as easily in the case of nonhuman animals as it can be in the case of humans. But (as Professor Cohen would be the first to agree) a moral position that implies that some human beings may be treated as chattel offers no reason to make chattel of animal beings, either. Any credible moral outlook will have to do better than this.

Rawlsian Contractarianism

The version of contractarianism just examined is, confessedly, a simple variety, and, in fairness to those of a contractarian persuasion, it needs to be said that more refined, subtle, and ingenious varieties are possible. For example, John Rawls, in his monumental *A Theory of Justice,* sets forth a strikingly original interpretation of contractarianism.[8] As is true of simple contractarianism, Rawls's version denies that we have any direct duties to animals; but unlike simple contractarianism, his position arguably will not sanction such prejudices as racism and sexism or permit evil institutions such as chattel slavery. Here is why.

As would-be contractors, Rawls invites us to ignore those characteristics that make us different—such characteristics as our race and class, intelligence and skills, even our date of birth and where we live. We are to imagine that our knowledge of such personal details is hidden from us by what Rawls calls a "veil of ignorance." Here is the way he describes the situation.

> No one knows his place in society, his class position or social status, nor does anyone know his fortune in the distribution of natural assets and abilities, his intelligence, strength and alike. I shall even assume that the parties do not know their conceptions of the good or their special psychological propensities. To [choose] the principles of justice [from] behind a veil of ignorance . . . insures that no one is advantaged or disadvantaged in the choice of principles by the outcome of natural chance or the contingency of social circumstances. Since all are similarly situated and no one is able to design principles to favor his particular condition, the principles of justice are the result of a fair agreement or bargain.[9]

Despite our ignorance of such details, Rawls does allow us to know that we will someday be a member of a community whose basic rules of justice we are being asked to formulate. All that is required to participate is that we have "a sense of justice," understood as a "normally effective desire to apply and act on the principles of justice, at least to a minimum degree."[10] Or, alternatively (for Rawls describes the qualifying conditions in another way) those who participate must have the "ability to understand and act upon whatever principles are adopted."[11]

What rules, or principles, contractors would select from behind the veil of ignorance is less important for our purposes than the procedure by which they make their selection. Rawls's procedure is clearly superior to the one favored by simple contractarianism, something we can appreciate if we reconsider the two objections raised against that view. Recall, first, how simple contractarianism distorts the idea of elementary justice by permitting the contractors to assign much greater importance to their interests than they assign to the equal interests of those who are denied the opportunity to participate in framing the contract. Rawlsian contractarianism arguably will not allow this. Because contractors do not know *who they will be,* they will want to make sure that *everyone's* interests are taken into account and counted equitably. To be satisfied with anything less would be to fail to look out for one's self-interest, *whosoever* one happens to be. In this respect, Rawls's version of contractarianism is superior to the simple variety.

Rawls also has a reply to the second objection, the one that noted how simple contractarianism has morally unacceptable implications, allowing, as it does, the systematic exploitation of those not covered by the contract, members of a racial minority being an obvious example. Rawlsian contractors arguably would not permit this. Positioned as they are behind the veil of ignorance, contractors cannot know what race they will be; as such, whether they will belong to the majority race or to a racial minority is something they do not know. Lacking such knowledge, the rational choice for self-interested contractors to make arguably is one that guarantees that no group of people, including those who belong to a racial minority, will be exploited. After all, for all the contractors know, the minority race could turn out to be *their* race. Once again, therefore, the Rawlsian contractarianism is arguably superior to what I have been calling the simple version.

Though Rawls focuses on justice in particular, he notes that the procedure he favors "hold[s] for the choice of all ethical principles and not only for those of justice."[12] Seen in this light, the same language used to characterize simple contractarianism can be used to describe the Rawlsian variety. Acts are right if they conform to a valid rule, wrong if they fail to conform to (if they break) a valid rule, the validity of the rules to be determined by asking whether the self-interest of rational contractors is advanced by having everyone obey them. Where Rawls's position differs procedurally from simple contractarianism, as has already been noted, is over *how* the rules are selected and, to some degree, regarding *who* gets to participate in the selection process.

Evaluating Rawlsian Contractarianism

Rawls's "veil of ignorance" has received a good deal of criticism at the hands of some philosophers.[13] Whether this criticism is well founded or not, the "veil of ignorance" arguably helps illuminate one way to think about what is just and fair. Because we are selecting principles of justice from the point of view of our rational self-interest, to know that we will be white and male, for example, will give us powerful self-interested reasons to select principles that give the interests of white men a privileged moral status. However, fairness should be color- and gender-blind. From the point of view of justice, the interests of some people should not be ignored because of facts about their race or gender, nor should their interests be counted for less than the like interests of others. To assign a privileged moral status to the interests of some people and, implicitly, to assign a lower status to the comparable interests of others, based solely on considerations about race or gender, are classic expressions of two of the worst forms of prejudice: racism in the one case, sexism in the other. Rawls's "veil of ignorance" is designed to prevent these and other prejudices from having an undue influence in the selection of principles of justice.

But while Rawlsian contractarianism arguably denies the moral legitimacy of some of the worst prejudices, it is not entirely free of prejudicial implications. In Rawls's view, we have direct duties to all and only those humans who have "a sense of justice," understood as a "normally effective desire to apply and act on the principles of justice, at least to a minimum degree." Human infants as well as seriously mentally disadvantaged human beings of all ages do not satisfy this requirement. Even if we recognize their mental capacities (e.g., sentiency, perceptual awareness, memory, and various emotions), there is no basis for crediting them with a "sense of justice," in Rawls's sense. In this respect, therefore, Rawlsian contractarianism is indistinguishable from simple contractarianism: both deny that we owe direct duties to these human beings. And in both cases, therefore, another moral prejudice is detectable, only this time a yet-to-be named prejudice against the most vulnerable members of the extended human family.

The following example highlights the prejudice I have in mind. Suppose a mugger has pushed you to the ground and stolen your money; you are left with a number of cuts and bruises—minor, to be sure, but still painful. Alongside your condition, consider the following testimony presented by Isaac Parker before Great Britain's House of Commons Select Committee. The year is 1790. The matter before the committee, the Atlantic slave trade. Parker describes the following episode involving a sick child, who would not eat, and a Captain Marshall, who was determined to make him do so.

> The child took sulk and would not eat. . . . [T]he captain took the child up in his hand and flogged it with the cat. . . . [T]he child had swelled feet; the captain desired the cook to put on some hot water to heat to see if he could abate the swelling, and it was done. He then ordered the child's feet to be put into the water, and the cook putting his finger into the water said, "Sir, it is too hot." The captain said, "Damn it, never mind it, put the feet in," and so doing the skin and nails came off, . . . I gave the child some victuals, but it would not eat; the captain took

the child up again, and flogged it, and said, "Damn you, I will make you eat," and so he continued that way for four or five days at mess time. . . . The last time he took the child up and flogged it, and let it drop out of his hands, "Damn you (says he) I will make you eat, or I will be the death of you," and in three quarters of an hour after that the child died.[14]

Death for this poor child surely was a merciful release from the all but unimaginable pain endured. When we learn that the object of Captain Marshall's abuse was all of *nine months old,* we are (if we are normal) sickened to the core. The depths of depravity to which we humans can descend never ceases to shock. And never should.

So here we have the two cases: your relatively minor pain caused by the mugger, on the one hand; the barely imaginable pain experienced by the child, on the other. Are we to say that your pain is of direct moral relevance, because it is the pain of someone with a sense of justice but that the child's pain is not of direct moral relevance, because children lack a sense of justice? Are we to say that your minor pain counts for more, from the moral point of view, than does the much greater pain of the child, because your pain is the pain of someone with a sense of justice, the child's not? Are we to say that part of the direct wrong done to you consists of the pain the mugger has caused but that no direct wrong is done to the child, again because you have a sense of justice, something the unfortunate child lacks?

Rawls commits himself to saying all of this; I do not think there can be any question that this is where his thinking leads him. Neither, then, can there be any question (in my mind, at least) that he is guilty of a prejudicial way of thinking about the moral status of children and other human beings lacking in rational capacities. (That he is not alone in this will be shown in chapter 16, both in the discussion of moral elitism and in the assessment of Kant's ideas.) In any event, if morality is interpreted in terms of interests, as Rawls assumes, the interests of some human beings cannot be ignored and cannot count for less than the like interests of other human beings simply because some do, while others do not, have a sense of justice.

As for other-than-human animals: they do not fare well, given the Rawlsian perspective. For while the veil of ignorance shields contractors from detailed knowledge of their personal identity, there is one rather important fact they are permitted to know. Each knows that they will enter and exit the world as a human being. There can be no surprise, therefore, when Rawls denies that we have direct duties to animals. Rational, self-interested contractors *cannot* have self-interested reasons for recognizing the direct moral relevance of the interests of animals nor, therefore, any direct duties owed in their case. Why not? Because contractors know that *they* (the human contractors) will never be one of *them* (a nonhuman animal). That Rawls denies direct duties to animals thus is preordained, the outcome, in the cards as dealt.

Some critics believe that the part of Rawls's position just summarized suffers from a moral prejudice analogous to racism and sexism. The prejudice is speciesism, understood as assigning greater weight to the interests of human beings, just because they are human interests, compared with the interests of nonhuman animals, just because they are not human interests. Rawls does do this; I do not think there can be any doubt that he does. The important question is whether, in doing so, his views may be correctly and fairly described as prejudicial. I think they can.

A variation on our earlier example will help explain why. A mugger has pushed you to the ground and stolen your money; you are left with a number of cuts and bruises—minor, to be sure, but still painful. Next, let us try to imagine the pain felt by the dogs who were vivisected by the scientists at Port Royal—the dogs who, without the benefit of anesthetic, had their four paws nailed to boards before being slit open. Are we to say that your pain is of direct moral relevance, because it is human pain, but that the dogs' pain is not of direct moral relevance, because it is canine pain? Are we to say that your minor pain counts for more, from the moral point of view, than the much greater pain of the dogs, because your pain is the pain of a human being, the dogs' not? Are we to say that a direct wrong was done to you because of the pain caused by the mugger but that no direct wrong was done to the dogs, again because your pain is human pain, their pain not?

Rawls commits himself to saying all of this, too; I do not think there can be any question that he does. Neither, then, can there be any question that he is guilty of a prejudicial (if all too common, at least among philosophers) way of thinking about morality. From the point of view of elementary justice, as noted above, the interests of some human beings cannot be ignored, and cannot count for less than, the like interests of other human beings simply because they do not belong to the "right" race or gender. The same is true when it comes to species membership. From the point of view of elementary justice, the interests of animals cannot be ignored and cannot count for less than the like interests of human beings simply because animals do not belong to the "right" species. And just as it is true that assigning a privileged moral status to some people and, implicitly, assigning a lower status to others, solely on the basis of race or gender, are classic expressions of racism or sexism, so it is true that assigning a privileged moral status to human beings and, implicitly, assigning a lower status to every other animal, solely on the basis of species membership, is a classic expression of an analogous prejudice: speciesism.

Once we recognize that, save at the cost of moral prejudice, the interests of animals cannot be ignored or discounted *because they are the interests of animals,* the way is cleared for recognizing direct duties in their case. As noted earlier, direct duties are owed to those whose interests are directly morally relevant. Contrary to the Cartesians among us, nonhuman animals *have* interests; and contrary to both simple and Rawlsian contractarians, the interests of animals *are* directly morally relevant. As such, animals who have interests are owed direct duties. This is the conclusion we reach, given the preceding analysis, a conclusion that finds additional corroboration by considering the following.

Suppose I maliciously break your leg, thereby causing you serious injury and a great deal of gratuitous pain. Next, suppose I maliciously break your dog's leg, thereby causing her serious injury and a great deal of gratuitous pain. My two actions are relevantly similar: in each I do something, for no good reason, that causes another individual serious injury and a great deal of pain. Now, relevantly similar cases should be judged similarly. This principle is axiomatic if our moral thinking is to be nonarbitrary and nonprejudicial. And our moral thinking is neither in the present case if we think as follows: my maliciously breaking your leg represents my failure to fulfill a duty I have directly to you, because you have an interest in being spared serious injury and gratuitous pain, but my maliciously breaking your dog's leg does not represent a failure to fulfill a duty I have directly to your dog, even though she has a comparable interest in being spared serious injury and gratuitous pain. It is only if we are willing arbitrarily or prejudicially to judge relevantly similar cases differently that we can suppose that the duty in the one case is direct, in the other not. One of this chapter's main purposes has been to show why we should not be willing to do this.

Of course, one could, and, as we have seen, Cartesians do, deny that non-human animals are aware of anything, including pain, a maneuver that would blunt the force of the objection that Rawlsian contractarianism is prejudicial. If animals do not feel anything no matter what we do to them, it would not be prejudicial to affirm that we have a direct duty to avoid causing human beings gratuitous pain, on the one hand, and to deny that we have this same duty directly to animal beings, on the other. To his credit, Rawls is too much in the grip of a robust common sense to believe that the dogs at Port Royal were devoid of consciousness and thus did not, because they could not, suffer. Rawls's problem is not that he consorts with today's neo-Cartesians, including those who, like Carruthers, use their Cartesianism as a basis for their contractarianism; his problem is that his moral outlook prejudicially excludes nonhuman animals from direct moral concern.

Conclusion

Indirect duty views, I believe, including the most ingenious among them, and despite their several merits, are and must be unsatisfactory in general, unsatisfactory when it comes to the moral status of animals in particular. In this latter context, those who favor indirect duty views have a choice: *either* they can rest their position on the claim that animals lack interests (the Cartesian option favored by Carruthers), *or* they can rest their position on the claim that, while animals have interests, their interests are of no direct moral concern (the non-Cartesian option favored by Rawls). For reasons given in the preceding discussion, both options are unsatisfactory.

Whatever else may be in doubt, this much is clear: those animals we raise for food, trap for fur, and use in scientific research are owed direct duties. Because (by definition) indirect duty views deny direct duties in their case, every indirect duty view is, and every indirect duty view must be, mistaken. The following chapter examines two ways of thinking about morality that, even while both deny that animals have rights against us, each affirms that we have direct duties to them.

Notes

1. Polling results concerning both meat consumption and attitudes toward using animals to test medical treatments are among those found in a 2 December 1995 Associated Press telephone poll of 1,004 randomly selected adult Americans. The percentages concerning wearing fur come from a 27 December 1993 nationwide poll of 1,612 adults conducted by the *Los Angeles Times*. Exaggerated claims sometimes have been made regarding the number of vegetarians in the United States. In 1997 the Vegetarian Resource Group commissioned a Roper poll. Respondents (1,960 women and men over age eighteen) were interviewed in their homes. The result: approximately 1 percent, or 2 million of the estimated 194 million Americans over eighteen, excluding those who are institutionalized, "never eat red meat, never eat poultry, never eat fish."

2. Descartes's views about animals may be found in selections from his work in Regan and Singer, eds., *Animal Rights*.

3. The quote from Nicholas Fontaine appears in Lenora Rosenfield, *From Beast-Machine to Man-Machine* (New York: Columbia University Press, 1968), 54.

4. For the views of Peter Carruthers, see his *The Animals Issue: Moral Theory in Practice* (Cambridge: Cambridge University Press, 1992), especially chapter 8. Carruthers allows for the possibility that extraterrestrials might be conscious despite the fact that they do not use a natural language; among terrestrials, however, the ability to use such a language is necessary for conscious experience. Another neo-Cartesian, Peter Harrison, offers a quite different argument for why animals do not feel pain in "Theodicy and Animal Pain," *Philosophy* 64 (January 1989): 79–92. The views of both Carruthers and Harrison are critically examined by Evelyn Pluhar in the first chapter of *Beyond Prejudice: The Moral Significance of Human and Nonhuman Animals* (Durham, N.C.: Duke University Press, 1995). Pluhar's book includes an excellent bibliography.

5. Darwin's views are summarized in Regan and Singer, eds., *Animal Rights and Human Obligations*, 27–31. This anthology also includes several other important contributions to the literature on animal minds. For a contemporary elaboration and defense of Darwin's approach and conclusions, along with an excellent bibliography,

see Colin Allen and Marc Bekoff, *Species of Mind: The Philosophy and Biology of Cognitive Biology* (Cambridge, Mass.: MIT Press, 1997).

6. Voltaire's response to Descartes may be found in Regan and Singer, eds., *Animal Rights and Human Obligations*, 20.

7. The simple form of contractarianism I sketch takes its inspiration from some of Jan Narveson's earlier writings. See his "Animal Rights," *Canadian Journal of Philosophy* 2 (March 1977): 161–78, and "Animal Rights Revisited," in *Ethics and Animals*, ed. H. Miller and W. Williams (Clifton, N.J.: Humana, 1983), 56–58.

8. John Rawls's *A Theory of Justice* was first published by Harvard University Press in 1971. It is possible to interpret his position either narrowly or broadly. The narrow interpretation assumes that what Rawls argues is restricted to justice only; the broad interpretation assumes that what he argues is not restricted to justice only but is, instead, offered as a general account of moral right and wrong. I favor the latter interpretation and believe that the criticisms I suggest, if modified appropriately, could be pressed equally forcefully against the narrow interpretation.

9. Rawls, *A Theory of Justice*, 130.

10. Rawls, *A Theory of Justice*, 505.

11. Rawls, *A Theory of Justice*, 137.

12. Rawls, *A Theory of Justice*, 130.

13. *A Theory of Justice* has occasioned a voluminous literature. Three important recent discussions are Mark Rowlands, "Contractarianism and Animals," *Journal of Applied Philosophy* 14, no. 3 (1997): 235–47; Mark H. Bernstein, *On Moral Considerability: An Essay on Who Matters Morally* (Oxford: Oxford University Press, 1998), 151–58; and Carruthers, *The Animals Issue*, 101–03.

14. Quoted in Roger Anstey, *The Atlantic Slave Trade and British Abolition: 1760–1810* (Atlantic Highlands, N.J.: Humanities Press, 1975), 32.

15

Direct Duty Views

Humans and animals are owed direct duties. This much we know. Can we know more than this? In particular, can we know what duties are owed and why we owe them? This chapter examines two answers to these questions, each of which dispenses with the idea of rights, human rights as well as animal rights. The cruelty–kindness view, which for reasons of simplicity I will sometimes refer to as "cruelty–kindness," is discussed first; this is followed by a discussion of a particular interpretation of the position known as utilitarianism. Both moral outlooks are examples of direct duty views—views that, in contrast to each and every indirect duty view, maintain that nonhuman animals are owed direct duties.

The Cruelty–Kindness View

Simply stated, the cruelty–kindness view maintains that we have a direct duty to be kind to animals and a direct duty not to be cruel to them. To say that the duty of kindness is direct means that kindness is owed to animals themselves, not to those humans who might be affected by how animals are treated. And the same is true of the prohibition against cruelty: our duty not to be cruel is owed to them directly.

Some philosophers who favor kindness and condemn cruelty to animals deny that the duty in either case is direct. These philosophers encourage kindness and discourage cruelty to animals because of the effect these behaviors have on human character and what this portends for how humans will be treated. Writes the great Prussian philosopher Immanuel Kant, "Tender feelings toward dumb animals develop humane feelings towards mankind." That is why we should be kind to animals. As for cruelty: "[H]e who is cruel to animals becomes hard also in his dealings with men." That is why we should not be cruel to them.[1]

Kant is not alone in thinking this way. The seventeenth-century English philosopher, John Locke, shares the same perspective. "One thing I have frequently observed in Children," Locke writes:

> that when they have got possession of any poor creature they are apt to use it ill. They often torment, and treat very roughly, young Birds, Butterflies, and such other poor Animals, which fall into their Hands, and that with a seeming kind of Pleasure. This I think should be watched in them if they incline to any such Cruelty, they should be taught the contrary Usage. For the Custom of Tormenting and Killing of Beasts, will, by Degrees, harden their Minds even towards Men; and they who delight in the Suffering and Destruction of Inferior Creatures, will not be apt to be very compassionate, or benign to those of their own kind.[2]

Both Kant and Locke are on the side of truth when it comes to human moral development. Recent studies confirm what people of common sense have long suspected, that a pattern of cruelty to animals in a person's youth is frequently correlated with a pattern of violent behavior towards humans in adult life.[3] This is certainly *a* reason to discourage cruelty to animals. Still, this cannot be the *only* reason, nor can it be the *main* one, if cruelty–kindness is interpreted as a direct duty view. Interpreted in this way, both the duty to be kind and the duty not to be cruel are owed to animals themselves.

The cruelty–kindness view makes an important contribution to our understanding of morality. First, by recognizing that direct duties are owed to non-human animals, it overcomes the prejudice of speciesism common to both simple and Rawlsian versions of contractarianism. Second, any credible moral outlook arguably should find a place for kindness and against cruelty, not only when it comes to how animals are treated but also when it comes to our treatment of one another. Cruelty–kindness succeeds in this respect, too, which is another reason it represents an important advance over the versions of contractarianism considered in the previous chapter.

If fully generalized, moreover, cruelty–kindness offers the broad outlines of a distinctive moral vision. Right acts are right because they are acts of kindness; wrong acts are wrong because they are acts of cruelty. Analogous direct duty views might select a different pair of comparable polar moral opposites. For example, an ethic of love would assert that acts are right if they are expressive of love, wrong if they are expressive of hate. Other candidates are compassion and indifference, or reverence for life and malice towards life. Although the focus here is on cruelty–kindness, I believe the logic of my criticisms encompasses these and other relevantly similar positions. All such views, I believe, confuse assessments of the *moral character* people display in acting as they do with assessments of the *morality of the acts* they perform.

To understand the cruelty–kindness view obviously presupposes that we understand the two key ideas: cruelty, on the one hand, and kindness, on the other. To take up the latter idea first: People express kindness when they act out of concern for or with compassion toward another. Kindness moves us to do things that advance the well-being of others, either by finding ways to satisfy their preference interests (what they are interested in having or doing) or by tending to their welfare interests (what is in their interests). For many of us, perhaps even for all, the best people we know are generous when it comes to kindness, freely giving of their time, effort, and, when possible, money to those in need. The world, we think, would be a much better place if there were more kind people in it.

The vice of cruelty occupies a moral space opposite to that of kindness. People or their acts are cruel if they display either a lack of sympathy for (what I will call "indifferent cruelty") or positive enjoyment in another's suffering (referred to as "sadistic cruelty"). Recall the words Locke uses when he describes the cruelty he sometimes finds in children: they "torment" their victim, treat their victim "very roughly," "use (their victim) ill," and do so "with a seeming kind of Pleasure." Some children, Locke is saying, are sadistically cruel. That he limits his comments to children who are cruel to animals should not obscure the fact that the same things define sadistic cruelty to humans. Anytime anyone enjoys making anybody suffer, sadistic cruelty rears its ugly head.

Evaluating Cruelty–Kindness

As has been remarked already, too few people have the virtue of kindness. Nevertheless, and notwithstanding its cherished status, the presence of kindness is no guarantee of right action. While being motivated by kindness is a good thing as far as it goes, there is no guarantee that a kind act is the right act. Someone who helps a child abuser find new victims doubtless acts kindly toward the abuser. But none of us will infer that helping the abuser is therefore the right thing to do. The virtue of kindness is one thing; the moral rightness of our actions another.

Cruelty fares no better as a general criterion of moral wrongness. Cruelty in all its guises is a bad thing, a lamentable human failing, something that, while it is not restricted to people who exploit animals, is not unknown in their case either. Consider the following passage from Joan Dunayer, describing observations made by sociologist Mary Phillips during her three-year study (1985–87) of practices in two research laboratories in the New York City area:

In one laboratory, a rat placed on a small box had his head immobilized by a vise. When a postdoctoral vivisector started drilling into his skull, the rat began to struggle. Held by the head, he attempted to run. His lower body fell over the box's edge. The rat dangled there, struggling. The drilling continued. Some minutes later, the rat kicked the box over, forcing the vivisector to stop and inject him with some anesthetic. Before the anesthetic took effect, the vivisector resumed drilling. Again the rat struggled. Finally, ten minutes into the vivisection, the rat quieted.[4]

Here we have a disturbing case of what appears to be indifferent cruelty: someone who, without empathy or sympathy, chooses to inflict pain even while in possession of the means to prevent it. Next, as an example of sadistic cruelty, consider the behavior Gail Eisnitz documents in her book about the American slaughter industry in general, hog slaughter in particular.[5]

Hog slaughter represents a variation on the main theme of the meat packing industry. Hogs are driven up a narrow restrainer where the "stunner" gives them an electric shock that is supposed to render them unconscious. They are then shackled with chains attached to their rear legs, hoisted so that they dangle upside down, and placed on a conveyor belt where they meet the "sticker," whose job is to slit the animals' throats. After being bled to death, the pigs are submerged in a tank of boiling water, then eviscerated, having never regained consciousness. At least this is the way things are supposed to work in theory. As a matter of practice, as Eisnitz found after speaking with workers, actual hog slaughter frequently does not measure up to theory.

The following is a not atypical example, from an interview with Donny Tice and Alec Wainwright (to protect her sources, Eisnitz changed their names). In an earlier conversation, Tice had described some of the things he did to the hogs. It was now Wainwright's turn. Writes Eisnitz:

> Not yet out of his teens, Wainwright had already been working as a day-shift shackler for two years.
>
> Wainwright talked about the same games as Tice had—the stun operator would intentionally misstun hogs so that Wainwright would have a hard time shackling them.
>
> "Sometimes," he said, "when the chain stops for a little while and we have time to screw around with the hog, we'll half stun it. It'll start freakin out, going crazy. It'll be sitting there yelping."
>
> Other times, when a hog would get loose outside the catch pen, [Wainwright] and his co-workers would chase it up to the scalding tank and force it to jump in. "When that happens," he said, "we tell the foreman he accidentally jumped in."
>
> Wainwright had little new to add to what Tice had already told me, but he did confirm Tice's claims of gratuitous cruelty to the animals. And while Tice's confession had seemed both painful and cathartic for him, Wainwright, in telling me

of his atrocities against the already doomed pigs, chortled with delight as if recounting a schoolboy prank.

"Why do you do it?," I asked.

"Because it's something to do," Wainwright said. "Like when our utility guy takes the ol' bar and beats the hell out of the hogs in the catch pen. That's kind of fun. I do it, too."

"How often do you do it?"

"I dunno," he replied. . . .[6]

To "beat the hell" out of an animal and find it "kind of fun" illustrates the depths of cruelty to which we humans can sink. Perhaps Eisnitz is correct when she sees workers like Tice and Wainwright, not just the pigs going to slaughter, as victims of the system of mechanized death that defines day-to-day activities in America's 2,700 slaughterhouses. But even if this is true, there can be no doubt that indifferent and sadistic cruelty are not strangers among the men and women who work in the packing industry, nor any doubt that the existence of such cruelty leaves a major moral question unanswered. For just as knowing that an act is kind does not guarantee that it is right, so the presence of cruelty does not guarantee that what is done is wrong. Here is an example from another quarter that illustrates the distinctions at issue.

Most physicians who perform abortions are not cruel people; they are not indifferent to the pain they cause, and neither do they enjoy causing it. Still, it is possible that some physicians bring a warped moral sense to their work; in their case, nothing pleases them more than making those in their care suffer. The existence of cruel abortionists certainly is a possibility. Suppose it is more than that; suppose there actually are such physicians. Even granting that there are, it should be clear that the existence of cruel abortionists would not make abortion wrong, any more than the existence of kind abortionists would make abortion right. To think otherwise is to confuse moral assessments of what people do (whether what someone does is right or wrong) with assessments of the their moral character, their virtues and vices. The two are logically distinct. People can do what is wrong while acting from a good motive (recall the person who as an act of kindness helps the child abuser find new victims) just as people can do what is right from a bad motive. It happens every day.

The logical distinction between (1) morally assessing people and (2) morally assessing their acts applies as much to cruelty and kindness to animals as it does to cruelty and kindness to humans. Here is an example that illustrates the general point. Suppose some researchers who experiment on cats are more considerate than some of their peers. They try to make the cats comfortable and use analgesics to eliminate their pain. Their peers, by contrast, are cruel; they are largely indifferent to or enjoy the pain they deliberately inflict on the cats. Without a doubt we would think better of the former researchers than we do of the latter. But what we think of them *as people* goes no way toward determining the morality of what they *do*—namely, use cats in research. Whether *that* is right or wrong depends on the morality of what they do, not on the qualities of character they exhibit in doing it. Indeed, even if it were true that none of the animals exploited for food, fashion, and knowledge are treated cruelly, that would not tell us whether exploiting them for these purposes is right. Or wrong. The existence of kind exploiters of animals does not make exploiting them right, any more than the existence of cruel abortionists makes abortion wrong. Moral assessments of people are, and they should be kept, distinct from moral assessments of what they do. Cruelty–kindness blurs this distinction. Wherever the truth about moral right and wrong might lie, it will not be found in the cruelty–kindness view.

Utilitarianism

Some people think the direct duty view we are looking for is utilitarianism. Like contractarianism, utilitarianism takes different forms, and while it is an exaggeration to say that there are as many forms of utilitarianism as there are utilitarians, the position does seem to be a breeding ground for internal dissent. Understandably, therefore, what I have to say will be selective. Having duly acknowledged this limitation, it is worth noting that the particular form of utilitarianism I discuss, preference utilitarianism (which, for reasons of simplicity, I sometimes refer to as "utilitarianism"), is the one favored by both Peter Singer and R. G. Frey, the two philosophers who have had the most influence in the area of ethics and animals, approached from a utilitarian perspective.[7]

Preference utilitarians accept two principles. The first is a principle of equality: everyone's preferences count, and similar preferences must be counted as having similar weight or importance. White or black, American or Iraqi, human or animal: what each individual is interested in, what each wants to do or have, matters, and matters just as much as the equivalent interests of anyone else. The second principle utilitarians accept (about which I will have more to say later) is that of utility: we ought to do the act that brings about the best overall balance between totaled preference satisfactions and totaled preference frustrations for everyone affected.

Preference utilitarians give a simple answer to questions about moral right and wrong. Acts are right if they lead to the best overall consequences (the best overall balance between totaled preference satisfactions and totaled preference frustrations) for everyone affected, while acts that result in less than the best overall consequences are more or less wrong, depending on how bad the consequences are. For utilitarians, our acts are like arrows that, when right, hit the moral "bull's-eye" and that, when wrong, miss the target by a greater or lesser amount.

Part of utilitarianism's enduring appeal is its uncompromising egalitarianism: *everyone's* preferences count, and count as much as the like preferences of anyone else. If you are interested in listening to Brahms, that counts. If someone else is interested in listening to Boys II Men, that counts, too. And if the preferences in both cases are equal, then their satisfaction or frustration count the same. The morally prejudicial discrimination that simple contractarianism can justify, where greater weight may be given to the interests of some human beings just because they belong to a favored race or gender, for example, is disallowed by utilitarianism. The same is true when it comes to prejudicial discrimination based on species membership, or speciesism, understood as assigning greater weight to the interests of human beings just because they are human interests. Both simple and Rawlsian contractarianism are hospitable to this latter prejudice. Not utilitarianism. For utilitarians, *we owe it to animals themselves* to take their preferences into account and to count their preferences fairly. Our duty in this case is a direct duty to animal beings, not an indirect duty to human beings. In these respects, utilitarianism is a more credible way to think about morality than the way favored by any indirect duty view.

Utilitarianism also represents an important advance over cruelty–kindness. That view, as we have seen, assumes that the morality of what people do is tied to the character traits they exhibit in doing it. This is not true, and utilitarians have an explanation of why it is not. From their perspective, acts are right or wrong depending on their consequences (their results, their effects). Clearly, *why* people act as they do is not one of the consequences, results, or effects of *what* they do. If the kind helper in the earlier discussion of cruelty–kindness is successful, the child abuser will have new children to torment; having these children available will be among the consequences, results, or effects of what is done. That the abuser's helper was motivated by kindness is in a different category altogether. For utilitarians, the character traits people express in acting as they do add nothing to the moral assessment of what they do. On this important matter, utilitarianism proves to be more credible than cruelty–kindness.

Two other important features of preference utilitarianism require further comment. The first concerns what has morally relevant value; the second, what "best overall consequences" means. Regarding the question of value first: preference utilitarians believe that morally relevant positive value resides in the satisfaction of an individual's preferences, while morally relevant negative value is found when an individual's preferences are frustrated. In both cases—that is, both in the case of what has positive value and in the case of what has negative value—it is the satisfaction or frustration of what individuals are interested in, what they want to do or have, that matters morally, not the individual whose preferences they are. A universe in which you satisfy your desires for water, food, and warmth is, other things being equal, morally better than a universe in which these desires are frustrated. And the same is true in the case of an animal with similar desires. But neither you nor the animal has any morally significant value in your own right.

Here is an analogy to help make the philosophical point clearer. Imagine that some cups contain different liquids, some sweet, some bitter, some a mix of the two. What has value are the liquids: the sweeter, the better; the bitterer, the worse. The cups have no value. It is what goes into them, not what they go into, that has value. For the utilitarian, human beings are like cups. We have no morally significant value as the individuals we are and thus no equal value. What has morally significant value is what "goes into us," so to speak, the mental states for which we serve as "containers." Our feelings of satisfaction have positive value; our feelings of frustration, negative value.

It is also important to be clear about what utilitarians mean by "best overall consequences." This does not mean the best consequences for me alone, or for my family and friends, or for any other person or group taken individually. Instead, to make a fully informed judgment about the best *overall* consequences, a threefold procedure should be followed. First, we need to identify the satisfactions and frustrations of everyone who will be affected by the choices we might make (e.g., by placing the satisfactions in one column, the frustrations in another). Second, we must total all the satisfactions and frustrations for each of the possible actions we are considering. Third, we must determine which act will bring about the best overall balance of totaled satisfactions compared to totaled frustrations. After we have satisfied these procedural requirements, but not before, we are in a position to reach a fully informed moral conclusion. Whatever choice leads to the best overall consequences is where our moral duty lies, and that choice—the one that will bring about the best overall results—will not necessarily lead to the best results for me personally, or for my family or my friends, or for a chimpanzee in a lab. The best *overall* consequences for everyone concerned are not necessarily the best for each concerned individual.

Evaluating Preference Utilitarianism

I believe preference utilitarianism, despite its appealing features, is not a satisfactory way to think about morality. The position, as I understand it, is seriously flawed, both procedurally and substantively. Procedurally, it is flawed because it requires that we count the worst sorts of preferences (what I will call "evil preferences") in reaching a fully informed judgment of moral right or wrong; substantively, it is flawed because, after the necessary calculations have been completed, the worst sorts of acts (what I will call "evil outcomes") can be justified. Later in this chapter, and again in chapter 16, I offer my own account of these two kinds of evil. In the present context, I assume that people of good will who are not already committed to utilitarianism will recognize what I mean by these ideas and will agree with the specific judgments I make. I begin with an example of evil preferences.[8]

A few years ago the nightly news followed a tragic story involving four young boys who gang-raped a mentally disadvantaged girl from their neighborhood. What the boys wanted was not sex in the abstract; what they wanted was sex forced on a defenseless girl. After each of the boys "took his turn," they beat their exhausted victim and then repeatedly shoved a baseball bat into her vagina.

Preference utilitarians will want to assure us that their moral outlook has the wherewithal to explain why what the boys did was wrong. In addition to the terrible things done to the victim, a fully informed moral judgment will have to consider the bad consequences for others, including the anxiety and fear experienced both by the parents in the neighborhood and by the other young girls who lived there. Let us assume, for the sake of argument, that utilitarians are able to cite enough bad consequences to support their judgment of wrongdoing. This certainly is the right result. Utilitarianism's first problem concerns the procedure used to get there. That procedure requires that *everyone's* preferences be taken into account and counted fairly. The poor victim's suffering? Yes. The anxiety of the neighborhood's parents? Yes. Their daughters' fears? Yes. The vicious rapists' preferences? Yes, indeed. Not to take *their* preferences into account would be to treat them unfairly.

How otherwise sensible, sensitive people, people whose philosophical abilities I admire and whose character I respect, can subscribe to a view with this implication always has been, is now, and always will remain a mystery to me. Are we to count the preferences of child abusers before condemning child abuse? Those of slaveholders before denouncing slavery? The very idea of guaranteeing a place for these preferences in the "moral calculus" is, as I am sure Professor Cohen would agree, morally offensive. We are not to evaluate the violation of human dignity by first asking how much the violators want to do it. The preferences of those who act in this way should play no role whatsoever in the determination of the wrong they do. That is part of what it means to judge the preferences evil.

For its part, preference utilitarianism is unable to deny a rightful place for such preferences, if our judgment is to be fully informed. Consistent preference utilitarians cannot say, "What the boys did was wrong, which is why we do not have to count their preferences." Consistent utilitarians cannot say this because, from their perspective, a fully informed moral judgment cannot be made before the necessary calculations have been carried out, and the necessary calculations cannot be carried out without including the preferences of the rapists. Consistency is a virtue, certainly. But consistency is no guarantee of truth. Any credible position concerning the nature of morality should be able to explain why some preferences simply do not count in the determination of moral right and wrong. Because utilitarians who are consistent will count the rapists' preferences in reaching a fully informed judgment concerning the morality of what the boys did, we have reason enough, I believe, to look for a better way to understand what makes right acts right, wrong acts wrong.

The logic of this line of criticism includes more than the preferences of the direct agents of wrongdoing. Imagine that other boys in the neighborhood wanted to watch the rape and derived satisfaction from doing so; then the procedure favored by utilitarians will oblige us to count their preferences, too, before reaching a fully informed moral judgment about the morality of what took place. This cannot be right. If the preferences of the rapists should play no role in the determination of the morality of their actions, the same is no less true of the preferences of those who support and approve of the wrongdoing of others; their preferences do not count, either.

In addition to its flawed procedure, preference utilitarianism also can be faulted for the conclusions it reaches. Not only can the worst sorts of acts be permitted; they can emerge as positively obligatory, judged by utilitarian standards. The murder of the innocent illustrates the general problem. All that is necessary to justify this evil is that the best overall consequences obtain, something that can happen in the real world, not just in futuristic works of science fiction. The elderly and people of all ages with serious disabilities, for example, often are a burden to their families and society in general. It is, I think, undeniably true that better *overall* consequences would result, in some of these cases, if some of these people had their lives humanely terminated. Would we be doing anything wrong if we participated in killing such a person, someone innocent of any serious moral or legal crime, someone not facing imminent death, someone who wants to go on living? Not according to a consistent preference utilitarianism. To kill the innocent in such cases—to murder them—not only is not wrong; assuming their murder brings about the best overall consequences, all things considered, murdering the innocent is morally obligatory. Few, if any, utilitarians will welcome this result.

In response to this line of criticism, some preference utilitarians (Singer is one of the principal architects of this way of thinking) note that, unlike flowers or snails, the victims in our example have various desires about the future, including the desire to go on living. To end their life, to murder them, means that these desires will never be satisfied. Even if we arranged to bring a new human being into existence, one whose life prospects were generally better than the quality of life the victims experienced, that, it may be argued, would not change two important facts: (1) if someone is murdered, then that person's desires, including the desire to go on living, will never be satisfied; and (2) the newly conceived "replacement," given the total absence of mind in the case of the human embryo, cannot have any desire, including the desire to go on living. In this sense, and for these reasons, individuals who want to go on living are said to be "irreplaceable."

Suppose this is true. What difference does it make, what difference can it make, to a preference utilitarian? If we are told that murdering an irreplaceable individual is always wrong no matter what the consequences, we no longer have a consistent utilitarianism. If utilitarianism means anything, it means this: Whether *any* act is right or wrong *always* depends on the consequences for all those affected by the outcome, something that cannot change just in case someone is "irreplaceable."

A consistent preference utilitarian, therefore, must recognize that the morality of murdering the innocent depends on the consequences, all things considered. So let us again describe the sort of case we are considering. Before us is someone who is a burden to family and society, someone who is not going to die soon, someone who prefers to go on living. Let us concede the existence of this important preference. Nevertheless, that is all the desire to go on living is: a preference, one that, like every other preference, must be included in the utilitarian calculus and one that, as is true of every other preference, can be outweighed by aggregating the preference satisfactions of others. To express the same point using different words: a consistent utilitarian must acknowledge that the desire to go on living cannot have the status of a "trump" and thus can be outweighed by the preferences other people have. Given the complexities of life, there is no reason to deny, and abundant reason to affirm, that, *in some cases*, others would be better off if steps were taken to end the lives of people who want to go on living.

From the perspective of a consistent preference utilitarianism, therefore, murdering the innocent not only is not always wrong; if the consequences for all concerned are "the best," murdering them is morally obligatory. It should not be surprising, therefore, that people with disabilities, who sometimes are a burden to family and society, have publicly expressed fears about their safety, should the day come when the public embraces a utilitarian moral outlook. In my opinion, their fears are entirely justified. A moral philosophy that subscribes to the principle that the end justifies the means potentially places everyone's life in jeopardy, the life of the least powerful in particular.

The moral logic of the preceding criticism of utilitarianism is not limited only to the murder of the innocent. On the contrary, this same kind of criticism can be repeated, in all sorts of cases, illustrating time after time how the preference utilitarian's position leads to results that impartial people of goodwill, people who are not already committed to utilitarianism, will find morally wrong. Lying, cheating, stealing, failing to carry out a solemn promise, arranging to imprison or execute people who are known to be innocent of any crime—all these and countless other acts emerge as right, even obligatory, if the benefits for others outweigh the preferences of the victims. Judged purely in terms of the evil outcomes it can permit or require, preference utilitarianism, even acknowledging its strengths when compared to the other moral positions reviewed in the preceding pages, is not an adequate way to think about how human beings should treat one another.

Utilitarianism's implications concerning how we should treat other animals, as is true of everything else, depends on the overall consequences, about which informed, fair-minded people can disagree. A cursory look at commercial animal agriculture illustrates the general point.

In the case of raising and slaughtering animals for food, relevant consequences include how these animals are treated, certainly. Also relevant are the effects of a meat-based diet on human morbidity and mortality; the environmental impact, both of factory farming itself and of the crop production required to feed animals raised in close confinement; the interests of distant strangers, people who live in the poorer nations of the world and who succumb to, or live on the edge of, the ravages of famine, and who might conceivably be fed if better-off people ate no or much less meat; and the interests of generations of the yet unborn, assuming that not-yet-existing people, and not-yet-existing animals, have interests.

From a utilitarian perspective, however, fairness requires that we consider much more. For example, the number of Americans whose lives are directly or indirectly linked to current forms of animal agriculture is hardly inconsiderable. Figures provided in the 1996 edition of *Statistical Abstract of the United States* place the number of those who operate and manage animal agricultural operations, along with those who work at such operations or hold jobs directly related to the meat industry, at over 4.5 million. Total farm income from animal production, including dairy and eggs, for that same period, is listed as $154 billion, while the U.S. Department of Labor gives the figure of $4.9 billion as the amount of taxes paid by farms of all types in 1994, the most recent year for which tax estimates are available at the time this is written. Add to these figures the millions of other people whose livelihood is indirectly tied to farm animal production, from truckers to young people flipping burgers at the neighborhood McDonald's; plus the millions of others who are the dependents of those whose economic situation is directly or indirectly related to meat production; plus the dietary tastes and preferences of the 99 percent of Americans who like eating meat and spend their money accordingly—add all this together and we begin to glimpse both the magnitude of the massive impact animal agriculture has on the United States economy and the costs, financial as well as personal, of abolishing commercial animal agriculture as we know it.

With such large numbers, representing far from trivial human interests, there is little wonder that different people can reach different conclusions about whether raising animals in factory farm conditions is right or wrong, judged from a utilitarian perspective. If it were possible for utilitarians to deny the moral relevance of human interests and to focus instead on how the animals are treated, then the utilitarian case against contemporary animal agriculture would be clear-cut. The aggregate of the harms done to the billions of animals raised and slaughtered annually in the United States is vast given any reasonable estimate. But a consistent preference utilitarianism cannot do this; by its very nature, it cannot exclude relevant human interests, including those of farmers, their families, and the majority of American consumers. Before the preference utilitarian can render a fully informed moral evaluation of animal agriculture, therefore, *all* the relevant interests must be taken into account and evaluated fairly.

Let us suppose that somebody is somehow able to carry out all the necessary calculations. Who can say what the results would be? Certainly no utilitarian to my knowledge has made a thoroughly convincing, a thoroughly documented, case either in defense of the morality of animal agriculture or in favor of the obligation to become a vegetarian. Those who in the past have argued for vegetarianism from a utilitarian perspective, in my judgment, have offered at most a promissory note in place of the massive amount of detailed empirical, especially economic, data their position requires and which advocates of the position are duty bound to provide.

Is it necessary to collect all this data? From a utilitarian perspective, the answer is obvious: without the data, objectively obtained, moral judgments have no objective basis. So reasons the utilitarian. But what of those of us who are not already committed to this moral outlook—should we agree? If the preceding discussion of utilitarianism is sound, this outlook is doubly flawed; flawed, first, because it gives evil preferences a role in the moral evaluation of what people do, and flawed, second, because it turns acts that are wrong (the murder of the innocent, for example) into acts that are right. These flaws are not minor by any means—just the opposite.

Here is an abstract way to illustrate this criticism. Suppose a given act, A, turns out to be morally right when assessed by preference utilitarianism's standards. And suppose this moral verdict is rendered on the basis of calculating the overall preference satisfaction score, using preferences x, y, z. Given the evil outcomes utilitarianism can sanction, are we to conclude that A is right? And given the evil preferences it must count, are we to say that the preferences x, y, and z are all morally aboveboard?

The answer to both questions clearly is no. To show that A is right, according to the utilitarian standard, is no guarantee that A *is right;* and to count preferences x, y, and z in the utilitarian calculus is no guarantee that *there is nothing morally evil, nothing morally problematic,* about these preferences.

This much acknowledged, the general conclusion toward which the earlier critique of utilitarianism has been leading should be clear. Notwithstanding its many merits, the position emerges as so seriously flawed that it fails to provide a reliable standard by reference to which moral right and wrong can be determined. Because it fails to provide such a standard, utilitarian calculation, while it may be relevant for some purposes, should play no role whatsoever when the purpose is to decide what is fundamentally morally right and wrong.

Rejection of utilitarianism has important consequences for our moral thinking in general, our thinking about how animals should be treated in particular. In the case of animal agriculture, to continue with this example, a careful, exhaustive analysis of overall consequences would support one of three conclusions: (1) The current system of animal agriculture leads to better overall consequences than any alternative. (2) The current system leads to worse overall consequences than other alternatives. (3) The current system leads to overall consequences that are equal to those that would flow from other alternatives. If the first option were shown to be true, nothing would follow regarding the moral acceptability of the current system; if the second, nothing would follow concerning the moral acceptability of the current system; and the same is true of the third alternative. In short, *whatever* the overall consequences happen to be, the central moral question, "Is the current system morally acceptable?" will remain unanswered.

When it comes to evaluating the morality of how humans *or* animals are treated, and, in the case of animals, whether the question concerns their treatment in contemporary agriculture or in some other exploitative context, we do well to resist utilitarian calculations. The next chapter offers a fresh start, one that, I believe, leads to a more satisfactory way to think about morality than any of the views considered up to now.

Notes

1. The quotes from Kant may be found in Regan and Singer, *Animal Rights and Human Obligations,* 24.

2. *The Educational Writings of John Locke,* ed. James Axtfell (Cambridge: Cambridge University Press, 1968), 225–26.

3. Social scientists have demonstrated a pattern of childhood abuse of animals among convicted violent criminals. See, for example, Stephen R. Kellert and Alan R. Felthouse, "Childhood Cruelty toward Animals among Criminals and Noncriminals," *Human Relations* 38 (1985): 1113–29. For a more recent work devoted to the same subject, see Randall Lockwood and Frank R. Ascione, eds., *Cruelty to Animals and Interpersonal Violence: Readings in Research and Application* (West Lafayette, Ind.: Purdue University Press, 1998).

4. Joan Dunayer, *Animal Equality: Language and Liberation* (Derwood, Md.: Ryce Publishing, 2001), 107. The work by Mary Phillips to which Dunayer refers is the former's unpublished dissertation, "Constructing Laboratory Animals: An Ethnographic Study in the Sociology of Science," New York University, 1991.

5. Eisnitz, *Slaughterhouse* (Amherst, N.Y.: Prometheus, 1997).

6. Eisnitz, *Slaughterhouse*, 97–98.

7. For Peter Singer's views regarding ethics and animals, see *Animal Liberation*, 2d ed. (New York: Random House, 1990), and *Practical Ethics* (Cambridge: Cambridge University Press, 1979). Singer's views regarding irreplaceability and the wrongness of killing are more fully developed in the latter work than they are in the former. Among R. G. Frey's relevant publications are *Interests and Rights: The Case against Animals* (Oxford: Clarendon, 1980), and *Rights, Killing, and Suffering* (Oxford: Basil Blackwell, 1983).

8. A possible account of evil preferences would include preferences other than those that are tied to rights violations. People who gratuitously deface or destroy works of art, for example, might be construed to be acting on evil preferences even if works of art lack rights. For present purposes, this matter can be left unresolved. It is enough that my account offers a sufficient condition for classifying preferences as evil.

16

Human Rights

The previous two chapters examined a number of influential moral outlooks; while each contains something of enduring importance, all are arguably deficient in fundamental respects. Is it possible to fashion a way to think about morality that has none of their weaknesses and all of their strengths? If so, where might one begin?

The place to begin, I think, is with the utilitarian's view of the value of the individual—or, rather, lack of value. That individuals lack morally significant value is a central tenet of utilitarianism, something that was illustrated in the previous chapter by means of the analogy of cups and their contents. It is not the cups themselves (not the individuals we are) that have morally significant value; rather, it is what the cups contain (the quality of our experiences, the satisfaction or frustration of our interests) that have such value.

Suppose we conceptualize the matter differently. Instead of thinking that *the interests individuals have* are what has fundamental moral value, we think that it is *the individuals who have interests* who have such value. To think about morality in this way is Kantian in spirit, though, as we shall see, not Kantian in letter. Kant gives the name "worth" to the kind of value under discussion; I prefer "inherent value"—"inherent" because the kind of value in question belongs to those individuals who have it (it is not something conferred on them as the result of a contract, for example) and "value" because what is being designated is not some merely factual feature shared by these individuals but is instead their equal moral status. To say that individuals are inherently valuable is to say that they are something more than, and in fact something different from, mere receptacles of valued mental states. In our case, it is the persons we are, not the positive or negative feelings we experience, that have fundamental moral value.

191

To refer to our working analogy, it is the cups, not the liquids they contain, that have such value.

In his philosophy, Kant interprets worth in terms of what he calls "end in itself." He means that human beings are not of merely instrumental value. Kant is not denying that we can be useful as a means to one another, as when a plumber fixes a leaky faucet or a dentist fills a tooth; instead, he is affirming that it is wrong to treat one another *merely* as means. The Tuskegee syphilis study described earlier illustrates how human beings are sometimes treated in this way. The men who volunteered were not told what their true condition was or what the pills they were given really contained; instead, they were treated merely as means to learning new facts about the effects of the disease if left untreated—facts that, it was thought, might benefit those who contracted syphilis in the future. For Kant, whenever we take informed choice away from persons or coercively impose our will on them, in pursuit of some selfish or social good, what we do is morally wrong. We reduce the moral worth of persons to what is instrumentally valuable, ignoring their inherent value. We treat *somebodies* as if they were *somethings*.

By way of general answers to the basic moral questions we have been asking, the initial statement of the position I favor comes to this. Those individuals who possess inherent value are owed the direct duty of respectful treatment, meaning they are never to be treated as if they are of merely instrumental value. In general, what makes right acts right is that individuals who possess such value are treated with respect, while what makes wrong acts wrong is that these same individuals, like the men used in the Tuskegee study, for example, are not treated respectfully.

The Duty of Respect

It is one thing to describe a moral outlook; it is quite another thing to offer reasons why anyone should accept it. What reasons can be given in the present case? And how compelling are they?

The grounds for recognizing the direct duty to treat one another with respect grow out of the objections raised against the moral outlooks discussed in the previous two chapters. As we have seen, simple contractarianism (Rawls's treatment of contractarianism is taken up near the end of this chapter) makes a valuable contribution when it emphasizes the importance of reason in determining what is morally right and wrong; but this same position can be faulted because it permits those who frame the contract prejudicially to exploit those who are excluded, the members of racial minorities being among the obvious candidates. Any adequate moral outlook should prohibit such prejudicial exclusion. The view I favor does. For reasons that will become clearer as we proceed, the duty of respect is owed to all persons, regardless of their race, gender, intellectual abilities, sexual orientation, and age, for example.

Any adequate moral outlook must not only avoid speciesism; it must also recognize that direct duties are owed to animals. Simple contractarianism fails to do this; cruelty–kindness succeeds, at least in intent. Cruelty–kindness also succeeds in recognizing what any adequate moral outlook must, that cruelty should be discouraged, and kindness encouraged, both in our dealings with one another and in our dealings with other animals. Nevertheless, an adequate moral outlook must be able to distinguish between moral assessments of what people do, on the one hand, and moral assessments of the character they display in doing it, on the other.

As has been argued, cruelty–kindness is unable to distinguish between these two very different kinds of moral assessment. By contrast, the position I favor clearly distinguishes between them. Recall the four rapists. Imagine that all four were sadistically cruel, each taking intense pleasure in abusing their victim, or imagine that all four were coolly indifferent to the pain and fear they caused. In either case, we could not help but look upon the four teenagers as seriously morally deformed, lacking those feelings that help define the minimal moral expectations of being human. Even so, the cruelty exhibited in such behavior is and must be kept distinct from the moral wrong done. Having a cruel character would help explain why the rapists did the wrong they did; it would not explain why what they did was wrong. The view I favor, by contrast, offers a clear explanation of the wrong done: what the rapists did was wrong because they treated their victim with a lack of respect, treating her as a mere thing, valuable only because she satisfied their desires.

Utilitarianism arguably overcomes the weaknesses of both simple contractarianism and cruelty–kindness while preserving the strengths of each. As is true of simple contractarianism, utilitarianism assigns reason a key role in determining moral right and wrong; and as is true of cruelty–kindness, utilitarianism recognizes that direct duties are owed to animals. In addition, the kinds of prejudice that simple contractarianism can permit, ranging from racism to speciesism, arguably are disallowed by utilitarianism's insistence on counting equal interests equally; and whereas cruelty-kindness is unable clearly to distinguish between moral assessments of what people do, and moral assessments of the character they display in doing it, utilitarianism satisfies this requirement, too. With so many important strengths to its credit, utilitarianism is an appealing moral outlook.

All things considered, I think we can do better. While the differences between the position I favor and utilitarianism are many, highlighting two will be enough for present purposes. As we have seen, consistent utilitarians are logically committed to counting any and every preference, no matter how bad these preferences are; only after we have done this can we make a fully informed judgment about what is right and wrong. This is why the preferences of the rapists count just as much as the comparably important preferences of anyone else, including those of their victim. An adequate moral outlook should be able to explain why preferences like those of the rapists are beyond the moral pale. On my view, they are. The preferences of the rapists, let alone their satisfaction, play no role whatsoever in the moral assessment of what they did. From the moral point of view, the question is not "What desires did the boys satisfy by treating their victim as they did?" but "How did they treat her?" *How* they treated her is straightforward: they treated her as if she were a thing, as if she lacked morally significant value in her own right; fundamentally, that is why what they did was the grievous wrong it was, something that is true, and something we can know to be true, independently of knowing what the rapists wanted. Thus, one way to characterize what evil preferences are is the following: Evil preferences are those preferences that, if acted on, lead people to treat inherently valuable individuals merely as means, as if they were things, having instrumental value only. (I offer an alternative analysis of evil preferences at the end of this chapter.)

Second, as an earlier criticism of utilitarianism attempted to show, that view permits harming innocent individuals in the name of producing benefits for others. An adequate moral outlook should prohibit exploiting the innocent in this fashion. Both my and, to a lesser degree, Kant's way of thinking about moral right and wrong satisfy this requirement. In Kant's terminology, to murder innocent people so that others might benefit is to treat the victims merely as means to the realization of ends chosen by others. Using my terminology, to murder the innocent for this reason is to treat those who possess inherent value as if they are of instrumental value only—as if their moral status was the same as a pencil or skillet, a pair of roller skates or a Walkman. Whatever language we use, the murder of the innocent is wrong because it wrongs the victim, regardless of the consequences for others.

To conclude this defense of the duty of respect, recall the question asked at the beginning of this chapter: Is it possible to craft a moral outlook that has none of the weaknesses and all of the strengths found in the positions examined in the previous two chapters? I believe it is. For the reasons just given, recognition of the inherent value individuals share and the direct duty of respect owed to those who have it avoids these weaknesses and preserves these strengths. In the absence of compelling arguments to the contrary, I shall assume that the duty of respect is a valid principle of direct duty, one that is owed to all those human beings who are inherently valuable. Which humans these might be is the next question that concerns us.

Moral Elitism

As is evident from the preceding, the moral outlook I favor involves two central ideas. The first is the inherent value of individuals, understood as a kind of value that is categorically distinct from whatever is merely instrumentally valuable. The second is the duty to treat others with respect, a duty that is honored whenever individuals who are inherently valuable are treated in ways that do not reduce their value, as the individuals they are, to (in Kant's words) "mere means."

To agree that some humans exist as ends in themselves or have inherent value leaves open the question whether this is true of all, most, or only a select few among us. Some philosophers favor this last option. This certainly seems to be what Aristotle thinks.[1] He believes that those who possess advanced rational capacities enjoy a more exalted moral status than those who lack them. This has serious implications for those found lacking in this regard. Using this basis, Aristotle classifies women as less morally worthy than men and argues that humans who are deficient when it comes to rational capabilities are born to be the slaves of those who are gifted in their rational endowments.

Aristotle does not err when he identifies reason as an important human capacity; his problems arise because of the inferences he makes after having done so. While moral elitism of the Aristotelian variety may have been an attractive view among members of the educated male aristocracy that flourished in Athens during the fourth century B.C.E., it will attract few adherents today. Women are not of less moral worth than men, and human beings who do not possess advanced rational abilities are not properly consigned to being the slaves of those who do. If we cannot agree on this, it is difficult to imagine any substantive moral truths on which we can agree.

There is a way to avoid moral elitism's unacceptable implications. This is to view all who possess inherent value as possessing it equally, *regardless* of their intellectual brilliance, gender, race, class, age, religion, birthplace, talent, disabilities, and social contribution, for example. The genius and the seriously mentally disadvantaged child; the prince and the pauper; the brain surgeon and the fruit vendor; Mother Teresa and the most unscrupulous used-car salesman—all who have inherent value possess it equally; all are owed the direct duty to be treated with respect and none is to be treated in ways that reduce them to the status of things, as if they existed merely as means to forward the individual or collective interests of others, including some self-proclaimed group of "moral elite."

Moral Rights

How do rights enter the picture? As already noted, whether humans (let alone animals) have rights is among moral philosophy's most contentious questions. Any proffered answer, including the one I favor, faces serious challenges. Nevertheless, like Professor Cohen, I believe recognition of individual moral rights is absolutely essential to an adequate moral outlook. My reasons for thinking so are as follows.

In the previous section, I explained why the duty of respect is a valid principle of direct duty, a duty owed to all those who are inherently valuable. In saying it is a valid principle of direct duty I mean it has the best reasons, the best arguments on its side. If this much is granted, how rights arise can be explained as follows.

As Professor Cohen maintains, correctly in my view, rights are valid claims. To say that they are claims means that rights represent treatment that one is justified in demanding, treatment that is strictly owed; to say that such a claim is valid means that the claim is rationally justified. Thus, whether a claim to right is valid depends on whether the basis of the claim is justified. And the basis of such a claim is justified if the basis is a valid principle of direct duty. For example, our claim to a right to life is valid if others have a direct duty not to take our life as they please (i.e., if the duty not to take life is a valid principle of direct duty), and our claim to a right to liberty is valid if others have a direct duty not to interfere with our liberty as they please (i.e., if the duty not to interfere is a valid principle of direct duty).

Thus, if, as has been argued, the obligation to treat one another with respect is a valid principle of direct duty; and if, as was just explained, the validity of a claim depends on the validity of the moral principle on which it rests; then it follows that we have a valid claim to be treated with respect. And if, as Professor Cohen and I both agree, rights are valid claims, it follows that we have a right to be treated with respect. Or (to express these same ideas differently) being treated respectfully is something we are morally entitled to claim as our due, something we are morally justified in requiring of others. Because individual rights occupy a central place in the moral position I favor, and for reasons of linguistic economy, I sometimes refer to my position as the "rights view."

The right to be treated with respect shares the two features of moral rights explained in chapter 13. Those who possess this right are protected by an invisible "No Trespassing" sign, about which more will be said in the following section. This right also has the status of a "trump"; people who have this right have a valid claim against being treated as mere means in the advancement of some selfish or social good chosen by others. In this sense, the right to be treated with respect is correlated with the duty to be treated with respect; the duty to receive respectful treatment is one side of the moral coin; the right to demand it, the other.

Does the preceding constitute a strict proof of the rights view? I would be the first to say that it does not. In fact, the very idea of a "strict proof"—analogous to the kind of proof we find in geometry, for example—is out of place in the context of assessing competing moral outlooks. What can be done, and what I have attempted to do, is to explain why the rights view has strengths that the other influential views examined lack; how, unlike these other views, it satisfies a family of reasonable requirements for assessing competing moral outlooks; and why, therefore, it offers a way to think about morality that is principled, nonarbitrary, nonprejudicial, and rationally defensible. Short of constructing a strict proof, my argument functions to shift the burden of appropriate proof to those who favor some other view, meaning: it will be the burden of others who disagree with the rights view to explain where and why it goes wrong. To advance the critical assessment of competing moral outlooks this far, especially given the nature of the present essay, it seems to me, may be the best one can hope to do.

What Rights Do Humans Have?

In chapter 13, when the topic of rights was broached for the first time, distinctions were made between (1) legal and moral rights and (2) positive and negative rights. I indicated there that the argument and analysis contained in these pages would mainly be concerned with negative moral rights, understood as rights not to be harmed or interfered with, whether or not these rights are recognized and protected by the common law. Something more can now be said about these rights at this juncture.

The moral right to be treated with respect, which is fundamental to the rights view, can be interpreted both as a positive and a negative right. Interpreted as a positive right, possession of this right would impose duties of assistance on others (e.g., duties to make educational, health, and other human services available to all). Whether this right has this status is among the most divisive issues in moral and political philosophy, one that, given the nature of my disagreement with Professor Cohen, need not be addressed on this occasion. For while the possible status of this right as a positive right is disputed by many human rights' advocates, to the best of my knowledge none of these advocates, including Professor Cohen, denies that the right to be treated with respect has the status of a negative moral right. This is the way I have been interpreting this fundamental human right in the preceding pages, and this is how I will continue to interpret it in what follows.

Now, negative moral rights, we know, have two noteworthy features: first, they have the status of invisible "No Trespassing" signs; second, they function as "trump." For reasons already given, the fundamental right to be treated with respect shares both of these features. The same is true of the more specific rights mentioned in that earlier discussion: the rights to life, bodily integrity, and freedom. These three rights correspond to the most important ways in which our value as the persons we are can be assaulted. Those who assume unjustified freedom for themselves may wrongfully deprive us of our life, invade or injure our body, or deny or diminish our freedom, all in the name of some "greater good," whether personal or social. The enumeration of these additional rights thus serves to remind us of more specific aspects of our individuality that are protected (or at least should be) because we share the right to respectful treatment. The "No Trespassing" and "trump" functions of moral rights shield our life, our body, and our freedom against the excessive freedom of others. To act in ways that are respectful of individual rights is to act in ways that are respectful of the individuals whose rights they are.

Does the recognition of these individual rights mean that it is always wrong to embark on or sustain social practices or institutions that seek to advance the good of society? Again, this is among the most divisive issues in contemporary moral and political theory, one that is intimately connected to asking whether the right to be treated with respect has the status of a positive right. As noted earlier, these matters are not addressed on this occasion. Here it is enough to remark that, from the perspective of the rights view, whatever benefits some might derive from various policies and institutions, these policies and institutions are wrong if they violate the rights of some in order to secure benefits for others. In this sense, the rights view gives priority to the right to be treated with respect, interpreted as a negative moral right, even if this same right also happens to have the status of a positive moral right.

A final point needs to be clarified before concluding this section. Because so much emphasis is being placed on respectful treatment, an interpreter of the rights view might infer that the pain people suffer at the hands of their abusers does not matter morally. This is not true. The suffering of those who are treated immorally matters, sometimes (as in the previously described case of the poor child who died at the hands of Captain Marshall) profoundly. Even so, it is important to understand why, according to the rights view, and according to Kant's view as well, causing others to suffer is not the fundamental moral wrong. The fundamental moral wrong is that someone is treated with a lack of respect. The suffering they are caused compounds the wrong done, making a bad thing worse, sometimes with tragic results. But that they are made to suffer is itself a *consequence* of their disrespectful treatment, not equivalent to such treatment; as such, causing the innocent to suffer is not the same as, is not identical with, disrespectful treatment. Some examples will help clarify this important point.

People are murdered in a variety of ways. Some victims meet their end only after prolonged torture; others are murdered without having suffered at all. For example, a drink might be laced with an undetectable lethal drug; then, without knowing what has happened, the victim dies painlessly, never having regained consciousness. If the wrongness of murder depended on how much the victim suffered, we would be obliged to say that painless murders are not wrong. But this is absurd. How, then, can we account for why the murder of the innocent is wrong even when the victims do not suffer? And how can this account be extended to cases where those who are murdered suffer a great deal?

The rights view answers these questions as follows. In cases in which innocent people are murdered painlessly, their right to be treated with respect is violated; that is what makes their murder wrong. In cases in which the victims suffer greatly, the fundamental wrong is the same: a lack of respect, only in these cases the wrong done is compounded by how much the victims suffer. The suffering and other harms people are made to endure at the hands of those who violate their rights is a lamentable, sometimes an unspeakably tragic feature of the world. Still, according to the rights view, this suffering and these other harms occur *as a consequence* of treating individuals with a lack of respect; as such, as bad as they are, and as much as we would wish them away, the suffering and other harms are not themselves the fundamental wrong.

Persons

The rights view, I believe, is rationally the most satisfactory way to think about human morality. The claim we make to respectful treatment is a valid claim, grounded in a valid principle of direct duty. All of us are directly owed treatment that respects our equal inherent value, and each of us possesses an equal right to be treated respectfully, as ends in ourselves, never as merely having instrumental value. To adopt the rights view, I believe, is to embrace a moral outlook that more adequately illuminates and explains the foundations of our duties to one another than the other outlooks we have considered. On this score, the rights view has the best reasons, the best arguments, on its side. One important question that remains to be addressed concerns which humans have rights, assuming that some do.

In his philosophy, Kant limits inherent value, or worth, to those humans who are persons.[2] Persons are individuals who possess a variety of sophisticated capacities—reason and autonomy, in particular. Because persons are rational, they are able critically to assess the choices they make before making them; because they are autonomous, persons are free to make the choices they do; and because they are both rational and autonomous, persons are morally responsible for what they do and fail to do. For Kant, then, there is an elegant reciprocity in how moral responsibility and moral rights are related. All and only those who are morally responsible have moral rights, just as all and only those who have rights are morally responsible. Moreover, because all and only persons are morally responsible, Kant believes that all persons, and only persons, have moral rights.

In view of the preceding, it should come as no surprise that Kant denies rights to other-than-human animals. These animals do not have rights because they are not persons. In fact, Kant believes that rational, autonomous beings and animals belong to two distinct, mutually exclusive moral categories; rational, autonomous beings belong to the category "persons"; cows and pigs, coyotes and mink, dogs and cats belong to a different category, the category (this is Kant's word for it) "things." When it comes to these animals, therefore, we do nothing wrong when we treat them merely as means. Indeed, for Kant, the *reason nonhuman animals exist in the first place* is to advance human interests; animals, writes Kant, "are there merely as a means to an end. That end is man." This is why we do nothing wrong to them when we slaughter them for food, trap them for reasons of fashion, or invade their bodies in the name of science.

Subjects-of-a-Life

Kant's position, as profound and insightful as I believe it is, and as much as it has influenced my own thinking, is not without its problems, some of them insurmountable, in my judgment. Here I consider only one major difficulty; it concerns which humans count as persons and what follows morally, given Kant's answer.

We begin by noting the obvious: not all that is human is a person, in Kant's sense. A newly fertilized human ovum and a permanently comatose human are human; but neither is what Kant means by person. The same is true of late-term human fetuses, infants, children throughout several years of their life, and all those human beings, whatever their age, who, for a variety of reasons, lack the intellectual capacities that define Kantian personhood. As such, all these humans lack the morally significant worth possessed by persons, and each lacks the right to be treated with respect. Were we to treat these human nonpersons *merely as means,* therefore, Kant would be unable to explain why and how we would be doing anything wrong to them.

Professor Cohen and I both agree that this last proposition expresses a profoundly unacceptable moral position. Not for a moment do we believe that it is impossible to do anything wrong to children and the mentally disadvantaged of all ages, for example. The challenge Professor Cohen and I face is how, in a principled, nonarbitrary, nonprejudicial, and rationally defensible way, we can avoid endorsing an outlook that neither of us believes is credible.

My response to this challenge involves abandoning the Kantian idea of personhood as a criterion of inherent value and replacing it with an idea for which we have no commonly used word or expression. The absence of such a linguistic marker, referred to by some philosophers as a "lexical gap," is not unique to the present situation. For example, the American philosopher Bill Lawson notes that we do not have a word for the white stringy fiber that clings to bananas. The existence of a lexical gap in this case carries no moral baggage; there is no reason to believe that the absence of a linguistic marker here suggests that moral duties are being shirked, morally important facts ignored. The existence of a lexical gap in other contexts is more problematic. Writing about social policies that affect African Americans, Lawson notes that while some of us "have the concept of the legacy of black subjugation, there is no generally accepted word that denotes this condition." For Lawson, the absence of a commonly used word or expression in this case is symptomatic of a failure to come to terms with a discomforting moral reality. To the extent that what is not named is not worth our attention, the absence of a commonly used word or expression with which to talk about "the legacy of black subjugation" suggests that this legacy is unimportant.[3]

I will have more to say about lexical gaps in the next chapter. At this point, I note only that, in the present context, there is something of real moral importance for which we have no commonly used word or expression. 'Person' does not fill the gap I have in mind; it covers too few individuals. 'Human' does not fill the gap; it covers too many. Necessity being the mother of invention, I use the words "subject-of-a-life" to fill the gap in question. Let me explain what I mean.

We bring to our life the mystery of consciousness. Never satisfactorily explained by philosophers or scientists, this fact remains: we are not only in the world; we are aware of it—and aware, too, of what transpires "on the inside," so to speak, in the realm of our feelings, beliefs, and desires. In these respects, we are something more than animate matter, something different from plants that, like us, live and die; we are the experiencing subjects-of-a-life, beings with a biography, not merely a biology. To employ words used in an earlier discussion, we are *somebodies,* not *somethings.*

This experiential life we live (and this is also part of the mystery) is unified, not chaotic. It is not as if the desires we have belong to someone (A), the beliefs to someone else (B), and the feelings to someone totally different (C); instead, our desires, beliefs, and feelings have a psychological unity; all belong to the distinct individual each of us is; all help define how the story of our individual life, our biography, unfolds over time; and all help illuminate how the story of any one individual's life differs from the stories of others.

Now, the life of each subject-of-a-life fares experientially better or worse for the individual whose life it is, logically independently of whether that individual is valued by others. This does not mean that the quality of our life is unaffected by our relationships with others. On the contrary, most of life's most important goods, including love, friendship, the closeness of family, a sense of community, trust, and loyalty, depend on the quality of such relationships. The same is true of most of life's most important evils, including hate, enmity, the disintegration of family, a sense of alienation, deceit, and betrayal. As a matter of fact, in short, the quality of our life waxes and wanes to a considerable degree depending on whether our relationships with others are amiable and supportive, the opposite, or somewhere in between. But *that we are individuals who have an experiential welfare*—this is a fact equally true of each of us. The *kind of being we are—subjects-of-a-life with an experiential welfare*—is something we all have in common, something we all share equally, something that makes us all the same, regardless of our gender, intelligence, race, class, age, religion, birthplace, talent, and social contribution, for example.

In place of Kant's criterion of personhood, the rights view uses the subject-of-a-life criterion as a basis for determining who has inherent value. All those who satisfy this criterion—that is, all those who, as subjects-of-a-life, have an experiential welfare—possess inherent value—thus are owed the direct duty to be treated with respect, thus have a right to such treatment. The rights view therefore recognizes moral rights in the case of humans excluded by the Kantian criterion of personhood. Given Kant's views, late-term human fetuses, newborn children, children throughout several years of their life, and human beings, whatever their age, who, because of various disadvantages, lack the requisite intellectual capacities, are nonpersons; for Kant, therefore, these humans are not ends in themselves and lack rights. Not true, given the subject-of-a-life criterion. These humans, one and all, are subjects-of-a-life. Young children and humans of any age who, while they suffer from disabilities that prevent them from being persons, qualify as subjects-of-a-life: each has a life that is experientially better or worse for the one whose life it is. Late-term fetuses and newborn children arguably occupy the same status; the more we learn about prenatal and neonatal humans, the more reason we have to attribute feelings, desires, and preferences to them, making it eminently plausible to regard them as having their own experiential welfare.[4] If true, then late-term human fetuses and human neonates satisfy the subject-of-a-life criterion, are inherently valuable, and are owed the direct duty of respect. *These* humans, not just the members of some "moral elite," possess the basic moral right to respectful treatment. Thus, whereas, given Kant's criterion of personhood, these humans in principle can be treated as mere means without any wrong being done to them, the rights view reaches a very different conclusion. To treat any of these humans as if they are of instrumental value only is to do something wrong to them, something that violates their right to be treated with respect.

Not all is clear sailing for the rights view; like every other way of thinking about moral right and wrong, the view I favor faces any number of serious challenges, one of which is analogous to the objection I have been pressing against Kant. Given his views, some humans are not persons; given the rights view, some humans (e.g., newly fertilized human ova and encephalic neonates, infants born without a brain or brain activity above the brain stem) are not subjects-of-a-life. According to the rights view, interpreted consistently, these humans do not satisfy the subject-of-a-life criterion and thus, judged on this basis, do not have a right to respectful treatment.

Does this mean that these human beings cannot possibly have rights? The rights view leaves this question open. The subject-of-a-life criterion is offered as a sufficient condition for having inherent value, meaning: *all* who are subjects-of-a-life possess inherent value. Whether *only* those who are subjects-of-a-life possess inherent value is a question the rights view does not foreclose. In other words, the rights view allows for the possibility that individuals who are not subjects-of-a-life might nonetheless have a kind of value that is not reducible to instrumental value only. However, the onus of proof will be on those who wish to attribute such value beyond subjects-of-a-life to offer a principled, nonarbitrary, nonprejudicial, and rational defense of doing so.

It is at this point that the rights view's strengths when compared with Rawlsian contractarianism are most apparent. Rawls's moral outlook has noteworthy virtues. In particular, the prejudicial discrimination against, as well as the permissible exploitation of, those who belong to the "wrong" race, the "wrong" class, and the "wrong" gender, for example, arguably are disallowed by Rawls's veil of ignorance. Given the moral prejudices validated by some of the other views we have considered—simple contractarianism and moral elitism, in particular—Rawls's outlook clearly is superior, and any philosopher working in the areas of moral and political theory owes Rawls an enormous debt of gratitude.

Prejudices linger in the Rawlsian vision nonetheless. Recall that Rawlsian contractors, each of whom must have "a sense of justice," are the only ones who are owed direct duties. Because young children and human beings of any age who suffer from quite serious mental disabilities do not satisfy this requirement, no direct duties are owed in their case. What duties we have in their case are indirect duties to others—namely, those with a sense of justice.

The rights view preserves the strengths and avoids the weaknesses of Rawlsian contractarianism. It preserves the strengths because it distances itself from prejudicial discrimination against, and the possible exploitation of, members of the extended human family that are based on race, gender, or ethnicity, for example; and it avoids the weaknesses because it denies that one must have a sense of justice in order to be owed direct duties. One has only to ask whether the mentally disadvantaged victim of the gang rape was treated wrongly to realize that Rawls's standard is too high. Without herself having a sense of justice, this unfortunate young girl was treated in ways that give humanity a bad name. Without herself having the ability to have duties to others, as a subject-of-a-life, *she* was owed the direct duty of respectful treatment; *she* possessed the right to be treated with respect, not some indirect protection grounded in the interests of others. It is the similarities between humans who have this right, not our differences, that matter. And the relevant similarities are these: we are each of us the subject-of-a-life, a conscious creature with an experiential welfare that has importance to us whatever our usefulness to others. When viewed from the perspective of the rights view, all human subjects-of-a-life have equal inherent value, and all possess an equal right to be treated with respect.

Final Thoughts

Three final substantive points need to be made before concluding this chapter. First, as was noted in the critical evaluation of utilitarianism, that view is committed to a procedure that counts all preferences, no matter from whence they arise. This is why a consistent utilitarianism must count evil preferences—like those of the four young rapists, as well as those of others who may have been supportive or complicit—and count them as being of equal importance to the comparable preference of their victim. I believe that this procedure is morally obscene; I believe that the preferences of those who violated the young woman, as well as the preferences of anyone who was supportive or complicit, should play no role whatsoever in the determination of the wrong that was done. The rights view is able to explain why. Evil preferences are those preferences that, if acted on, either lead agents to violate someone's rights or cause others to approve of, or tolerate, such violations. This is why, according to the rights view, the preferences of the rapists, as well as any others who may have approved or tolerated what they did, do not count. Not at all.

Second, to act on evil preferences does not mean that those who act on them are evil people. People are evil (at least this is the clearest example of what we mean) when, as an expression of their settled personal character, they make a habit of violating others' rights *and* to do so cruelly, either by taking pleasure in or by feeling nothing (being indifferent) to the suffering or loss caused by the violation. Contrast this with those who are otherwise decent people but who, in an isolated case, act on preferences that lead them to violate someone's rights, an act that they later regret. Such was the case with the four teenage rapists. Granted, what they did was horribly wrong; granted, giving in to their evil preferences led them to do it; nevertheless, a single evil act does not a moral monster make. People who do evil (and we all do) often have other redeeming qualities. So even while we are right to judge rights violations wrong, we should guard against a rush to judgment concerning the moral character of the violators.

Third, and finally, otherwise decent people can be supportive of and complicit in evil as part of their day-to-day life, not just in isolated incidents. This arguably was true of some white southerners who benefited from slavery, for example. That great wrongs were done to slaves because their fundamental rights were routinely, often ruthlessly violated is unquestionably true; and that these violations occurred because of the evil preferences of the white majority also is unquestionably true. But not all white beneficiaries of slavery were evil people; not all possessed a morally deficient character that led them habitually to enjoy violating others' rights or to regard all violations committed by others with moral indifference. As was observed in the earlier discussion of cruelty–kindness, moral assessments of what people do should be kept distinct from moral assessments of the people who do them. This is a principle that applies in the present case, too. To act on evil preferences, while this is tied to the wrong associated with violating rights, is one thing; to find someone of evil character is another.

In the following chapter I present my argument for animal rights and respond to a variety of criticisms. Before turning to these important tasks, it is worth noting what the rights view offers in the case of human morality. What it offers is a way to think about moral right and wrong in which human rights are central; a way that represents the life, the bodily integrity, and the liberty of individuals as being worthy of maximum protection; a way that provides this same protection to all human subjects-of-a-life regardless of their race, gender, class, age, or advanced intellectual capabilities, for example; and a way that grounds this equal protection in considerations that are principled, nonarbitrary, nonprejudicial, and rationally defensible.

In chapter 11, I expressed the hope that these pages would demonstrate that my commitment to human rights, including, as we have now seen, the rights of infants, children, and other powerless members of the extended human family, is as central to my moral outlook as is my commitment to animal rights. I trust the former commitment has been demonstrated. Even if it should turn out that the conclusions reached in the next chapter are false or foolish, I hope that the conclusions reached in this one, and the arguments used to reach them, because they stand or fall on their own, will be judged accordingly.

Notes

1. Excerpts from Aristotle's work, where his commitment to moral elitism is starkly evident, are included in Regan and Singer, eds., *Animal Rights and Human Obligations*.

2. Kant's most relevant work is *The Fundamental Principles of the Metaphysic of Morals*, available in many editions. Kant himself would not extend rights to nonhu-

man animals. For a statement of his indirect duty view, see the selection from his writings in Regan and Singer, eds., *Animal Rights and Human Obligations.*

3. For Bill Lawson's discussion of lexical gaps, see "Moral Discourse and Slavery," *Between Slavery and Freedom: Philosophy and American Slavery,* ed. Howard McGary and Bill Lawson (Bloomington: Indiana University Press, 1992), 71–89.

4. For an exhaustive review of recent work on fetal and neonatal brain development, which includes an extensive bibliography, see Charles D. Laughlin, "Pre- and Perinatal Brain Development and Enculturation: A Biogenetic Structural Approach," available on the Web at http://superior.carleton.ca/~claughli/dn-art1a.htm. Writes Laughlin:

> The literature in pre- and perinatal psychology (including aspects of cognitive psychology, developmental psychology, developmental neuropsychology, psychobiology, social psychobiology and clinical psychology) now provides ample evidence that the perceptual and cognitive competence of the fetus and infant is significantly greater than was once thought. This evidence suggests that neurocognitive development in the pre- and perinatal human being produces structures that make the world of experience "already there" for the advanced fetus, neonate and infant. For instance, objects, relations between objects, faces and speech sounds appear to be already meaningful to the neonate.

17

Animal Rights

We turn now to a consideration of the rights of other-than-human animals. From the outset I have emphasized the cumulative nature of my argument. Whether animals have rights is a topic that cannot profitably be broached before other, more fundamental questions have been answered. These questions include, but are not limited to, those that critically assess moral outlooks that deny rights to animals and, as we have seen, sometimes to humans, too. After the weaknesses of these ways of thinking about morality have been reviewed, and after it has been explained how the rights view preserves their respective strengths, the reasons for recognizing human rights can be understood; once these reasons are understood, then—but not before, in my judgment—the reasons why animal rights should be recognized can be understood as well. It has taken this long to arrive at the point where an answer to the question about the rights of animals makes rational sense. Whether the answer I give is or is not correct, the need to approach the issue carefully and fairly, as the previous chapters have attempted to do, demonstrates what was meant earlier when it was noted that the case for animal rights cannot be given in twenty-five words or less.

Controversial moral issues—and few are more controversial than the one that asks whether animals have rights—characteristically have four separate but related kinds of question that help define where and how people can agree or disagree. There are (1) questions of fact; (2) questions of value; (3) questions of logic; and (4) practical questions, those that ask what changes, if any, should be made, given how the other questions have been answered. This chapter explores questions of each kind, explains why the conclusion that other-than-human animals have rights is reached, responds to a variety of criticisms, and concludes first by looking back, then by looking ahead.

Questions of Fact

Concerning questions of fact: People of goodwill who offer opposing answers to controversial moral questions sometimes disagree about what should be done morally because they disagree about what is true factually. For example, some people think it would be morally wrong to legalize active euthanasia, understood as deliberately killing competent, terminally ill patients who suffer greatly, and who ask that their lives be ended. Some oppose legalizing active euthanasia, even in cases like the one just described, because they believe that if we legalize active euthanasia in a limited number cases, we will end up legally "euthanizing" people who are not suffering greatly, are not terminally ill, and do not prefer death over remaining alive. To express their concern simply and starkly, these opponents of legalization believe that legalizing active euthanasia for some will lead to legalizing murder for others.

But *will* legalizing active euthanasia in some cases lead to murder in others? This is a question of fact, one that illustrates how complicated "mere questions of fact" sometimes can be. With our limited knowledge about the long-term effects of situations, such as the one we find in Holland, where active euthanasia was legalized in 1973, who is to say, with great confidence, what the long-term effects of legalization are?

The central factual questions in the animal rights debate differ in important respects from those that help define the debate over the legalization of active euthanasia. In the latter case, we are being asked to speculate about human behavior in the future; in the former, we are being asked to say what we know about animal psychology here and now. Earlier, in chapter 14, considerations were offered in support of a variety of judgments of fact about animal minds. There it was argued that mammals and birds (at least), in addition to being sentient, share with us a family of cognitive, attitudinal, emotional, and volitional capacities. Cognitively, they are able to form beliefs about the world; attitudinally, they are able to take an interest in things, wanting and desiring, as they do, some things more than others; emotionally, these animals respond to what transpires in their life with a rich variety of feelings, including fear and joy, for example; volitionally, they are capable of making choices, relative to what they believe and feel, in pursuit of what they want. These animals are our psychological kin, and the minds they have are not unsophisticated by any means.

How do we know this? As was noted in that earlier discussion, the grounds for attributing minds to these animals are analogous to those we have for attributing minds to one another. Their behavior resembles our behavior. Their physiology and anatomy resembles ours. And their having a mind, their having a psychology, not only accords with common sense, it is supported by our best science, the implications of evolutionary theory in particular. No one of these considerations by itself need be claimed to be proof of animal minds; when taken together, however, they provide compelling grounds for attributing a rich, complex mental life to other-than-human animals.

Questions of Value

Questions of value do not concern mere matters of fact, though facts can be highly relevant. This certainly is true in the present case, in which one of the central questions of value concerns the moral status of other-than-human animals. Here is what I mean.

The previous chapter included a discussion of the idea of those who are subjects-of-a-life. As explained there, not only are subjects-of-a-life in the world; they are aware of it—and aware, too, of what transpires "on the inside," in the realm of feelings, beliefs, and desires. As such, subjects-of-a-life are something more than animate matter, something different from plants that live and die; subjects-of-a-life are the experiencing centers of *their* lives, individuals who have lives that fare experientially better or worse for the ones whose lives they are, logically independently of whether they are valued by others. At least in the case of mammals and birds, then, the conclusion we reach is that, *as a matter of fact,* these animals, as is true in our case, are subjects-of-a-life.

The preceding makes it possible to say something more on the topic of lexical gaps. In general, the traditional vocabulary of moral philosophy has had to make do with three different but related concepts: (1) humans, (2) animals, and (3) persons. No one of the three coincides perfectly with the other two. For example, while it is true that all humans are animals, it is false that all animals are humans; and while it is true that some human beings are persons, in the Kantian sense, no animal beings are. What our language lacks is a commonly used word or expression that applies to the area where humans and animals overlap psychologically. This is the lexical gap "subject-of-a-life" is intended to fill. The introduction of this concept permits us to identify those humans and other animals who share both a family of mental capacities and a common status as beings who have an experiential welfare. The word *human* is inadequate to the task; some subjects-of-a-life are not human. The word *animal* is inadequate to the task; some animals are not subjects-of-a-life. And the word *person* is similarly deficient; some subjects-of-a-life, whether human or not, are not persons. And yet there is no mistaking the reality in question, a reality shared by literally billions of human and animal beings.

If the identity of those who are subjects-of-a-life was morally unimportant, the existence of a lexical gap in the present case would be of no greater moral significance than the existence of a lexical gap in the case of "white stringy fiber that clings to bananas." But the identity of those who are subjects-of-a-life is far from being morally unimportant. On the contrary, for reasons offered in the previous chapter, the subject-of-a-life criterion offers a basis for answering the question "Who is inherently valuable? Who is never to be treated merely as a means, as if they are of instrumental value only?" A more fundamental question of value is difficult to imagine.

As for the suggestion that the subject-of-a-life criterion is a credible criterion only for determining which human beings have inherent value: such a suggestion is symptomatic of the prejudice of speciesism. If what we are being asked to believe is that humans who satisfy this criterion are inherently valuable *because they are human beings,* whereas other animals who are subjects-of-a-life lack value of this kind *because they are not human beings,* then what we are being asked to believe, more than suggesting this prejudice, actually embodies it. Just as it is speciesist to count human interests as being morally significant, and to deny this same status in the case of the similar interests of nonhumans, because the former are human interests, the latter not, so it is speciesist to affirm inherent value in the case of human subjects-of-a-life who have interests and to deny this in the case of nonhuman subjects-of-a-life who have interests, because the former are human subjects-of-a-life, the latter not.

What, then, shall we say of the animals who concern us—cows and pigs, cats and dogs, hamsters and chimpanzees, dolphins and whales, coyotes and bears, robins and crows? Are they like us in being subjects-of-a-life? Do they have an experiential welfare that is of importance to them independently of their possible usefulness to us? Let those with Cartesian inclinations step forward and deny this. The convictions of common sense and an informed science will (as they should) take a contrary view. These animals are our psychological kin. Like us, they bring to their life the mystery of a unified psychological presence. Like us, they are *somebodies,* not *somethings.* In these fundamental ways, they resemble us, and we, them. In this fundamental sense, all subjects-of-a-life are equal because all equally share the same moral status.

Questions of Logic

Questions of logic ask whether one statement follows from another. There are more or less elaborate methods for determining this; fortunately, their details need not concern us here. Here it is enough to explain how the conclusion that animals have rights follows from a number of other statements for which supporting arguments have been offered in the preceding. By way of summary:

1. Moral outlooks that deny that we owe direct duties to animals (e.g., both simple and Rawls's version of contractarianism) are unsatisfactory. Any plausible moral outlook must therefore recognize that animals are owed direct duties. The rights view satisfies this requirement.

2. Moral outlooks that are speciesist (e.g., those that maintain that all and only human interests matter morally simply because they are the interests of human beings) are unsatisfactory. Any plausible moral outlook must therefore recognize that other-than-human interests matter morally. The rights view satisfies this requirement.

3. Moral outlooks that attempt to explicate the direct duties we owe to animals by reference to human character traits (e.g., the cruelty–kindness view) are unsatisfactory. Any plausible moral outlook must therefore be able to distinguish between moral assessments of what people do and the moral character they display in doing it. The rights view satisfies this requirement.

4. Moral outlooks that attempt to explicate human morality while dispensing with the idea of moral rights (e.g., preference utilitarianism) are unsatisfactory. Any plausible moral outlook must therefore recognize the rights of humans, including the right to respectful treatment in particular. The rights view satisfies this requirement.

5. Moral outlooks that attempt to explicate human morality by attributing inherent value to all and only those humans who are persons (e.g., Kant's position) are unsatisfactory. Any plausible moral outlook must therefore recognize the inherent value of humans who are not persons. The rights view satisfies this requirement.

6. Moral outlooks that deny that no other-than-human animals have an experiential welfare (e.g., Carruthers's position) are unsatisfactory. Any plausible moral outlook must therefore recognize that there are other-than-human animals who have an experiential welfare. The rights view satisfies this requirement.

7. Moral outlooks that attempt to limit inherent value to all and only humans who are subjects-of-a-life, thereby denying this same value to other animals who are subjects-of-a-life, are speciesist and unsatisfactory. Any plausible moral outlook must therefore recognize that anyone with an experiential welfare matters morally, whatever the species. The rights view satisfies this requirement.

8. Moral outlooks that affirm inherent value and rights in the case of humans who are subjects-of-a-life are preferable to positions that deny this. The rights view satisfies this requirement.

With statements 1 through 8 serving as the argument's foundation, the rights view's case for animal rights concludes as follows:

9. Because the relevant similarity shared by humans who have inherent value is that we are subjects-of-a-life, in the sense explained; because the nonhuman animals who concern us are like us in that they, too, are subjects-of-

a-life; and because relevantly similar cases should be judged similarly, it follows that these nonhuman animals also possess inherent value.

10. Because all those who possess inherent value possess the equal right to
be treated with respect, it follows that all those human beings *and* all
those animal beings who possess inherent value share the equal right
to respectful treatment.

Does this constitute a strict proof of animal rights? My answer here echoes
my answer to the earlier question about arguments for human rights. "Strict
proofs" are not possible in these quarters. What can be done, and what I have
attempted to do, is to explain how the ascription of rights to animals is supported by a way of thinking about morality that is principled, nonarbitrary, nonprejudicial, and rationally defensible—one that both preserves the strengths and
avoids the weaknesses of the influential moral outlooks examined along the way.
Short of constructing a strict proof, my argument here again functions to shift
the burden of appropriate proof to those who favor some other view. In other
words, it will be the burden of others who disagree with the conclusions I reach
to explain where and why my argument goes wrong.

Practical Questions

From the outset of this essay I have noted the abolitionist character of my
views, both in the case of animal rights and regarding the animal rights movement. "This movement," I noted, "seeks not to reform how animals are
exploited, making what we do to them more humane, but to abolish their
exploitation—to end it, completely." Why humane reforms are not enough
should be clear. In the case of the use of animals in science, for example, the
rights view is categorically abolitionist. Animals are not our tasters. We are not
their kings. Because animals used in research are routinely, systematically
treated as if their value is reducible to their usefulness to others, they are routinely, systematically treated with a lack of respect; thus are their rights routinely, systematically violated. This is just as true when they are used in trivial, duplicative, unnecessary, or unwise research as it is when they are used in
studies touted as holding real promise of human benefits. We cannot justify
routinely harming or killing human beings for these sorts of reasons. Neither
can we do so in the case of nonhuman animals in a laboratory. It is not refinement in research protocols that is called for; not mere reduction in the number of animals used; not more generous use of anesthetic or the elimination
of multiple surgery; not reforms in an institution that is possible only at the
price of systematic violations of animal rights; not larger, cleaner cages. It is
empty cages. Total abolition. The best we can do when it comes to using ani-

mals in science is not to use them. That is where our duty lies, according to the rights view.

As for commercial animal agriculture, the rights view takes a similar abolitionist position. The fundamental moral wrong here is not that animals are kept in stressful close confinement or in isolation or that their pain and suffering, their needs and preferences are ignored or discounted. All these are wrong, of course, but they are not the fundamental wrong. They are symptoms and effects of the deeper, systematic wrong that allows these animals to be viewed and treated merely as means to human ends, as resources for us—indeed, as renewable resources. Giving animals on farms more space, more natural environments, more companions does not right the fundamental wrong, any more than giving animals in laboratories more anesthesia or bigger, cleaner cages would right the fundamental wrong in their case. Nothing less than the total dissolution of commercial animal agriculture will do this, just as, for similar reasons, the rights view requires nothing less than the total eradication of the fur industry. The rights view's abolitionist implications, as I have said, are both clear and uncompromising.

That beliefs such as these will be seen by many people as radical and extreme is not a judgment I have sought to avoid; given the dominant customs of the culture in which we live, these beliefs cannot be perceived in any other way. To say that animals have rights means something more than that we should be nice to them. Given that they, like us, are protected by invisible "No Trespassing" signs, and given that their integrity, as is true of ours, "trumps" any selfish or social interest we might have, however important that interest might be, the "radical," "extreme" abolitionist implications of the rights view are unavoidable. Morally, we are never to take the life, invade or injure the body, or limit the freedom of any animal just because we personally or society in general will benefit. If we mean anything by the ascription of rights to animals, we mean this.

Some Objections, Some Replies

Many people resist the idea of animal rights. Some of the objections are raised by academic philosophers; for example, some question the cogency of attributing a unified, complicated psychology to animals who are unable to use a language. Other objections are the stuff of everyday incredulity; objections of this type are voiced not only by philosophers but also by skeptical members of the general public. As referenced in the accompanying notes, I have replied to objections of the former (the distinctively philosophical) kind in other places;[1] I will also be responding to Professor Cohen's philosophical objections in my reply. Here I limit myself to answering some of the most common objections of the second type.

The Absurdity of Animal Rights

Some critics challenge the idea of animal rights head-on. If animals have rights, they contend, we will have to acknowledge their right to vote, marry, and file for divorce, all of which is absurd. Thus, animals have no rights.

Now, part of what is said is true: any view that entails that animals have the right to vote, marry, and file for divorce is absurd. Clearly, however, the rights view entails nothing of the sort. Different individuals do not have to have all of the same rights in order to have some of the same rights. An eight-month-old child, for example, does not have either the right to vote or the other rights enumerated in the objection. But this does not mean that the child lacks the right to be treated with respect. On the contrary, young children possess this right, at least according to the rights view. And since these children possess this right while lacking the rights mentioned in the objection, there is no reason to judge the status of animals differently. Animals need not have the right to vote, marry, or file for divorce, if they have the right to be treated with respect.

No Reciprocity

Critics of animal rights sometimes maintain that animals cannot have rights because animals do not respect human rights. Again, part of this objection is correct: animals do not respect our rights. Indeed, animals (we have every good reason to believe) have no idea of what it even means to respect someone else's rights. However, this lack of understanding and its behavioral consequence (namely, the absence of animal behavior that exhibits respect for human rights) do not undermine attributing rights to animals.

Once again, the moral status of young children should serve to remind us of how unfounded the requirement of reciprocity is. We do not suppose that young children must first respect our rights before we are duty bound to respect theirs. Reciprocity is not required in their case. We have no nonarbitrary, nonprejudicial reason to demand that animals conform to a different standard.

Line Drawing

"But where do you draw the line? How do you know exactly which animals are subjects-of-a-life (and thus have a right to be treated with respect) and which animals are not?" There is an honest, simple answer to these vexing questions: we do not know exactly where to draw the line. Consciousness, which is presupposed by those who are subject-of-a-life, is one of life's great mysteries. Whether mental states are identical with brain states or not, we have massive evidence that our having any mental states at all presupposes our having an intact, functioning central nervous system and brain activity above the brain stem. Where exactly this physiological basis for consciousness emerges on the phylogenic scale, where exactly it disappears, no one can really know with certainty. But neither do we need to know this.

We do not need to know exactly how tall a person must be to be tall, before we can know that Shaquille O'Neal is tall. We do not need to know exactly how old a person must be to be old, before we can know that Grandma Moses was old. Similarly, we do not need to know exactly where an animal must be located on the phylogenic scale to be a subject-of-a-life, before we can know that the animals who concern us—those who are raised to be eaten, those who are ranched or trapped for their fur, or those who are used as models of human disease, for example—are subjects-of-a-life. We do not need to know everything before we can know something. Our ignorance about how far down the phylogenic scale we should go before we say that consciousness vanishes should not prevent us from saying where it is obviously present.

Other Animals Eat Other Animals

Sometimes an objection to animal rights addresses a particular practice, such as meat eating. Critics point out that lions eat gazelles, after all, and then ask how it can be wrong if we eat steak. The most obvious difference in the two cases is that lions *have* to eat other animals to survive. We do not. So what a lion *must* do does not logically translate into what we *may* do.

Besides, it is worth noting how much this kind of objection diverges from our normal practice. Most Americans live in houses that have central heating and indoor plumbing, drive cars, wear clothes, and write checks. Other animals do not do any of these things. Should we therefore stop living as we live, stop doing what we do, and start imitating them? I know of no critic of animal rights who advocates anything remotely like this. Why, then, place what carnivorous animals eat in a unique category as being the one thing they do that we should imitate?

Only Humans Are Inherently Valuable

Other objections to animal rights take different forms. For example, some critics maintain that because all and only human beings have inherent value, all and only human beings have a right to be treated with respect. How might this view be defended? Shall we say that all and only humans have the same level of intelligence, or autonomy, or reason? But there are many humans who lack these capacities and yet who, according to the rights view, have value above and beyond their possible usefulness to others. Will it then be suggested that this is true only in the case of human beings because only humans belong to the right species, the species *Homo sapiens?* But this is blatant speciesism.

Animals Have Less Inherent Value

Some critics contend that while animals have some inherent value, they have less, even far less, than we do. Attempts to defend this view can be shown to lack rational justification. What could be the basis of our having more inherent value than animals? Their lack of reason, or autonomy, or intellect? Only if, as is true of moral elitists like Aristotle, we are willing to make the same judgment in the case of humans who are similarly deficient. But it is not true that human subjects-of-a-life who have significantly less mental ability than is normal therefore have less inherent value than we do. It is not true (at least it is not true according to the rights view) that these humans may be treated merely as means in cases where it would be wrong to treat more competent humans in the same way. Those humans who are less mentally endowed are not the natural slaves of those of us who, without our having done anything to deserve it, are more fortunate when it comes to our innate intelligence. That being so, we cannot rationally sustain the view that animals like these humans in the relevant respects have less inherent value. All who have inherent value have it equally, all who exist as subjects-of-a-life have the same morally significant value—whether they be human animals or not.

Only Humans Have Souls

Some people think that the crucial difference between humans and other animals is that we do, whereas they do not, have a soul.[2] After all, we are the ones who are created "in the image of God"; *that* is why all humans have inherent value and why every nonhuman animal lacks value of this kind. Proponents of this view have their work cut out for them. I am myself not ill disposed to the proposition that there are immortal souls. Personally, I profoundly hope I have one. But I would not want to rest my position on a controversial issue like this one about inherent value, on the even more controversial question about who or what has an immortal soul. Rationally, it is better to resolve moral issues without making more controversial assumptions than are needed. The question of who has inherent value is such a question, one that is resolved more rationally by reference to the subject-of-a-life criterion, without the introduction of the idea of immortal souls, than by its use.

But suppose we grant, for the sake of argument, that every human has an immortal soul and that every other animal lacks one. Would this justify the way we treat animals? More specifically, would this justify using mice in LD50 tests or raising calves after the fashion of the milk-fed veal trade? Certainly not. Indeed, if anything, the absence of a soul arguably makes such conduct even more reprehensible than it already is. For consider: If we have immortal souls, then however bad our earthly lives have been, however much suffering and personal tragedy we have had to endure, we at least can look forward to the prospect of having a joyful existence in the eternal hereafter. Not so a milk-fed veal calf or a mouse whose internal organs burst in response to heavy doses of paint stripper. Absent a soul, there can be no other life after this one that compensates them for their misery while on Earth. Denied the possibility of such compensation, which we are assuming all humans enjoy, the pain, loneliness, terror, and other evils these animals suffer are, if anything, arguably worse than those experienced by human beings. So, no, the soul argument will not serve the purposes of those seeking a justification of the tyranny humans exercise over other animals. Just the opposite.

What about Plants?

Inherent value, according to the rights view, belongs equally to all those who are subjects-of-a-life. Whether it belongs to other forms of life, including plants, or even to rocks and rivers, ecosystems, and the biosphere,[3] are questions the rights view leaves open for others to explore, noting only that the onus of proof will be on those who wish to attribute inherent value beyond subjects-of-a-life to offer a principled, nonarbitrary, nonprejudicial, and rational defense of doing so.

Wherever the truth might lie concerning these matters, the rights view's implications concerning the treatment of animals are unaffected. We do not need to know how many people are eligible to vote in the next presidential election before we can know whether we are. Why should we need to know whether plants and the biosphere are inherently valuable before we can know that animals are?

And we do know that the billions of animals that, in our culture, are routinely eaten, trapped, and used in laboratories, for example, are like us in being subjects-of-a-life. And since, to arrive at the best account of our duties to one another, we must recognize *our* equal inherent value and *our* equal right to be treated with respect, reason—not mere sentiment, not unexamined emotion, but reason—compels us to recognize *their* equal inherent value and *their* equal right to respectful treatment.

The Magnitude of Evil

Whether the ways animals are treated by humans adds to the evil of the world depends not only on how they are treated but also on what their moral status is. Not surprisingly, the rights view represents the world as containing far more evil than it is customary to acknowledge. First, and most obviously, there is the evil associated with the ordinary, day-to-day treatment to which literally billions of animals are subjected; representative examples from the food industry, the fashion industry, and the research industry were summarized in chapter 12. If it is true, as has been argued, that these animals have a right to be treated with respect, then the massive, day-to-day invasion of their bodies, denial of their basic liberties, and destruction of their very lives suggest a magnitude of evil so vast that, like light-years in astronomy, it is all but incomprehensible.

But this is not the end of the matter. For the magnitude of evil is much greater than the sum of the violations of animal rights and the morally wrong assaults on their independent value these violations represent. Recall that one of the weaknesses of preference utilitarianism is that it cannot rule out counting evil preferences in the process of reaching a fully informed judgment of moral right and wrong. This is a weakness that any plausible moral outlook must remedy, and the rights view has a way of doing so. As was noted near the end of the previous chapter, according to the rights view evil preferences are those preferences which, if acted on, either lead agents to violate someone's rights or cause others to approve of, or tolerate, such violations.

From the perspective of the rights view, therefore, the magnitude of the evil in the world is not represented only by the evil done to animals when their rights are violated; it includes as well the innumerable human preferences that are satisfied by doing so. That the majority of people who act on such preferences (e.g., people who earn a living in the fur industry or those who frequent KFC) do not recognize the preferences that motivate them as evil—indeed, that some will adamantly assert that nothing could be further from the truth— settles nothing. Whether the preferences we act on are evil is not something to be established by asking how strenuously we deny that they are; their moral status depends on whether by acting on them we are party to or complicit in the violation of someone's rights.

Are all those who act on evil preferences evil people? Not at all. As was observed in the previous chapter, people are evil (at least this is the clearest example of what we mean) when their general character leads them to habitually violate others' rights *and* to do so cruelly, either by taking pleasure in or by feeling nothing (being indifferent) about the suffering or loss caused by the violation. While some who benefit from animal rights' violations may meet this description, the majority of people, including those who, as part of their day-to-day life, are supportive or tolerant of this evil, are not. In the vast majority of cases, I believe, those associated with the meat industry, for example, and those who support it by acting on their gustatory preferences, are not evil people. And the same is true of the vast majority of other people who either are themselves actively engaged in industries that routinely violate the rights of animals or are supportive or complicit in these violations.

The judgment that otherwise decent people act on evil preferences in these ways may invite anger and resentment from some, hoots of derisive laughter from others; but it may also awaken still others to a larger sense of the moral significance of our life, including (even) the moral significance of our most mundane choices: what we put in our mouths and wear on our backs. Imperfect creatures that we are, living in an imperfect world, no one of us can be entirely free from our role in the evil around us. That recognition of the rights of animals reveals far more evil than was previously suspected is no reason to deny the magnitude of the evil that exists in the world at large or how much, on close examination, we find in ourselves; rather, our common moral task is to conscientiously search for ways to lessen both.

The Grounds of Hope

How has it come to pass that people who genuinely care about animals, companion animals in particular, nonetheless find themselves supporting practices that are evil not only in their result but also in their origin? This is a question to give the most ardent animal rights advocate pause. Certainly I do not have an answer ready at hand. In fact, recent work by sociologists studying human attitudes and behavior suggests that animal rights is not an idea whose time has come.

In their studies of diverse human populations, Arnold Arluke and Clinton R. Sanders cite many of the "conflicts" and "contradictions" that characterize human–animal interactions. Do these "conflicts" and "contradictions" bother people? Hardly ever, according to the authors. Write Arluke and Sanders: "While inconsistency does occasionally come into an individual's awareness as a glaring problem calling for correction, most of the time, most people live comfortably with contradictions as a natural and normal part of everyday life." And, again: "[Living with contradictions] is not troublesome for ordinary persons because commonsense is not constrained to be consistent."[4] For the great mass of humanity, then, loving animals and eating them, or respecting animals and wearing them, are not matters to lose any sleep over.

History suggests that humans are made of sturdier stuff. If most of us, most of the time, really had no trouble living with contractions, slavery would still be with us and women would still be campaigning for the vote. While some people some of the time may be able to live with some contractions, some inconsistencies, there must be thresholds above which the daily business of living is affected. As explained in the opening chapter to Part II, I clearly remember when this happened in my life. My reading of Gandhi awakened me to the realization that I held inconsistent beliefs and attitudes about unnecessary violence to human beings, on the one hand, and unnecessary violence to animal beings, on the other. And the death of a canine friend led me to the realization that I was placing some animals (dogs and cats, in particular) in one moral category and other animals (e.g., hogs and calves) in another, even as I realized that, when viewed in terms of their individual capabilities, there really was no morally relevant difference between them. I have no reason to believe my wanting to craft a coherent set of values for my life makes me any different from anyone else. None of us is so acculturated that we sleep-walk through our moral life. We know a contradiction in our values when we see one. If too few of us today are seriously troubled by our contradictory beliefs and attitudes toward animals, that may be because too few of us recognize where and why our beliefs and attitudes are contradictory. What is invisible must first be made visible before it can be seen; contradictions must first be seen before they can be honestly and directly addressed. One of the present essay's central purposes has been to help make some things more visible than before.

Evidence suggests that more and more people are beginning to come to terms with such inconsistencies and are changing their lives as a result. Take the fur industry, for example. As recently as the mid-1980s, seventeen million animals were trapped for their fur in the United States; by the early 1990s, that number was approximately ten million; for 1997–98, the total had fallen to four million and estimates for 1998–99 place the total at half that of the previous year. During this same period the number of caged-mink "ranches" declined from 1,000 to 401. In 1988, active trappers numbered 330,000; by 1994, there were fewer than half that number. And while there were almost eight hundred fur manufacturers in America in 1972, their ranks had dwindled to just over two hundred in 1992. Arizona, California, Colorado, Florida, Massachusetts, New Jersey, and Rhode Island have joined eighty-nine nations, from Austria to Zimbabwe, in banning use of the steel-jaw leghold trap. Internationally, Austria has banned fur ranches, both Denmark and Norway have declared that ranch-raised fur is "ethically unacceptable," and the British government has declared its intention to pass legislation to prohibit all fur farming. In the United States House of Representatives, legislation that would ban the use of the steel-jaw leghold trap on all federal lands garnered eighty-nine cosponsors from both major political parties. All the indicators point to the fur industry's steady downward spiral. Fur, once as "in" as anything could be in the world of fashion, increasingly is "out."

American consumption of most varieties of meat also is declining. Whereas fourteen million veal calves were slaughtered in 1945, the number declined to eight hundred thousand in 1995. Except for poultry, overall per capita meat consumption continues to decline. USDA figures for "red meat" (beef, lamb, veal, and pork) for 1996 and 1998 were 119.5 and 112.0 pounds, respectively; fish, 15.1 and 14.7 pounds; and poultry, 51.9 and 64.3 pounds. This same period has witnessed a decline in per capita consumption of eggs and dairy products. Granted, some people who have stopped eating meat and meat products, or who have decreased the amount that they eat, have done so for reasons other than respect for animal rights. Legitimate health and environmental concerns, for example, can lead some people to make changes in their diets. Nevertheless, the national trend away from an animal-based diet and toward one richer in vegetables, legumes, grains, and nuts is unmistakable.

Is reliance on the animal model in research, testing, and education undergoing a comparable transformation? Because the numbers are hard to come by (recall the earlier discussion regarding the limitations of the Animal Welfare Act), no one can say with certainty. What is known is that the research community is increasingly willing to look for ways of replacing animals in the lab, researchers experience accelerated success in finding them, and a steadily rising number of Americans want to see this happen. A 1996 poll conducted by the Associated Press and the *Los Angeles Times* found that 72 percent of those responding said that it is sometimes wrong to use animals in research, and fully 29 percent said it is always wrong.

Even the American public's attitude toward the idea of animal rights is changing. Once the object of ridicule and sarcasm, animal rights increasingly is accepted as an appropriate moral norm. According to the poll just alluded to, fully two-thirds of adult Americans agree that "an animal's right to live free from suffering should be just as important as a person's." Even the courts are beginning to respond. In the past, advocates of animal rights have been prevented from having their case heard because they have not had legal standing. A recent verdict of the U.S. Court of Appeals for the D.C. Circuit reversed this pattern of denial. Henceforth, individuals and advocacy groups will have the legal freedom to bring suit against the USDA on grounds of its failure to enforce the provisions, limited though they may be, of the Animal Welfare Act. And two determined English activists, Dave Morris and Helen Steel, the "McLibel two," in the longest (314-day) trial in English history, successfully defended themselves against charges of libel brought by McDonald's. Among the court's findings: McDonald's is "culpably responsible for animal cruelty."

Is it, then, hopelessly unrealistic to imagine a day when fur coats will follow whale-bone corsets into fashion oblivion, when slaughterhouses will exist only in history books, and when all the scientific laboratories of the world will have a sign over their entrance proclaiming "No Animals Allowed"? Those who are pessimistic about the moral possibilities of humanity will answer yes. And perhaps they are right. But those who believe in the human capacity to change one's whole way of life, because both justice and compassion require it, will answer, no. Not in my lifetime, perhaps, but someday surely, I believe, the principled journey to abolition will be complete. As the evidence presented in the previous paragraphs suggests, for many people who understand and respect other animals, that long journey already has begun.[5]

Notes

1. I have replied to philosophical critics of my position in "*The Case for Animal Rights:* A Decade's Passing" in *A Quarter Century of Value Inquiry: Presidential Addresses of the American Society for Value Inquiry,* ed. Richard T. Hull (Amsterdam: Rodopi, 1994), 439–59. This same essay is included in a collection of my recent papers and lectures, *Defending Animal Rights* (Champaign: University of Illinois Press, 2001).

2. Whether animals have a soul is a much debated question; some well-regarded theologians answer in the affirmative. For a sampling of the relevant literature, see Tom Regan and Andrew Linzey, eds., *Animals and Christianity: A Book of Readings* (New York: Crossroads, 1989).

3. A number of philosophers have argued for the extension of inherent value to non-sentient nature. Of particular note are Holmes Rolston III, *Environmental Ethics: Duties to and Values in the Natural World* (Philadelphia: Temple University Press, 1988); J. Baird Callicott, "Non-Anthropocentric Value Theory and Environmental Ethics," *American Philosophical Quarterly* 21 (1984): 299–309; and Paul Taylor, *Respect for Nature* (Princeton, N.J.: Princeton University Press, 1986). For my critical reservations about the possible success of this enterprise, see "Does Environmental Ethics Rest on a Mistake?" *The Monist* 75 (1992): 161–82.

4. The quotations from Arluke and Sanders are from their jointly authored *Regarding Animals* (Philadelphia: Temple University Press, 1996), 190 and 188, respectively.

5. I wish to acknowledge the permission of Basil Blackwell, Ltd., to use several paragraphs from my essay "The Case for Animal Rights," which first appeared in *In Defense of Animals,* ed. Peter Singer (Oxford: 1985), 13–27.

Part III

REPLY TO TOM REGAN
Carl Cohen

An Overview

The dispute between Tom Regan and myself is well defined. Do animals have *rights*? He holds that animals like rats and chickens do have rights and that their rights entitle them to protection against any use of them by humans. I hold that although rights are morally central in human lives, they have no place in the lives of rodents and birds.

Our conflicting views have sharply conflicting consequences for everyday behavior. Write "animals" and most folks think of dogs—but it is chickens (and cows) that humans eat, and rats (and mice) used in medical research that are Regan's principal beneficiaries. For the sake of concreteness I will refer mainly to them.

The "animal rights movement" supposes that cruelty to animals will be avoided only when they are protected by "rights" universally recognized as inhering in them. I believe this to be false. We all want animals to be treated humanely, but a decent regard for animal suffering does not oblige us to apply to rats and chickens the concept of a moral *right*—a concept that makes good sense only in the human moral world. "Animal rights"[1] are a fiction.

Rodents and birds, on Regan's view, are surrounded by invisible "No Trespassing" signs (p. 152, 197). We humans are therefore duty bound, he thinks, to keep our hands completely off all rats and chickens; they are "some*bodies* and not some*things*" (p. 201). Rats and chickens have moral selves on his view, just as humans have moral selves; therefore, he contends, they are entitled to *moral respect* just as humans are entitled to moral respect.

This position I think to be both mistaken and dangerous. It is mistaken because the notion of a moral self, and of rights possessed by a moral agent, are concepts that arise in and apply to the world of human conduct, but they do not apply to animals like rats and chickens that cannot make moral judgments and never are or could be moral agents. It is a dangerous position because if taken seriously, it would interfere with our serious need to use animals for the protection and improvement of the lives of human beings, to whom we have far more weighty obligations.

Our duty to protect rats and chickens, on Regan's view, is absolute. It makes no difference to him what purpose lies behind our use of them. The killing of some mice, even one mouse, that contributes to the saving of thousands of lives, or to the alleviation of intense human pain, is still *wrong* on his view. That the mice are killed in the development of a vaccine to protect children from malaria or polio makes no difference because *all* uses of animals in science he thinks to be immoral. The use of animals in medical research he condemns categorically; animals, he writes scornfully, "are not our tasters" (p. 212).

This philosophical view is meant to be kind and humane, but in reality it is *un*kind and *in*humane. The outcome of its consistent application would be literally catastrophic. In my judgment, while it is right to protect animals from abuse and from pain where that is feasible, it is also right, *morally* right, to use animals in the service of human needs where the great value of such use has been proved.

In contrast to Regan's absolutism, I hold that our obligations to animals, of which there are many, are often overridden by our obligations to human beings. Our obligations to animals arise not from their rights, I believe, but from the fact that they can feel pain and from the fact that we, as moral agents, have a general obligation to avoid imposing needless pain or death. We are also obliged to fulfill the responsibilities of care that we have voluntarily assumed. I accept the obligation to care for my dog and be kind to him because I am a moral agent and recognize principles that govern my conduct—not because my dog has rights.

This critical distinction must be borne in mind throughout: rights and obligations are not fully reciprocal.[2] Although some of our obligations are a consequence of the rights held by other humans (for humans surely do have rights!), many of the obligations we owe do not arise from the *rights* of the beings (humans or nonhumans) to whom they are owed.

Although the capacity of rats and chickens to feel and suffer does not give them rights, it remains the case that we are not free to do anything we please to them. Out of respect for our own moral principles, the sentience of some animals results in some restrictions on our conduct. In dealing even with creatures like rats and chickens, which have no rights, we have the obligation to act humanely, to act in accord with our dignity as moral agents.

Some of Regan's followers, acting on behalf of what they claim to be the rights of animals, blow up research laboratories, throw paint on persons wearing furs, threaten the lives of opponents, and assault them.[3] Tom Regan himself does no such things; he is a law-abiding citizen, not a hoodlum. He is indeed a zealot, but he is not to be blamed for the atrocious misconduct of those who share his passion. It is Regan's philosophical views that are to be condemned. My reply to him will be as generous as his words permit, but his insensitivity to *human* needs makes it difficult for one to respond with sympathy. His reasoning produces conclusions that are morally perverse; this reasoning is taken seriously by members of his movement with outcomes that are sometimes outrageous.

The very cruelest outcomes of his views are those that, in the interests of rats and chickens, hinder the development of medical relief for humans who are sick and in pain. In Regan's larger view, those among us who use rodents to develop cures for human disorders, or vaccines to protect human children from disease, do *evil*. And those who "frequent KFC" (meaning all those who eat chicken) also do evil. Indeed, all those who use animal products for any human purpose—whether for clothing or medicines or nutrition or any other—are *complicit* in evil when these preferences are indulged. Regan believes it is our moral duty to refrain from all such conduct and preferences, no matter the cost in human pain or discomfort.

In contrast, I believe that using animals to protect and serve important human interests is morally right. Mindful of our duty to treat them humanely I contend, as the prime example, that killing mice and rats in the effort to develop drugs and vaccines to combat disease is profoundly right.

These are the philosophical and practical positions, clearly and sharply in conflict, on which readers individually and our society generally must pass judgment.

Universal Assertions, Particular Denials

Any claim of universal breadth is disproved by showing that in at least some cases it is not true. Tom Regan defends conclusions that he himself describes as having universal force. He thinks, for example—and tells us on his very first page—that the rights of animals require the *total* abolition of animal use: in medical science, in agriculture, everywhere. I contest these universal claims. Some uses of animals are shameful, I agree—but there are very many practical contexts in which the use of animals is entirely justifiable, and the assertion of their supposed rights in these contexts is absurd. His claims and mine differ greatly in scope.

Rejecting all uses of animals, Regan expects his critic to defend their use with like universality; he has repeatedly expressed to me his distress because I will not defend all that he attacks. But his expectations in this matter are unwarranted as a matter of logic. If X contends that all birds can fly, Y proves him mistaken by showing that some birds cannot fly; Y need not contend in opposition that *no* birds can fly. If it is correct to conclude, as I do, that some uses of animals for human gain are worthy and not wrong, Regan is mistaken about the total abolition of animal use. To show him mistaken we need not defend everything that is done to animals.

My concern about the consequences of Regan's abolitionism arises largely from my recognition of the central role of animal use in medical research. "But," he says to me in effect, "your essay says nothing about trapping wild animals for furs, or raising calves for veal!" He has no cause for complaint. Some cruel things done to some animals by some humans are indeed unjustifiable. There are entertainments using animals—dog fights and cock fights and camel fights—that are in my judgment indefensible. Hunting animals for sport may be indefensible. All this is perfectly consistent with my position that cocks, foxes, and camels have no rights. Tom Regan would like his critic to defend practices that he can point to as cruel, but he cannot oblige his critics to say what he would like them to say.

This shape of our dispute gives our readers a straightforward way to render judgment. Regan contends that rats have rights demanding our respect. If they do, then every killing of a rat for the sake of medical advance is morally wrong. So, dear reader, if you believe that there are cases (indeed, that there is any single case) in which the killing of rats in medicine may be judged morally right (and in truth there are very many such cases, of course), then you may know that the rats in question *could* not have had the moral rights Regan claimed for them. Either rats have rights that must be respected as Regan claims, or they do not. The judgment here is important, as we both agree in the preface to this volume—but it is not a judgment difficult to make.

Which Animals Are to Be Protected?

Regan does not assert that *all* animals have rights; regarding the moral status of many he is frankly unsure. On his view creatures have rights if they are "subjects-of-a-life," but he simply cannot say with confidence "how far down the phylogenetic scale we should go" (p. 215) in identifying creatures who really are "subjects-of-a-life"—so the class of "rights-holding" animals has, for him, no specifiable lower limit.

Some bottom boundary there must be, however, even for him. To suppose that every animal in the world has rights would outrun all credibility. Regan confesses an inability to draw the limiting line, but his exposition indicates that even his tentative efforts to do that must rely on the system of orders, families, genera, and species that constitute the animal kingdom. Drawing that bottom line, when he finds himself able to do it, will therefore unavoidably turn out to be a kind of speciesism. Regan can't admit that, but he is quite unable to suggest any other way to delineate the class of animals who do not possess rights. Very plainly he believes that there are some so far "down" the scale of animal life that rights do not apply to them (p. 215).

This vagueness is a serious problem for the animal rights movement. Stern moral rules are proposed to protect animal lives; *which* animals are thus protected is therefore a matter of some consequence. To deflect attention from this reasonable question Regan insists that there are at least some animals, like rats and chickens, whose rights are evident and must be respected. This does not respond to the troubling issue raised. What is the *extent* of the duties pressed upon us? He simply evades the issue.

Regan appears to believe that there is one great linear ladder of animal life, on the higher reaches of which lie the "subjects-of-a-life" who have rights.[4] Modern systematic zoology incorporates an evolutionary scheme a good deal more complex than this, one in which development is seen to have advanced in different directions—along one fork to the phyla *Echinodermata* (the sea urchins and starfishes, etc.) and *Chordata* (which include the vertebrates, and therefore the mammals as well), and along an entirely separate fork to the phyla *Arthropoda* (including the insects, spiders, and crustaceans) and *Mollusca*, which include the snails, squid, and shellfish.

So we ask: Which animals (on Regan's view) might be those "too far down the phylogenetic scale" to warrant our moral regard? Insects, he would likely agree, are creatures without rights—although he does not say that explicitly.[5] The octopi, on a very different evolutionary branch, are no "higher" than insects on the phylogenetic scale although they have nervous systems, the apparent capacity to solve simple problems, and probably subjective experience of a kind sufficient to count them as "subjects-of-a-life"—in which case they would (on Regan's view) have rights demanding respect. But the octopi are mollusks, and if some mollusks have rights other mollusks are surely entitled to the same regard[6]—which would expand the realm of rights-holders to include the billions of tiny krill that populate the polar oceans, millions of which, every day, lose any rights they might have had to the great whales which consume them by the ton. A rational account of the class of animals that do not possess rights would appear impossible for Regan to give, and the class of those who do possess them would appear to be, on his view, more vast than he had imagined—or then again it may not be, but he is unsure.

This difficulty cannot be evaded by claiming ignorance about the consciousness of primitive animals. Animals that are commonly eaten either deserve our respect, in which case we must not eat them, or do not. Right conduct in dealing with them can be prescribed only after Regan confronts with candor the fact that *there are differences in the moral status of different species.* This is an admission he is loathe to make, of course, because once we have agreed that there are differences (among species) having moral import, it no longer makes sense to refuse to draw moral distinctions between humans and other mammalian species. If his own theory relies on phylogenetic categories, then Regan cannot consistently deride (as prejudiced "speciesism") the distinctions drawn by his critics. Name-calling does not help; ordinary folks with common sense, most biologists and other scientists among them, are speciesists, make moral distinctions among species regularly and without difficulty.

In any event, Regan harbors no doubts about rodents and birds. Their rights he finds utterly compelling. *We are morally forbidden to kill them under any circumstances,* he contends, unless they are threatening our lives. Since chickens and mice are not known to threaten human lives, and rats only occasionally do so, it is fair to say that while Regan would hold it *always* immoral to kill a chicken or a mouse, killing rats he thinks generally wrong, but not wrong in every *possible* circumstance. The rat or mouse that invades our basement we would not be justified in killing. We might seek to trap it and move it to safety out of our house, but that also could infringe on what Regan calls the rat's "basic liberties" (p. 218). The extent of those liberties he may also be unsure about, but he is dead certain about this: to kill a rat in the effort to perfect a drug that may combat diabetes or cancer or heart disease is unconditionally wrong, categorically immoral.

From remarks he makes about various species we may reasonably infer that Regan thinks a great many aquatic animals do have rights. A trout, like a crab or an octopus, will struggle to break free from the fisherman's line—from which one may suppose that fish also lead internal lives that (on Regan's view) would make them somebodies. He himself will not eat fish. If fish have rights, the diets of human beings who would abuse those rights by eating fish must be sharply restricted. The fact that humans have sustained themselves on fish for thousands of generations is no reason to permit them to continue to do so if, as we are constrained to conclude on Regan's theory, eating fish is morally wrong.

If Regan is correct, all human beings are morally obliged, right now, to stop eating all meat, fish, and seafood and should cease to wear or use any animal products of any kind.[7] Henceforward, humans are obliged to depend on *plants* for food and clothing. Plants, Regan suggests, have no subjective lives demanding respect. But he is not *absolutely* certain about this, either.[8]

The Full Price of Animal Rights

The supposed rights of rats and chickens take precedence, in Regan's view, over all concerns for human health, *however great the benefit to humankind that may result from the use of animals.* Improving the lives or saving the lives of even millions of human beings is *overridden* (on his view) by the moral claims of *any single rat,* since that rat has (he believes) the *right* not to be killed. These conclusions are preposterous.

First, the rejection of all uses of animals in medicine—past, present, and future medicine—would be nothing short of catastrophic. The achievements of medical science using animals in the recent past, and the achievements of medicine requiring the use of animals in the years to come, are and will be so very great and so precious to humankind as to be beyond calculation. If these medical advances are morally right, as most rational folks will agree, then Regan's defense of alleged animal rights is unworthy of respect.

Second, the dietary changes that Regan would impose on the world's population would be fatal for many humans. Regan's convictions leave no place for the consideration of such consequences. He may be pained by the fact that his demands would cause much human suffering, even death—but he cannot allow that outcome to soften his strictures. *Animals must not be killed.* The burdens of morality must be borne. Rights do trump interests.

It is never open to Regan to respond—when faced with a particular consequence of his view that appears absurd—that an exception may be made in that case. The rights of rats are like the rights of his readers; they do not yield to the troubles of those having the obligation to respect them. The rights of a rabbit or a trout may never be sacrificed to advance the interests of a starving human. If rabbits and trout have rights, then mice and tuna do also, and their invisible " 'No Trespassing' signs" forbid our catching them, and all other mammals and fish, for the sake of human nutrition. Tom Regan is an unqualified abolitionist; no consequences give him pause.

The moral distinctions among animal species that most of us make every day without hesitation Regan categorically refuses to recognize. I love my dog very much; he sleeps in my bedroom. Some evenings, before retiring, I set a trap that I hope will kill an uninvited mouse. I find no difficulty in this behavioral contrast because, in my view, there are momentous moral differences between dogs and mice; what it is right to do to a mouse is often wrong to do to a dog. But of course I am, as I think every morally sensitive person must be, a speciesist.

Some distinctions between rats and humans even Regan cannot deny, but he recognizes no distinctions between them with respect to the reality of the rights they possess. Distinctions of that sort he finds morally intolerable. Eating the meat of cows he thinks "unspeakably repulsive." The human consumption of animals he probably wouldn't call "cannibalism"—but eating meat is for him grossly immoral *in the way that cannibalism is.*

In many human communities animal products are essential for survival. Ceasing to use them would entail a wholesale transformation of diet, of work, of life itself. Such a transformation would probably prove impossible for many and would result in uncountable deaths. Part of the price of implementing animal rights would be the resultant impact on entire human cultures.

What advice might Regan give to those who, on his view, have the duty to alter so fundamentally their way of life? What might he say, for example, to aboriginal populations in various parts of the globe who now barely sustain themselves on hard-won animal products? He cannot offer them an indulgence in view of their great need, for the chief thrust of his argument is that *however* important our *interests* in using animals may be, humans *do not have the right* to kill them. They have the *right* to live, and their rights must be respected.

The Inuit peoples of the Arctic are utterly dependent on hunting and fishing; their very bodies have evolved so as to be able to survive on the high-calorie fats that alone make life possible in so frigid an environment. Even Regan admits that wearing furs might be necessary for their survival (p. 139), although he does not tell us how we are to reconcile this need with the duty to respect animal rights. But survival in the far north requires more than warmth; it requires food. Life-sustaining plants do not grow there. Only by the incessant killing and eating of innocent animals can the Inuit survive. The urgent moral imperative they confront is therefore plain: they must *stop* living that way and move south.

In the Horn of Africa, where also agriculture cannot sustain the population, and drought results in periodic famines because livestock suffer, cattle are *the* principal source of food. In Ethiopia and Eritrea and Somalia and Sudan, and also in Kenya and Uganda farther south, respecting the "rights" of those cattle will result in the early death of millions of people. Replacing the nutrition that animals provide is simply not possible there, and elsewhere. Regan tells us that all the nutrition needed for human life may be obtained "without eating meat or any other food derived from animals, including milk, cheese, and eggs" (p. 139). One has only to look at the face of recurrent starvation in Africa to decide whether this animal rights diet is humane or inhumane.

The very existence of these animal-dependent cultures only shows (Regan might say) how deeply the world is sunk in evil. He's very serious about this; the tone of the language at the close of his essay ("not in my lifetime, perhaps, but some day surely," and "that long journey has begun") makes evident his view of himself as one who brings moral enlightenment to the rest of us. However great the transformation and suffering it may entail, every human community, aboriginal and sophisticated, must come to realize at last that adopting a strict vegetarian diet is our *duty*. Doing our duty may prove difficult, perhaps even fatal for some—but there is nothing Regan can do about that. He can only make plain the demands of his austere vegetarianism. Everyone—whether in Greenland or in Ethiopia or in North Carolina, and that includes you, the reader—must come to recognize the moral truth that the rights of chickens and cows override all interests in preserving human livelihood. Rights trump interests. Let justice be done "though the heavens fall."[9]

But it is not as food that humans rely most critically and most widely on animals. The great curse in all human lives is *sickness*—and to protect against dreadful diseases most of the world's children are inoculated as infants with vaccines—vaccines that would not exist but for the use of experimental animals. Immunization against diphtheria, whooping cough, polio, and other diseases is possible only because the dangerous trials of their safety and efficacy were completed using animal subjects.[10] The animal rights movement gives a clear and unequivocal response to this practice: stop it. The use of animals to test vaccines or drugs must end immediately and completely. "The best we can do when it comes to using animals in science," Regan writes "is not to use them. That is where our duty lies" (p. 213).

When animal rights have been given the respect Regan urges, there will be no more new vaccines—unless human families are prepared to allow their babies to be used for the needed tests of efficacy and safety. And that supposes we would think it permissible for altruistic parents to put the lives of their infants at risk. Not likely. If animals are out, most of the trials of drugs and vaccines are out; and if the trials are out, the new vaccines (and new drugs of every other kind) are out as well. We must face up to the full price of animal rights.

Is Medical Research Using Animals Intellectually "Bankrupt"?

Losing the use of animals in medical research would not be a troubling burden if that use were worthless anyway. Regan would like to have us believe that it is worthless. Nothing in his advocacy of animal rights is as misleading and unworthy as his deliberate suggestion that the use of animal models in medicine is a "bankrupt scientific methodology." Of course Regan dare not *assert* that it is, but he insinuates that it is by asking rhetorical questions framed in such a way as to suggest that animal research is obviously disreputable (p. 147).[11] About tests or studies that use animal models, he writes, "Questions arise about their *scientific validity:* Is it scientifically credible to believe that what is discovered by using a cat or a dog, a mouse or a rat, can be extrapolated to human beings? Or might it be true that the use of the animal model is a bankrupt scientific methodology? (p. 147). The innuendo here is reprehensible.

Some responses: First, the extensive reliance on laboratory animals in successful medical research was recounted at length in my essay earlier in this book. Readers may refer again to it (p. 3) and to the long chain of historic medical achievements in which the use of animals as subjects was essential. Readers may also refer to every issue of the *New England Journal of Medicine,* or the *Journal of the American Medical Association,* or *Science,* or *Nature,* or the *hundreds* of other periodicals in the world of biomedical research reporting successful research using animals. In the *New York Times* and other leading newspapers accounts of breakthroughs involving animal use are reported frequently; hardly a week goes by during which some progress in biology or medicine *using animals* is not reported by reputable researchers. In all of medical science the use of animals is the one most common and most successful methodology, the most seminal and the most concretely productive. Regan finds this very disconcerting, and we understand why he would—but for him to insinuate, as he does, that animal research is a "bankrupt scientific methodology" (p. 147) is inexcusable. In the light of what Tom Regan either knows or ought to know about the role of animals in the advance of medical science, the rhetorical devices in these passages are shameful. His suggestion that animal research is "bankrupt" is, as a substantive matter, ludicrous.

Second, a major element in Regan's evidentiary support is a long passage taken from a 1975 out-of-print book by Richard Ryder,[12] a zealous British animal rights advocate who argued that the Nazis' use of Jews as experimental subjects had more to recommend it than the use of rats in the laboratory.[13] Ryder's monograph appears to be one of Tom Regan's principal sources; Ryder inveighs against the living conditions of laboratory animals in that book and repeatedly assails what he calls the "*pseudo-medical*" uses of animals.[14] Using human volunteers in medical research Ryder finds more defensible than using mice and rats, because rodents cannot give their consent. He asserted in 1975, and in the year 2000 Regan appears to remain convinced, that medical research using animals is "trivial," and "that the knowledge gained *has no medical importance*."[15] The quality of Ryder's angry treatise is not difficult to appraise, but he is the best authority that Regan can muster to support the condemnation of animal research.

By way of contrast, here is the considered judgment of the National Academy of Sciences, writing jointly in 1991 with the Institute of Medicine of the National Institutes of Health:

> Methods to combat infectious diseases have not been the only dividends of animal research. Surgical procedures, pain relievers, psychoactive drugs, medications for blood pressure, insulin, pacemakers, nutrition supplements, organ transplants, treatments for shock trauma and blood diseases—all have been developed and tested in animals before being used in humans.[16]

The most authoritative medical voices are unswerving in their insistence on the necessity of animal use in medical research. Here is the eloquent judgment of the American Medical Association, rendered in 1989: "Virtually every advance in medical science in the 20th century, from antibiotics and vaccines to antidepressant drugs and organ transplants, has been achieved either directly or indirectly through the use of animals in laboratory experiments."[17]

And Regan's teacher said what? That the knowledge gained using animals was "trivial" and that "the knowledge gained has no medical importance." Regan and his friends have no credibility in this matter, and they deserve none.

Third, Regan writes as though medical researchers are commonly fools, concluding like simpletons that what is true of a mouse or a rat must be true of a human. He reveals a painful ignorance of the research strategies with which animals are used in medicine and of the physiological foundations of those strategies.

Is it scientifically credible to believe, he asks, that what is found true in a mouse or a dog is true also of humans? That question obscures great biological complexity. There are cases in which we do rightly extrapolate, very cautiously, from animal data to the human context, in the interests of safety. When, for example, it is found that a given compound is highly toxic in rats, or carcinogenic in mice, we have good reason to think it is at least likely to be poisonous or cancer-causing in humans also, and we are well advised to seek another compound that does not have such outcomes in rodents. Extrapolation in some contexts is far from silly.

More common, however, is the use of animal results as *leads,* suggestions for further research into compounds that *may* succeed in treating human disease. Animal research may uncover causal factors, environmental or genetic, that give researchers an approachable target, a promising path, in caring for humans or protecting them. When we learn that certain environmental factors cause disorders in mice very similar to those suffered by humans, we rightly seek to determine whether factors of that kind have a like impact on humans and, if so, how that adverse impact can be reduced or avoided. When we learn of new causal relations in the organic systems of rats or previously unknown genetic influences in mice, we may search for the same relations and influences in humans whom we know to possess similar organs and similar genes with similar functions.[18] "Knockout mice" in which certain genes (having close analogues in the human gene pool) have been deleted are used to unravel the mechanics of disorders otherwise indecipherable. The analysis of the chromosomes of mice, now well under way, greatly advances the understanding of chromosome regions in humans that closely correspond to them, and in that way opens the search for the role of genetic factors in many human diseases. Mice and humans, and other animals as well, have very many important organic and genetic features in common.[19]

Of course, no reputable scientist draws the simple-minded conclusion that because something is true in some animal species, it will be true in humans. But it very well may be true. Where there is ignorance and uncertainty (and there is plenty of that in medicine), it is essential that investigators undertake risky explorations in animals before they are done in humans. Comparative molecular biology has become very highly sophisticated, its reasoning penetrating and acute. Regan writes as though medical scientists using animals are blockheads.

When a new drug or a new antibiotic does succeed in the treatment of animals, investigators do not automatically suppose that it will succeed in the care of humans. But from such animal studies promising alternatives are often uncovered, and many of these have later borne fruit in the care of humans. Leads of this kind are precious in the advance of medicine. Success in animal research is obviously not a sufficient condition for success in human medicine, and animal successes can at times mislead—although Regan's examples of this are archaic. Nevertheless, careful trials using animals are exceedingly useful; they may even be demanded before investigators are prepared (or will be allowed) to put human subjects at risk. Subsequent research involving human subjects who have given their consent is not entirely without risk, but that risk would be far greater, and might even be unacceptably high, had not critical animal data been gathered beforehand. That is why, for compounds newly developed, the law *requires* that animal trials precede human use. Tom

Regan's account of the value of animals in medicine is so simple-minded and unrefined that it is hardly worth taking seriously.

A Very Short Treatise on Toxicology

Regan's angriest thrust is against a particular toxicity test once widely used to appraise the dangers created by chemicals with which humans come into contact. This toxicity screen, called the LD50, troubles him greatly, but he does not appear to understand it fully or to know its present status in the world of laboratory research. A short disquisition on that test, and the role of animals in the science of which such testing is a part, is needed here.

Many of the chemicals humans must deal with are poisonous, some very poisonous. Toxicology is the science of poisons. To define the intrinsic toxicity of various chemicals, to predict their hazards for humans, to provide information about the risk of exposure to various chemicals, to help physicians design and select dose levels in administering drugs, and above all to help diagnose and treat damaging exposure to chemicals, it is essential to have some measure of their toxicity. Early in the twentieth century the LD50 test was designed for that purpose, to determine relative toxicities and to answer physicians when they asked: "How poisonous is that?" This test, rarely used today, is a statistical method for determining what single dose of a given substance can be expected to cause death in 50 percent of any given population. Because it gave a quantitative measure of intrinsic toxicity, it was useful in the handling of highly toxic substances, where slight variations could be lethal to humans. LD50 results, expressed as milligrams per kilogram of body weight, report how much of that stuff (whatever it may be) is likely to kill with a single dose. The answer for rats is a very useful signal to humans who may be obliged to handle that chemical. For strychnine sulfate, for example, still used in some pesticides, 3 milligrams per kilogram of body weight is all that is needed to kill; for nicotine, 24 milligrams per kilogram; for DDT, 135 milligrams per kilogram; for botulism toxin, found in some spoiled foods, *0.00001 milligram per kilogram is the lethal dose.*

But the LD50 screen had serious limitations, widely recognized by 1959;[20] the quantitative results of the LD50 tests were imprecise, and they varied with the sex and the condition of the test animals and with various environmental factors. Other ways were sought, and found, to test for acute toxicity. Attention shifted from lethal consequences to milder ones. Rather than ask what dose of the chemical will kill, toxicologists now more commonly ask what dose of the chemical would bring on symptoms of poisoning. This proves more useful because the chemicals of concern often have troubling manifestations and wide-ranging consequences that fall far short of death. By 1980, the LD50 test had largely ceased to be relied on in acute toxicity testing, although some of the older data derived from it remain useful. In 1981, the Organization for Economic Cooperation and Development (OECD) in Paris formulated and adopted alternative assays of acute toxicity[21]—of which there are several, all now replacing the LD50 test in most contexts. In the following years the refinement of toxicity testing progressed vigorously.[22] Some of the new assays rely on the known chemical properties of the various classes of toxins; some identify the signs of toxicity, and the range of its levels and its pathology, but avoid lethal dosing. Acute toxicity testing still goes on extensively, as of course it must, but the end points of the tests are no longer the deaths of the animals, and many fewer animals—rats or mice—are now needed. The change in emphasis in acute toxicity testing from quantity to symptoms was summed up in 1989, in one major text in toxicology: the shift has been approved and accepted by "general consensus in academia, industry, and government."[23]

Toxicology is a huge branch of medical science, of enormous value to human beings. Pesticides and herbicides, metals and solvents, radioactive materials, animal toxins (venoms) and plant toxins—all are ubiquitous poisons whose hazards we ignore at great peril. Food additives, air pollutants, soil pollutants, and water pollutants add to the toxic dangers that surround us. Safety requires the fullest understanding of the damage that can be done by these substances to human and animal organs: the liver, kidneys, eyes, and skin and organic systems—the central nervous system and the immune system, the cardiovascular and respiratory and reproductive systems. We have learned a very great deal in this arena, most of our knowledge coming from studies with rats and mice. As the number of hazards grows with the inexorable growth of human populations, we will need to learn much more, and our ability to do so will depend almost entirely on the work of toxicologists continuing to use rats and mice.

Tom Regan appears to understand very little of this. In what he seems to think a telling blow he advises the reader, "Hospital personnel who work in emergency rooms, where the majority of accidental poisonings are dealt with, do not consult LD50 results before treating their patients" (p. 146). Well, of course they do not. Even when they were in wide use decades ago, LD50 tests were not designed for emergency room application. He then continues with language implying that his critics are not to be trusted: "To suggest otherwise reflects profound ignorance of the practice of emergency medicine." But no thoughtful defense of animal research ever would "suggest otherwise"; this careful phrasing implies that those who use animals contend what they do not in fact contend. How ought one respond to such rhetoric?

Regan appears not to know that the LD50 test—a central object of his ire— is no longer commonly used by toxicologists, that it has been replaced by toxicity tests of different kinds, relying on rats and mice in different ways and in much smaller numbers. If he does know it, he refrains from saying so, for he writes as though toxicology ceased to advance after 1940. Either Regan's understanding of scientific toxicology is very shallow, or his account of toxicity testing is deliberately deceptive.

Many tests for chemical hazards are in use today, rightly used every day to ensure the safety of drugs and other compounds designed for administration to humans. But the use of animals in toxicological studies to advance safety differs vastly from the use of animals to acquire basic scientific understanding and to uncover and explore possible treatments for human disease. Regan seems not to appreciate even that enormous difference. He thinks the rights of rats are infringed upon in all cases and so does not trouble to distinguish the varieties of the sin. Whether out of ignorance or design, therefore, his criticism of animal research of *every* kind goes forward on the basis of the alleged faults of that one, out-dated, quantitative test for acute toxicity, the LD50. He writes, "the *same questions* [as those asked about this test] can be asked of *any test or research that uses the animal model*" (p. 147; emphasis added). Poor stuff, but it gets yet worse.

The "Basic Moral Questions"

Having presented what he calls the two "basic scientific questions,"[24] Regan advances to what he calls "the basic moral questions" which are also two. The first is a beauty: "First, if animal model tests or research are scientifically indefensible, then how, morally, can their continued use be justified?" (p. 147). The wording is plainly designed to suggest that the premise (that animal research is scientifically indefensible) had been established, while in fact the contradictory of that premise is true. The uses of animal models in research, and toxicity tests using animals, are in fact as defensible and as worthy as any branch of medicine; laboratory animal medicine is one of the very most productive modern scientific instruments. And although not foolproof, its reliability is very high. That is the verdict of the history of science and of the entire medical world. To frame the question as Regan does, in a way that deliberately implies the indefensibility of animal research, is the plainest sort of manipulation. The intelligence of his readers, I believe, he has badly underestimated.

Having asked the question in this manipulative way, he reports that he will "consider the first question in my reply to Professor Cohen" (p. 147). Why delay? Is there something he plans to say about animal research in his reply that cannot be said at this point? Why hold it back? Does he fear that if presented forthrightly at that appropriate point, his critic will have too full an opportunity to respond? Nothing is held back in my criticism of his views.

Tom Regan has been fully aware of my critique of the animal rights movement for years. He appears to think that safeguarding his reply to me by postponing it will yield strategic advantage. Here again I think he underestimates his readers.[25]

In any event, his artfully constructed "first question" needs no laborious response. Taken literally it may be answered crisply and put aside: *if* research using animals were "scientifically indefensible," it could not be justified, of course. That's perfectly obvious to everyone, and there is no need for him to be coy about it. But this so-called "basic moral question" he framed very carefully, *building in* the false assumption that animal research is indefensible. This is argument of which I believe Tom Regan ought to be ashamed.

The second of the "basic moral questions" is much more interesting. But to it we get no answer at all. Regan asks, "Second, even if this methodology is scientifically defensible—indeed, even if, by relying on it, important human interests in safety and health are advanced to a degree that would be otherwise unobtainable—does that make animal tests or research right?" (p. 147). We know that Regan believes that the answer to this question is no. He told us on the very first page of his first essay that he stands for "the total abolition of the use of animals in science." But at this point he does not answer; he backs away, changes the focus. Why? Perhaps he fears that if he tells his readers straight out that they must reject the uses of rats in medicine "even if important human interests in safety and health are advanced by that use to a degree that would be otherwise unobtainable," they will shake their heads and close the book. He must temporize. This question, we are advised, "cannot be answered in a vacuum"; in such moral disputes, he tells us, "which side is correct is hard to say" (p. 147–48).

But the answer to this second question is not hard at all; it may be given readily and clearly, without unfairness or inaccuracy: *if it is true* that the use of animals in medicine is a methodology that is scientifically defensible, and *if, using it, important human interests in safety and health are advanced to a degree that would be otherwise unobtainable*—premises established and confirmed and reconfirmed repeatedly with abundant and compelling detail, and asserted without reservation by the very finest scientific minds in the very finest medical centers the world over[26]—then the use of animal models is *right*, and the use of animals in testing vaccines and new drugs is most certainly right.

And it must be emphasized: *Animals cannot be replaced as subjects in most medical research.* At one point Regan asks rhetorically whether reliance on the animal model in research might not be undergoing "transformation." It may indeed be undergoing transformation because, with the Human Genome Project now nearing completion, and the known genetic similarities between humans and other animals suggesting medical investigations that have not been imagined to this date, the number of scientific studies using animals is rising and will continue to rise. New horizons are opening in medicine, and with them new and more productive avenues of research into human disease and disorder, much of which will require animal use.

This is not the transformation Regan has in mind, of course. His vision of the great moral awakening, of which he sees himself as a founder, is one in which "all the scientific laboratories of the world will have a sign over their entrances proclaiming 'No Animals Allowed' " (p. 221).

Regan reports correctly that there is a "growing willingness on the part of the research community to look for ways of replacing animals in the lab." This is for him another of those "grounds of hope" with which his essay comes to climax. He is correct in noting that in some restricted contexts some reduction of animal use is indeed feasible. Animal lives ought not be sacrificed to no purpose, and there is therefore no dispute about the desirability of such replacements when the quality of the results achieved are not adversely affected. *Replace* living subjects where feasible, *reduce* the numbers of lives expended where feasible, *refine* experiments so as to put those lives to best use—these are the three *R*s of good animal laboratory science, reasonable ideals of humane practice.

But it is sheer folly to think that the replacement of animals is possible generally in medical science. If Regan believes that in the testing of new drugs and vaccines computers or discarded tissues or synthesized materials or some other artifacts will be substituted for rats and mice, he is living in a fantasy world. The reasons for this were given at length earlier (pp. 70–72). The short of the matter is this: the very great complexity of a living animal cannot be reproduced with tissue samples, or computer simulations, or with any other synthetic models.[27] Without trials on subjects having the needed complexity, we cannot gather sufficient evidence that a new compound is likely to be safe or effective. Human subjects have the needed complexity, but using them first would be unconscionable. Primary testing of the safety and efficacy of new compounds will *require,* as far into the future as we can see, nonhuman living animals as subjects. Their use is generally not conclusive (except where toxicity is plainly shown), but if rodents (or other animals) are not used to evaluate new compounds, humans would have to be used—or those compounds will not be evaluated at all.

Yes, the use of animals in medical science is incontrovertibly essential, and the human interests in view—the elimination of misery and pain and sickness and death—are so plainly paramount that the use of animals in medicine is morally *right,* deeply right.

Tom Regan claims that the interests of human safety and health are simply *trumped* by the rights of rats. In the sections that follow, therefore, I look very closely at the reasons he gives us to believe that this is so, to believe that it is our moral duty to respect the rights of rodents. After all, Regan's willingness to sacrifice the interests of untold millions of humans (us included), now and in the future, in order to safeguard the rights of rats and chickens, surely obliges him to establish the reality of those rights with compelling argument. Nothing of the sort is offered; his arguments are fallacious and without merit.

The Burdens of Consistency

One preliminary matter: To decide rationally how much confidence we must have in his arguments before we would accept them, we will want to know how the adoption of his principles will affect our lives. Regan himself (to the best of my knowledge) lives the life his categorical prohibitions require: he eats no meat or meat by-products; he wears and uses no animal products of any kind, no leather belts or furniture, no woolen clothing. He opposes *all* medical research involving animals ("not larger cages but *empty* cages" is his goal)—and therefore, I presume, he accepts no benefits from such research. His philosophical convictions make him an abolitionist without any reservation whatever. He believes that it is his duty to live in this way, protecting animal rights scrupulously, and that it is your duty and my duty to do as he does.

Many advocates of animal rights are less consistent than Regan and are ridiculed for wearing leather shoes or eating hamburgers. Such *ad hominem* jibes I deplore because they are directed at flaws of character instead of substantive issues. Our proper concern is the *falsity* of claims about the alleged rights of animals, not the integrity of those who make those claims. If defenders of animal rights do fail to live up to their own teaching, the anguish of personal inconsistency is their problem, not ours.

But Tom Regan is consistent, and that consistency is instructive. He is prepared to accept all the consequences of his abolitionist convictions; the rights of any rats, horses, cows, or chickens touching his life Regan will protect, *come what may*. If he must suffer because of these duties, well, that's just a burden that must be borne. The prohibitions by which he thinks himself bound reveal what *we* would be morally obliged to refrain from doing if animals really did have rights as he believes they do.

Not eating meat or wearing leather are not the heaviest parts of that burden. Far more grave is the obligation to eschew, for one's self and one's children, the use of all drugs and vaccines developed using animal research. It is not *ad hominem* argument to observe that Regan and his friends, respecting "animal rights" consistently, must refrain from the use of compounds that may be needed to protect their health or the health of their loved ones. For in this case his arguments are claimed to give *us* sufficient reason to refrain from such use as well, and we must decide whether those arguments are strong enough to oblige *our* abstinence too. So I ask: Have the children of these zealots been vaccinated against disease? I presume not.

The following thought experiment reveals more fully the consequences of committing one's self consistently to the protection of animal rights. Tom Regan enjoys outdoor activities, and we can well imagine that on some cross-country hike a child of his may be bitten by one of the Eastern diamondback rattlesnakes abundant in those North Carolina woods, or a cottonmouth or copperhead perhaps, or during a winter holiday in Martinique his wife may be struck by the *fer-de-lance*, a snake whose bite is often fatal if not swiftly treated with an antivenin. Happily, there is treatment readily available for such excruciatingly painful bites, an antivenin that is waiting for the Regan family or any family in need of it, at any good hospital in North Carolina or the Caribbean. But would Tom Regan's child be allowed to receive it? Here is his problem: The needed treatment for the bites of that family of pit vipers is Antivenin (crotalidae) Polyvalent—serum globulin obtained from the blood of healthy horses that have been injected with snake venoms to cause the development, in their blood, of the needed antibodies. Those horses have been *used* without their consent, with some pain to them. But if the antivenin is not administered quickly, children bitten by rattlesnakes (or other pit vipers) will suffer terribly, may lose an arm or leg, and may even die. What would be the fate of Regan children so bitten? Their father's words lack no clarity: the rights of animals must be respected "though the heavens fall." The animals he refers to surely include those horses whose life-giving blood could not have been taken without blatantly violating their rights, if they have rights.

Perhaps Regan and friends do use vaccines tested on animals, or antivenins produced in living animals, and defend that use by pointing out that these are long-established realities, no longer requiring animal sacrifice. Whatever happened long ago, these compounds have been in standard use for decades; no protection is given to animal rights today by forgoing their use. Is this a fair response? Not in the case of the antivenin, surely, whose production requires the ongoing use of healthy horses.

But would it justify the use of standard vaccines? Might those who eat hamburgers defend their doing so by noting that they are consuming the meat of animals killed some time back? Eating the beef (they might say) doesn't violate animal rights because the fact of consumption entails no additional slaughter. Regan's reply is obvious and forceful. That defense of eating meat is plainly disingenuous, since we know that slabs of meat will quickly be procured to replace the ones consumed. The practice of eating beef today (he will insist) virtually ensures that more cows will have their rights infringed upon tomorrow. This rejoinder has merit. *If* we are obliged not to support the killing of animals for meat, we are certainly obliged *also* to refrain from eating the meat of animals killed earlier. Not to refrain will surely promote repeated killing.

But if this is a good reason to refuse to eat the beef already in the kitchen, it is an equally good reason to forgo the use of the vaccine already in the clinic.

We don't save any rat's life by refusing the vaccine already prepared, but every use of benefit from that slaughter of rats is direct encouragement to seek and test other vaccines in the same way. More rats will die in the effort to discover and certify the vaccines that are not yet in the laboratory. If it is wrong to eat the steak now in the restaurant, it must be wrong to use the drug (developed using animals) now in the doctor's office.[28] For the consistent advocate of animal rights virtually every medication in a modern pharmacy—certainly including antivenins—is simply forbidden.

What the actual practice of Regan and his friends may be, in this connection, is not important. The serious and honest application of their principles would require that *we* not use any vaccines, or drugs, or antivenins developed at any time in the past through the use of animals, directly or as subjects for the test of safety or efficacy. We must refuse to use such compounds now, or ever, whether in the interest of our own health or the health of our children. Since virtually every vaccine and modern drug has in fact been developed or tested using animal studies, and since federal law (rightly) compels the animal testing of every drug before it is administered to human patients, and since the manufacture of many compounds requires the continuing use of animals, a consistent defense of animal rights would oblige us, as it obliges Tom Regan, to refrain absolutely from the use of modern antibiotics, antivenins, and other medicines, and also to refrain from the vaccination of our babies to safeguard them from disease.

The price of consistent adherence to the animal rights movement is *very* high. Before we seriously contemplate the transformation of our lives urged on us by that movement, therefore, we owe it to ourselves and our families to examine, with a very skeptical eye, the philosophical arguments by which it is claimed that "animal rights" are established.

The Structure of Regan's Case

Regan's arguments for animal rights occupy very little space. More than four-fifths of all that he has to say, in this volume as in his earlier book,[29] is devoted to the discussion of human rights but does not mention animals at all. Most of these matters are not in dispute. Rights are indeed a central feature of human moral life and are of profound importance; rights do demand respect even at the cost of the convenience or the interests of those who are the targets of those rights. The issue that is in dispute, on which we sharply disagree, is whether *rats and chickens* have rights as humans do. This subject Regan reaches only in the final pages of his essay; to it he devotes approximately five pages (pp. 207–12).

Some plausible foundation for the claim that rats and chickens really do have rights is what Regan needs. He thinks he has uncovered this foundation in an alleged moral fellowship of rodents, humans, birds, and other animal species. All these, he asserts, are members—essentially equal members—of a common moral community. Evidence of their alleged moral fellowship he thinks revealed in certain aspects of the *subjective* experience of rats and chickens that are no different from the same aspects of human experience.

This enterprise is doomed to failure. Philosophers have long pointed out that *facts* about the subjective experiences of any beings never can justify *moral* conclusions about those beings. From what *is* the case there are no conclusions to be drawn about what *ought to be* the case. To draw a conclusion that something *ought* to be done (or ought not be done), the argument needs to have some *premise* that, at minimum, brings "oughtness" into the arena. The passage from the wholly *a*moral to the moral, from subjective awareness to objective rights, must be a non sequitur because the realm of physiological subjectivity is entirely distinct from the realm of moral rights. When that gap between the region in which Regan builds premises and the region in which he would like to draw conclusions is discerned, his undertaking is seen to be hopeless. Its hopelessness is partly obscured by an elaborate argumentative strategy.

Here is the structure of his case: Regan begins with what he calls factual matters—what he believes to be the facts of the rat's *subjective experiences.* From this animal consciousness he infers that the rat is one of those beings he calls "subjects-of-a-life." From the claim that the rat is a "subject-of-a-life" Regan next infers that the rat possesses *inherent value.* From the rat's alleged inherent value Regan concludes that the rat has *moral rights.*

This is the essence of the argument that must be closely examined.

Facts and Conjectures

The empirical base on which Regan builds is a set of judgments about what he thinks actually goes on in the brains of rats and chickens. These are animals plainly capable of taking an interest in things and of wanting things; in their behavior we witness aversions and attractions and choices. These are taken to provide "compelling grounds" for attributing to rats and chickens "a rich, complex mental life."

Everyone is likely to agree that at least some animals do experience something analogous to human fear and volition. We should be very careful, however, in drawing inferences about the internal lives of animals from the record of their external behavior.

First, very different species are clumped together in Regan's claim. Animals with extremely limited capacities are presumed to have internal lives essentially like the lives of animals far more highly evolved.[30]

Second, it is very doubtful that any of the animals in question *reflect,* as humans do, on the fact that they are the subjects of their own experience.

Third, it is very easy to be misled, to draw unwarranted conclusions about animal thought process from animal conduct that is externally like human conduct. Sophisticated students of animal behavior are very cautious in making claims about what animals are really thinking. We witness actions that bear some resemblance to our own; we may interpret these as revealing emotions or attitudes like our own. Sympathy leads us to infer that the chicken's internal experience is essentially like our own internal experience. Such inferences are very speculative.

One example of the leap from external behavior to conjectured feelings is given by Professor Marc Hauser, a Harvard psychologist and expert in animal behavior.[31] Pet owners will commonly suppose, when they find a half-eaten pizza on the floor and the dog's head hanging down with eyes downcast, that the dog feels "guilty." But guilt is a feeling that cannot be concluded from external behavior only; guilt requires a sensitivity to the thoughts and beliefs of those who are judging the conduct in question. Humans can reflect on their own conduct, and their own beliefs, and then appraise these in the light of their understanding of the beliefs of others. To suppose that dogs go through this process, similarly juxtaposing conduct and beliefs, and then feeling guilt because of an awareness of some dissonance, is pure conjecture. For that conjecture, Hauser points out, we have no evidence whatever.

Readers will come to their own judgment of what is likely to be the thought process of rats and chickens. Some complexity of experience in the minds of animals there surely is. The reach and significance of the complexity realized in their minds remains very uncertain.

Why "Subjects-of-a-Life"?

Regan's need is to create some *link* between the imputed subjective experience of animals and the alleged rights of those animals. To this end a class of beings is marked off that Regan calls "subjects-of-a-life." These are the beings who are believed to have some subjective awareness of their own lives, and for whom, as a result, it may be said that things "fare well or badly." Of course we may not conclude, from the fact that things fare well or badly for an animal, that it can formulate the proposition expressing this, or can even grasp that notion in some sub-linguistic way. The judgment that "things are faring well *for me* these days" is not likely to be among the repertoire of chicken reflections. But some crude subjective experience there must be, since the chicken is drawn toward the food tray and runs away from the fox. This indicates, says Regan, that the chicken (like every "subject-of-a-life") has *interests*.

The strategy here is to devise some category into which both animal lives and human lives may be assimilated. Within this newfound category, since it is designed to include humans too, some of the lives led (the human ones) are plainly moral. From this he will go on to infer that *all* the lives in that class, lives so categorized by virtue of his definition, are moral. But this maneuver could succeed only if the criteria for admission to the newly invented category were themselves intrinsically moral—which of course they are not.

"Subjects-of-a-life" is a category of beings that Regan defines by his own stipulation; membership in that class requires only the crudest subjective experience. Having devised the category by fastening upon certain kinds of primitive experience that rats and humans do share, he goes on to assume that moral rights, possessed by humans, arise from just those interests. Some human interests (e.g., in food and sex) are no different in essence from those of rats, and since we all agree that humans do have rights, he infers that rats must have them, too.

In the sense that a sentient animal—even an octopus or a trout—seeks to avoid pain, it does indeed have interests; many animals obviously have interests in that sense. Were Regan to leap directly from the possession of interests to the claim that such interests establish moral rights, his argument—like those far-fetched claims of Bernard Rollin and Steven Sapontzis earlier recounted[32]—would be a transparent failure. To avoid this transparency Regan takes a more convoluted path.

A Closer Look at Inherent Value

The rights that are to be established flow, Regan contends, from the "*inherent value*" of rats and chickens, and their inherent value is held to be a consequence of their being "subjects-of-a-life." So he makes the passage from interests to rights *by way of* "subjects-of-a-life" and then "inherent value." Both these concepts, as in his 1983 book,[33] are critical links for him: what has subjective experience must have inherent value, and what has inherent value must have rights. This can explain, he argues, why moral respect is owed to rats and chickens.

Reasoning in this way supposes that the rights of rats and chickens are *derived* from the primitive capacities that give them interests. Like Rollin and Sapontzis, Regan is at bottom convinced that rights are the product of animal interests, that a being has rights because it has interests—and he cannot fathom how we could assert of humans, who surely do have interests, that their rights could flow from anything else.

But the conviction that human rights flow from human interests (a conviction shared expressly or tacitly by virtually all animal rights advocates) is one for which there is simply no foundation. The lives we humans lead are indeed moral lives, pervaded by duties and rights. But this moral character of our lives is not a byproduct of our subjective awareness. Our rights are not ours because we experience our lives as our own. Nonhuman creatures may have subjective interests like ours in survival and reproduction, and they may be supposed to have subjective experience of some sort. But from those interests moral rights cannot be inferred.

The plausibility of Regan's reasoning depends on the inference that animals have "inherent value" and then on what may be inferred from the possession of such value. The failure of the argument is a consequence of the fact that the "inherent value" that he infers from the reality of subjective experience is not the same "inherent value" from which rights are later derived. An academic shell game is afoot, in which readers are the marks. Having given our assent to what is plausible in one sense of the expression "inherent value," we are told that dramatic conclusions follow respecting rights. But these conclusions do *not* follow from the inherent value that we may have assented to in animals, although they may follow from inherent value in a very different sense of that term.

Readers will recall the critical distinction, explained earlier in this volume, between what was there called sense 1 and sense 2 of the words "inherent value" (pp. 53–56). Both are plausible uses of the words; neither is objectionable in itself. But what is true of inherent value in the one sense is not true of inherent value in the other sense, and by slipping from one to the other meaning of the phrase Regan commits an egregious fallacy.

We earlier distinguished:

1. Inherent value in the very widely applicable sense that every unique life, not replaceable by other lives or things, has some worth in itself. In this sense every rat, and every octopus too, has inherent value. This value may be minimal; it certainly has no awesome moral content—but it is fair to say that, being irreplaceable and unique, even primitive living things ought not be destroyed for no reason whatever.

2. Inherent value in the far narrower sense arises from the possession of the capacity to make moral judgments, the value of beings with duties and the consciousness of duties. This is the rich philosophical sense of value made famous by Immanuel Kant and employed by many moral thinkers since; it is the sense of inherent worth flowing from the special *dignity* of those who have a moral will. The value of agents who have a moral will does indeed *inhere* in them and entitles them to be treated as ends, and never as means only. Beings with value in this sense—human beings, of course—have rights.

Now it is plain that most beings with inherent value in the first sense—live creatures in the wild, for example—although they may merit some protection, do not begin to possess inherent value in the second, moral sense. Trees and rats have value in the common sense, and we may plausibly call that value "inherent"—but that is no ground for ascribing moral agency to them. The gap in the argument is here exposed: subjective experiences of rats and chickens lead us to conclude that they really do have interests, but subjective experiences cannot serve to justify the claim that they have rights.

Human beings, on the other hand, have inherent value in both senses. We have worth in that second, Kantian sense, to be sure, but value also in the simpler, common sense as well. The equivocal uses of these two senses of the same phrase in *The Case for Animal Rights* was explained in some detail earlier in this book. The restatement of that argument, in Regan's contribution to the present volume, relies in the same way on slippage between these two senses of the same phrase. That slippage is obscured by reaching rights from subjectivity *through* the concept "subject-of-a-life." Within that category lie beings with inherent value in both senses (humans), and beings with inherent value in the first sense only (rats). The stage is set for slippage.

We humans are subjects of our own lives, of course, so we have inherent value in that simple first sense; and surely we do have moral rights. Regan then asks: if the rat is the subject of its own life, must it not also have the same "inherent value" that we have? In the first sense of inherent value it does. And if it does have inherent value as we do, does it not also have moral rights as we do? No, not at all! By moving *into* the concept of "inherent value" in the first sense (in which that value is shared), then drawing inferences *from* inherent value in the second sense (in which it is not shared), Regan pulls the rabbit from the hat, miraculously extending the realm of moral rights to include the rats and the chickens.

Underlying his equivocation is the tacit supposition that we humans have rights only as a *consequence* of our being "subjects-of-a-life." But this is false, and we have not the slightest reason to think it true. Having assumed it true, Regan and his friends take themselves to have *amalgamated* the world of human moral experience with the world of rodent experience. That cannot be done with words, or with anything else.

The Argument Step by Step

Here follow the steps of Regan's argument, essentially as he sets them forth, with brief comment on each. Close scrutiny will show that his critical steps rely on double meanings, his objectives reached by using whichever sense of the equivocal term is convenient for the purpose at hand.

1. Humans and rats are both "subjects-of-a-life."

   Comment: If all that is being said here is that other animals as well as humans have subjective interests and awareness, this premise is not in dispute. In having subjective interests "non-human animals are like us," Regan says. Yes, in the sense that they also have appetites, feel pain, and so on.

2. Beings that are "subjects-of-a-life" are beings having inherent value.

   Comment: This is the introduction of the central equivocal phrase. Animals with subjective experience do indeed have "inherent value" in the common sense that all living things, including humans, are unique and irreplaceable. But the vast majority of beings having subjective experiences do *not* have "inherent value" in the Kantian sense that would be needed to ground moral rights.

3. Since rats, like humans, have inherent value because they are "subjects-of-a-life," the inherent value that rats possess is essentially no different from the inherent value that humans possess.

   Comment: The distinction between the two very different senses of inherent value being here ignored or obscured, it seems plausible for Regan to assert here what is true (but innocuous) if the words are taken in one way, yet false (and very harmful) if taken in another. In the common sense both rats and humans do have inherent value. But this "inherent value" possessed by them both (sense 1) is profoundly different from the "inherent value" that is bound up with human moral agency (sense 2).

   Regan writes, "The relevant similarity shared by humans who have inherent value is that we are subjects-of-a-life" (p. 211). No, that similarity is not relevant to moral matters at all. On the contrary, we may say that the relevant *dissimilarity* between humans and rats is that, although both may have value as lives, only humans have inherent value in the sense from which rights may be inferred. Regan conflates the two very different senses of value, referring to both with the same words, and his argument depends upon this conflation.

5. The inherent value that we humans possess is what accounts for our moral rights. (In his words: "All those who possess inherent value possess the equal right to be treated with respect.")

   Comment: So long as we understand that it is Kantian inherent value (sense 2) here referred to, the claim that from it great moral consequences flow is not in dispute.

6. Since rats possess inherent value for the same reasons that humans do, rats must have moral rights just as human do.

   Comment: Not at all! Here the switch is cashed out. Rats possess inherent value *in sense 1* for the same reason humans do, because they have subjective interests as humans also have. But from these primitive interests no moral rights can be inferred. Regan writes, "Relevantly similar cases should be judged similarly" (p. 212). But the circumstances of rats and humans are in the most essential matters *not* relevantly similar. Indeed, with regard to moral status they could hardly be more sharply dissimilar. The argument thrives on repeated equivocation.

7. Regan concludes, "It follows that all those human beings and all those animal beings who possess inherent value share the equal right to respectful treatment" (p. 212).

Comment: Not on your life! The inherent value shared is value in the common sense, but what can entail respect for rights is *not* shared by rats. What is true of both rats and humans is the fact that they are living beings, the life of each unique, each having interests of its own. From this, nothing about moral rights may be validly inferred.

Infected throughout by the equivocation between inherent value that "subjects-of-a-life" may possess and the entirely different sense of inherent value that may indeed ground human rights, the argument is worthless. The lives of rats and chickens are indeed like the lives of humans in some primitive ways, but it certainly does not follow from those likenesses that rats and chickens share membership in the community of moral beings. Repeatedly we encounter the same fallacious passage from the premise that animals have interests to the conclusion that animals have rights.

What about Plants?

That trees and bushes have rights is too much even for Regan to swallow. But might not trees, as well as rats, have inherent value? And might not such inherent value warrant their protection also? The question "What about plants?" (p. 217) is opened by Regan himself, but with obvious reluctance because answering the question is for him problematic. When he tries to fit plants into his scheme of things, the difficulty created by his unwillingness to distinguish different senses of inherent value bears down on him.

The alternatives he faces in this revealing passage are very awkward. Regan does not really think that plants are "subjects-of-a-life" of course, yet he cannot forthrightly say that they are not, because (given his definitions) to do so would seem to deny the commonly recognized inherent value of trees and other living things. Humble creatures do indeed have inherent value: threatened fishes, ancient trees, all living things have some worth in themselves, value that inheres in each of them. On the other hand, Regan cannot affirm this forthrightly, either, because, since he recognizes only one kind of inherent value, any admission that plants have it would oblige him to conclude that plants have rights as well.

The question ("What about plants?") that he may have thought innocuous confronts Regan with a very troubling dilemma. If there is only one sense of inherent value, either plants have it or they do not have it. And yet he cannot answer his own question straightforwardly. To affirm that plants do have inherent value would, on his own account, lead him to conclude that they too are subjects-of-a-life and have rights. But he cannot deny that plants have inherent value because he is too honest to lie, and the inherent value (sense 1) of living creatures is plainly seen by us all. Either response, were he to give it explicitly, would be devastating.

No quandary would confront him if only Regan would distinguish between the common sense of value in which trees (and rats and threatened fishes, etc.) do have it inherently, and the moral sense of value in which humans have it inherently but trees do not. Then he could reasonably allow (as most of us would) that trees have inherent value in one sense, but not in the sense that gives them rights. This distinction he is quite unwilling to make, however, for once the multiple senses of the phrase are called to attention his earlier argument, leaning heavily on their unacknowledged interchange, must collapse.

Regan's escape requires that he avoid answering his own question. Regan's dodge is charming: Whether inherent value "belongs to other forms of life, including plants [he writes] . . . are questions the [Regan] rights view *leaves open for others to explore*" (p. 217; emphasis added)!

The Alleged Blind Spot of Immanuel Kant

"Subject-of-a-life," Regan tells us, is the conceptual key to morality itself, the category that answers the deepest of all moral questions. It alone, we are told, "offers the basis for answering the great question posed by Immanuel Kant, 'Who is inherently valuable?' " (p. 210). How in the world did Regan make this marvelous discovery? The term is one that he invents. Why should anyone believe his claims about it? The cephalopods, invertebrates including the octopus and squid, have complex nervous systems that give clear indications of subjective experience. On Regan's criteria we are likely to conclude that they also are "subjects-of-a-life." So they must have rights, too. But whether squid—or rats or chickens—are inherently valuable in the Kantian sense that may ground moral rights is precisely the question in dispute. Never was there a clearer case of an author begging the question, assuming the very thing that was to have been shown.

The only gap that "subjects-of-a-life" can fill is the "lexical" gap created by Regan's own play with words. Its definition is entirely arbitrary, *stipulated* by him. The stipulation is not precise and has an air of mystery, but the term itself, *subject-of-a-life,* must bear enormous weight in his worldview. All philosophers before him, we are to understand, have failed to recognize this most central of moral concepts, the one concept that applies to all persons, all humans, and very many (but not all) lower animals; this category, "subject-of-a-life," accounts for their shared moral status. When Alice complains to Humpty Dumpty (in *Through the Looking Glass*) about a particularly convoluted definition he had given, he responds, "When I make a word do a lot of work like that, I always pay it extra."[34]

Kant understood very well that *duty,* the moral imperative, cannot possibly be deduced from the bare facts of physical life. When Kant asked, "Who are never to be treated merely as means?" he fully understood that the answer, whatever it was, could not be grounded in *subjectivity,* in the kinds of experience shared by a rat and Socrates. Those whom one must never treat as mere means are *persons,* he concluded, those having autonomous moral wills. It is not awareness of self, or the having of interests, but *being a member of the community of moral agents,* as rats and birds can never be, that gives moral dignity.

Regan's introduction of Kantian thought helps us to see why his arguments must fail. Using the newly invented category, "subjects-of-a-life," Regan would like to expand the Kantian conclusion to a huge and ill-defined class of beings who have some measure of subjective experience. This expansion of the moral realm to include all the rodents and birds, and all the cephalopods as well, would be utterly ridiculous in Kant's eyes. Subjective experience in the lives of creatures for whom there is and can be no morality is not surprising, but the uniqueness of their lives does not elevate them to membership in the realm of ends in themselves. Things may fare well or badly for a chicken, but that fact does not give the chicken the *dignity* of a being with moral rights and duties.

The answer to Kant's question was given crisply by Kant himself: *human beings* (but not all beings with subjective experience) must be treated as ends-in-themselves. This was not a myopic blunder. The critical role of the capacity to make moral choices Kant explains in the third section of the *Foundations of the Metaphysics of Morals.* It is the capacity to choose freely that distinguishes members of the moral world. We humans are members of that world, but not of that world only. If we were moral agents purely and had no animal interests our acts would always be right, always in accord with duty. But we are also members of the world of sense, having desires and interests that often conflict with what we know to be right. We understand that our actions in the everyday world *ought* to conform to a moral standard that we can recognize but cannot steadily maintain in practice. This consciousness of the gap between our *inclinations* and the choices we *ought* to make, between our interests and our duties, Kant thinks to be what accounts for *imperatives* that constrain our will, and for our status as moral agents with inherent value beyond all price.

Rats and chickens recognize no moral imperatives, cannot possibly pass moral judgment of any kind. The suggestion that rats and chickens are fellow members of the community of moral agents is totally absurd, as Regan—seeking to ward off that complaint preemptively—half recognizes. He does this by suggesting that the complaint of absurdity is based on a mistaken assumption by his critics, who are supposed to believe that he thinks that rats and chickens should have the right to vote and to marry, which of course he does not think.[35]

But that is not the complaint made; Regan's response here is just smoke. The confusion underlying his views—for Kant and for us—lies not in the supposition that rats and chickens might claim the right to vote or marry but in the supposition that they have the moral standing presupposed by rights of any kind. The claim that such animals are fellow members of the moral community is what thoughtful reflection finds indigestible. The notion that rats and chickens could hold rights Kant would dismiss with disdain. It is indeed absurd.

The "lexical gap" that Regan manufactures tells us nothing about authentic duties; Kant would dismiss the entire notion as obfuscation. "Lexical" categories may be stipulated without limit, but genuine morality is concerned with rights that are objective, not invented. Regan is presumptuous to suppose that he has given to Kant's great moral question the correct answer that (he appears to think) Kant himself was not deep enough to grasp.

The Underlying Difficulty

The fact that there is in human life a moral dimension that cannot be accounted for by simply being alive, as a trout or a chicken is alive, is one with which Regan cannot come to grips.[36] He focuses only on the kinds of interests that rats and humans *share* and then assumes that rights arise from interests of just that kind. *We* feel ourselves the subject of our own lives; *they* (he conjectures) feel themselves the subjects of their own lives; if subjective awareness (as he supposes) is the ground of our moral condition, the subjectively aware chicken must have moral rights in the same sense that the subjectively aware human has them. Not the same rights, he allows of course, but rights held in the same sense, and rights deserving of the same moral *respect*.

We all agree that humans do have rights, and certainly they have interests also. Since *some* human interests are no different in essence from some interests of rats, he concludes that rats must have rights as we do. He writes, "It is speciesist to affirm inherent value in the case of human subjects-of-a-life who have interests, and deny this in the case of non-human subjects-of-a-life who have interests" (p. 210).

But humans, although we share some physiological features with rats and chickens, remain importantly different from them, different in having moral capacities and leading moral lives. This reply he finds anathema: "such a suggestion is symptomatic of the prejudice of speciesism." Speciesism it surely is. Sound judgments require moral distinctions among species. The species *Homo sapiens* and the species *Rattus norvegicus* do not share the same moral circumstances, do not live in the same moral world. To call the recognition of the contrast between them a "prejudice" is again to beg the question. Regan is blinded by his unshakable commitment to the proposition that no moral distinctions among species can ever be made.

Practical Questions

Having presented his case for the derivation of animal rights from the reality of animal interests, Regan turns to the practical consequences of his views. Were animal rights to be widely accepted, the impact on human lives would be, as he realizes, stunning. Regan sees himself as a moral teacher, an abolitionist through and through, applying prohibitions categorically and sternly. Our duty to respect the rights of rats and chickens may prove burdensome, but it does not excuse us. Just as human slavery was intolerable, so also rat slavery, sheep slavery, and chicken slavery are intolerable and must be abolished at any cost. Abolition must be complete, without exception, and without delay.

"In the case of animals in science," Regan writes, "the rights view [i.e., Regan's own view] is categorically abolitionist"[37] No benefit of medical research, however probable or however great, can justify the disrespectful treatment of mice. In medical science mice and rats are *used;* "their rights are routinely, systematically violated" (p. 212). Such use Regan finds utterly unacceptable; whatever benefits to humanity (or to animals) the use of animals may have produced or may some day yield, it is and will always be unacceptable.

A rhetorical problem confronts Regan here. The admission that the benefits of much research using animals have indeed been enormous he finds too awkward to make forthrightly. The truth of that he knows quite well, but for him to recognize those benefits candidly while insisting upon the complete abolition of the research that has produced them must surely cause readers to doubt his good sense. A way must be found to soften the blow of his abolitionism. What to do? He *insinuates* that the benefits of animal research are only illusory. Without lying he can again intimate what he dare not assert. Mice and rats must not be used, he writes, even "when they are used in studies *touted* as holding real promise of human benefits" (p. 212; emphasis added). This indirect suggestion that the promise of animal research in medicine is no greater than the promise of a racetrack tout is one of Regan's least winning passages.

The prohibition of animal use, in his view, is a consequence of the principle—a sound principle—that rights trump interests. Human health, longevity, freedom from pain are all interests of ours, to be sure—but "however important that interest might be," the rights of the rats and mice that we would use to advance it prevail over them and preclude all such research. We *may not* sacrifice the rights of mice to our interests. "We are never to take the life, invade or injure the body, or limit the freedom of any animal just because we personally or society in general will benefit. If we mean anything by the ascription of rights to animals, we mean this" (p. 213).

Farm animals are for him in the same case. By referring repeatedly to "commercial" animal agriculture, he would leave the suggestion that his condemnation will burden only greedy businessmen. But of course the family farmer who keeps chickens for the home use of their meat and eggs *uses* animals just as the mass producer of dairy products uses animals. All farmers, small and large, and most of the rest of us as well, view animals as renewable resources for our use. That view of them, Regan believes, is downright *evil*, a sin of which we are all guilty. "Nothing less than the total dissolution of commercial animal agriculture" is his explicit aim. "The [Regan] rights view's abolitionist implications, as I [Regan] have said, are both clear and uncompromising" (p. 213).

How fully Regan really does understand the practical consequences of his views in this connection is not clear. Animal agriculture is a major segment of the economies of most regions and nations of the globe. All the peoples of central Asia, much of China, East Asia, and the Indian subcontinent, much of South America, all of New Zealand, and much of Australia, Canada, and the American West, and all the peoples of the Arctic north depend on animal agriculture. Most of the inhabitants of our planet are either involved in raising animals or use animal products. The human suffering entailed by the total dissolution of animal agriculture would be incalculable.[38]

None of this troubles Tom Regan. The pains of eliminating animal use count no more in his scheme of things than the pains of eliminating human slavery counted in the worldview of abolitionists then. But the proposal to eliminate all animal agriculture, all animal use, is not noble, not humane. It is fatuous; and when its consequences are weighed thoughtfully, it will be judged callous.

Reducing the Magnitude of Evil in the World

The human world is shot through with evil, in Tom Regan's view. His passionate phrases—the "massive, day-to-day invasion" of the bodies of animals, the "denial of their basic liberties," the "destruction of their very life"—call to mind sermons of threat and condemnation, like that of Melville's Father

Mapple: "Jonah teaches *me,* as a pilot of the living God . . . to sound those unwelcome truths in the ears of a wicked Nineveh."[39] Our sinfulness is so depraved, the horror of our ways so vast, that "like light years in astronomy, it is all but incomprehensible" (p. 218).

The evil doings of hunters, fur trappers, and the like, are but a small part of the problem. The true magnitude of evil in the world, he thinks, includes every human *preference* for the use of animals that any person may express or seek to satisfy. Are you, dear reader, complicit in this evil? That may depend on what you eat or wear. Do you drink milk or wear wool? Are you one of those who yield to "gustatory temptations associated with lamb chops, fried chicken, and steak" (p. 130)? Then it is bootless to deny your guilty thoughts and acts. Confess them. Transform your life so that you take no nourishment, wear no garment, engage in no conduct that fails to respect the rights of animals. For the zealous puritan, fornication is but the manifestation of the sin of lust in the heart; for the zealous advocate of animal rights the use of animals is but the manifestation of the sin of preferences no less damnable. Only by cleansing ourselves of these, he teaches, we may significantly reduce the magnitude of human evil.

This teaching is not only ungrounded, but thoroughly mistaken and seriously damaging to the well-being of humankind. Abolishing every use of mice and rats and chickens and cows, as Regan would have us do, would indeed have great impact upon the magnitude of evil in the world—an impact that the animal rights movement is unwilling to confront.

Consider: The evils inflicted on human beings by *cancer,* the pain and misery, and the premature death of loved ones that is carried in its train, are evils we may seriously hope soon to reduce. We have reduced them greatly in recent years. Many sorts of cancer can now be *cured.* But the drugs and surgery widely used in this campaign were developed only through the use of animals, mostly mice.

There is vastly more to learn. The continuing war against cancer is waged in the laboratories of our medical centers; the battles in those wars are the careful studies of new compounds and diets, their safety and their effectiveness; the most effective weapons in those battles are the mice and rats without which we cannot hope to learn what reducing the evil of cancer requires.

The evils inflicted by *diabetes* on human beings, widespread evils inflicting pain, and misery, and the premature death of loved ones are also among those we may seriously hope to reduce. We will need to learn how to transplant insulin-producing cells safely and effectively, how to suppress the immune systems of the recipients of those transplants without causing damage, and so on and on. But before very long we will cure diabetes—*cure* it. This will require the use of a great many mice whose lives we will sacrifice, and should sacrifice, to save and improve the lives of our children.

One could go on in this vein at great length: the evils inflicted by the *genetic disorders* of human beings: cystic fibrosis, multiple sclerosis; the evils of *infectious diseases,* tuberculosis and AIDS; the evils of *heart disease* and *malaria;* the evils of *depression* and *mental disorder;* the evils of *aging* suffered by our parents, of Parkinson's and Alzheimer's—the evils of a thousand other diseases and disorders whose products are pain, and misery, and the premature death of loved ones. All these are evils we may hope soon to reduce.

We will do it. But to do it we will most certainly have to undertake very many studies involving animal subjects. The laboratory use of mice and rats and other animals is and will be absolutely critical in our continuing efforts to promote human health. Reducing the magnitude of evil in the world—alleviating human misery—is an aim that all may share. Even as we write and read this book great strides are being taken to advance this end, strides only possible because of animal research.

Using animals in this way is morally right. Refusing to use them because to do so is thought an infringement of the "rights" of rats and mice is morally wrong. That refusal, even though well intended, is conduct as inhumane as it is confused. Members of the animal rights movement—Regan and friends—are mostly decent folks who love animals. But their personal goodness cannot begin to justify the dreadful failure to reduce the magnitude of evil in the world that the adoption of their views would entail.

Notes

1. The use of quotation marks to indicate the fictitious status of animal "rights" is cumbersome; I forgo that convention from this point forward, but I note that any subsequent reference to alleged rights must not be supposed to presume their reality.

2. This point, often missed, was discussed at some length earlier in this volume. See pp. 27-30.

3. A professor of physiology at the University of Oxford, Colin Blakemore, who studies brain development and human childhood blindness, has been the target of the "Animal Liberation Front" for thirteen years; he and his family have received death threats and kidnapping threats, and bombs have twice been delivered to his home. In February 2000, a British magistrate convicted and sentenced one animal rights activist for standing outside his house for several weeks, shouting at him through a megaphone. See *Chronicle of Higher Education,* 17 March 2000, A58.

4. In the eighteenth century, when Regan's view was common, that scheme was called the *scala naturae.*

5. The number of insect species, the total number of insects, and the total biomass of insects all *vastly* exceed the totals of all other animals. Of all the species of animals that there are, 62 percent are of beetles. It would be understandable if Regan were not to claim that insects are among the animals allegedly having rights.

6. The lives of mollusks (oysters, clams, etc.) would be protected by Peter Singer

also, whose defense of strict vegetarianism is based on his utilitarian convictions. See Cohen at p. 60. Singer argues not that mollusks (or any animals) have *rights* but that mollusks ought not be eaten nevertheless, since they may suffer.

7. An animal defense organization called People for the Ethical Treatment of Animals (PETA) carries on an active campaign against the drinking of milk, which is obtained, on their view, only by invading the rights of cows.

8. Whether the inherent value that (in his view) entails the possession of rights "belongs to other forms of life, including plants" Regan "leaves open for others to explore" (p. 217). More will be said about this apparent uncertainty later in this reply.

9. The obligation to cease eating animals is not one that constrains other animals, on Regan's view. Of course not. That is because animals have no obligations whatever; they live in a totally *amoral* world. He is certainly right about that.

10. Vaccinations for smallpox are no longer given—but that is because smallpox has been *eradicated* from the globe, eliminated as a threat to humans by the almost universal vaccination against smallpox over a period of many decades.

11. Interrogatives are not propositions; they assert nothing. So asking a question whose answer assumes the truth of what one wants to have believed is safe; deniability is protected. Regan never *said* that laboratory animal medicine (an established department in most medical centers) is bankrupt, did he? As a backhanded technique of argument, questions that make some factual assumptions implicitly while avoiding responsibility for their forthright assertion—loaded questions—are a technique as old as sophistry itself. See Irving M. Copi and Carl Cohen, *Introduction to Logic*, 10th ed. (Upper Saddle River, N.J.: Prentice Hall, 1998), 18–21.

12. *Victims of Science* (London: Davis-Poynter, 1975). The passage Regan cites appears on p. 47. On p. 5 of Ryder's book he defines and attacks "speciesism" in a way that Regan closely echoes. Peter Singer's use of that same pejorative term in *Animal Liberation* (also published in 1975) appears to have been influenced by Ryder. Acute toxicity testing, which Ryder does not seem to understand, he can tolerate only if humans but not animals are put at risk. Regan is no deeper. Screening out dangerous compounds *before* they are tested on human beings is a problem Regan and Ryder never confront.

13. The uses of this analogy by animal rights advocates was discussed earlier. See Cohen, at pp. 19,21.

14. Ryder, *Victims of Science*, 85*ff*.; emphasis added.

15. Ryder, *Victims of Science*, 22; emphasis added.

16. *Science, Medicine and Animals* (Washington, D.C.: National Academy Press, 1991), 6.

17. *Use of Animals in Biomedical Research* (Chicago: American Medical Association, 1989).

18. The very day that this sentence was written (1 March 2000), the report of a new mouse model for the most common variety of human cancer was published in the journal *Nature Genetics*. More than one million skin cancers are diagnosed in the United States each year, most of these basal cell carcinomas. Associated with the development of basal skin cancer is the mutation of a gene called PTCH—but how this genetic change causes the normal cell to become a tumor cell is not known, although an excess of the protein Gli2 is plainly implicated. A research team at the University of

Michigan, working with researchers from the Hospital for Sick Children at the University of Toronto, have developed a strain of mice with abnormally large amounts of Gli2 in their skin, mice that spontaneously develop multiple skin tumors closely similar to human basal cell tumors. Because the same proteins, the same RNA markers, are found in both, we now have for the first time a robust animal model with which the cause and treatment of human cancers of that kind can be readily and fully explored.

19. Even fruit flies (*Drosophila melanogaster*), whose genome has recently been fully decoded, have genetic similarities to humans from which much can be learned. Of the 289 genes in humans known to cause disease in mutated form, scientists at the University of California at Berkeley (as reported in *Science*, 31 March 2000) have found direct counterparts of 177—more than half!—in the fruit fly. Of enthusiastic fruit-fly researchers it is sometimes said that they think of people as large flies that lack wings. Genetically speaking, mice are very much closer to humans, of course.

20. In that year W. M. S. Russell and R. L. Burch published a full treatment of the issues, *The Principles of Human Experimental Technique* (London: Methuen).

21. Organization for Economic Cooperation and Development, *Guidelines for Testing of Chemicals: Acute Oral Toxicity*, No. 401 (Paris: 1981). The OECD continues to publish guidelines for this purpose. Most recently appeared the *Guidance Document on Humane Endpoints for Experimental Animals Used in Safety Evaluation Studies* (1999).

22. Some of the principal contributors were these: G. Zbinden and M. Flury-Roversi, "Significance of the LD50 Test for Toxicological Evaluation of Chemical Substances," *Archives of Toxicology* 47 (1981): 77–99; E. Schutz and H. Fuchs, "A New Approach to Minimizing the Number of Animals Used in Acute Toxicity Testing and Optimizing the Information of Test Results," *Archives of Toxicology* 51 (1982): 197–220; G. L. Kennedy R. Ferenz, and B. A. Burgess, "Estimation of Acute Oral Toxicity in Rats by Approximate Lethal Dose Rather Than LD50," *Journal of Applied Toxicology* 6 (1986): 145–48.

23. *Principles and Methods of Toxicology*, 2d ed., ed. A. Wallace Hayes (New York: Raven, 1989). The other major text, *Toxicology: The Basic Science of Poisons*, 3d ed., ed. Louis M. Cassarett and John Doull (New York: Macmillan, 1984), makes essentially the same observation.

24. Those discussed just above: (1) "Is it scientifically credible to believe that what is discovered by using . . . a rat can be extrapolated to human beings?" and (2) "Might it be true that the use of the animal model is a bankrupt scientific methodology?"

25. Postponing reply is a maneuver Regan employs on a number of occasions. With respect to my rejection of his arguments for animal rights he says at one point, "I shall postpone . . . why I believe his arguments go wrong for my reply." Why? And early in his essay when he suggests that research using animals is sometimes tragically misleading, his reasons for making that claim are not given; he says only that "I shall return to this topic in my reply to Professor Cohen." I can hardly wait, although I do not see why I should have to. There are of course some cases in which animal research is misleading; no methodology is without failings. We are probably going to hear, in his reply, hoary accounts of injurious drugs, like thalidomide, that were not caught by animal screening some decades ago. We won't hear about the thousands of dangerous compounds that *have* been caught by animal screening. What really counts, of course,

is not this anecdote or that but the weight of evidence over the years. The weight of the evidence in support of medical research using animals is *overwhelming*.

26. The formal judgment of the National Academy of Sciences and the Institute of Medicine is dispositive:

> Animals will continue to be essential in combating human illness. . . . Cancer, atherosclerosis, diabetes, Alzheimer's disease, and AIDS remain inadequately understood. Debilitating conditions such as traumatic injury, strokes, arthritis, and a variety of mental disorders continue to exact a severe toll on human well-being. Animal research will be no less important in the future than it has been in the past. Indeed, it may be even more important because the questions remaining to be answered generally involve complex diseases and injuries that require whole organisms to be studied.

Science, Medicine and Animals (Washington, D.C.: National Academy Press, 1991). See also Cohen in this volume, "What Good Does Animal Experimentation Do?" (p. 85*ff*.).

27. In the world of medical science this is not in doubt. One confirming passage, written jointly by the director of the British Central Toxicology Laboratory and the head of the Acute Toxicity section of that laboratory, will suffice here:

> Researchers must use the best available methods to assess toxic hazards. In most cases, this means experiments on laboratory animals. . . . For a pesticide or drug, 30 or 40 different toxicity studies are necessary to cover all the significant areas of potential concern. . . . In the longer term it is difficult to see how living organisms can be reproduced in any laboratory system. It seems unlikely that even a combination of *in vitro* systems could model, for example, the results from 100 organs, 1,000 cell types or 10,000 enzymes, which represent the intact animal or human. Those that argue otherwise must be . . . encouraged to be more realistic in identifying attainable targets for the science of toxicology.

See Phil Botham and Iain Purchase, "Why Laboratory Rats are Here to Stay," *The New Scientist*, 2 May 1992. *Toxicity* testing is the concern of these authors; testing for *effectiveness* is a separate layer of concern, and without animal data that give some reasonable probability that a new compound will have the hoped-for results, the administration of that compound to humans will of course be rejected as unjustifiable.

28. But for each new lot of the standard vaccines, including those developed long ago, there is the *continuing* need for the pharmaceutical manufacturer *to test for quality control* before distribution for human use. Guinea pigs and other rodents are used for this purpose. This continuing need for animal "tasters" gives Regan (but not you and me!) another powerful reason to abjure all use of vaccines and other drugs for his children.

29. Tom Regan, *The Case for Animal Rights* (Berkeley: University of California Press, 1983). Careful comment on this book appears earlier in this volume (pp. 50–56.).

30. There are enormous differences in the capacities of different species, of course, and these varying capacities and sensitivities have a direct bearing on what we think humane care requires for each. Dogs may not be used as chickens are rightly used, but such differences, having moral consequences, Regan simply refuses to recognize.

31. Marc D. Hauser, *Wild Minds* (New York: Holt, 2000). Professor Hauser is a widely respected neuroscientist who admires animals greatly and has laboriously catalogued their remarkable skills. He agrees with Tom Regan that animals can be "moral patients but not moral agents." That is, they can suffer, but their inability to attribute mental states to others leaves them always blameless for their conduct. The world they

live in knows no ethics, no rights. Much current enthusiasm for animal morality he thinks unwarranted.

32. See my earlier discussion of their views in this volume at pp. 41–50.

33. Regan, *Case*—discussed at length earlier in this volume.

34. Lewis Carroll, *Through the Looking Glass*, chap. 6.

35. Treating a criticism as something other than it is, and then replying only to that other, answerable complaint, is an old sophistical technique for dealing with serious objections too difficult for direct response. Many of Regan's claims are indeed ridiculous—but the claim that rats should have the right to vote and marry are not among them. Claims of *that* kind he does not make. He does contend that all the benefits of modern medicine cannot justify the killing of a single rat. *This* is the sort of claim that truly does justify ridicule.

36. The uniquely moral character of human lives has been given many different philosophical explanations, as recounted at length earlier in this volume (pp. 32-34). Some would rely on a fundamental metaphysical dualism and a supernatural realm of spirit. Others think our moral lives to be the wholly natural product of higher levels of internal organization emerging as the outcome of evolution. One need not insist on the truth of any one philosophical account to recognize the reality of this *moral dimension* of human life and to appreciate how fundamentally different it makes us from animals in whose lives there can be no wrongs, no rights, no moral considerations whatever.

37. The vast majority of those who believe that rights are central in moral thought do not for a moment accept the "abolitionist implications" of Regan's very special convictions. It is therefore presumptuous of Regan (and not quite correct, either) for him to refer repeatedly to his own somewhat far-fetched opinions as "the rights view." It is properly referred to, I submit, as "the Regan rights view."

38. Also incalculable would be the consequent suffering of living animals that are not likely to be cared for and whose abandonment is likely to produce great suffering before their death.

39. *Moby Dick*, chap. 9. Melville italicizes the *me*.

Part IV

REPLY TO CARL COHEN

Tom Regan

It is a singular privilege to have this opportunity to reply to Professor Cohen's brief against animal rights. Among the literature critical of this idea, his critique, set forth on several occasions in the past and repeated in its essentials in this volume, is far and away the most famous and influential. In responding to his challenge, therefore, one is responding to the best thinking produced by those who deny rights to animals; that is why being able to reply is such an uncommon privilege.

Understandably, my main interest lies in assessing Professor Cohen's arguments against animal rights. But no response could possibly do full justice to his brief if it failed to comment on other aspects of his presentation. Some of my comments in this regard are offered in chapter 1 in this reply. Chapters 2 and 3 interpret and evaluate his anti–animal rights arguments, the former containing my assessment of his general criticisms, the latter my response to his specific criticisms of my position. These chapters are followed by two others, in one of which I examine his defense of speciesism, in the other his defense of vivisection. A brief, final chapter, in the nature of a summary and conclusion, completes my reply.

Chapter 1

Preliminaries

In the opening pages of his essay, Professor Cohen notes that humans use animals in a variety of ways, adding that "for each specific use, as for each kind of use, it may always be asked, '*Should* that be done? Is it right?' " (p. 3). Asking these questions is not of merely theoretical interest. As he writes a few paragraphs later, "Whatever the moral status we conclude animals deserve, that conclusion will surely affect the range of things we are permitted to do with them and will therefore play a significant role in guiding our personal lives" (p. 4). That animals do not have rights, Professor Cohen is quite certain; but that "we humans surely ought cause no pain to [animals] that cannot be justified" and that "we [ought not] to kill them without reason" (p. 46), of this, too, he has no doubt.

Given that billions of animals are raised in confinement on factory farms before being slaughtered for food, given that millions of other animals are trapped or ranched for their fur, given that these animals are made to suffer and are killed, and given that these specific uses are mentioned explicitly both in the preface and in the body of his opening essay (recall how he there characterizes the beliefs that humans should not eat meat or use animal products as "fanatical convictions" [p. 25]), readers might naturally expect that Professor Cohen would explain whether these ways of using animals cause them gratuitous pain or take their lives without justifiable cause. What could be more directly relevant, more helpful in "guiding our personal lives" than Professor Cohen's thoughtful assistance, grounded in those principles he favors, concerning the ethics of the food we eat and the clothes we wear?

Professor Cohen disappoints in this regard. In fact, I am obliged to say he does so willfully. For despite repeated requests that he directly address the ethics of commercial animal agriculture and the fur industry, for example, he refused to do so, electing instead to concentrate on "the rightness or wrongness of using animals in medical science" which, he asserts, "is the central focus of this book" (p. 4).

This assertion is false, and Professor Cohen has known that it is for the better part of two years. "The rightness or wrongness" of this particular use of animals is not, nor was it ever intended to be the *book's* central focus. That focus concerns (1) whether animals do or do not have rights and (2) what follows concerning how we should conduct our personal lives from the answer we give. One area of our "personal lives" that may be affected by our answer (and I note, parenthetically, that Professor Cohen never explains what guidance we are to receive, for our personal lives, from his defense of vivisection) involves the use of animals in a scientific setting; but one such area does not the central focus make, no matter how insistently Professor Cohen says that it does, and no matter how much he might wish that it was.

"Beyond Calculation"

Why would Professor Cohen elect to keep his interest so narrow even at the price of knowingly misdescribing our book's central focus? The answer is not hard to find. His defense of using animals in research and testing is of a utilitarian variety. Not only are the benefits humans derive, he believes, "beyond calculation" (p. 3); they cannot be secured in any other way. Thus, neither the pain animals are caused in pursuit of these benefits nor their untimely deaths are gratuitous.

Now, to claim that a range of benefits for some is "incalculable," whatever the harms done to others, does not discharge the obligation to explain how the relevant benefits and harms are to be assessed. Are the benefits and harms for humans and animals equally important, so that the pain or pleasure of one counts for as much (is of equal importance, from the moral point of view) as the equal pain or pleasure of the other? Or are human pains and pleasures, human harms and benefits morally more important than the equal pains and pleasures, the equal harms and benefits of other animals?

Professor Cohen is of the latter opinion. "I certainly do not mean to suggest," he writes (p. 63), "that the pain of animals is unworthy of consideration. Their pain *is* morally considerable. . . . But in making a calculation of long-term utility, it is one thing to say that the pains of animals must be *weighed* and another thing entirely to say that all animal and human pain must be weighed *equally*." In Professor Cohen's view, which I discuss at length in chapter 4, belief in the equal moral importance of human and animal pleasures and pains, even when these pleasures and pains are equal in other respects, is "mistaken" (p. 60).

How, then, if not in terms of equality, are we to weigh the pains and pleasures of animals in comparison to those of humans? In the case of cock fighting and pigeon shoots, for example, does the pain these animals experience equal one-quarter, one-half, five-eighths or some other fraction of the pleasure enjoyed by the human participants? Does the increased pleasure in their sex lives some men attribute to ingesting powders made from crushed bear penises or rhino horns equal two, three, or four times the pain suffered as these animals go to their death?

That Professor Cohen does not answer *these* questions is not what is important; after all, limits of space guaranteed that neither of us could address "each kind of use," let alone "each specific use" humans make of other animals. What is important is that he fails to offer any rational basis for answering *all* such questions; and he fails to do this because he fails to explain how human and animal pleasures and pains, human and animal benefits and harms are to be compared and weighed. In Professor Cohen's moral universe, where there is no rational basis for making the necessary calculations, no calculations can be rationally made, with the result that *much* more than the alleged benefits humans derive from using animals in biomedical research—indeed, *everything* involving relevant comparisons across species—is "incalculable."

It should not be surprising, therefore, even while it remains acutely disappointing, that Professor Cohen has chosen to ignore the questions "Should that be done? Is it right?" when asked about the treatment of animals in commercial animal agriculture and the fur industry. Having failed to provide a rational basis for comparing human and animal pleasures and pains, human and animal benefits and harms, he *cannot* address these questions thoughtfully and directly. His failure to answer these questions, as an exercise in practical ethics, in short, is a direct consequence of his failure to discharge his obligations, at a theoretical level, as a moral philosopher.

Professor Cohen's Semantics

This is not Professor Cohen's only failure, by any means, a finding I attempt to support throughout what follows. Before turning to that task, however, something needs to be said about the language he uses to describe ideas that differ from his own as well as the people whose ideas they are. In Professor Cohen's semantics, those who believe in animal rights are said to be "out of their mind" (p. 24), while what they believe is characterized as "silly" (p. 29), "absurd"

(p. 35), "preposterous" (p. 65), " a fanatical conviction" (p. 25), and "a popular slogan for the ignorant" (p. 121). The belief in the moral equality of humans and animals? This he describes as "preposterous" (p. 65) and "absurd" (p. 35). The rejection of speciesism? It is "pernicious" (p. 63), "silly" (p. 60), and embodies "a gruesome moral confusion" (p. 63). Even individual philosophers, Professor Cohen's professional peers, do not escape unscathed. Steven Sapontzis, for example, whose views are described as "wrong-headed" (p. 50) and "ridiculous" (p. 48), is (readers will be relieved to learn) "not completely mad" (p. 49). And Bernard Rollin, whom Professor Cohen misidentifies as "a sensitive veterinarian" (Rollin, in fact, is a philosopher who teaches courses in veterinary ethics at Colorado State University), offers a defense of animal rights that is said to be more than "preposterous" (p. 45); it is "an intellectual catastrophe" (p. 45).

Readers will have to decide for themselves what to make of the meretricious tendencies of Professor Cohen's writing. Speaking for myself, I find his rhetoric to be of a kind with which I am unfamiliar in philosophy, its frequent indulgence, incompatible with principles mutually agreed on and jointly endorsed in our reface. "We are both moral philosophers," we write there:

> who believe that ad hominem attacks are no substitute for reasoned argument; that important moral questions, like those we explore in these pages, can only be resolved when the inquiry is as patient as it is fair; that special care must be taken to understand those with whom we disagree; and that it is possible to show respect for people whose values differ from our own, even when the difference is great and the values fundamental.

Suffice it to say that, in my judgment, Professor Cohen's practice does not always exemplify these high ideals.

Duties to Animals

Professor Cohen, we know, thinks animals count for something morally. "[We] humans do have many obligations to animals," he writes (p. 27). In particular, "the obligation to act humanely *we owe to them*" (p. 29; emphasis in original). Mammals (at least) are "morally considerable," and "[we] humans have a moral obligation not to cause [them] unjustified pain" (p. 50).

As the passages just quoted confirm, Professor Cohen subscribes to a direct, as distinct from an indirect, duty view. Those who hold some version of the latter type (an indirect duty view) believe we have duties involving animals, but no duties to them. To use an example from my opening statement: If your neighbor mistreats your dog, you will be upset. Because it is wrong to upset you, your neighbor does something wrong. To you, that is; not to your dog. On such a view, dogs and other animals have the same moral standing, the same moral considerability as sticks and stones. Assessed from the moral point of view, animals themselves count for nothing.

To his credit, Professor Cohen rejects each and every indirect duty view. If your neighbor mistreats your dog, your neighbor wrongs the dog. That you are upset is a consequence of the wrong done, not the basis of it. The duty violated is a duty owed to the dog directly. This is Professor Cohen's belief, and mine as well. However, for reasons I advance later (see chapter 2's discussion of the amorality–rights argument), this is something he cannot consistently believe if he continues to accept what he alleges in other places.

Before turning to an examination of his anti–animal rights arguments, it will be useful to describe three additional points of agreement—one concerning the relationship between duties and rights, a second relating to animal psychology, and a third having to do with the prerequisites of moral responsibility.

Duties and Rights

From the fact (assuming it to be a fact) that we have duties directly to animals, it does not follow that they have rights against us. This is not unique to our duties to animals. In the case of the moral ties that bind humans to one another, there are many cases in which our duties do not have correlative rights. For example, we have a duty to render assistance to those in need, but no particular needy people have a right to demand that we discharge our duty by assisting them. Moreover, even when the duty is owed to a specific individual (e.g., someone who has been especially kind or thoughtful), there need be no correlative right. "A *spontaneous kindness* done," Professor Cohen recognizes, "may leave us with the obligation to acknowledge and perhaps return that gift, but the benefactor to whom we are thus obliged has no claim of *right* against us" (p. 29; emphasis in original). Many are the duties owed to those who have no right to require performance.

It would therefore be a mistake, as Professor Cohen recognizes, to infer that animals have rights *simply on the ground* that we have direct duties to them. While it is true that all rights have correlative duties, it is false that all duties have correlative rights, let alone that all duties (in his words) "arise from rights" (p. 27). On this point, Professor Cohen will get no argument from me.

More, he will get no argument from anyone, at least not anyone with whom I am familiar, including those philosophers who attribute rights to animals. Even in the case of a position like mine, where duties are treated as the basis of rights, it is not claimed that rights are correlated with or arise from each and every duty. As I am at pains to explain in *The Case for Animal Rights*, it is only when duties are (1) basic and (2) unacquired—only in the case of duties such as the duty of respect, for example, as distinct from our duties to render assistance or to repay kindness—that correlative rights may be validly inferred. Possibly I am mistaken. Certainly I would be obliged to carefully consider an argument that purported to show that I am. In the case of Professor Cohen's analysis of correlatively, however, since it fails to address my views, there is nothing to consider. One does not show that all duties lack correlative rights by showing that some duties lack correlative rights.

Animal Psychology

Professor Cohen does not make his argument against animal rights an easy one, as it would be if, following Descartes or today's neo-Cartesians, he denied a mental life to animals. Unlike Peter Carruthers, for example, who attributes little if any mental life to nonhuman animals (recall how even the pain they experience is said by him to be "unconscious"), Professor Cohen has a robust view of animal psychology, one that, in all essential respects, coincides both with the one I favor and with the outlook of people of common sense everywhere. Animals (e.g., mammals and birds) have cognitive, communicative, affective, and other noteworthy psychological capacities, including sentiency. These animals can reason. They have an emotional life. They can plan and choose. And some things they experience give them pleasure, while others cause them pain. In these and other respects, these animals are like us, and we, like them: both are (in the sense in which I use this idea) subjects-of-a-life.

The Prerequisites of Moral Responsibility

Still, there are important differences between these animals, on the one had, and the people reading these words, on the other. In particular, Professor Cohen believes, as do I, that nonhuman animals are not morally responsible for how they behave. Whatever they do, it is not morally right; nor can it be morally wrong. Moral right and wrong, like moral responsibility and accountability, apply to humans and (at least among terrestrial forms of life) to humans only.

Professor Cohen and I both favor interpreting moral responsibility along Kantian lines. We humans, he writes, have the "capacity . . . to formulate moral *principles* for the direction of our conduct . . . [to] grasp the maxim of the principles we devise, and by applying these principles to ourselves as well as to others, [to] exhibit the autonomy of the human will" (p. 35; emphasis in original). Nonhuman animals, we agree, lack these capacities. Even philosophers like Sapontzis who discern the workings of a protomorality in the loyal, courageous, and empathetic behavior of animals, stop short of supposing that wolves and elephants ever ask themselves if the maxims of their actions can be willed to be universal laws.

In general, then, those of us who read these words, on the one hand, and other animals, on the other, while we resemble one another in many ways, differ in others. Like us, other animals have a complicated, unified psychology, involving cognitive, affective, volitional and other capacities; and, as subjects-of-a-life, they have an experiential welfare of their own apart from any possible utility they may be to us. But unlike the people reading these words, other animals lack the prerequisites that make moral responsibility possible. These animals are, in my terminology, moral patients, beings who are directly owed duties by us, without owing any duties to us; on the other hand, we are moral agents, beings who, in addition to having duties owed directly to us, owe duties directly to others.

But it is not only animals who lack the prerequisites of moral responsibility, in my view. Many humans do, as well. The newly born, the soon-to-be born, and young children, for example, are unable (in Professor Cohen's words) "to formulate moral *principles* for the direction of [their] conduct . . . [to] grasp the maxim of the principles [they] devise, and by applying these principles to [them]selves as well as to others, [to] exhibit the autonomy of the human will."

Does this mean that these human beings are therefore beyond the moral pale? Not in my view, certainly. Humans do not need to be moral agents to be owed direct duties; neither do they need to be moral agents to have correlative rights. On the contrary, because these humans are subjects-of-a-life, such duties are owed, and correlative rights possessed. And because other animals are like these humans in the relevant respects, the same is true in their case. Or so I believe, and thus have I argued. It remains to be explained why Professor Cohen disagrees.

Chapter 2

General Arguments against Animal Rights

With the preceding serving as relevant background, we now turn to our book's central philosophical focus, the debate over animal rights. Professor Cohen's brief against their rights proceeds on two fronts. Sometimes he criticizes the ideas of individual philosophers (e.g., Sapontzis and Rollin); at others he attempts to show, in a general way, why all humans but no animals have rights. I leave it to the other philosophers whose arguments he disputes to decide whether and when to reply. In this chapter I limit my attention to his general arguments; his specific criticisms of my position are considered in the chapter that follows.

An Appeal to Authority

As was noted in my opening statement, Professor Cohen and I are of one mind on a number of controversial issues. One concerns the importance of rights. "Rights always trump interests," he writes at one point (p. 18). What this means is not obscure. If I have a right to life, then you are not morally entitled to kill me because you stand to benefit. My right trumps your interests. The same is true of society at large: my life is not to be taken in pursuit of improvements in the general welfare. On Professor Cohen's view, as in mine, the rights of the individual trump the otherwise noble goal of advancing the good of society.

But *do* humans have rights? What *arguments* may be advanced in support of the conviction that we do?[1] While he has no doubt that we have rights (humans "certainly have rights," he insists at one point [p. 21]), and while he is no less certain that "rights belong to all humans because they are human" (p. 21), Professor Cohen relieves himself of the task of providing "a definitive account of the human moral condition" or "to offer here the resolution of the deepest questions confronting human beings" (p. 32). Instead, he offers a number of argument-sketches, so to speak, each one of which helps explain why no animal but every human has rights.[2]

One such sketch involves an appeal to authority, where the judgment of "the greatest moral philosophers" is solicited. Professor Cohen's list of "the greatest" is eclectic by any measure, including philosophers as diverse as St. Thomas Aquinas and Karl Marx, St. Augustine and Vladimir Ilyich Lenin, F. H. Bradley and John Dewey, philosophers who, he alleges, despite their many and obvious differences, agree in thinking that there is something uniquely morally important about being human. "However much great thinkers have disagreed about fundamental principles," he writes, "*the essentially human (or divine) locus of the concept of right* has never been doubted. Of the finest moral philosophers from antiquity to the present, not one would deny—as the animal rights movement does seek now to deny—that there is a most profound difference between the moral stature of humans and that of animals, and that rights pertain only to the former" (p. 34; emphasis in original).

Now, Professor Cohen is logician enough to understand why appeals to authority are not and never can be probative, either in general or in the particular case of animal rights. Great moral philosophers, like the rest of us, not only can be, they sometimes are profoundly mistaken. John Locke is a great moral philosopher. So are David Hume and Immanuel Kant. But no one (one hopes) will conclude that they judge truly when, as is true of each, they deny equal moral stature to people of color. There is no reason why philosophical "greats" cannot be mistaken, and ample historical evidence exists to support the finding that they sometimes are.

Moreover, not all of the "finest moral philosophers from antiquity to the present" would agree that "there is a most profound difference between the moral stature of humans and that of animals." From Pythagoras and Porphyry, to Jeremy Bentham and John Stuart Mill, some of our "finest moral philosophers" have advanced views that grant equal moral stature, at the most fundamental level, to humans and other sentient beings. Had Professor Cohen been fair to the facts as we know them, he would have acknowledged that some great moral philosophers deny what he evidently wishes all great philosophers would affirm.

The logical shortcomings and selectivity of his summary aside, it is important to recognize a related deficiency in his treatment of human rights. Basic moral rights, he and I agree, are valid claims; but whereas in my work, including my opening statement in this volume, I endeavor to explain *what makes claims to rights valid*, Professor Cohen fails to offer any explanation. *Why* we should accept his assertion that rights are valid claims, and *what he means* when he says that they are, thus are and, in his hands, must remain matters of pure conjecture, lacking anything by way of requisite explanation let alone thoughtful justification.

When it comes to human rights, then, Professor Cohen is certain that we have them ("by nature") and knows what they are ("valid claims"). On examination, however, he offers no explanation of what makes claims to rights valid and begins his argument against animal rights by producing a demonstrably partisan list of "great" philosophers whose presumed agreement with his judgment fails to provide a credible reason for thinking that either their or his judgment is correct. Clearly, if we are to have sound reasons for believing that all humans but no animals have rights, Professor Cohen will have to do better than this.

The Amorality–Rights Argument

Although he himself does not clearly distinguish between them, Professor Cohen deploys at least three additional arguments, each of which, although it is related in some ways to the others (e.g., all three involve the idea of moral responsibility), stands or falls on its own. His first argument, which purports to show that no animal has rights, not to explain why all humans do, grows out of the fact that animals are (this is his word) *amoral,* an idea he introduces after asking us to imagine a lioness who kills a baby zebra. He writes:

> Do you believe the baby zebra has the *right* not to be slaughtered? Or that the lioness has the *right* to kill that baby zebra to feed her cubs? Perhaps you are inclined to say, when confronted by such natural rapacity (duplicated in various forms millions of times each day on planet Earth) that *neither* is right or wrong, that neither the zebra nor the lioness has a right against the other. Then I am on your side. Rights are pivotal in the moral realm and must be taken seriously, yes; but zebras and lions and rats do not live in a moral realm; their lives are totally *a*moral. There *is* no morality for them; animals do no moral wrong, ever. In their world there are no wrongs and there are no rights. (pp. 30–31; emphasis in original)

The essential point being argued here, in so far as it concerns animal rights, is a simple one and may be summarized as follows:

The Amorality–Rights Argument
1. Animals live in an amoral world (a world where nothing is right or wrong).
2. Those who live in an amoral world cannot have rights against one another.
3. Therefore, animals cannot have rights against one another.

Sapontzis's reservations about the moral agency of animals to the contrary notwithstanding, Professor Cohen and I agree that animals are incapable of doing what is right and wrong. We agree as well that it makes no sense to say that the baby zebra has a right not to be killed by the lioness or that the lioness has a right to kill the baby zebra. This much granted, what may we logically conclude? It is in our respective answer to this question that Professor Cohen and I part company.

What Professor Cohen believes follows is that animals cannot have rights against us. In other words, because animals, living as they do in an amoral world, cannot have rights against one another, we must conclude, he thinks, that animals "[have] no rights that [we] can possibly infringe" (p. 32). Thus we have the following:

4. If animals cannot have rights against one another, they cannot have rights against us.
5. Therefore, animals cannot have rights against us.

That Professor Cohen does reason in this fashion is evident; that he cannot consistently reason in this fashion may be less so. To make the inconsistency clearer, consider an argument having the same logical structure as the amorality–rights argument, only this one dealing with duties.

The Amorality–Duties Argument
1. Animals live in an amoral world (a world where nothing is right or wrong).
2. Those who live in an amoral world cannot have duties to one another.
3. Therefore, animals cannot have duties to one another.
4. If animals cannot have duties to one another, we cannot have duties to them.
5. Therefore, we cannot have duties to animals.

Professor Cohen unquestionably accepts 1′ through 3′, 1′ repeating a claim he makes himself; 2′ making the obvious point that amoral beings cannot have duties to one another; and 3′ concluding that animals cannot have duties to one another. What Professor Cohen cannot consistently accept is 4'. And he cannot consistently accept this because *he* believes that we have duties to animals. Thus, when it comes to duties, Professor Cohen must believe—logically, he is committed to believing—that *our* having duties to animals is perfectly consistent with *their* not having duties to one another.

Logically, the possibility of nonhuman animals having rights is no different. From the fact that animals cannot have rights against one another, it does not follow that they cannot have rights against us. I think they can and do. Professor Cohen thinks they cannot and do not. Who is correct is open to debate. What is not open to debate is whether the issue can be resolved by establishing that animals cannot have rights against one another.

Regarding Professor Cohen's first argument against animal rights, therefore, we may conclude as follows: Not only does he fail to demonstrate what he sets out to prove (that animals cannot have rights); what he succeeds in demonstrating is that he cannot consistently argue against their rights in the way he does.

The Right-Kind Argument

Professor Cohen's second argument is embedded in a response he gives to an objection critics raise against thinkers who deny rights to animals because they lack those capacities presupposed by moral responsibility and moral judgment ("full moral functions," in his terminology).

> It cannot be [the critic says] that having rights requires the ability to make moral claims, to grasp and apply moral laws, because, if it that was true, many human beings—the brain-damaged, the comatose, infants, and the senile—who plainly lack those capacities must be without rights. But that is absurd. This proves [the critic concludes] that rights do not depend on the presence of moral capacities. (p. 36)

To this objection, Professor Cohen has a lengthy reply:

> Objections of this kind are common but miss the point badly. They arise from a misunderstanding of what it means to say that humans live in a moral world. Human children, like elderly adults, have rights *because they are human*. Morality is an essential feature of human life; all humans are moral creatures, infants and the senile included. Rights are not doled out to this individual person or that one by somehow establishing the presence in them of some special capacity. This mistaken vision would result in the selective award of rights to some individuals but not others, and the cancellation of rights when capacities fail. On the contrary, rights are *universally* human, arise in the human realm, apply to humans generally. This criticism (suggesting the loss of rights by the senile or the comatose, etc.)

mistakenly treats the essentially moral feature of humanity as though it were a screen for sorting humans, which it most certainly is not. The capacity for moral judgment that distinguishes humans from animals is not a test to be administered to humans one by one. Persons who, because of some disability, are unable to perform the full moral functions natural to human beings are not for that reason ejected from the moral community. The critical distinction is one of kind. Humans are of such a kind that rights pertain to them *as humans;* humans live lives that will be, or have been, or remain *essentially* moral. It is silly to suppose that human rights might fluctuate with an individual's health, or dissipate with an individual's decline. The rights involved are human rights. On the other hand, animals are of such a kind that rights never pertain to them; what humans retain when disabled, rats never had. (p. 37; emphasis in original)

Even when read in a sympathetic manner, much in this passage is unclear. To begin with, readers must decide whether we are being offered one or several different arguments. I believe there are at least two, each of which purports to explain why all humans but no animals have rights. One is based on how and where rights "arise" (they "arise in a human realm"); the second logically distinct argument is based on the "kind" of being humans and animals are. I discuss each separately, focusing on the latter argument in this section, the former in the one that follows.

Concerning what I term the right-kind argument, two things are reasonably clear. First, Professor Cohen sees himself as offering a positive argument: he believes there is something about the *kind* of being humans and animals are that has a logical bearing on why all humans but no animals have rights. Second, he sees himself as offering a critical argument: he believes the consequences that flow from rejecting his positive argument (e.g., that some humans would be "ejected from the moral community") show that it is a "mistake" or "silly" to reject it. I consider his positive argument first.

The Positive Argument

Central to Professor Cohen's positive argument is his belief that "humans are of a kind that rights pertain to them because they are human." If we can decipher what this means, we might better understand what drives the argument. One thing it cannot mean is that all humans are the same (kind) biologically—that, for example, all humans, and only humans share a full complement of human genes. For from "All and only humans share a full complement of human genes" nothing follows concerning our moral status, least of all that "humans are of a kind that rights pertain to them because they are human."

But if it is not some universal, unique biological fact, what is there about being human that might ground our universally shared, our unique moral status? Professor Cohen's answer, so far as it can be determined, will be found in his assertion that "humans live lives that will be, have been, or remain *essen-*

tially moral." To say that the lives humans live are *essentially* moral must mean that we could not live a human life if we did not live our lives as moral beings. In other words, being in the world as a moral being, unlike being in the world as a male or female, a student or teacher, a plumber or philosopher is so central to living a human life that, absent the exercise of full moral functions, we *cannot live* a human life.

This view is not without its attractions. To exercise our moral capacities—to involve ourselves in moral deliberation and to take responsibility for our actions, for example—arguably is necessary if we are to live a human life. Certainly this is true of those who read these words, utilizing, as we do, our moral capacities everyday of our life. Moreover, in the case of infants who have the potential to exercise these capacities, it is undeniably true that, barring incapacitating injury or premature death, they will use these capacities in the future. And as for those who, though presently senile or comatose, once lived their lives as we live ours: they most certainly used these same capacities in the past. Thus would it seem that Professor Cohen thinks truly when he writes that "human beings live lives that will be, or have been, or remain *essentially* moral."

I believe this is a fair interpretation of Professor Cohen's positive argument, an interpretation that is supported by what he writes and the spirit in which he writes it, and one that may be summarized as follows:

The Right-Kind Argument
1. Individuals have rights if and only if they are a kind of being who live lives that will be, have been, or remain essentially moral.
2. All and only humans (at least among terrestrial beings) are this kind of being.
3. Therefore, all and only humans (at least among terrestrial beings) have rights.
4. Other animals are not human.
5. Therefore, other animals do not have rights.

Once we understand the content and structure of the positive argument, we can begin to recognize where and why it goes wrong. An obvious place to begin is with the argument's first premise: "Individuals have rights if and only if they are a kind of being who live lives that will be, have been, or remain essentially moral." Even if we grant that all humans have rights because they are the "right kind" of being, it does not follow that *only* humans have them. The central question in dispute asks, "Do *animals* have rights?" To this we receive no answer if we are told, "Morality is essential to human but not to animal life" or "Humans, but not animals, are morally responsible for what they do." That morality is essential to human life *leaves every question open* regarding the moral status of animals. That humans will be, have been, or are morally responsible for their actions *leaves every question open* regarding the identity of those to whom we are responsible—and, in any given case, whether the nature of our responsibility involves our duties to them or their rights against us. In short, even if morality is essential to human but not to animal life, and even if all humans have rights because of this essential aspect of our being, it does not follow that only humans have rights.

Moreover, as is true of his other efforts, this argument of Professor Cohen's fails in more ways than one. Not only does it fail to illuminate why no animals have rights; it fails to offer a credible reason for thinking that all humans do. Here is why.

Logically, it is fallacious to infer that because something is true of a group (class, species, kind), considered as a whole, the same thing is true of each member of the group (class, species, kind), considered individually. Fallacious reasoning of this kind is so common it even has a name: the fallacy of division. For example, from "The orchestra can play louder than the organ," it does not follow that "The concertmaster can play louder than the organ," just as from "The offensive line can lift a ton," it does not follow that "The left guard can lift a ton." Thus, even if we grant that (a) "Morality is essential to human but not to animal life," it does not follow that (b) "Morality is essential to *each* human life." Because Professor Cohen does reason in this way, and because this way of reasoning commits the fallacy of division, he reasons fallaciously. And because his attribution of rights to all humans depends on our accepting this fallacious inference, the universality of human rights is neither established nor explained.

In response, Professor Cohen might agree that (b) does not follow from (a), protest that he never says that it does, insist that (b) is true anyhow, and use (a) to ground rights for all humans. While possible, this response has the disadvantage of containing something false: morality is not essential to each human life. Conceptually, there are important differences between (1) being a human being who lives a human life and (2) being a human being who is alive. Everyone who is a human being in sense 1 is a human being in sense 2, but not everyone who is a human being in sense 2 is a human being in sense 1. Anencephalic infants, born with a brain stem but no brain, are an example of this latter possibility. Beyond question they are human beings; without a doubt they are alive; yet they do not, have not, and never will be able to *live a human life*—never will be able, for example, in Professor Cohen's words, "to formulate moral *principles* for the direction of [their] conduct."

Professor Cohen would have us believe that anencephalic humans have rights, not because the life *they* live is essentially moral (it is not and never will be) but because *human life* (*when it is lived*) is essentially moral. Such an inference defies logic. One might as well say that anencephalic infants have intellectual curiosity, aesthetic preferences, and long-term plans about their futures because these are essential to living a human life. But it is false that anencephalic infants at one time had, presently have, or at some time in the future will have intellectual curiosity; false that they at one time had, presently have, or at some time in the future will have aesthetic preferences; false that they at one time had, presently have, or at some time in the future will have long-term plans about their future; and false that they at one time had, presently have, or at some time in the future will have rights if *their* having rights requires that *they* live a life that will be, has been, or is "essentially moral." Even if it is true that human lives, when lived, are essentially moral, the same is not true of those who, though human and alive, cannot live a human life.

Once we recognize that Professor Cohen's positive argument, judged on its own terms and if we assume it does not beg essential questions, fails to ground the rights of *some* human beings, we should be open to the possibility that it fails to guarantee rights for *many* human beings, including, for example, those who, from birth, suffer from mental disabilities that foreclose the possibility of moral agency. These humans not only are not *now* living a human life (a life that involves "full moral functions"), but as is true of anencephalic humans, these humans *never will* lead such a life. As such, it is false that *their* life is "essentially moral," and false, as well, that they have rights, if possessing them depends, at the very least, on having the potential to live such a life.

As for Professor Cohen's assertion that, unlike what is true of animals, the humans we have been discussing, despite their disabilities, retain their rights: this, too, is false. Because individuals cannot retain what they never possessed, and because, given Professor Cohen's reasoning, purged of its fallacies, these humans never had rights, it is false that they retain what they never had in the first place.

The preceding critique of Professor Cohen's positive argument has important implications for the general inquiry into who has rights, and why. In particular, it undermines his view that all humans have rights because they are human; rather, individual humans have rights, if they do, because of what is true of them as the individuals they are, not because of what is true of the kind of being they happen to be. Any prima facie credible basis for the possession of rights must avoid making explicit reference to humans or any other species as such; in this sense, and for that reason, the species identity of those individuals who have rights is not something the basis itself can determine. My position satisfies this requirement; Professor Cohen's position does not.

The Critical Argument

Professor Cohen, as was noted earlier, believes that rejecting his positive argument has consequences that show why it is "mistaken" or "silly" to do so. If we are to avoid these consequences, he thinks, we must agree with him that "the capacity for moral judgment that distinguishes humans from animals is not a test to be administered to humans one by one." The imputed consequences are of two kinds. First, if we maintain that the capacity for moral judgment is a test to be administered to humans "one by one," we will be obliged to agree that "rights are . . . doled out to this individual person or that one by somehow establishing the presence in them of some special capacity." But, Professor Cohen protests, "this mistaken vision would result in the selective award of rights to some individuals but not others and the cancellation of rights when capacities fail."

With all due respect to Professor Cohen, this is at best a caricature of the important issues at hand. No one, and certainly not I, presumes to be in a position to "dole out" rights, whether as an act of charity (one meaning of the verb, *to dole*) or to distribute them sparingly (another meaning of the verb). On any prima facie credible account of rights, individuals either have them or they do not; and they either have them or not because of what is true of them, not because someone "doles out" (or "selectively awards") rights to some, while denying rights to others.

The preceding is as true of Professor Cohen's arguments about rights as it is of anyone's. If I were to object to his denial of rights to animals by saying that he "doles out" rights to humans only, I have no doubt that he would deny, and deny most strenuously, that he was doing anything of the kind. On the contrary, he would insist, and this with predictable alacrity, that he denies rights to animals because of what is true of them and affirms rights in our case because of what is true of us.

No less, and no more, applies to those who might deny rights to some humans: to describe what they do as "doling out" rights is not to describe what they do. Possibly they are mistaken. Possibly not. The issue is open to debate. What is not open to debate is whether philosophy tolerates double standards. It does not. And because it does not, Professor Cohen cannot consistently represent other philosophers as "doling out" rights if they deny rights in the case of some humans, and at the same time represent himself (as he surely would) as doing something else when he denies rights in the case of every other animal.

Professor Cohen has a second critical reason for accepting his view that "the capacity for moral judgment that distinguishes humans from animals is not a test to be administered to humans one by one." "Persons who, because of some disability, are unable to perform the full moral functions natural to human beings," he writes, "are not for that reason ejected from the moral community." The implication is not obscure: those who reject Professor Cohen's views are committed to "ejecting" these humans from the moral community.

As Professor Cohen surely must realize, this certainly is not true of my position, which affirms rights in the case of humans "who, because of some disability, are unable to perform the full moral functions natural to human beings." Moreover, as he again surely must realize, it certainly is not true of positions that deny human rights in such cases. Professor Cohen himself—and the point that he makes this argument cannot be stressed too strongly, since he stresses it so strongly himself—Professor Cohen himself argues that *there are many instances in which duties are owed in the absence of correlative rights.* Even if it is true, therefore, that some humans, because they are "unable to perform the full moral functions natural to human beings" and thus, on some views, do not have rights, it by no means follows either that we have no duties to them or that they are to be "ejected" from the moral community.

As a matter of fact, therefore, and despite his insistence to the contrary, there is no good reason to accept and eminently good reason to reject Professor Cohen's critical argument. Moreover, since, for reasons already offered, his positive argument also should be rejected, the conclusion we reach is this: at a minimum, the right-kind argument fails to show that all humans and no animals have rights.

The Community Argument

Professor Cohen has another argument for why all humans but no animals have rights. Unlike the amorality–rights argument, which builds on the allegedly amoral condition of nonhuman animals, and unlike the right-kind argument, which rests on allegedly essential features of being human, this final argument is grounded in how and where rights arise. "[R]ights," he declares, in the longish passage quoted earlier, "are *universally* human, arise in the human realm, apply to humans generally." Other animals, alas, are not "members of [this] community," which is why they lack rights. Bring forth whatever impressive list of capacities and achievements one might wish (communicative skills among nonhuman primates, the cleverness of cats, the sagacity of wolves); compare these animals with a human bereft of all cognitive and volitional abilities; it matters not. The human has rights, the other animals do not. "It is beside the point to insist that animals have remarkable capacities," Professor Cohen observes, in one of his previously published essays,

> that they really have a consciousness of self, or of the future, or make plans, and so on. And the tired response that because infants plainly cannot make moral claims they must have no rights at all, or that rats must have them too, we ought forever put aside. Responses like these arise out of a misconception of right itself. They mistakenly suppose that rights are tied to some identifiable individual capacities, or sensibilities, and they fail to see that rights arise only in a community of moral beings, and that therefore there are spheres in which rights do apply and spheres in which they do not.[3]

I think any honest reading of these passages will have to conclude that Professor Cohen's meaning is not as clear as one might wish. But let me explain what I think he means; then I will be able to explain why I believe he is mistaken.

Rights, we are told, "arise in the human realm," the "human moral community." This is both true and important. The very idea of a moral right assumes a social context without which the idea could not arise. To explain: Professor Cohen and I agree that rights place justified limits on how individuals may be treated; for example, we agree that our right to life entails that others are not at liberty to kill us except in very unusual circumstances (in self-defense, say). That being so, the idea of rights can arise only if (1) individuals are living together and interacting with one another, and if (2) these individuals can understand what it means to have justified limitations placed on what they are morally free to do to one another. Human beings, Professor Cohen thinks, satisfy both these conditions. Arguably, no other animals do.

True, nonhuman animals who live in groups in the wild satisfy condition 1, but to claim that they also satisfy condition 2 is implausible. Granted, we may limit their liberty, for justifiable cause; but it is doubtful that members of a pack of wolves, for example, can understand the idea of imposing justified moral limits, based on respect for individual rights, on how they behave. This is why zebras and gazelles, for example, arguably cannot understand what a right is and also why rights arguably cannot arise in a community of these animals.

The same is no less true of those animals who live in community with us. For example, Professor Cohen shares his life with a beloved son and dog. And there can be no doubt that both father and son lavish their love and affection on this lucky animal. But while it is true that the dog is a member of the "Cohen community," in one sense, this is not the sense in which the human members of the Cohen family belong to the human moral community. For the Cohen dog, like every other dog who has existed, currently is alive, or will one day roam the Earth, never has, does not now, and never will understand that moral rights place justified limits on what individuals are free to do. The idea of rights can no more arise among domesticated than it can among wild animals.

But what of those human beings (e.g., the severely mentally disadvantaged) who, like both wild and domesticated animals, are unable to understand what moral rights are? After all, these humans are members of the human community, not in some extended sense (as when we say, e.g., that the Cohen dog is an "honorary member" of the Cohen family), but literally: they all *are* human beings. However, as is true of the "honorary" canine members, these humans do not now, and many of them never will understand what a right is. Do these humans have rights?

As we have seen, Professor Cohen thinks they do. He believes that while the inability of animals to understand what rights are is sufficient to exclude them from the class of right holders, this same lack of understanding does not disqualify any human being. *Every* human being has rights because *all* are members of the community in which the idea of rights arises, whereas *every* nonhuman animal lacks rights because *none* belongs to this community. Clearly, then, the decisive criterion for possessing rights being proposed here is not whether one understands what rights are; it is whether one is a member of the community in which rights arise. And since the only community in which rights arise, at least in the terrestrial sphere, is the community composed of human beings, being human (belonging to the species *Homo sapiens*) is both a necessary and a sufficient condition of possessing rights.

I think the foregoing is a fair reading of what Professor Cohen believes as well as why he believes it; and I think the following is a fair representation of the argument he places before us:

The Community Argument
   1. All and only those individuals have rights who are members of communities in which the idea of rights arises.
   2. Within the terrestrial sphere, the idea of rights arises only in the human community.
   3. Therefore, within that sphere, all and only humans have rights.
   4. Animals are not members of the human community.
   5. If animals are not members of the human community, they have no rights.
   6. Therefore, animals have no rights.

This argument will not withstand a moment's critical scrutiny. Conceptually, there is a distinction between (a) the necessary and sufficient conditions of the origin or formation of an idea and (b) the scope of the idea. The former concerns how it is possible for an idea (to use Professor Cohen's word) to "arise"; the latter concerns the range of objects or individuals to which or to whom the idea may be intelligibly applied. The central point to recognize is that these two matters are logically distinct: the scope of an idea is something that must be determined independently of considerations about the origin of the idea.

By way of example: As far as we know, ideas such as "central nervous system" and "genes" arise only among humans because only humans have the requisite cognitive capacities to form them. But the range of entities to which these ideas apply is not necessarily limited to all and only members of the community in which they originate. Indeed, not only is the scope of these ideas not necessarily limited to all and only humans; there are literally billions of nonhuman animals to whom the ideas are correctly applied—who have, that is, genes and a central nervous system.

Considered conceptually, discussions regarding rights are no different. We grant that, as far as we know, the idea of rights arises only among humans because only humans live in the requisite kind of community and have the requisite cognitive capacities. But the range of entities to which this idea applies is not necessarily limited to members of the community in which the idea originates. Logically, one might as well infer that wolves cannot have genes or that the Cohen dog lacks a central nervous system because these animals do not belong to a community in which these ideas arise.

The community argument therefore fails to prove that no animal has rights. Worse, its logic is unremittingly neutral when it comes to explaining why all humans do. To make this clearer, consider ghosts. As far as we know, this is an idea that arises only among humans, but no one should point to this fact as providing the slightest reason for believing that there actually are ghosts, questions about the origin of the idea belonging to one category of our understanding, questions about the idea's instantiation belonging to another. Nothing less than this is true in the case of rights. As far as we know, individual rights is an idea that arises only amongst humans, but no one should point to this fact as providing the slightest reason for believing that we actually have rights, questions about the origin of the idea belonging to one category of our understanding, questions about the idea's instantiation belonging to another.

All things fairly considered, then, Professor Cohen fails to show, in a general way, that all humans but no animals have rights. Each of the arguments he fashions (e.g., the right-kind argument and the community argument), and each for its distinctive reasons, fails to make the case for human and against animal rights. In this respect, if in no other, his arguments are noteworthy for the depth and breadth of what they do not show, not for the depth and breadth of what they do.

Chapter 3

Professor Cohen's Critique of My Position

In addition to his general objections, Professor Cohen devotes part of his sixth chapter to a critical examination of my position, as set forth in *The Case for Animal Rights* and summarized, in its essentials, in this volume. To say that he has limited respect for my work is an understatement. Readers will, he writes, find my book "long and tortuous and in places obscure" (p. 51); the arguments in its pages, "largely smoke" (p. 51); the argument for animal rights, "utterly fallacious," "dreadfully unsound" (p. 54), "worthless" (p. 56), "profoundly mistaken" (p. 56), and "entirely unpersuasive" (p. 56); its central conclusion (that animals have rights), "reached with almost magical speed" (p. 54). To anyone who, in the face of his critical discernment, might still be tempted to open its pages, there to take on the laborious task of actually reading what is written, Professor Cohen offers his (this is his word) assurance: "there is," he writes, "no argument or set of arguments in *The Case for Animal Rights* that successfully makes the case for animal rights" (p. 55). For reasons I advance here, Professor Cohen fails to provide any credible reason to accept his assurance as well grounded.

My response is divided into two main sections. In the first, I explain where and how Professor Cohen misrepresents my position, not occasionally but systematically, and not at the margins but with respect to ideas that are absolutely central to my position. In the second, I respond to his charge that my argument for animal rights commits a fallacy of equivocation.

Issues of Interpretation

Professor Cohen's critique of my position begins on an inauspicious note when he writes that I attempt "to show, patiently and laboriously, that to *justify* [our] existing obligations to animals, it must be the case that animals have rights" (p. 51; emphasis added). This is not true. Nowhere will anyone find any such claim made by me. My position, explained in *The Case for Animal Rights* and repeated in my opening essay, is that (a) our obligations (or duties) to animal are fundamental, and (b) in some cases (when the duties owed are both basic and unacquired) animals have correlative rights against us. Correct or not, my position manifestly is not that the rights of animals *justify* the duties we have to them; rather, my position is very different: it is that (c) the basic, unacquired duties we have to them ground (are the basis of) the rights they have against us, and (d) recognition of their rights is essential if we are to understand the nature of our duties. Nowhere—not in *The Case for Animal Rights*, not in any other of my previously published work, not in these pages—do I argue that we must acknowledge the rights of animals "to justify [our] existing obligations to [them]."

Professor Cohen's misrepresentation of my position does not stop here by any means. After complaining that "there is not even a single *mention* of animals rights (save in the preface) in the first two-thirds of [*The Case for Animal Rights*]" (p. 51; emphasis in original), he registers his displeasure because, he claims, my ascription of rights to animals "is built on one single principle" (p. 52) and is presented, "with magical speed," "in less than two pages" (p. 52). What this principle is will concern us shortly. First, the "magical speed" of my argument deserves comment.

Without requiring anyone to read the whole of *The Case for Animal Rights* before judging the accuracy of what Professor Cohen says, let me remind readers of how I argue for animal rights in the present volume. Recall how I stress, not once but several times, that my argument is cumulative in nature, one that evolves by overcoming shortcomings in positions examined along the way. In its present formulation, necessarily shortened because of the limits of space, the argument for animal rights, which is not set forth until the seventeenth chapter, is given in less than two pages. But recall (I quote, in full, to emphasize the point I am making) what is said there.

1. Moral outlooks that deny that we owe direct duties to animals (e.g., both simple and Rawls's version of contractarianism) are unsatisfactory. Any plausible moral outlook must therefore recognize that animals are owed direct duties. The rights view satisfies this requirement.

2. Moral outlooks that are speciesist (e.g., those that maintain that all and only human interests matter morally simply because they are the interests of human beings) are unsatisfactory. Any plausible moral outlook must therefore recognize that other-than-human interests matter morally. The rights view satisfies this requirement.

3. Moral outlooks that attempt to explicate the direct duties we owe to animals by reference to human character traits (e.g., the cruelty–kindness view) are unsatisfactory. Any plausible moral outlook must therefore be able to distinguish between moral assessments of what people do and the moral character they display in doing it. The rights view satisfies this requirement.

4. Moral outlooks that attempt to explicate human morality while dispensing with the idea of moral rights (e.g., preference utilitarianism) are unsatisfactory. Any plausible moral outlook must therefore recognize the rights of humans, including the right to respectful treatment in particular. The rights view satisfies this requirement.

5. Moral outlooks that attempt to explicate human morality by attributing inherent value to all and only those humans who are persons (e.g., Kant's position) are unsatisfactory. Any plausible moral outlook must therefore recognize the inherent value of humans who are not persons. The rights view satisfies this requirement.

6. Moral outlooks that deny that no other-than-human animals have an experiential welfare (e.g., Carruthers's position) are unsatisfactory. Any plausible moral outlook must therefore recognize that there are other-than-human animals who have an experiential welfare. The rights view satisfies this requirement.

7. Moral outlooks that attempt to limit inherent value to all and only humans who are subjects-of-a-life, thereby denying this same value to other animals who are subjects-of-a-life, are speciesist and unsatisfactory. Any plausible moral outlook must therefore recognize that anyone with an experiential welfare matters morally, whatever their species. The rights view satisfies this requirement.

8. Moral outlooks that affirm inherent value and rights in the case of humans who are subjects-of-a-life are preferable to positions that deny this. The rights view satisfies this requirement. (pp. 210-11)

With statements 1 through 8 serving as the argument's foundation, the rights view's case for animal rights concludes as follows:

9. Because the relevant similarity shared by humans who have inherent value is that we are subjects-of-a-life, in the sense explained; because the nonhuman animals who concern us are like us in that they, too, are subjects-of-a-life; and because relevantly similar cases should be judged similarly, it follows that these nonhuman animals also possess inherent value.

10. Because all those who possess inherent value possess the equal right to be treated with respect, it follows that all those human beings *and* all those animal beings who possess inherent value share the equal right to respectful treatment. (pp. 211–12)

The soundness of my argument is not the issue; what is, is the accuracy of claims Professor Cohen makes about it. Nothing more need be said, I believe, to remind readers of the cumulative nature of my argument for animal rights or to defuse any suggestion that the case I make for their rights, in this volume, is made with "magical speed." Nor should anyone doubt that anything less (in fact, readers will find that a great deal more) is true of my cumulative argument, as presented in *The Case for Animal Rights*, where the logical climax of the argument is not reached until, as Professor Cohen reminds us, we are "two-thirds [of the way through] this big [400+-page] book." Given the cumulative nature of my project, I think readers will agree that a conclusion reached after more that 250 pages of argument hardly qualifies as a conclusion reached with "magical speed."

In addition to his displeasure at the speed with which the conclusion of my argument for animal rights is reached, Professor Cohen also is disturbed because that argument turns on a "single principle," which, quoting from *The Case for Animal Rights*, he identifies as follows: "The validity of the claim to respectful treatment, and thus the right to respectful treatment cannot be any stronger or weaker in the case of moral patients than it is in the case of moral agents" (p. 279).[4]

Now, there is no denying that I do say this or that what I say here (henceforth referred to as my "summary principle") summarizes the conclusion toward which my cumulative argument has been leading. So Professor Cohen is correct in recognizing the importance of this passage. But his interpretation of what my summary principle means is more than seriously mistaken.

Who are the "moral agents" to whom I refer? Who the "moral patients"? Remarkably, Professor Cohen interprets my understanding of "moral agents" to be equivalent to "human beings" and my understanding of "moral patients" to be equivalent to "animals." Here is the relevant portion of the relevant quote: "Regan's case (for animal rights) is built entirely on one principle. . . . What principle is that? It is the principle . . . by which '*moral agents*' (*humans*) and '*moral patients*' (*animals*) are held unconditionally equal" (p. 52; emphasis added).

What Professor Cohen says here is more than not true; it is beyond being false, attributing to me, as it does, equivalencies I not only deny but ones I deny repeatedly. A few representative quotations from *The Case for Animal Rights* (the number could easily be multiplied) will suffice to confirm this.

> Human infants, young children, and the (seriously) deranged or enfeebled of all ages are paradigm cases of human moral patients. (153)

> To the extent that the case can be made for describing and explaining the behavior of a human being (by reference to their beliefs and desires), to that extent, assuming that we have further reasons for denying that the human in question has the abilities necessary for moral agency, we have reason to regard that human as a moral patient. (154)

> [A]ny position that denies that we have direct duties to those moral patients with whom we have been and will continue to be concerned (normal mammalian animals, age one or more, and those human moral patients like these animals in the relevant respects) is rationally defective. (239)

Nothing could be clearer, even to those who read my work in the most superficial manner, than that in my hands "*moral patient*" is not equivalent to "*animal*" and "*moral agent*" is not equivalent to "*human being.*" Indeed, one of the main objectives of my argument, both in *The Case for Animal Rights* and throughout my other writings, is to show that these pairs of concepts are not equivalent. Why not? Because (1) many human beings (e.g., the newly born and the soon-to-be-born) are not moral agents, meaning in their present condition, they are not capable of acting in ways for which they are morally responsible; and (2) these human beings are moral patients, meaning they are directly owed such basic duties as the duty of respect.

Granted, someone might object to my position by arguing that all human beings are moral agents (which is false) or that no humans are moral patients (which also is false). But it is one thing to challenge my position, quite another accurately to say what that position is.

Professor Cohen's misrepresentations of my views, which prove to be more systematic than episodic, extends to his characterization of another idea central to my position: inherent value. In the following section I respond to his charge that I use this idea in an equivocal fashion; here I am content to note that he misrepresents how I understand it. I quote:

> The concept of "inherent value" . . . first entered Regan's account in the seventh chapter [of *The Case for Animal Rights*], at the point at which his principal object was to fault or defeat utilitarian moral arguments. Utilitarians, with lesser or greater sophistication, depend ultimately on some calculation of the pleasures and pains that moral agents experience. But, Regan argued there, the real value of human beings must rest not in their experiences but in themselves. It is not

the pleasures and pains that go "into the cup" of humanity that give value but the cups themselves; *all humans are in a deep sense equal in value because of what they are: moral agents having inherent value.* (p. 53; emphasis added)

Someone may say or believe what Professor Cohen attributes to me. As a matter of demonstrable fact, I am not that someone. Never have I either affirmed or implied that "all humans are in a deep sense equal in value because of what they are: moral agents having inherent value." For reasons already given, *I explicitly and repeatedly deny that all humans are moral agents,* just as *I explicitly and repeatedly deny that moral agency is the basis of human equality.* Mistaken or not, this is the position I hold; it is not the one Professor Cohen attributes to me.

Professor Cohen's Objection

Readers of Professor Cohen's critical discussion of my position may be surprised to find that, stripped of its pejorative rhetoric and systematic misrepresentations, we find only one serious objection: my case for animal rights, he argues, is "utterly fallacious" because it involves "an egregious example of the fallacy of equivocation—that informal fallacy in which two or more meanings of the same word or phrase are confused in the several propositions of an argument" (p. 54).

The equivocation of which I am said to be guilty involves the expression "inherent value," concerning which Professor Cohen distinguishes two meanings. One is moral in nature; the second is not. According to Professor Cohen, my argument for attributing inherent value to animals, and thus my case for their rights, is "utterly fallacious," "dreadfully unsound," and so forth, because it involves "a unmarked shift from one meaning of 'inherent value' to another" (p. 54).

What are the two meanings in question? The morally neutral sense is said to mean that "each living creature [is] unique [and] irreplaceable" (p. 54). As for the moral sense of "inherent value," Professor Cohen, in a passage quoted earlier, provides the following: "Regan argue[s] [that] the real value of human beings must rest not in their experiences but in them*selves*. It is not the pleasures and pains that go 'into the cup' of humanity that give value but the 'cups' themselves; all humans are in a deep sense equal in value because of what they are: moral agents having inherent value" (p. 53).

For reasons offered in my previous discussion of this passage, what Professor Cohen says here is true, if true at all, of someone else. Nowhere do I use "inherent value" to mean what he says it means. It must be false, therefore, that I equivocate in the manner in which Professor Cohen says I do; and it is, in any event, false that I equivocate at all.

Among the many relevant obligations Professor Cohen fails to discharge in this quarter, one concerns his failure to identify where in the text the alleged equivocation is supposed to occur. The most plausible place to look, if we accept ordinary standards of scholarship, is where I set forth my reasons for extending the scope of inherent value to include individuals other than human moral agents. That place is not hard to find. It occurs in the seventh chapter of *The Case for Animal Rights,* where I write the following:

> [I]f we view all moral agents as having equal inherent value, if we rely on this account of the value of these individuals to avoid the counterintuitive implications of act utilitarianism, denying that the harms done to some moral agents can be justified merely on the grounds that harming them brings about optimal consequences for all concerned, if some of these harms done to moral agents are of the same kind as harms done to moral patients, and if the duties not to harm moral agents and moral patients in these ways is prima facie owed directly to each, then it would be morally arbitrary to regard moral patients as lacking inherent value or to suppose that they have the status of mere receptacles. If, in short, we postulate inherent value in the case of moral agents, then we cannot non arbitrarily deny it in the case of moral patients. (239–40)

Just where is the alleged equivocation supposed to occur? Where is it, exactly, that I will be found using "inherent value" to mean "each living creature is unique and irreplaceable," at one place, only to use this very same expression, at some other place, to mean "all humans, as moral agents, have value in themselves"? The place will not be found because the place does not exist. It is inherent value in its moral sense, as I understand it, not some morally neutral way of understanding this idea that informs the argument. The question the argument addresses is not whether moral patients, including animals, are unique (everything and everybody is, in some sense); it is whether we can nonarbitrarily refuse to recognize the inherent value (the noninstrumental, the independent moral value) of moral patients if we ascribe this same kind of value to moral agents. Equivocation? Professor Cohen's accusation to the contrary notwithstanding, there is not a shred of evidence to support the charge.

Chapter 4

Why Speciesism Is Wrong

Professor Cohen's seventh chapter is entitled "The Moral Inequality of Species: Why 'Speciesism' Is Right." While he here limits his criticisms among philosophers to Singer, whom Professor Cohen mistakenly identifies as "a member of the philosophy faculty at Princeton University" (Singer in fact is DeCamp Professor of Bioethics in Princeton's University Center for Human Values), they apply equally to the other philosophers whose ideas he criticizes in other places and who, whatever our differences, are united in opposing speciesism. We all are mistaken, if any one of us is, in judging speciesism both prejudicial and indefensible. I propose, therefore, to discuss Professor Cohen's critique in general terms.

What Speciesism Is

It is important to understand what the debate is not about. It is not about whether we are ever justified in treating some animals differently than we treat other animals, and it is not about whether we are ever justified in treating human beings differently than we treat animal beings. No one critical of speciesism questions the justifiability of differential treatment of either kind. We are not obliged to give bananas to cats because we give them to monkeys, not required to teach dogs to read and write because we teach children to do so.

But if not about this, what is the issue? What *is* speciesism? Professor Cohen offers help in this quarter when he characterizes the outlook of nonspeciesists: "When the interests of humans and animals are of a similar kind, there is no reason to favor the human over the animal" (p. 60). Not surprisingly, Professor Cohen disagrees, positioning himself squarely on the side of the speciesist. "The suffering of members of our species," he writes, "is somehow more important than the suffering of members of other species" (pp. 60–61). His challenge is to explain why this is so.

To meet this challenge, someone might deny that human and animal interests, human and animal suffering ever are "of a similar kind"; more pointedly, someone might deny that the pain animals experience, judged in terms of its intensity and duration, ever equals or exceeds the pain experienced by humans. Such an outlook certainly would qualify as one kind of speciesism— and an extreme variety at that. Except for latter day Cartesians, however, it is difficult to understand how such an extreme view could be supported. To make this clearer, consider a variation on an example used in chapter 14 of my opening statement:

> A mugger has pushed you to the ground and stolen your money; you are left with a number of cuts and bruises—minor to be sure, but still painful. Next, let us try to imagine the pain felt by the dogs who were vivisected by the scientists at Port Royal—the dogs who, without the benefit of anesthetic, had their four paws nailed to boards before being slit open. Are we to say that your minor pain is qualitatively worse than the much greater pain experienced by the dogs, because your pain is the pain of a human being, the dogs' pain not?

Perhaps someone like Peter Carruthers, who believes that the pain animals experience is "unconscious," might be moved to say, "Yes, the minor pain you experience is qualitatively worse." Not Professor Cohen; he gives no evidence that he would deny, and ample evidence that he would agree that sometimes the pain animals experience, judged in terms of its intensity and duration, equals or exceeds the pain experienced by human beings. It is in their respective moral judgments about such cases that Cohenian speciesists and nonspeciesists part company.

For their part, Cohenian speciesists believe that when humans and animals both experience the same amount of pain, of the same intensity, for the same amount of time, for example, there is nothing wrong in assigning greater moral weight, greater moral importance to the pain the humans experience, because it is humans who experience it; if anything, speciesism of the type Professor Cohen favors would think it wrong not to do so.

Nonspeciesists, on the other hand, believe that equal pains count equally, no matter whose pains they are, and that it is wrong to assign greater moral weight, greater moral importance to human pain just because it is a human who experiences it. For reasons explained in the following sections, Professor Cohen wishes to distance himself from this "gruesome moral confusion" (p. 63).

Professor Cohen's Defense of Speciesism

Professor Cohen's defense of speciesism takes two forms. First, reasons are advanced that purport to make a positive case in its favor; second, reasons are advanced that criticize a nonspeciesist moral outlook. I examine both, beginning with the former.

Positive Arguments

Two positive arguments are presented, the more important of the two citing what Professor Cohen believes are morally relevant differences between human beings, on the one hand, and animal beings, on the other. He writes:

> [A]mong the species of animate life—between humans and rats, between dogs and sea urchins—the morally relevant differences are enormous and almost universally appreciated. Sea urchins have no brains whatever, while dogs have very powerful brains. Humans engage in moral reflection, while rats are somewhat foreign to that enterprise. Humans are morally autonomous; the lower animals are not. Humans (as noted earlier) are members of moral communities, recognizing just claims even when those claims work against their own interests. Human beings have rights by nature; and those rights do give humans a moral status very different from that of sea-urchins, rats or dogs. (p. 63)

Thus, given the type of situation described earlier—a human being and an animal both experience the same amount of pain, of the same intensity, for the same amount of time—Professor Cohen would count the pain the human experiences for more, from the moral point of view, than the equal pain experienced by the animal; and he would do this because human beings, who engage in moral reflection, are morally autonomous, have rights, and enjoy "a moral status very different from that of sea urchins, rats[,] . . . dogs," or any other animal. Expressed another way: In assessing the moral importance of pains assumed to be equal (and the same applies to, e.g., equal pleasures, benefits, harms, and interests), we need to take into account both the pain that is experienced and the moral status of those who experience it. Because humans have a higher moral status than other animals, our pain counts for more than their pain, even when the pains are equal in all other respects.

This defense of speciesism is no defense at all. That it lacks a rational basis is especially obvious if (as the passage quoted earlier strongly suggests) the superior moral status of humans is supposed by Professor Cohen to depend on moral autonomy. Granted, those humans who live a human life in the fullest sense exercise their moral autonomy; but it is fallacious to infer, and in fact it is false (for reasons offered in chapter 2) that the same is true of all human beings, anencephalic humans, for example. To insist, in the face of the plain facts before us, that severely mentally disadvantaged human beings, because they are human, are morally autonomous is no more and no less credible than to insist that they are intellectually curious. The plain truth is that they are not the one, and not the other.

Professor Cohen offers what appears to be a second argument by way of positive support of his version of speciesism. "Humans, I submit," he writes, "owe to other humans a degree of moral regard that cannot be owed to animals. I love my dog very much, but it would be very wrong of me to protect my dog at the cost of the life of my neighbor's child or of any human child. Obligations are owed to humans that are not owed to dogs" (p. 63).

Readers might wonder why they should accept, as truth, what Professor Cohen is moved to submit. More, they might wonder how the remainder of what he writes bears on the issues before us. No one, not even an animal rights abolitionist like myself, would deny that we have obligations to humans that we do not have to dogs. Nor is it credible to interpret Professor Cohen to mean that he has an obligation to protect someone else's child but no obligation to protect his dog.

What, then, does he mean? What he means, presumably, is this: If we must choose between our obligation to protect our dog, on the one hand, and our obligation to protect someone else's child, on the other, we ought to protect the child. This must be why, in Professor Cohen's view, we have "obligations [to] humans that are not owed to dogs."

This observation, even granting its truth, is not equal to the task of offering a general defense of speciesism. Why this is so is perhaps best understood by way of analogy. Suppose we find ourselves in a situation where we can save either the life of our child or the life of a neighbor's child; for example, suppose both our house and our neighbor's house are on fire, the children are trapped inside their respective homes, and there is no possibility of saving both. Without a doubt people of goodwill would understand the decision to save our own child even though, by doing so, the neighbor's child will perish. What they would not understand is our generalizing on this extreme case—our maintaining that, because our obligation to our child takes priority in an extreme case like this one, it follows that we are always justified in counting the interests of our child as being morally more important than the equal interests of every other child. In fact, of all the people who would deny this, Professor Cohen must rank among those who would do so most emphatically. Thus, even if it is true that, *sometimes*, in *some* situations, the duties we have to our children override the duties we have to other children, it does not follow that, at *all* times, in *all* situations, the interests of our children should always be given greater moral weight, greater moral importance than the equal interests of every other child.

Once we recognize why it would be illogical to generalize on the basis of extreme cases when our duties to humans conflict, we can recognize why it would be no less illogical to do so when our duties to animals are added to the mix. Even if it is true that, were we faced with having to choose between saving a child and saving our dog, we ought to save the child, speciesism gains no logical support: that we *always* ought to give greater weight to the interests of human beings over the equal interests of animal beings simply does not follow.

The Critical Argument

In addition to presenting positive arguments in its defense, Professor Cohen also supports speciesism by highlighting what he thinks are some of the undesirable consequences of adopting a nonspeciesist perspective. That perspective, he maintains, not only is "a terrible mistake," it is "a gruesome moral confusion that encourages insensitivity, interferes with reasoned conduct, and may lead to unwarranted cruelty" (p. 63). In support of these assertions, noteworthy for the confident insistence with which they are made, Professor Cohen offers not a shred of evidence. To whom or to what are nonspeciesists "insensitive"? To whom or to what does any one of them exhibit "unwarranted cruelty"? By what manner or means does their belief in the moral equality of interests across species "interfere with [their] reasoned conduct"? Is any of this true of Singer, Rollin, or Sapontzis? Of myself? Professor Cohen is without question free to make any claim he chooses to make about those philosophers with whom he disagrees; he is not free of the obligation to offer credible evidence to support such claims when he makes them. In general, one does not refute a position one believes to be mistaken just by saying unflattering things about the people who accept it.

Racism, Sexism, and Speciesism

Those who adopt a nonspeciesist moral perspective sometimes allude to the similarities they find between speciesism, on the one hand, and racism and sexism, on the other. This certainly is true in my case, as the following quote, taken from my opening essay, attests:

> From the point of view of elementary justice . . . the interests of some human beings cannot be ignored, and cannot count for less than, the like interests of other human beings simply because they do not belong to the "right" race or gender. The same is true when it comes to species membership. From the point of view of elementary justice, the interests of animals cannot be ignored, and cannot count for less than, the like interests of human beings simply because animals do not belong to the "right" species. And just as it is true that assigning a privileged moral status to some people and, implicitly, assigning a lower status to others, solely on the basis of race or gender, are classic expressions of racism and sexism, so it is true that assigning a privileged moral status to human beings and, implicitly, assigning a lower status to every other animal, solely on the basis of species membership, is a classic expression of an analogous prejudice: speciesism. (p. 170)

Professor Cohen objects, arguing that the case against speciesism and the case against racism "are *very* far from parallel; the analogical argument is insidious. Racism is evil because humans really are equal and the assumption that some races are superior to others is false and groundless" (p. 62; emphasis in original). Why? Because "there is no morally relevant distinction among human ethnic groups" (p. 62).

When it comes to human and other forms of animate life, however, Professor Cohen believes that "the morally relevant differences are enormous" (p. 62). And if we ask what these differences are, we are told, in a passage we have already had occasion to quote on two previous occasions, that "humans engage in moral reflection"; "humans are morally autonomous"; "humans are members of moral communities"; and "human beings have rights by nature" (p. 62). In this sense, and for these reasons, we are to agree that humans and other animals really are not equal.

I have already explained why moral autonomy, for example, is not a capacity shared by all human beings. What I now want to explain is why neither moral autonomy nor any of the other factors Professor Cohen mentions has any logical bearing on the issues before us.

Imagine someone says that Jack is smarter than Jill because Jack lives in Syracuse, Jill in San Francisco. Where the two live is different, certainly; and where different people live sometimes is a relevant consideration (e.g., when a census is being taken or taxes levied). But everyone will recognize that where Jack and Jill live has no logical bearing on whether Jack is smarter. To think otherwise is to commit a fallacy of irrelevance familiar to anyone who has taken a course in elementary logic.

The same is no less true when a speciesist says that Fido's suffering counts for less than the equal suffering of Fred because Fred, but not Fido, is morally autonomous or because Fred, but not Fido, engages in moral reflection. If the question we are being asked is whether Jack is smarter than Jill, we are given no relevant reason for thinking one way or the other if we are told that Jack and Jill live in different cities. Similarly, if the question we are being asked is "Does Fido's pain count as much as Fred's?" we are given no relevant reason for thinking one way or the other if we are told that Fred is morally autonomous, while Fido is not, or that Fred, but not Fido, engages in moral reflection.

This is not because the capacity for moral autonomy, for example, is never relevant to our moral thinking about the interests of humans and other animals. Sometimes it is. If Jack and Jill have this capacity, they (but not Fido) will have an interest in being free to act as their conscience dictates. In this sense, the difference between Jack and Jill, on the one hand, and Fido, on the other, *is* morally relevant. But just because moral autonomy is morally relevant to the assessment and weighting of *some* interests, it does not follow that it is relevant to the assessment and weighting of *all* interests. And one interest to which it is not relevant is the interest in avoiding pain. Logically, to discount Fido's pain because Fido is not morally autonomous is fully analogous to discounting Jill's intelligence because she does not live in Syracuse.

The question, then, is whether any defensible, relevant reason can be offered in support of the speciesist judgment that the moral importance of the pains of humans and those of animals, equal in other respects (I note, again, that the same applies to, e.g., equal pleasures, benefits, harms, and interests), always should be weighted in favor of the human being over the animal being? To this question, Professor Cohen—even if we concede to him all the moral differences he alleges, even if we agree with him that we sometimes have duties to humans that we do not have to animals, and even if we permit him to make unsupported attacks on the character of those with whom he disagrees—offers no logically relevant answer whatsoever.

Speciesism: A Final Word

The nonspeciesist believes, writes Professor Cohen, that "when the interests of humans and animals are of a similar kind, there is no reason to favor the human over the animal." He disagrees. "The suffering of members of our species is somehow more important than the suffering of members of other species" (p. 60–61). It is not. "From the point of view of elementary justice," to quote again words already cited,

> the interests of some human beings cannot be ignored, and cannot count for less than, the like interests of other human beings simply because they do not belong to the "right" race or gender. The same is true when it comes to species membership. From the point of view of elementary justice, the interests of animals cannot be ignored, and cannot count for less than, the like interests of human beings simply because animals do not belong to the "right" species.

To persist in judging human interests as being more important than the like interests of other animals, because they are human interests, is speciesism. It is not rationally defensible. It is a moral prejudice. And (contrary to Professor Cohen's assurances to the contrary), it is wrong, not right.

Chapter 5

Utility and Vivisection

As noted in the opening pages of my reply, Professor Cohen falsely represents the use of animals in science as "the central focus" of this book; it is, however, the central focus of his contribution, with more than half of its pages devoted to this topic. The use of animals in research and testing (vivisection) is justified, he believes, because of the benefits humans derive. Animal liberationists, who rest their case against vivisection on utilitarian principles, while they use the right principles, reach the wrong conclusion. "[T]heir weighing of the advantages and disadvantages of animal experimentation," he maintains, "is woefully incomplete" (p. 69). For reasons I advance here, this is a no less apt description of the defense he offers.

Before presenting my reasons, it is worth mentioning that they are not ones I am obligated to give. Rights, Professor Cohen and I agree, trump interests, including the interests we have in being helped when sick or disabled. If animals have rights (and I note that Professor Cohen uniformly fails to provide a single valid reason against their having them), their rights trump our interests; thus, if animals have rights, questions about how much we might benefit from their use in research and testing, or how much we might lose if their use came to an end, emerge as morally irrelevant—as indeed, from my perspective, they surely are. It is not, therefore, the obligation of someone who believes in animal rights to make the utilitarian case against vivisection; rather, it is the obligation of someone like Professor Cohen, who denies their rights, to make the utilitarian case in its favor. Even so, the case he presents is so badly flawed, for so many different reasons, that it should not be permitted to stand without comment.

My remarks address five topics: (1) misrepresentations of the kind and number of animals used, (2) misrepresentations of the protection these animals receive, (3) misrepresentations of human harms attributable to vivisection, (4) misrepresentations of human benefits attributable to the same practice, and (5) misrepresentations of the complexity of the human health care question. After these misrepresentations are described, I explain why and how, to use Professor Cohen's words, his "weighing of the advantages and disadvantages of animal experimentation is [at best] woefully incomplete."

Misrepresentations of the Kind and Number of Animals Used

According to Professor Cohen (no footnote is provided to clarify what "recently" means here, but the figure would seem to refer to the estimate for fiscal year 1994), "the U.S. Department of Agriculture recently estimated the number of animals used in medical and pharmaceutical research to be about 1.6 million, of which the vast majority, approximately 90 percent [1,440,000], were rats, mice, and other rodents" (p. 14), including ferrets (p. 23). These figures are more than a little mistaken, and anyone even modestly familiar USDA regulations, as they pertain to enforcement of the Animal Welfare Act, will understand why. Whereas some rodents (specifically, gerbils, hamsters, and guinea pigs; contrary to Professor Cohen, ferrets are not rodents) are reportable, rats and mice are not. For purposes of reporting, in other words, rats and mice (and birds, too) *do not count* as animals. Facilities that use these animals thus *have nothing to report;* and they have nothing to report because, given operative federal regulations, *no animals were used.*

That this is a shocking disregard, not only of elementary biology but of plain commonsense, no one can seriously dispute. But the foolish denial of the truth by some offers no excuse for misrepresentation of the facts by others, and it is the misrepresentation of the facts, in Professor Cohen's hands, that cannot be permitted to stand. For what the USDA figure (1.6 million) estimates is *not the total number of animals used* in the year in question; it estimates *the total number used, subject to USDA regulations,* a method of reporting that excludes (among others) rats and mice.[5]

How many animals actually were used during the year in question? For reasons explained in my opening statement, this is a question that has no definitive answer. Estimates range from twenty to one hundred million. Suppose we adopt the lower number, which is in line with the American Medical Association's estimate of seventeen to twenty-two million; in that case, Professor Cohen's figure of 1.6 million underestimates the number of animals used by 18.4 million.[6]

Given his speciesist views about the subordinate moral status of nonhuman animals, Professor Cohen might think it unimportant to get the facts right when it comes to the number and kind of animals used for research purposes in a given year. If ferrets are not rodents, and if twenty million, not 1.6 million animals were used, what difference does it make?

Getting the facts right makes a difference to Professor Cohen for at least two reasons. First, the number of animals used, whatever that number is, at some point *must* make a difference to the moral assessment of using them, given his position. Granted, the number used would make no difference if animals count for nothing morally. But this is not his view. Their pleasures and pains, their benefits and harms, while they are not equally important when compared with ours, nevertheless do count for something. Theoretically, then, there *must* be a point, given his position, when research that uses animals would have to stop because the benefits humans derive do not exceed the harms done to the animals. Professor Cohen fails to say what that point is; he also fails to explain how we could know if we reached it.

Second, a mistake of the magnitude Professor Cohen makes, on the order of eighteen million animal deaths in a given year, matters to his credibility. In general, it is difficult to muster much confidence in what someone says, in every respect, when they make mistakes of great magnitude, in any respect. If Professor Cohen is not equal to task of answering the relatively simple factual question concerning how many animals were used for a given purpose, in a given year, readers might well ask what credence should be placed in his answer to the complex ethical question concerning whether animals should be used for this purpose in the first place. That a healthy skepticism is warranted will become more evident as we proceed.

Misrepresentations of the Care and Treatment of Animals

Professor Cohen assures his readers that all is well in the laboratories of the world in general, the United States in particular. "Death is inflicted, and some pain too," he notes, "on rats and other animals whose lives are used in medical research" (p. 122). This "is regrettable"; it "ought to be minimized" (p. 70); and, because of federal regulations and laboratory inspections, it is. Writes Professor Cohen:

> Sentient animals must be treated with careful regard for the fact that they feel pain; decent people will always exhibit that concern and will rightfully insist that the animals we use be fed and housed properly, handled considerately. Regulations insuring such humane treatment are not in dispute; they are entirely justified and (in this country) universally in force. Principles of good animal husbandry rule, as they ought to rule, among the scientists who rely on animals in their investigations. Every medical center, every pharmaceutical company, every research institute using animals has (and under American law must have) its own Institutional Animal Care and Use Committee whose legal duty it is to ensure that the animals in that facility are cared for properly and that experiments using

those animals are conducted humanely. Frequent inspections by federal agencies, as well as by professional peers, enforce and reinforce high standards for animal (pp. 5–6)

Each and every substantive policy claim contained in this passage is misleading at best, false at worst:

- Professor Cohen would have us believe that "regulations ensuring . . . humane treatment (of animals used in experiments) are not in dispute; they are entirely justified and (in this country) universally in force." The facts of the case would have us believe otherwise. Three independent government investigations,[7] including one by the General Accounting Office, another by the Office of Technology Assessment, reach the same conclusion: enforcement of operative government regulations is systematically deficient. The third, a 1995 audit conducted by the Office of the Inspector General, agrees: of randomly selected institutions, almost half (twelve of twenty-six) were "not adequately fulfilling their responsibilities" in enforcing government regulations concerning "humane treatment." So, no, we should not place great confidence in what Professor Cohen says on this matter.
- To say, as Professor Cohen does, that "every medical center, every pharmaceutical company, every research institute using animals has (and under American law must have) its own Institutional Animal Care and Use Committee [IACUC] whose legal duty it is to insure that the animals in that facility are cared for properly"—to say this sounds reassuring until one recalls that some animals are not animals, given relevant federal regulations. A facility that uses only rats and mice, for example, does not use any animals and so is not required to have an IACUC. It is just false, therefore, to say that *every* such entity has its own IACUC.
- Moreover, among those entities that do have IACUCs, it is profoundly false to maintain that their members are charged with insuring that "experiments using (covered) animals are conducted humanely." "*Humanely* conducted experimentation" presumably means "experimentation in which animals are not made to suffer without moral justification." In point of fact (and of law, as well), however, IACUCs have no authority to impose *ethical* limits on what researchers may or may not do and thus no authority to stop even a single experiment on ethical grounds. As Rutgers University law professor Gary Francione notes:

[T]he only time that the IACUC may act with respect to the conduct or content of an experiment is if the experimenter (who has complete ethical and scientific autonomy) cannot justify the infliction of pain and the IACUC determines that the infliction of pain is "unnecessary." And that judgment can *never* occur in the context of an *ethical* analysis. Rather, any IACUC action *necessarily* involves a determination that the experimenter is wasting animal resources and threatening the production of reliable data by inflicting "unnecessary" pain on an animal.[8]

In short, deliberations and decisions of IACUCs manifestly fail "to ensure that experiments using those animals are conducted humanely," in any ethical sense of that word.

- Furthermore, even if the pain animals experience during an experiment could be judged ethically by IACUCs, there is more than a little reason to question the reliability of the judgments they would make. In 1997, for example, IACUCs throughout the United States reported that 54 percent of regulated animals experienced neither pain nor distress, 38 percent received painkillers because of the pain or distress they experienced, and 8 percent experienced pain or distress without relief.[9] Not only are those who make these judgments doing so without a common harm scale, already in place in many European countries as well as Canada, Australia, and New Zealand; paradigms of animal suffering, including toxicity tests, commonly are classified as nonpainful. Moreover, because mice and rats are the animals of choice in some of the most painful investigations (e.g., LD50 tests and tumor research), and because research using these animals is not reportable, the estimate of 8 percent hardly commands confidence. The plain fact is, given current regulations, and despite Professor Cohen's assurance that animals used in research and testing "are seldom caused pain" (p. 1), *nobody knows* how many animals experience how much pain or distress and how many do so without the benefit of relief.

By contrast, one thing we do know is that researchers do not seem to be overly concerned about animal suffering. At least this is the conclusion the sociologist Arnold Arluke, relying on the work of his own and of others, reaches after more than a decade of studying the culture of animal research and the people involved in it. "Even before [animals] arrive in laboratories," he writes:

[their] naturalistic identity . . . is stripped away, when breeding companies market lab animals as superobjects—pure and standardized as virtual clones of each other, manufactured and customized to meet science's needs, and submissive and cooperative to make their use in experiments easy. Once they are ordered from breeding companies as "supplies," they are systematically incorporated into experiments by assigning them numbers or meaningless names, handled in large batches by giving them corporate rather than individual identities, and

defined by laboratory norms as objects. . . . The result is that the animal's body is transformed into data and it is regarded as a different kind of entity from the naturalistic animal. Mary Phillips, for instance, found that scientists rarely provided analgesics after surgery. She argues that, like the nineteenth century savage and drunk that were thought not to need anesthesia because they felt little pain, the contemporary lab animal gets no pain relief. Although scientists will admit that animals are sensitive to pain, it rarely occurs to scientists that animals might feel pain because they are defined as scientific data. The view of these animals as existing solely for research overrides concern for their subjective experience.[10]

Let it be agreed, then, that Professor Cohen speaks truly when he says that, in a laboratory context, "[s]entient animals must be treated with careful regard for the fact that they feel pain." But let it be agreed also that Professor Cohen has failed to discharge the obligation of showing that they are.

Misrepresentations of Human Harms Attributable to Reliance on the Animal Model

Professor Cohen further erodes his credibility when he turns his attention to human benefits and harms attributable to the use of the animal model. In developing and testing drugs, we are told, "successful administration to mice does not guarantee harmlessness [for us]" (p. 73). "It may even turn out— though it happens very rarely—that what has been shown to be nontoxic in animals proves toxic in humans" (p. 74); only "a very few dangers are not screened out by animal trials" (p. 77). These "occasional failures" (p. 74) should not obscure or diminish the fact that "the role of animal experimentation in medical research is not misleading" (p. 72).

These assertions, made without supporting evidence, have no basis in fact. Just the opposite. Professor Cohen surely must know that many drugs that have cleared animal tests are later found to be toxic for humans. A 1990 report issued by the General Accounting Office found that approximately 50 percent of the FDA-approved drugs investigated either had to be taken off the market or relabeled because of their toxic effects on the people who were using them.[11]

More recent studies paint an even less reassuring picture. It is estimated that more than one hundred thousand Americans die and another two million are hospitalized every year because of the adverse effects of the prescription drugs they are taking. Even while acknowledging that deaths and disabilities attributable to adverse drug reactions are grossly underreported (the FDA itself estimates that the number reported is only 1 percent[12]), these are not inconsiderable sums. At more than one hundred thousand deaths annually (a figure that is roughly equivalent to having a jumbo jet crash each day, day after day throughout the year, with no survivors), the number of fatalities resulting from prescription drugs ranks as the fourth leading cause of death in America, behind only heart disease, cancer, and stroke.

Nor are these deaths and the millions of hospitalizations due to human error. Cases in which drugs were *misprescribed* were excluded from the studies; all the patients who died (one in every three hundred hospital patients) received the right drug, in the right amount, at the right time; the same was true of the millions who were hospitalized.[13]

For his part, Professor Cohen might view these figures as being consistent with his observation that it "*sometimes* turns out—though it *happens very rarely*—that what has been shown to be non-toxic in animals proves to be toxic in humans" (p. 74; emphasis added). Retention of this belief must require a radically different meaning of "happens very rarely" than what these words have in everyday life. The plain fact is, people frequently are harmed, and many die from prescription drugs that were tested on animals. It is just false to say, as Professor Cohen does, that "the role of animal experimentation in medical research is not misleading."

The harmful consequences for humans who use drugs tested on animals is not the only kind of relevant harm; another is the harm done to humans because no animal can be found to "model" a debilitating human condition. By way of example, consider the role of tobacco in the etiology of human cancers. As early as the 1950s, human epidemiological studies revealed a causal link between cigarette smoking and lung cancer; nevertheless, repeated efforts to induce tobacco-related cancers in mice, rats, and other animals failed. This "inability to induce experimental cancers, except in a handful of cases, during 50 years of trying," writes the American pathologist Eric Northrup, in his 1957 book *Science Looks at Smoking,* "casts serious doubt on the validity of the cigarette–lung cancer theory," adding, "it is reassuring . . . that public health agencies have rejected the demand for a mass lay educational programme against the alleged dangers of smoking. Not one of the leading insurance companies, who consider health hazards in terms of monetary risk, has raised the life insurance rates for heavy smokers."[14]

Times have changed, when it comes not only to "mass . . . educational programme[s]" but also to life insurance rates for smokers and nonsmokers. Even so, it is estimated that 60 percent of the direct health care costs in the United States today go to treat tobacco-related illnesses and that one in five of all deaths in the United States is attributable to smoking. The percentages could not have been less, and doubtless were a good deal higher during those "50 years of trying" (unsuccessfully) "to induce experimental cancers" in animals.

Vivisection's role in tobacco-related illness and death is not an isolated incident. For example, despite clinical evidence that exposure to asbestos and low-level radiation was harmful or fatal to humans, precautionary steps were delayed because no animals modeled these conditions. Time and time again important, life-saving policies and procedures have been delayed because of reliance on the whole animal model. In the face of such harm done to humans, at once so massive and protracted, those who persist in claiming that "the role of animal experimentation in medical research is not misleading" risk losing whatever credibility they might retain.

Misrepresentations of Human Benefits Attributable to Reliance on the Animal Model

No one (at least no one with whom I am familiar) denies that sometimes, some people benefit from using some drug or from receiving some medical intervention originally developed and tested using animals. What is in dispute, in this context, is how much we have benefited.

Professor Cohen makes a number of claims on this topic. I consider two. First, he states that "in the history of modern medicine . . . virtually all of the greatest advances have relied essentially on animal research" (p. 85). This is false. Public health scholars who have studied improvements in human health attribute only a modest contribution (somewhere between 3.5 and 5 percent) to standard medical interventions that depend on animal model research. In particular, declines in mortality resulting from both infectious and chronic diseases are best explained by improvements to the environment and to changes in personal hygiene rather than because of the kinds of therapies Professor Cohen describes in his essay.[15]

Professor Cohen's second claim arguably is different because more specific. Instead of saying something about "all the greatest advances" of modern medicine, he writes, "Vaccines, antibiotics, prosthetic devices, therapeutic drugs of every description, the basic science that will make possible advances not yet dreamed of, as well as the safety of products we consume every day—all are owed to animal research" (p. 120). Because this second point concerns specific medical therapies and tests, whereas the first point concerns much more, it is possible that the second is true while the first is false.

To test the truth of point 2, consider the claimed importance of animal experimentation for the development and testing of therapeutic drugs. Professor Cohen would have us believe that we would not have access to these drugs unless they were first tested using animal models. Interpreted thus, what Professor Cohen says is true but trivial, fully comparable to my saying, "We would not have newly elected representatives in Congress today if people had not voted in the last election." Is that true? Yes. Does it tell us anything important? No. Why not? Because the only way to have newly elected representatives in Congress is for voters to have elected them.

The situation respecting prescription drugs is similar. Throughout its regulatory history, there is not a single instance of the Food and Drug Administration's approving a drug that has not been tested on animals. So, yes, given the history of FDA regulatory practice, we would not have the prescription drugs we have today if they had not been tested on animals. That is true. But it is also trivial. Because the only way FDA has been willing to approve such drugs is after they were first tested on animals, it cannot be surprising that this is the only way drugs have become available on the market.

Professor Cohen can be counted on to protest, insisting that his intention is to say something that is true and profound, not true and trivial. What might that be? How to answer is unclear. If his claim is that as a matter of fact, ignoring regulatory policies and other extrascientific influences, we would not have the prescription drugs we do if they had not been tested on animals, he invites skepticism concerning how he could presume to know so much when the rest of us know so little. Who is to say what technologies might have been developed, and at what speed, if modern science had foresworn the use of animals and looked resolutely, as a community of investigators, for other ways to advance human understanding of disease and health? (Of course, many researchers already do this; but this is a point that can be set aside, given present interests.) Were Professor Cohen to reply that generations of dedicated researchers would have failed, that they would have found nothing, the discussion is not moved forward. In general, we are not reassured that someone knows more than we think he does when he says he does for a second time.

Misrepresentations of the Complexity of the Human Health Care Question

Suppose we grant to Professor Cohen all that he might wish: the benefits humans derive from animal experimentation not only are "extraordinary" but could not have been obtained in any other way. What, then? Has vivisection been justified, on utilitarian grounds? No. Why not? Because all those harms causally linked to reliance on animal model research must find their rightful place in the utilitarian mix. To fail to enter them into the calculations is manifestly to fail to make the utilitarian case in favor of vivisection.

And there's the rub. Throughout his lengthy disquisition in praise of vivisection, one looks in vain to find so much as a hint that Professor Cohen is aware of the massive harm done to humans because of vivisection; one looks in vain as well for even the most modest effort to weigh the relevant harms preparatory to comparing them with the alleged benefits. Are the harms "calculable," the benefits not? Or are the harms, as the benefits are said to be, "incalculable," too? In either case, where is the honest effort made to meet the demands of rational justification?

Those demands concern more than a fair reckoning of the harms attributable to reliance on animals in research. As a society, we have limited funds with which to maximize the best health for the greatest number, assuming we favor using funds for this purpose. How to do this well and wisely is a complex question. Professor Cohen would have us think otherwise. "It is," he writes, "probably true that, in the large, too little money and energy is expended in the effort to prevent disease as compared to the energies and funds expended to cure it" (p. 81). To take refuge in what is "probably true" will not pass muster here. How *much* money is spent on efforts to prevent disease? How *much* on efforts to cure it? What *are* the returns for dollars spent, depending on whether the focus is on prevention or on cure? A utilitarian will want to know the answers to such questions before coming down on the side of funding the search for cures based on animal model research, an expensive, time-consuming methodology, given any fair judgment. That the necessary calculations will support this type of research, judged from a utilitarian perspective, is not something a utilitarian can simply assume without begging the question. Indeed, to do so might suggest that one's utilitarianism is captive to an ideology that requires no facts in order to know what is right.

Readers will again look in vain to find any of the required data, any of the necessary calculations in Professor Cohen's essay. What we find instead are different standards of proof applied to others than the ones Professor Cohen applies to himself. On the one hand, he repudiates those animal liberationists who are critical of vivisection, on utilitarian grounds, because their "weighing of the advantages and disadvantages of animal experimentation is woefully incomplete"; on the other, his utilitarian defense of vivisection is no less and, in many respects, even more "woefully incomplete."

Awash in incompleteness, whichever side we take, one thing is clear: Professor Cohen cannot have it both ways. Unless or until he responds to the challenge before him—meaning unless or until he canvasses and compares the full range of the costs associated with the relevant harms, as well as the full range of the costs of the relevant benefits; unless or until he makes good on his promise to present "the full consequences of animal use" (p. 8)—he will have done less than offer an inadequate utilitarian defense of vivisection; he will have failed to offer a utilitarian defense at all.

Chapter 6

Summary and Conclusion

As I noted at the outset of my reply, it is an uncommon privilege to have this opportunity to respond to Professor Cohen's brief against animal rights. Among the literature critical of this idea, his critique is far and away the most famous and influential. In responding to his challenge, therefore, one is responding to the best thinking produced by those who deny rights to animals.

To demonstrate how deficient that thinking is has been my unifying theme. Throughout I have endeavored to identify and explain Professor Cohen's many failures, including

- his failure to explain how human and animal pleasures and pains, human and animal benefits and harms are to be compared and weighed;
- his failure to use his general moral principles to offer guidance in "our personal lives";
- his failure to explain why people who abstain from eating meat or using animal products as a matter of moral principle are in the grip of "fanatical convictions";
- his failure to explain what it means to say that rights are "valid claims";
- his failure to explain what makes claims to rights valid;
- his failure to support his conviction that all humans have rights;
- his failure to support his conviction that no animals have rights;
- his failure to represent accurately the views of those with whom he disagrees;
- his failure to support his conviction that speciesism is "right";
- his failure to represent accurately the number and kind of animals used in vivisection;
- his failure to represent accurately the protection animals receive when used for purposes of vivisection;
- his failure to offer a credible justification for his assurance that, in a laboratory setting, "sentient animals are treated with careful regard for the fact that they feel pain";
- his failure to represent accurately the human harms attributable to vivisection;
- his failure to represent accurately the human benefits attributable to vivisection;
- his failure to represent accurately the complexity of the human health care question;
- his failure to apply standards of proof to himself that he applies to others; and
- his failure to present an even modestly complete utilitarian defense of vivisection.

Though not complete by any means, the aforementioned failures might go some way toward suggesting how seriously deficient is Professor Cohen's case against animal rights. Of course, to explain his many failures does not prove that animals have rights; positive arguments for that conclusion are found elsewhere. What recognition of his many failures does prove is how poorly reasoned and researched is his brief against their rights.

At the end of my opening statement, I cited some concrete reasons for thinking that some people are beginning to change how they live in order to show respect for some of the rights of some animals. These changes are occurring because of the conscientious efforts of animal rights activists throughout the world; many hands are applying themselves to many oars, as the struggle for animal rights moves forward. Habits of thought and action, formed over thousands of years of human history, have no simple cause, and it would be naive beyond words to believe that they all will be changed simply by having someone explain how bad are the philosophical arguments offered in their defense. This does not make such explanations worthless; it only puts them in proper perspective.

Unless or until the great mass of humanity evolves beyond the speciesist ideology that defines both our history and the great majority of our current practices, there is little hope that animal beings will have a better life. The work of philosophers arguing in defense of animal rights is one way, though not the only way, to attempt to effect the necessary transformation from where we are today, as a culture and a species, to where we might hope to be tomorrow. One person at a time.

Notes

Jonathan Balcolm, Andrew Breslin, Murray Cohen, Gary Comstock, Sidney Gendin, Joseph Levine, Barbara Orlans, Andrew Rowan, Peter Singer, and Dean Smith offered helpful comments and suggestions. It is a pleasure to acknowledge their assistance. My thanks as well to Laura Larson for her valuable editorial assistance.

1. Professor Cohen might be interpreted in such a way that he offers no reasons, no arguments for ascribing rights to humans universally, arguing only against rights in the case of animals. This hardly seems a fair way of reading him, given his aspirations. In general, one does not advance a controversial position merely by assuming the truth of what one believes.

2. An earlier version of my discussion of his general arguments against animal rights is "Mapping Human Rights" in *Global Ethics,* ed. N. Low (London: Routledge, 1999), 158–74; reprinted, with revisions, in my *Defending Animal Rights* (Champaign: University of Illinois Press, 2001), 66–84.

3. Carl Cohen, "Do Animals Have Rights?" *Ethics and Behavior 7*, no. 2:94–95.

4. Page references in the text are to *The Case for Animal Rights* (Berkeley: University of California Press, 1983).

5. For information concerning the number of reportable animals used in research, from 1973 (the first year such reporting was required) to 1997 (the most recent year for which numbers are available), consult www.aphis.usda.gov/oa/pubs/awrpt/awrpt97.html.

6. The AMA estimate of seventeen to twenty-two million animals used in research, including mice, rats, and birds, is for 1992; see *Statement on the Use of Ani-*

mals in Biomedical Research: The Challenge and the Response (rev. ed.) (Chicago: American Medical Association, 1992), 15. For the National Association for Biomedical Research's current estimate of twenty-three million, see their home page at <www.nabr.org>, and Lynne Lamberg, "Researchers Urged to Tell Public How Animal Studies Benefit Human Health," *Journal of the American Medical Association* 282, no. 7 (18 August 1999), http://jama.ama-assn.org/issues/v281n4/full/jlt0127-1.html.

7. See U.S. General Accounting Office, *Report to the Chairman, Subcommittee on Agriculture, Rural Development and Related Agencies, Senate Committee on Appropriations: The Department of Agriculture's Animal Welfare Program* (1985); U.S. Congress, Office of Technology Assessment, Rep. No. OTA-BA-273, *Alternatives to Animal Use in Research, Testing, and Education* (Washington, D.C.: U.S. Government Printing Office, 1986); and Office of Inspector General, *Animal and Plant Inspection Service Enforcement of the Animal Welfare Act* (Washington, D.C.: U.S. Government Printing Office, 1995).

8. Gary Francione, *Animals, Property, and the Law* (Philadelphia: Temple University Press, 1995), 206; emphasis in original.

9. For information regarding the incidence of pain caused to animals in research, for FY 1997, see www.aphis.usda.gov:80/oa/pubs/awrpt/awbusi.html. See also A. Rowan, F. Loew, and J. Weer, *The Animal Research Controversy* (Tufts, Mass.: Tufts University School of Veterinary Medicine, 1995), iii.

10. Arnold Arluke and Clinton R. Sanders, *Regarding Animals* (Philadelphia: Temple University Press, 1996), 173–74.

11. The statistics concerning the toxicity of FDA-approved drugs will be found in U.S. General Accounting Office, *Report to the Chairman, Subcommittee on Human Resources and Intergovernmental Relations, Committee on Government Operations, House of Representatives, FDA Drug Review, Postapproval Risks, 1976–1985* (Washington, D.C.: U.S. Government Printing Office, 1990).

12. The estimate of 1 percent of adverse drug reactions that are reported is given in D. A. Kessler, "Introducing MedWatch: A New Approach to Reporting Medication and Device Adverse Effects and Product Problems," *Journal of the American Medical Association.* 269 (1993): 2765–68.

13. For statistical studies of toxic and fatal reactions to FDA-approved drugs, see J. Lazarou, B. H. Pomeranz, and P. N. Corey, "Incidence of Adverse Drug Reactions in Hospitalized Patients: A Meta-analysis of Prospective Studies," *Journal of the American Medical Association* 279 (1998):1200–04.

14. Northrup, *Science Looks at Smoking* (New York: Coward-McCann, 1957), 133.

15. The limited contributions to human health attributable to animal research are summarized in Hugh LaFollette and Niall Shanks, *Brute Science: Dilemmas of Animal Experimentation* (London: Routledge, 1996), 12–14. The Physicians Committee for Responsible Medicine (www.pcrm.org) and the Medical Research Modernization Committee (www.mrmcmed.org) are excellent resources for exploring many claims Professor Cohen makes about the role of animal studies in specific research, both past and present. Of particular relevance to assessing the human harms attributable to vivisection is MRMC's "A Critical Look at Animal Experimentation," available at their

Web site. See also Robert Sharpe, *The Cruel Deception: The Use of Animals in Medical Research* (London: Thorsons, 1988), and *Science on Trial: The Human Cost of Animal Experiments* (Sheffield: Awareness Books, 1994).

In addition to these matters, readers are encouraged to investigate how reliance on the animal model actually retarded the development of a polio vaccine, on the one hand, and how little use of vaccines actually contributed to the decline of the disease. See, for example, Physicians Committee for Responsible Medicine, "Poliomyelitis: Background Paper" (Washington, D.C.: Author, 1996). For an important corrective to the exaggerated claims Professor Cohen makes about the role of animal studies in the work of recipients of the Nobel Prize, see Martin Stephens, "The Prize Goes to Alternatives: Noble Prize Awards in Medicine and Physiology," *Advances in Animal Welfare Science* 2, no. 1 (1986): 19–31(revised 1996); reprinted in *The Animals' Voice Magazine* (Winter 1997): 14–16.

Index

abolitionism, 212–13, 227, 241;
consequences of, 22–24, 25, 52,
56; consistency of, 241–43; goals
of, 127; violence of, 257n3. *See also*
agriculture (animal); animal
liberation movement; animal rights
movement; medical research
abortions, 179
acquired immunodeficiency syndrome
(AIDS), 90–91
adenovirus, 98
adrenal hormones, 120
adverse drug reactions, 302–3. *See also*
prescription drugs
African Americans, 153–54, 201
agents, moral. *See* moral agents
agreement, method of, 79–80
agriculture (animal), 9, 24, 188, 213,
255; human diet, 127–28, 135–38;
moral evaluation of, 186–87;
preference utilitarianism
perspective, 186–87
AIDS. *See* acquired immunodeficiency
syndrome
alopecia areata, 106–7. *See also*
genetics
ALS. *See* amyotrophic lateral sclerosis
alternatives to animal use, 12–13, 71,
72, 240
alveoli, 112. *See also* emphysema

Alzheimer's disease, 92–93. *See also*
neurodegenerative diseases
amorality, 273–75. *See also* morality
amyotrophic lateral sclerosis (ALS),
93–95
anencephalic infants, 278–79
angiogenesis, tumor, 107–8,
117n51–53. *See also* cancer
angioplasty, 86–88
angiostatin, 107–8, 117n51. *See also*
cancer
Animal and Plant Health Inspection
Service, 144
animal liberation movement, 46, 59–61;
arguments against animal use,
70–82; on disease prevention,
80–81; on equality of species,
59–61, 62, 63; on experimentation,
animal, 69, 76, 297; on medical
research, 59–60; overview of, 6–8;
on pain and suffering, 121–22; and
utilitarianism, 69. *See also* animal
rights movement
Animal Liberation (Singer), 6, 59–60,
61
animal rights, 5, 7, 8, 9, 228; amorality
of animals, 273–75; animal
liberation movement, 8, 59, 60;
arguments against, 5, 6, 214–17,
271–84; consequences of, 22–24,

About the Authors

Carl Cohen is professor of philosophy at the University of Michigan in Ann Arbor, Michigan.

Tom Regan is professor of philosophy at North Carolina State University in Raleigh, North Carolina.